Fear and Nature

Lucinda Cole and Robert Markley, General Editors

Advisory Board:
Stacy Alaimo (University of Texas at Arlington)
Ron Broglio (Arizona State University)
Carol Colatrella (Georgia Institute of Technology)
Heidi Hutner (Stony Brook University)
Stephanie LeMenager (University of Oregon)
Christopher Morris (University of Texas at Arlington)
Laura Otis (Emory University)
Will Potter (Washington, DC)
Ronald Schleifer (University of Oklahoma)
Susan Squier (Pennsylvania State University)
Rajani Sudan (Southern Methodist University)
Kari Weil (Wesleyan University)

Published in collaboration with the Society for Literature, Science, and the Arts, AnthropoScene presents books that examine relationships and points of intersection among the natural, biological, and applied sciences and the literary, visual, and performing arts. Books in the series promote new kinds of cross-disciplinary thinking arising from the idea that humans are changing the planet and its environments in radical and irreversible ways.

Fear and Nature

Ecohorror Studies in the Anthropocene

Edited by
Christy Tidwell
and Carter Soles

The Pennsylvania
State University Press
University Park,
Pennsylvania

Library of Congress Cataloging-in-Publication Data

Names: Tidwell, Christy, editor. | Soles, Carter, 1971– editor.
Title: Fear and nature : ecohorror in the Anthropocene / edited by Christy Tidwell and Carter Soles.
Other titles: AnthropoScene.
Description: University Park, Pennsylvania : The Pennsylvania State University Press, [2021] | Series: AnthropoScene : the SLSA book series | Includes bibliographical references and index.
Summary: "A collection of essays analyzing ecohorror motifs in literature, manga, film, and television, illuminating ambiguities that arise from human encounters with nonhuman nature and examining the scale and effect of ecohorror in, and of, the Anthropocene"—Provided by publisher.
Identifiers: LCCN 2021006871 |
ISBN 9780271090214 (hardback) |
ISBN 9780271090221 (paper)
Subjects: LCSH: Horror tales—History and criticism. | Horror films—History and criticism. | Horror in literature. | Human ecology in literature. | Human ecology in motion pictures. | Nature in literature. | Nature in motion pictures. | Ecocriticism.
Classification: LCC PN3435 .F434 2021 |
DDC 791.43/6164—dc23
LC record available at https://lccn.loc.gov/2021006871

Copyright © 2021 The Pennsylvania State University
All rights reserved
Printed in the United States of America
Published by The Pennsylvania State University Press,
University Park, PA 16802-1003

The Pennsylvania State University Press is a member of the Association of University Presses.

It is the policy of The Pennsylvania State University Press to use acid-free paper. Publications on uncoated stock satisfy the minimum requirements of American National Standard for Information Sciences—Permanence of Paper for Printed Library Material, ANSI Z39.48–1992.

Contents

Acknowledgments | vii

Introduction: Ecohorror in
the Anthropocene | 1
Christy Tidwell and Carter Soles

Part 1 | Expanding Ecohorror

1 Tentacular Ecohorror and the Agency of Trees
in Algernon Blackwood's "The Man Whom
the Trees Loved" and Lorcan Finnegan's
Without Name | 23
Dawn Keetley

2 Spiraling Inward and Outward: Junji Ito's
Uzumaki and the Scope of Ecohorror | 42
Christy Tidwell

3 "The Hand of Deadly Decay":
The Rotting Corpse, America's Religious
Tradition, and the Ethics of Green Burial in
Poe's "The Colloquy of Monos and Una" | 68
Ashley Kniss

Part 2 | Haunted and Unhaunted Landscapes

4 The Death of Birdsong, the Birdsong of Death:
Algernon Charles Swinburne and the Horror
of Erosion | 91
Keri Stevenson

5 An Unhaunted Landscape: The Anti-Gothic Impulse in Ambrose Bierce's "A Tough Tussle" | 110
Chelsea Davis

6 The Extinction-Haunted Salton Sea in *The Monster That Challenged the World* | 133
Bridgitte Barclay

Part 3 | The Ecohorror of Intimacy

7 From the Bedroom to the Bathroom: Stephen King's Scatology and the Emergence of an Urban Environmental Gothic | 153
Marisol Cortez

8 "This Bird Made an Art of Being Vile": Ontological Difference and Uncomfortable Intimacies in Stephen Gregory's *The Cormorant* | 174
Brittany R. Roberts

9 *The Shape of Water* and Post-pastoral Ecohorror | 195
Robin L. Murray and Joseph K. Heumann

Part 4 | Being Prey, Being Food

10 Superpig Blues: Agribusiness Ecohorror in Bong Joon-ho's *Okja* | 217
Kristen Angierski

11 *Zoo*: Television Ecohorror On and Off the Screen | 237
Sharon Sharp

12 Naturalizing White Supremacy in *The Shallows* | 257
Carter Soles

Contributors | 281

Index | 285

Acknowledgments

This book reflects an ongoing and vibrant conversation about ecohorror that we are happy to have been a part of. Many of those who have helped shape our ideas about the topic and prompted the creation of this book are featured in its pages—either as contributors or as frequently cited sources. We are grateful for the generosity and support of the scholars we have worked with in this collection; those we have presented with, presented to, and conversed with at conferences; and those whose work we have engaged with and built upon. In particular, conversations at multiple ASLE (Association for the Study of Literature and Environment) meetings and connections made via the ASLE Ecomedia Interest Group have been formative, challenging, and encouraging.

Christy Tidwell: I would also like to thank Bridgitte Barclay for thoughtful feedback at every stage (critical when necessary but also always supportive!); Laura Kremmel and Kayla Pritchard for innumerable meetings at coffee shops and bars to work together and talk through both ideas and frustrations; and Neil Robinson, Elliott Robinson, and Djuna Tidwell for their patience and love.

Carter Soles: I would also like to thank Kom Kunyosying, Stephen A. Rust, Bridgitte Barclay, Sara Crosby, and especially my brilliant, hardworking collaborator Christy Tidwell, without whose efforts and guidance this collection would not be remotely as interesting or clear. I additionally acknowledge Alicia Kerfoot, Peggy Kerfoot-Soles, and our menagerie of cats—Charlie, Roscoe, Dorian, and Rosy—for making everything I do worthwhile and joyful. And for letting me monopolize the TV when I need to watch horror movies.

Introduction
Ecohorror in the Anthropocene

Christy Tidwell
and Carter Soles

We live in ecohorrific times.

Wildfires are spreading across the US West, burning more land every year and endangering the lives of millions—human and nonhuman, both in the present and into the future.[1] Record-breaking heat waves are dramatically affecting Europe, disrupting transportation and agriculture and threatening people's lives.[2] India is suffering from both droughts and floods;[3] hundreds of people died in 2019 and tens to hundreds of millions of people have been affected. Greenland is melting, losing 12.5 billion tons of ice in one day in August 2019 and breaking the record for a one-day melt.[4] The planet's sixth mass extinction of species is ongoing—25 percent of species are currently threatened with extinction, while the current rate of extinction is tens to hundreds of times higher than the normal background rate of extinction and accelerating.[5] Meanwhile, the US government has taken action to weaken environmental protections, including the Endangered Species Act.[6] As this planetary ecohorror has become more visible, it is unsurprising that ecohorror narratives have become more widespread as well.

Contemporary ecohorror narratives can be read as a response to real-world environmental fears, but this connection is not new; horror and the Anthropocene share a longer history.[7] John Clute places the start of fantastic literature—including horror—between 1750 and 1800, "a span of time during which the inhabitants of the West begin to understand that the world is in fact a planet and begin almost immediately to develop the planet they have grasped."[8] This is, as Sarah Dillon observes, approximately the same period proposed as the start of the Anthropocene, "in which case, fantastic literature would be, by definition, the Literature of the Anthropocene."[9] This connection becomes more explicit in contemporary horror, which, Dillon argues, "is moving from a literature of cosmic fear to a literature of planetary fear."[10] In the early twenty-first century, she writes, we have a "*self-consciousness* that we are living in the Anthropocene" that was not present before.[11]

This self-consciousness builds upon long-established anxieties about science and scientific development in both horror in general and ecohorror specifically. As Jason Colavito writes, "Horror cannot survive without the anxieties created by the changing role of human knowledge and science in our society."[12] In the past, these anxieties have been reflected in mad science narratives or stories of scientific experimentation gone awry. This trend can be traced as at least as far back as Mary Shelley's *Frankenstein*, which Colavito calls "the godfather to the overreaching mad scientist plot," a Gothic novel whose focus on science, the role of the scientist, and matters of physical life and death set it apart from other Gothic works.[13] These anxieties about science and scientists are also present in early ecohorror films like *Godzilla* (1954) and *Night of the Lepus* (1972), which look beyond mere scientific overreach to the specifically environmental consequences of such overreach. The monstrous bunnies of *Night of the Lepus*, for instance, are created as a result of scientific experimentation (and poor lab safety practices), and the problem is contained only through the removal of the bunnies and restoration of ecological balance.

Ecohorror in the Anthropocene—and ecohorror *of* the Anthropocene—is not solely concerned with scientific knowledge or overreach on a small scale, however. More and more, the problems and anxieties of ecohorror texts are the result of broader forces, represented not only as mad scientists, creatures, or animal attacks but also as far-reaching events or processes such as pollution, species extinction, or extreme weather. Many twenty-first-century ecohorror narratives involving animal attacks illustrate this by placing such attacks in the context of larger climate change–related issues. *Crawl* (2019), for instance, is ostensibly a movie about gigantic alligators attacking people, but these attacks are enabled by the larger event, a climate change–induced hurricane. This echoes Matt Hills's argument that "a surprising range of horror films fail to present us with definite 'monsters' as entities," and in many cases "a monstrous agency cannot be reduced to any given 'entity.'"[14] *Crawl* and other twenty-first-century animal attack narratives do feature monsters, but those monsters are often only symptoms of a threat that exceeds their scale.[15] The Anthropocene, after all, is not a clear monster or singular occurrence, and it is not limited to a single time or place. It occurs over a long period of time and everywhere on earth (although not everywhere equally).

With this shifting sense of scale—both in time and in place—ecohorror and the Anthropocene reveal a concern with the ways in which the planet is changing. Ursula K. Heise writes of the Anthropocene that "it focuses on the reality of a terraformed planet that the genre [speculative fiction in general] has long held out as a vision for the future of other planets, but which has already arrived."[16] Ecohorror in the Anthropocene presents a vision of that terraformed planet as frightening rather than promising and reflects both the horrors we face now and those we fear will occur in the future. Similarly, Nicole M. Merola has argued that "the Anthropocene is fundamentally estranging: what we thought we knew about the continuance of a habitable biosphere for currently evolved creatures has turned out to be a mirage."[17] Ecohorror reflects this estrangement and reveals the horror of *knowing* we live on a terraformed planet, one not terraformed for our benefit. Therefore, ecohorror may be the dominant mode in which we talk to ourselves about the global climate crisis and the real-life ecological horrors of our current Anthropocenic moment.

The examples of ecohorror provided thus far are straightforward instances of ecohorror as a genre, texts that share certain conventions, but ecohorror is both a genre and a mode, meaning it has identifiable characteristics of its own while also appearing within other genres.[18] Stephen A. Rust and Carter Soles have identified some of ecohorror's central characteristics, noting that although ecohorror includes nature-strikes-back narratives (the type that may first come to mind), it also includes "texts in which humans do horrific things to the natural world, or in which horrific texts and tropes are used to promote ecological awareness, represent ecological crises, or blur human/non-human distinctions more broadly."[19] As such, ecohorror already incorporates a wide variety of texts, but considering it as a mode expands its reach. For instance, there are moments of ecohorror in the time-lapse footage of melting glaciers at the end of the documentary *Chasing Ice* (2012), in action blockbusters like *Geostorm* (2017), in the well-known opening of Rachel Carson's *Silent Spring* (1962), and in countless other horror films and Gothic narratives.

Thus, ecohorror functions as melodrama does for Linda Williams. While acknowledging the important history of melodrama-as-genre (e.g., the woman's film of the 1930s to 1950s) and its roots in the nineteenth-century sentimental novel, Williams stresses that melodrama is a mode that constitutes "the typical form of American popular narrative in literature, stage, film, and television," regardless of genre.[20] Williams emphasizes that melodrama emerges at times of ideological crisis, and ecohorror evinces this same pattern of emergence, appearing in clusters related to nuclear concerns in the 1950s, pollution and the environmental movement in the 1970s, and climate change and the concept of the Anthropocene now.

Just as in melodrama, emotion is crucial to ecohorror, and the most obvious emotional response provoked by ecohorror texts is fear. As such, ecohorror reflects (and sometimes reinforces) ecophobia, defined by Simon C. Estok as "an irrational and groundless hatred of the natural world, as present and subtle in our daily lives and literature as homophobia and racism and sexism."[21] Ecophobia has also played a significant role in conversations about the ecogothic, as noted by Dawn Keetley and Matthew Wynn Sivils, who emphasize intersections between the two "not only because ecophobic representations of nature will be infused, like the Gothic, with fear and dread but also because ecophobia is born out of the failure of humans to control their lives and their world. And control, or lack thereof, is central to the Gothic."[22] In addition to this anxiety about control, Estok argues that uncertainty—and the threat represented by uncertainty—"is the life-blood of ecophobia."[23] In this way, ecophobia as an element of ecohorror and the ecogothic reinforces Noël Carroll's argument that horror is "founded upon the disturbance of cultural norms,"[24] fundamentally concerned with impurity and category confusion.

As with horror writ large, ecohorror's focus on fear (or ecophobia) often generates a troubling ambivalence. Despite many creators' and audience members' very real concerns about environmental issues and their desires to prevent the worst from happening, ecohorror runs the risk of reinforcing fearful responses to the nonhuman or—equally dangerous—leading to a feeling of hopelessness. Ecohorror, after all, is not primarily a call to action. Even the most pointed ecohorrific critique of environmental degradation is ultimately couched in mere entertainment.

It's worth considering, then, what role fear plays in ecohorror's influence. Estok argues in *The Ecophobia Hypothesis* that ecophobic representations have serious impacts on the real world, even arguing they should be criminalized:

> Why are ecophobic representations of and actions toward nature not subject to the law? Why are they not under the category of hate speech and hate crimes? Having them so would seem a reasonable outcome of the expanding circle of moral concern that has already produced greater protections against sexism, racism, and speciesism.[25]

But is all fear ecophobic? Estok argues that "representations of nature as an opponent that hurts, hinders, threatens, or kills us ... are ecophobic."[26] However, Rayson K. Alex and S. Susan Deborah map a significant distinction between ecophobia and eco-fear, arguing that "it is not always useful to understand the fearful relation between humans and their ecology as ecophobia."[27] Focusing primarily on the role of eco-fear in traditional Indigenous communities, Alex and Deborah draw a line between the Indigenous reverential eco-fear exhibited there and the pathological ecophobia seen in modern, neoliberal cultures. As they illustrate, there is no reason to assume that all fear of nature in modern or Western culture is phobic. Some fears of the nonhuman world are justified, not irrational. If fear of the natural world is not necessarily phobic, then at least some instances of ecohorror might be productive—or at least not dangerous.

Greta Thunberg's call for fear rather than hope provides another useful perspective. At the World Economic Forum in January 2019, the climate activist said, "Adults keep saying we owe it to the young people to give them hope. But I don't want your hope, I don't want you to be hopeful. I want you to panic, I want you to feel the fear I feel every day. And then I want you to act, I want you to act as if you would in a crisis. I want you to act as if the house was on fire, because it is."[28] This call for a negative affective response to climate change highlights the power of fear to create change. Fear is not simply a reflection of deep-seated hatred. Sometimes it is justified and necessary.

Further, ecohorror is not defined solely by human fear *of* nonhuman nature but is also frequently concerned with human fear *for* nonhuman nature. Jennifer Schell notes that ecogothic literature is often "dedicated to exploring the horrifying implications of various ecological events and natural disasters, some of which are anthropogenic and some of which are not," and is "very critical of human beings and their destructive attitudes toward the natural world," tending "to regard environmental problems with a complicated mixture of anxiety, horror, terror, anger, sadness, nostalgia, and guilt."[29] Reflecting what Keetley and Sivils describe as "a culture obsessed with and fearful of a natural world both monstrous and monstrously wronged,"[30] ecohorror also consistently explores the effects of humans' actions on the natural world. Many 1950s films examine the consequences of nuclear testing on animals and the natural world (e.g., *Godzilla* [1954], *Them!* [1954], and *The Monster That Challenged the World* [1957]); 1970s ecohorror films take up pollution (*Frogs* [1972], for instance) and the depletion of the ozone layer (*Day of the Animals* [1977]); and twenty-first-century Syfy Channel and Asylum productions like *Mega Shark vs. Giant Octopus* (2009) and *Sharknado* (2013) anchor their monsters and happenings in anthropogenic climate change while other—more serious—films like *WALL-E* (2008) and *The Host* (2006) continue to address pollution. Because of their emphasis on the harm caused by humans, these films may frighten audiences with monstrous animals and dramatic weather events, but they also frequently prompt sympathy for the creatures, which can lead to guilt and anxiety about our responsibility toward the natural world and about the future. These films thus complicate audiences' fear responses, moving ecohorror beyond ecophobia, but they are still not necessarily effective at prompting action.

Another approach to ecohorror evinces a cautious optimism that emphasizes our human connection to the nonhuman and all that we stand to lose during the Anthropocene. This approach also builds upon Stacy Alaimo's concept of trans-corporeality, "the literal contact zone between human corporeality and more-than-human nature ... in which the human is always intermeshed with the more-than-human world."[31] Trans-corporeality can be frightening; as Alaimo argues, "the sense of being permeable to harmful substances" that is inherent in trans-corporeality "may provoke denial, delusions of transcendence, or the desire for a magical fix."[32] These denials and delusions appear regularly in horror when we imagine that the natural world—animals, weather, pollutants, and so on—can be separated from us, can be conquered. But although some ecohorror indulges in this fantasy, allowing us to imagine "a magical fix," much of the ecohorror considered here presents a more complex relationship between human and nonhuman and "may also foster a posthuman environmentalism of co-constituted creatures, entangled knowledges, and precautionary practices."[33] As such, ecohorror has the potential to help create relationships of care between human and nonhuman, even if these relationships are complicated by fear.

Ecohorror therefore reflects our anxieties about science and the nonhuman while revealing how much we value these things. We fear science and its attempts to control the natural world; we fear the natural world and the way it exceeds our control. We also value science as a way of understanding the world, however, and return to it repeatedly in these narratives; we value the natural world and fear its loss at least as much as we fear nonhuman nature itself. It's complicated.

These complex ideas about nature and science have a long history in horror, which has addressed nature and the environment since the beginning. *Where* horror occurs matters, and the settings of horror shape audience expectations as well as the genre's monsters. There is a reason, after all, why so many horror films begin with the protagonists leaving civilization and traveling to a new and unfamiliar location (a cabin in the woods, perhaps). Animals have also long played a significant role in horror—just think of Dr. Moreau's human-animal hybrids, the giant ants of *Them!*, or the monstrous shark of *Jaws*. And fears of an unfamiliar, uncontrolled space and the animal both easily reflect larger fears of death or the loss of self and humanity that frequently recur in horror.

Horror scholarship, however, has only recently begun to consistently and directly address such ecological elements. Historically, it has relied heavily on psychoanalytic theory and on gender studies, with other concerns treated as secondary (not just the environment but also race, class, etc.), but the growth of ecocriticism as a field has opened a space for horror scholars to engage with horror in ecocritical terms. Alongside the growing discourse about ecohorror, there is also an ongoing conversation about Gothic nature and the ecogothic.[34] Our contributors engage with both ecohorror and ecogothic conversations, and we make no attempt here to clearly outline or define a relationship between the two. Just as with horror and the Gothic more broadly, they overlap and speak to one another in complicated and ever-shifting ways.

An early contribution to ecohorror criticism is the ecohorror cluster published in *ISLE: Interdisciplinary Studies in Literature and Environment*, edited by Stephen A. Rust and Carter Soles (2014). The introduction to this cluster includes a definition of ecohorror that we, along with many contributors to this book, build upon. Rust and Soles argue that ecohorror "assumes that environmental disruption is haunting humanity's relationship to the non-human world" and "is present in a broad set of texts grappling with ecocritical matters."[35] The essays in the *ISLE* cluster provide an early sense of the many possibilities ecohorror affords: contributors look at texts ranging from Edgar Allan Poe and Mira Grant, 1960s horror films and the postmodern horror film, and horror comics; they consider ecophobia and mechanophobia, trans-corporeality and material ecocriticism, apocalypse and anthropocentrism. We intentionally adopt a similarly wide-ranging approach in this collection.

In addition, there have been four full-length critical works on ecohorror to date, three of which deal solely with ecohorror about creatures and animals. The first, William Schoell's *Creature Features: Nature Turned Nasty in the Movies* (2008), provides a clear (if somewhat limited) overview of creature-feature movies. Schoell's book is more descriptive than critical, and his scope is somewhat limited by his focus on "behemoths (discovered in time-lost worlds or ancient societies and somehow unleashed upon modern civilization) or normal-sized animals such as birds and bears that behave in strange ways" and by his unwillingness to include monster movies that he judges boring or sadistic.[36] Lee Gambin's *Massacred by Mother Nature: Exploring the Natural Horror Film* (2012) takes a more thoughtful approach. Gambin writes, "From the bugs and the bees and the dogs and the cats and the whales and the rats—Mother Nature is not happy, and she will slaughter the human population with the help of her friends, her loyal minions of feather, fur and fin."[37] Gambin focuses solely on animal horror films (he does not include other types of ecohorror), and he sees the revenge-of-nature narrative as central; therefore, his focus is also somewhat limited. Robin L. Murray and Joseph K. Heumann's *Monstrous Nature: Environment and Horror on the Big Screen* (2016) also focuses solely on film, but their book advances the critical conversation about ecohorror and considers a broader range of films (not just animal horror and creature features). Rather than narrowly focusing on a genre or subgenre, Murray and Heumann address "a monstrous nature that evolved either deliberately or by accident and incites fear in humanity as both character and audience,"[38] doing so across genre lines and including not just horror films but also documentary and other nonhorror drama films. Finally, Dominic Lennard's *Brute Force: Animal Horror Movies* (2019) returns to the ground covered by Schoell and Gambin—focusing specifically on animal horror and on film—while engaging more fully with contemporary scholarship about animal horror and placing these films in the context of evolutionary psychology.

Another significant contribution to the conversation about ecohorror can be found in Maurice Yacowar's analysis of the "natural attack film." Without using the term *ecohorror*, Yacowar defines the natural attack film as a narrative scenario that "pits a human community against a destructive form of nature."[39] He considers the natural attack film a subgenre of the disaster film, calling it "the most common disaster type,"[40] and subdivides the natural attack film into three types: attacks by animals (normal, giant, or otherwise) on a human community, attacks by the elements (as in 1974's *Earthquake*), and attacks by atomic mutants (including *Them!* and *The Beast from 20,000 Fathoms*).[41] As Yacowar writes, regardless of type or subgenre, "the natural disaster film dramatizes people's helplessness against the forces of nature."[42] Oddly, Yacowar does not directly mention horror, even though many of his key examples—for example, *King Kong*, *Godzilla*, *Them!*, and *The Birds*—are widely acknowledged as canonical horror genre entries.

Where Schoell, Gambin, and Lennard focus narrowly on animal horror, we provide a more expansive view of ecohorror; where Murray and Heumann discuss monstrous nature across genres, we maintain a focus on horror (on its own and in conjunction with other genres) and consider not just nature as monstrous but also nature as sympathetic or as victim; where Yacowar sees these narratives as a subset of the disaster film, we cultivate an approach to ecohorror that emphasizes the *horror* over the disaster and seeks out narratives of more subtle natural horror. Finally, where all these critics attend specifically to film, we put film in conversation with other media, including television, novels, manga, short fiction, and poetry.

Several edited collections have also addressed ecohorror, often by focusing on specific subsets of the genre. Katarina Gregersdotter, Johan Höglund, and Nicklas Hållén's *Animal Horror Cinema: Genre, History and Criticism* (2015), for instance, focuses on animal horror movies "that centre on the relation between 'human' and 'animal' as categories unrelated to their places in the ecosystem."[43] Dawn Keetley and Angela Tenga's *Plant Horror: Approaches to the Monstrous Vegetal in Fiction and Film* (2016) turns to another specific type of ecohorror, examining "the perennial and terrifying ability of vegetal life to swallow, engulf, overrun, and outlive humans."[44] These collections have made significant contributions to the discourse on ecohorror, even while focusing more narrowly on animal horror and plant horror.

Other collections have included chapters or sections devoted to ecohorror, indicating the growing attention to ecohorror within horror studies. For instance, *The Canadian Horror Film: Terror of the Souls*, edited by Gina Freitag and André Loiselle (2015), includes a section specifically addressing ecohorror and features the environment as a recurring theme throughout. Similarly, *Beasts of the Deep: Sea Creatures and Popular Culture* (2018), edited by Jon Hackett and Seán Harrington, addresses such topics as oceanic horror, the depths of the sea as sublime, fan response to sea creatures in horror fiction, *Jaws Unleashed*, and *Jurassic World*. The book's emphasis is not on ecohorror specifically, however, so it provides a set of interesting intersections with the genre rather than contributing consistently to ecohorror studies. Most recently, *The Palgrave Handbook to Horror Literature* (2018), edited by Kevin Corstorphine and Laura R. Kremmel, includes two valuable chapters on ecohorror: Bernice M. Murphy provides a thorough outline of the uses of the animal in horror literature, filling a scholarly gap left by the attention to animal horror *cinema* in particular, and Elizabeth Parker presents seven theses on "why we fear the forest."[45]

Our collection builds on the work done by previous scholars and takes advantage of an ecohorror-as-mode approach in order to analyze ecohorror tropes wherever they are found. The built-in flexibility and transhistorical dimension of mode-based analysis promotes fruitful cross-genre and cross-media analysis. Each contributor is attentive to matters of historical and generic specificity, yet our work as a group points to how productive ecohorror as a cross-generic and cross-media mode can be for seeing broad trends and developments in the ways our culture uses media to scare itself with ecological terrors.

The collection opens with a section dedicated to "Expanding Ecohorror." Here, contributors propose new types of ecohorror and seek out connections between ecohorror and other types of horror. In the collection's opening chapter, "Tentacular Ecohorror and the Agency of Trees in Algernon Blackwood's 'The Man Whom the Trees Loved' and Lorcan Finnegan's *Without Name*," Dawn Keetley argues for a new type of ecohorror, *tentacular ecohorror*, in which nonhuman nature "reaches out to grab and entangle the human." Building upon Stacy Alaimo's concept of trans-corporeality, Keetley argues that tentacular ecohorror stages a merging of the human and the vegetal that can be both terrifying and transformative.

Christy Tidwell's "Spiraling Inward and Outward: Junji Ito's *Uzumaki* and the Scope of Ecohorror" seeks to extend ecohorror's range, analyzing the intersections between three interrelated horror subgenres—ecohorror, body horror, and cosmic horror—to highlight the centrality of ecohorror to horror as a whole. Through an analysis of Junji Ito's *Uzumaki*, Tidwell argues that ecohorror cannot fully be separated from body horror or cosmic horror and, further, that *Uzumaki*'s combination of the three indicates the importance of shifting scales: from individual bodies to ecosystems, or from the life-span of a human to the life-span of the planet.

Rounding out the opening section is "'The Hand of Deadly Decay': The Rotting Corpse, America's Religious Tradition, and the Ethics of Green Burial in Poe's 'The Colloquy of Monos and Una,'" in which Ashley Kniss urges ecocritics to consider the corpse as a primary source of horror in the ecohorror genre. While Poe is not typically considered an ecohorror writer, his tale engages with the modern ethics of green burial, Kniss argues, reinforcing an ethic that values connections between the material body and the nonhuman world and "does not shy away from the physicality of death and the reality of rot."

Keri Stevenson's "The Death of Birdsong, the Birdsong of Death: Algernon Charles Swinburne and the Horror of Erosion" opens the collection's second section: "Haunted and Unhaunted Landscapes." Stevenson's chapter identifies erosion and the sea as sources of ecohorror, a fear heightened by climate change–related ocean-level rise. Stevenson traces erosion—and its companion figure, the relentlessly devouring sea—in works of Victorian poet Algernon Charles Swinburne. Her analysis stresses Swinburne's use of the disanthropic mode, depicting a world "completely and finally *without people*."[46]

In "An Unhaunted Landscape: The Anti-Gothic Impulse in Ambrose Bierce's 'A Tough Tussle,'" Chelsea Davis notes the horror of a world not only without humans but without human *influence*. She argues that Bierce's story represents a subset of ecohorror that draws its fear from the lack of human presence and even human hauntings. Drawing a distinction between anti-Gothic works and anti-*horror* narratives, Davis argues that the American Civil War period gave rise to literary unhaunted landscapes because it made us anxious about whether our species is significant enough to leave a lasting mark on the indifferent nonhuman world.

Bridgitte Barclay's "The Extinction-Haunted Salton Sea in *The Monster That Challenged the World*," however, examines a landscape that is dramatically haunted by human activity. Barclay contends that midcentury films featuring attacks by prehistoric creatures connect mid-twentieth-century understandings of prehistoric extinctions to concerns about atomic-caused human extinction. These fears of extinction appear both in the film's prehistoric mollusk and in the Salton Sea setting itself, the result of an apparently successful engineering feat that decades later is clearly a product of scientific hubris. In this film, Barclay argues, the Salton Sea's real-world environmental devastation is the source of ecohorror for twenty-first-century viewers—not the prehistoric creature itself.

The third section, "The Ecohorror of Intimacy," turns to the horror located in the home and/or family. Marisol Cortez opens this section with an examination of two Stephen King works—*It* and *Dreamcatcher*—that she identifies as key literary texts of the urban environmental Gothic. King's deployment of the bathroom in these two novels draws attention to infrastructural, technological, and historical ecophobia, pointing to the need for ecohorror studies to engage with these forms of ecophobia and asking readers to remember "what an ecophobic culture would prefer to forget."

Brittany R. Roberts turns to the relationship between human and nonhuman companions in "'This Bird Made an Art of Being Vile': Ontological Difference and Uncomfortable Intimacies in Stephen Gregory's *The Cormorant*." In *The Cormorant*, Gregory creates a complex, multispecies relationship marked by both companionship and fear. Roberts reads Gregory's novel as an exploration of ethical relationships between human and nonhuman animals that indicates the consequences of abandoning the responsibilities of such a relationship, "insinuat[ing] that true monstrosity is found not in the strange Others with whom we live but rather in humans who abandon their cross-species kin."

In their chapter, "*The Shape of Water* and Post-pastoral Ecohorror," Robin L. Murray and Joseph K. Heumann argue that Guillermo del Toro's *The Shape of Water* draws upon ecohorror conventions for multiple ends. Centrally, the film connects ecohorror conventions with a post-pastoral vision of nature that emphasizes a more positive relationship with the natural world. The film, they argue, creates this possibility through an emphasis on domestic spaces and familial and romantic relationships that highlights relationships of interdependence rather than abuse or violence.

The final section of the book—"Being Prey, Being Food"—examines narratives of food and predation between human and nonhuman in ecohorror texts. Kristen Angierski's chapter, "Superpig Blues: Agribusiness Ecohorror in Bong Joon-ho's *Okja*," uses the designation "anti-pastoral ecohorror" to describe a filmic world that uses sentimentality and satire to critique factory farming as itself a form of ecohorror. Although this combination of satire and ecohorror might seem to undermine the seriousness of its animal rights message, Angierski argues that this approach creates connections to the nonhuman world as well as to those who act on its behalf. "Even as the film encourages viewers to laugh at the silly personalities and inflexibilities of the ALF vegans," she writes, "it is much harder to argue with them."

In "*Zoo*: Television Ecohorror On and Off the Screen," Sharon Sharp turns to representations of animals on television, analyzing the way the animal horror show *Zoo* critiques institutional practices of animal captivity and estranges meat-eating via its graphic representations both of the human fear of consumption and of the horrific process of animals becoming meat. At the same time, Sharp argues, the series' critique is limited and focused on individual action, failing to address the industrial production of meat and engaging in practices of animal exploitation in early seasons. This relationship between critique and failure to critique indicates that an understanding of television ecohorror requires attention to human-animal relationships both on-screen and off.

Concluding this section and the collection, Carter Soles examines the interplay between animal horror and whiteness studies. His chapter, "Naturalizing White Supremacy in *The Shallows*," exposes how the nonhuman of *The Shallows* isn't only the shark but a more conceptual nonhuman that includes the film's abject Mexicans. This conceptual boundary between white humanity and all other living beings arises from a white Euro-American culture that views itself as superior to all other cultures and species. *The Shallows* is part of a long tradition of killer white shark movies that project human fears of "loathsome" extreme whiteness onto sharks. Sadly, by misrepresenting sharks as ecohorror monsters, these movies contribute to negative material consequences for the white shark as a species.

As this collection illustrates, ecohorror appears in many forms and provides an opportunity to better understand not only our human relationship to the natural world but also the effects of climate change. The book thus reinforces Christy Tidwell's description of ecohorror in the *Posthuman Glossary*:

> Perhaps animals will attack us, perhaps we will lose our place at the top of the animacy hierarchy, or perhaps we will have to acknowledge our interconnectedness with other beings. In doing so, ecohorror risks reinforcing those fears and the categories they are built upon, but ecohorror also asks us to reconsider some of those fears and to imagine what might happen if we were not to insist so vehemently upon such divisions.[47]

The content and title of this book—*Fear and Nature*—indicate that ecohorror is not defined only by fear *of* nature but also encompasses fear *for* nature. Ecohorror is not simply a venue for ecophobia.

Furthermore, these fears can direct us toward multiple outcomes, some prompted by fear for ourselves and some prompted by hope for a different future. Ryan Hediger writes, "Particularly in the age of the Anthropocene, as familiar and beloved places are affected by climate change and rendered foreign, we can make a virtue of necessity by engaging the strangeness as an opportunity to recast forms of living."[48] Ecohorror highlights the strangeness and horror of living in the Anthropocene and of engaging in less-than-positive ways with the nonhuman world. It therefore has the potential to reinforce our fears and estrange us further from the nonhuman world.

But it might also do the opposite. As Donna J. Haraway writes, the time in which we now live "is made up of ongoing multispecies stories and practices of becoming-with in times that remain at stake, in precarious times, in which the world is not finished and the sky has not fallen—yet. We are at stake to each other."[49] Although, as Haraway argues, "both the Anthropocene and the Capitalocene lend themselves too readily to cynicism, defeatism, and self-certain and self-fulfilling predictions, like the 'game over, too late' discourse,"[50] this is not the only possible narrative or outcome. Future work in ecohorror must be wary of such cynicism and defeatism—both in ecocriticism itself and in the works analyzed. As several of our contributors have done, we must look for ways to tell stories—*within* ecohorror and *about* ecohorror—that do not foreclose the future or discourage activism. Ecohorror offers an opportunity to help us see the ways in which we are "at stake to each other" and then "to recast forms of living."

Notes

1. CBS News, "Smoke from Wildfires Increases Health Risks for Millions of Americans," last modified June 25, 2019, https://www.cbsnews.com/news/2019-wildfire-season-smoke-from-wildfires-increases-health-risks-for-millions-of-americans/.

2. Iliana Magra, "Europe Suffers Heat Wave of Dangerous, Record-High Temperatures," *New York Times*, July 24, 2019, https://www.nytimes.com/2019/07/24/world/europe/record-temperatures-heatwave.html.

3. Jessie Yeung, Swati Gupta, and Michael Guy, "India Has Just Five Years to Solve Its Water Crisis, Experts Fear. Otherwise Hundreds of Millions of Lives Will Be in Danger," CNN, July 4, 2019, https://edition.cnn.com/2019/06/27/india/india-water-crisis-intl-hnk/index.html; Jessie Yeung, Swati Gupta, and Sophia Saifi, "227 Dead After Monsoon Floods Devastate South Asia," CNN, July 18, 2019, https://edition.cnn.com/2019/07/18/asia/monsoon-flood-south-asia-intl-hnk/index.html.

4. Jenessa Dunscombe, "Greenland Ice Sheet Beats All-Time 1-Day Melt Record," *Eos* 100, no. 2 (August 2019), https://doi.org/10.1029/2019EO130349.

5. Sandra Díaz et al., *Summary for Policymakers of the Global Assessment Report on Biodiversity and Ecosystem Services of the Intergovernmental Science-Policy Platform on Biodiversity and Ecosystem Services*, IPBES, last modified May 6, 2019, https://www.ipbes.net/sites/default/files/downloads/spm_unedited_advance_for_posting_htn.pdf.

6. Lisa Friedman, "U.S. Significantly Weakens Endangered Species Act," *New York Times*, August 12, 2019, https://www.nytimes.com/2019/08/12/climate/endangered-species-act-changes.html.

7. As a term, *Anthropocene* uses the language of stratigraphy to indicate the planet-changing ecological impact of the human species. For the Anthropocene to be adopted as the name of our geological epoch (following the Holocene), human actions must be measurable in the geological record. For this reason, it has not yet been officially approved by the International Commission on Stratigraphy, although a proposal is being developed. There is also debate about this term among humanists, some of whom argue that the term maintains an anthropocentric worldview and obscures differences between cultures, lifestyles, social classes, ethnic groups, etc. See, among others, Eileen Crist's "On the Poverty of Our Nomenclature," Andreas Malm's *Fossil Capital*, Jason W. Moore's *Capitalism in the Web of Life*, Kathryn Yusoff's *A Billion Black Anthropocenes or None*, Richard Grusin's collection *Anthropocene Feminism*, and Donna J. Haraway's *Staying with the Trouble: Making Kin in the Chthulucene*.

8. John Clute, "Physics for Amnesia: Horror Motifs in SF," *New York Review of Science Fiction* 21, no. 2, issue 242 (October 2008): 4.

9. Sarah Dillon, "The Horror of the Anthropocene," *C21 Literature: Journal of 21st-Century Writings* 6, no. 1 (2018): 7.

10. Ibid., 5.

11. Ibid., 8.

12. Jason Colavito, *Knowing Fear: Science, Knowledge and the Development of the Horror Genre* (Jefferson, NC: McFarland, 2008), 4.

13. Ibid., 79.

14. Matt Hills, "An Event-Based Definition of Art-Horror," in *Dark Thoughts: Philosophic Reflections on Cinematic Horror*, ed. S. J. Schneider and D. Shaw (Lanham, MD: Scarecrow, 2003), 145, 146.

15. Dawn Keetley's analysis of *The Happening* (2008) provides an example of the usefulness of Hills's event-based horror for ecohorror. Keetley points out that the threat shown in the film—plants and their agency—has no clear explanation or agency behind it. Instead, in the film, "there is no discernible monster: it may indeed be the vegetation—the trees, bushes, grasses—

releasing toxins as the wind sweeps through them. But even this is not clear." "Introduction: Six Theses on Plant Horror; or, Why Are Plants Horrifying?," in *Plant Horror: Approaches to the Monstrous Vegetal in Fiction and Film*, ed. Dawn Keetley and Angela Tenga (London: Palgrave Macmillan, 2016), 23.

16. Ursula K. Heise, *Imagining Extinction: The Cultural Meanings of Endangered Species* (Chicago: University of Chicago Press, 2016), 219.

17. Nicole M. Merola, "'What Do We Do but Keep Breathing as Best We Can This / Minute Atmosphere': Juliana Spahr and Anthropocene Anxiety," in *Affective Ecocriticism: Emotion, Embodiment, Environment*, ed. Kyle Bladow and Jennifer Ladino (Lincoln: University of Nebraska Press, 2018), 26.

18. We take genre to mean a contract between viewer and audience, any set of setting-specific, iconographic, and/or narrative conventions that congeal into recognizable forms for a certain period. Every genre—whether a film cycle, popular literary genre, or new subgenre of an existing genre—has a specific history and emerges at a particular time in response to contemporary cultural issues and concerns as well as to certain media-specific trends and industry conditions. Every genre also has a shelf life and a series of typical shifts it undergoes: from an initial formative period to a well-recognized classic one and finally to a self-reflexive or mannerist phase, which usually includes parodic approaches to genre conventions formerly taken seriously. In some genres, including many horror-related ones, this third phase translates into a camp phase.

19. Stephen A. Rust and Carter Soles, "Ecohorror Special Cluster: 'Living in Fear, Living in Dread, Pretty Soon We'll All Be Dead,'" *ISLE: Interdisciplinary Studies in Literature and Environment* 21, no. 3 (Summer 2014): 509–10.

20. Linda Williams, "Melodrama Revised," in *Refiguring American Film Genres*, ed. Nick Browne (Berkeley: University of California Press, 1998), 50.

21. Simon C. Estok, "Theorizing in a Space of Ambivalent Openness: Ecocriticism and Ecophobia," *ISLE: Interdisciplinary Studies in Literature and Environment* 16, no. 2 (Spring 2009): 208.

22. Dawn Keetley and Matthew Wynn Sivils, "Introduction: Approaches to the Ecogothic," in *Ecogothic in Nineteenth-Century American Literature*, ed. Dawn Keetley and Matthew Wynn Sivils (New York: Routledge, 2018), 3. Jennifer Schell, however, separates the two terms, noting that although many ecogothic scholars seem to have been inspired by Estok's concept of ecophobia, most reject it, using *ecogothic* as a way "to avoid the problematic conflation of fear and hatred inherent in Estok's definition of ecophobia and to draw on the substantial, already existing archive of research on gothic literature" (Jennifer Schell, "Ecogothic Extinction Fiction: The Extermination of the Alaskan Mammoth," in *Ecogothic in Nineteenth-Century American Literature*, ed. Dawn Keetley and Matthew Wynn Sivils [New York: Routledge, 2018], 176).

23. Simon C. Estok, "Ecophobia, the Agony of Water, and Misogyny," *ISLE: Interdisciplinary Studies in Literature and Environment* 26, no. 2 (Spring 2019): 476.

24. Noël Carroll, *The Philosophy of Horror: Or, Paradoxes of the Heart* (New York: Routledge, 1990), 214.

25. Simon C. Estok, *The Ecophobia Hypothesis* (New York: Routledge, 2018), 71.

26. Estok, "Theorizing," 209. Estok notes in "Ecophobia" that "an aversion to imagined threats to our survival is not ecophobia" (475), but this is not stated so clearly in most of his other articles on ecophobia, and most scholars who take up the concept do not make this distinction.

27. Rayson K. Alex and S. Susan Deborah, "Ecophobia, Reverential Eco-fear, and Indigenous Worldviews," *ISLE: Interdisciplinary Studies in Literature and Environment* 2, no. 2 (Spring 2019): 423.

28. Greta Thunberg, "'Our House Is on Fire': Greta Thunberg, 16, Urges Leaders to Act on Climate," *The Guardian*, January 25, 2019, https://www.theguardian.com/environment/2019/jan/25/our-house-is-on-fire-greta-thunberg16-urges-leaders-to-act-on-climate.
29. Schell, "Ecogothic Extinction Fiction," 176.
30. Keetley and Sivils, "Introduction," 11.
31. Stacy Alaimo, *Bodily Natures: Science, Environment, and the Material Self* (Bloomington: Indiana University Press, 2010), 2.
32. Ibid., 146.
33. Ibid. See Christy Tidwell's "Monstrous Natures Within: Posthuman and New Materialist Ecohorror in Mira Grant's *Parasite*" for an examination of this possibility in parasite-focused horror fiction.
34. See Bernice M. Murphy's *The Suburban Gothic in American Popular Culture* and *The Rural Gothic in American Popular Culture*, Tom Hillard's "'Deep into That Darkness Peering,' An Essay on Gothic Nature," Andrew Smith and William Hughes's collection titled *EcoGothic*, Dawn Keetley and Matthew Wynn Sivil's *Ecogothic in Nineteenth-Century American Literature*, and Elizabeth Parker's *The Forest and the EcoGothic: The Deep Dark Woods in the Popular Imagination*. The journal *Gothic Nature* also published its first issue in September 2019.
35. Rust and Soles, "Ecohorror Special Cluster," 510.
36. William Schoell, *Creature Features: Nature Turned Nasty in the Movies* (Jefferson, NC: McFarland, 2008), 1.
37. Lee Gambin, *Massacred by Mother Nature: Exploring the Natural Horror Film* (Baltimore: Midnight Marquee, 2012), 18.
38. Robin L. Murray and Joseph K. Heumann, *Monstrous Nature: Environment and Horror on the Big Screen* (Lincoln: University of Nebraska Press, 2016), xiv.
39. Maurice Yacowar, "The Bug in the Rug: Notes on the Disaster Genre," in *Film Genre Reader III*, ed. Barry Keith Grant (Austin: University of Texas Press, 2003), 277.
40. Ibid., 277.
41. An ecohorror critic might also parse *The Beast from 20,000 Fathoms* as a de-extinction narrative. See Bridgitte Barclay, chapter 6 in this volume, for more on de-extinction narratives.
42. Yacowar, "Bug in the Rug," 278.
43. Katarina Gregersdotter, Johan Höglund, and Nicklas Hållén, eds., introduction to *Animal Horror Cinema: Genre, History and Criticism* (New York: Palgrave Macmillan, 2015), 1–18.
44. Dawn Keetley, "Introduction: Six Theses on Plant Horror; or, Why Are Plants Horrifying?," in *Plant Horror: Approaches to the Monstrous Vegetal in Fiction and Film*, ed. Dawn Keetley and Angela Tenga (London: Palgrave Macmillan, 2016), 5.
45. Elizabeth Parker, "Who's Afraid of the Big Bad Woods? Deep Dark Forests and Literary Horror," in *The Palgrave Handbook to Horror Literature*, ed. Kevin Corstorphine and Laura R. Kremmel (Cham, CH: Palgrave Macmillan, 2018), 406.
46. Greg Garrard, "Worlds Without Us: Some Types of Disanthropy," *SubStance* 41, no. 1, issue 127 (2012): 40. Emphasis in original.
47. Christy Tidwell, "Ecohorror," in *Posthuman Glossary*, ed. Rosi Braidotti and Maria Hlavajova (London: Bloomsbury Academic, 2018), 117.
48. Ryan Hediger, "Uncanny Homesickness and War: Loss of Affect, Loss of Place, and Reworlding in *Redeployment*," in *Affective Ecocriticism: Emotion, Embodiment, Environment*, ed. Kyle Bladow and Jennifer Ladino (Lincoln: University of Nebraska Press, 2018), 157.
49. Donna J. Haraway, *Staying with the Trouble: Making Kin in the Chthulucene* (Durham, NC: Duke University Press, 2016), 55.
50. Ibid., 56.

References

Alaimo, Stacy. *Bodily Natures: Science, Environment, and the Material Self*. Bloomington: Indiana University Press, 2010.

Alex, Rayson K., and S. Susan Deborah. "Ecophobia, Reverential Eco-fear, and Indigenous Worldviews." *ISLE: Interdisciplinary Studies in Literature and Environment* 2, no. 2 (Spring 2019): 422–29.

Carroll, Noël. *The Philosophy of Horror: Or, Paradoxes of the Heart*. New York: Routledge, 1990.

CBS News. "Smoke from Wildfires Increases Health Risks for Millions of Americans." Last modified June 25, 2019. https://www.cbsnews.com/news/2019-wildfire-season-smoke-from-wildfires-increases-health-risks-for-millions-of-americans/.

Clute, John. "Physics for Amnesia: Horror Motifs in SF." *New York Review of Science Fiction* 21, no. 2, issue 242 (October 2008): 1–12.

Colavito, Jason. *Knowing Fear: Science, Knowledge and the Development of the Horror Genre*. Jefferson, NC: McFarland, 2008.

Corstorphine, Kevin, and Laura R. Kremmel, eds. *The Palgrave Handbook to Horror Literature*. Cham, CH: Palgrave Macmillan, 2018.

Crist, Eileen. "On the Poverty of Our Nomenclature." *Environmental Humanities* 3, no. 1 (2013): 129–47. https://doi.org/10.1215/22011919-3611266.

Díaz, Sandra, et al. *Summary for Policymakers of the Global Assessment Report on Biodiversity and Ecosystem Services of the Intergovernmental Science-Policy Platform on Biodiversity and Ecosystem Services*. IPBES. Last modified May 6, 2019. https://www.ipbes.net/sites/default/files/downloads/spm_unedited_advance_for_posting_htn.pdf.

Dillon, Sarah. "The Horror of the Anthropocene." *C21 Literature: Journal of 21st-Century Writings* 6, no. 1 (2018): 1–25.

Dunscombe, Jenessa. "Greenland Ice Sheet Beats All-Time 1-Day Melt Record." *Eos* 100, no. 2 (August 2019), https://doi.org/10.1029/2019EO130349.

Estok, Simon C. "Ecophobia, the Agony of Water, and Misogyny." *ISLE: Interdisciplinary Studies in Literature and Environment* 26, no. 2 (Spring 2019): 473–85.

———. *The Ecophobia Hypothesis*. New York: Routledge, 2018.

———. "Theorizing in a Space of Ambivalent Openness: Ecocriticism and Ecophobia." *ISLE: Interdisciplinary Studies in Literature and Environment* 16, no. 2 (Spring 2009): 203–25.

Freitag, Gina, and André Loiselle, eds. *The Canadian Horror Film: Terror of the Soul*. Toronto: University of Toronto Press, 2015.

Friedman, Lisa. "U.S. Significantly Weakens Endangered Species Act." *New York Times*, August 12, 2019. https://www.nytimes.com/2019/08/12/climate/endangered-species-act-changes.html.

Gambin, Lee. *Massacred by Mother Nature: Exploring the Natural Horror Film*. Baltimore: Midnight Marquee Press, 2012.

Garrard, Greg. "Worlds Without Us: Some Types of Disanthropy." *SubStance* 41, no. 1, issue 127 (2012): 40–60.

Gregersdotter, Katarina, Johan Höglund, and Nicklas Hållén, eds. *Animal Horror Cinema: Genre, History and Criticism*. New York: Palgrave Macmillan, 2015.

Grusin, Richard, ed. *Anthropocene Feminism*. Minneapolis: University of Minnesota Press, 2017.

Hackett, Jon, and Seán Harrington, eds. *Beasts of the Deep: Sea Creatures and Popular Culture*. East Barnet, UK: John Libbey, 2018.

Haraway, Donna J. *Staying with the Trouble: Making Kin in the Chthulucene*. Durham, NC: Duke University Press, 2016.

Hediger, Ryan. "Uncanny Homesickness and War: Loss of Affect, Loss of Place, and Reworlding in *Redeployment*." In *Affective Ecocriticism: Emotion, Embodiment, Environment*, edited by Kyle Bladow and Jennifer Ladino, 155–74. Lincoln: University of Nebraska Press, 2018.

Heise, Ursula K. *Imagining Extinction: The Cultural Meanings of Endangered Species*. Chicago: University of Chicago Press, 2016.

Hillard, Tom J. "'Deep into That Darkness Peering': An Essay on Gothic Nature." *ISLE: Interdisciplinary Studies in Literature and Environment* 16, no. 4 (2009): 685–95.

Hills, Matt. "An Event-Based Definition of Art-Horror." In *Dark Thoughts: Philosophic Reflections on Cinematic Horror*, edited by S. J. Schneider and D. Shaw, 138–57. Lanham, MD: Scarecrow, 2003.

International Commission on Stratigraphy. "Working Group on the 'Anthropocene.'" Subcommission on Quaternary Stratigraphy. Last updated May 21, 2019. http://quaternary.stratigraphy.org/working-groups/anthropocene/.

Keetley, Dawn. "Introduction: Six Theses on Plant Horror; or, Why Are Plants Horrifying?" In *Plant Horror: Approaches to the Monstrous Vegetal in Fiction and Film*, edited by Dawn Keetley and Angela Tenga, 1–30. London: Palgrave Macmillan, 2016.

Keetley, Dawn, and Matthew Wynn Sivils, eds. *Ecogothic in Nineteenth-Century American Literature*. New York: Routledge, 2018.

———. "Introduction: Approaches to the Ecogothic." In *Ecogothic in Nineteenth-Century American Literature*, edited by Dawn Keetley and Matthew Wynn Sivils, 1–20. New York: Routledge, 2018.

Lennard, Dominic. *Brute Force: Animal Horror Movies*. Albany: SUNY Press, 2019.

Magra, Iliana. "Europe Suffers Heat Wave of Dangerous, Record-High Temperatures." *New York Times*, July 24, 2019. https://www.nytimes.com/2019/07/24/world/europe/record-temperatures-heatwave.html.

Malm, Andreas. *Fossil Capital: The Rise of Steam Power and the Roots of Global Warming*. London: Verso, 2016.

Merola, Nicole M. "'What Do We Do but Keep Breathing as Best We Can This / Minute Atmosphere': Juliana Spahr and Anthropocene Anxiety." In *Affective Ecocriticism: Emotion, Embodiment, Environment*, edited by Kyle Bladow and Jennifer Ladino, 25–49. Lincoln: University of Nebraska Press, 2018.

Moore, Jason W. *Capitalism in the Web of Life: Ecology and the Accumulation of Capital*. London: Verso, 2015.

Murphy, Bernice M. *The Rural Gothic in American Popular Culture: Backwoods Horror and Terror in the Wilderness*. London: Palgrave Macmillan, 2013.

———. *The Suburban Gothic in American Popular Culture*. London: Palgrave Macmillan, 2009.

———. "'They Have Risen Once: They May Rise Again': Animals in Horror Literature." In *The Palgrave Handbook to Horror Literature*, edited by Kevin Corstorphine and Laura R. Kremmel, 257–73. Cham, CH: Palgrave Macmillan, 2018.

Murray, Robin L., and Joseph K. Heumann. *Monstrous Nature: Environment and Horror on the Big Screen*. Lincoln: University of Nebraska Press, 2016.

Parker, Elizabeth. *The Forest and the EcoGothic: The Deep Dark Woods in the Popular Imagination*. Cham, CH: Palgrave Macmillan, 2020.

———. "Who's Afraid of the Big Bad Woods? Deep Dark Forests and Literary Horror." In *The Palgrave Handbook to Horror Literature*, edited by Kevin Corstorphine and Laura R. Kremmel, 275–90. Cham, CH: Palgrave Macmillan, 2018.

Rust, Stephen A., and Carter Soles. "Ecohorror Special Cluster: 'Living in Fear, Living in Dread, Pretty Soon We'll All Be Dead.'" *ISLE: Interdisciplinary*

Studies in Literature and Environment 21, no. 3 (Summer 2014): 509–12.

Schell, Jennifer. "Ecogothic Extinction Fiction: The Extermination of the Alaskan Mammoth." In *Ecogothic in Nineteenth-Century American Literature*, edited by Dawn Keetley and Matthew Wynn Sivils, 175–90. New York: Routledge, 2018.

Schoell, William. *Creature Features: Nature Turned Nasty in the Movies*. Jefferson, NC: McFarland, 2008.

Smith, Andrew, and William Hughes, eds. *EcoGothic*. Manchester, UK: Manchester University Press, 2013.

Thunberg, Greta. "'Our House Is on Fire': Greta Thunberg, 16, Urges Leaders to Act on Climate." *The Guardian*, January 25, 2019. https://www.theguardian.com/environment/2019/jan/25/our-house-is-on-fire-greta-thunberg16-urges-leaders-to-act-on-climate.

Tidwell, Christy. "Ecohorror." In *Posthuman Glossary*, edited by Rosi Braidotti and Maria Hlavajova, 115–17. London: Bloomsbury Academic, 2018.

———. "Monstrous Natures Within: Posthuman and New Materialist Ecohorror in Mira Grant's *Parasite*." *ISLE: Interdisciplinary Studies in Literature and Environment* 21, no. 3 (Summer 2014): 538–49.

Williams, Linda. "Melodrama Revised." In *Refiguring American Film Genres*, edited by Nick Browne, 42–88. Berkeley: University of California Press, 1998.

Yacowar, Maurice. "The Bug in the Rug: Notes on the Disaster Genre." In *Film Genre Reader III*, edited by Barry Keith Grant, 277–95. Austin: University of Texas Press, 2003.

Yeung, Jessie, Swati Gupta, and Michael Guy. "India Has Just Five Years to Solve Its Water Crisis, Experts Fear. Otherwise Hundreds of Millions of Lives Will Be in Danger." CNN, July 4, 2019. https://edition.cnn.com/2019/06/27/india/india-water-crisis-intl-hnk/index.html.

Yeung, Jessie, Swati Gupta, and Sophia Saifi. "227 Dead After Monsoon Floods Devastate South Asia." CNN, July 18, 2019. https://edition.cnn.com/2019/07/18/asia/monsoon-flood-south-asia-intl-hnk/index.html.

Yusoff, Kathryn. *A Billion Black Anthropocenes or None*. Minneapolis: University of Minnesota Press, 2018.

Part 1
Expanding Ecohorror

1.
Tentacular Ecohorror and the Agency of Trees in Algernon Blackwood's "The Man Whom the Trees Loved" and Lorcan Finnegan's *Without Name*

Dawn Keetley

The most common form of ecohorror since at least the 1950s is the revenge-of-nature narrative.[1] Humans have spent centuries cultivating and exploiting land and animals, deforesting vast swathes of the globe, destroying habitats, and driving species to extinction. Bernice M. Murphy has argued that "nature strikes back" films are rooted not only in these attempts to dominate nature but also in a twinned guilt and contempt.[2] As Murphy puts it, revenge-of-nature films imagine humans' own disdain for nature "violently turned back upon" them.[3] These films give nature agency. The tagline for 1978's *Long Weekend*, for instance, proclaims, "Their crime was against nature. Nature found them guilty." The agency such films grant nature, however, is a very human agency. The tagline for 1977's *Day of the Animals* explicitly describes the animals' motivation as a mirror image of the humans': "For centuries they were hunted for bounty, fun and food. . . . Now it's their turn." And posters for 1987's *Jaws: The Revenge* inform us that "this time it's personal."[4] Human motives, "personal" motives, are inscribed onto what is presumed to be the blank canvas of nonhuman lives. Revenge-of-nature films thus manifest an erasure of nature—a denial of autonomous and immanent forms of life—at the same time that they dramatize its retribution. Moreover, this fantasy of nature, as Christy Tidwell has pointed out, frames "a nature that is exterior to humanity."[5] Nature stands as a humanlike entity, separate from and in perennial conflict with the human, the violence of one reflected in the violence of the other.

Because they are more easily imagined in human terms and thus more amenable to anthropocentric narratives, animals tend to dominate the revenge-of-nature narrative.[6] Vegetation, however, shapes a different form of ecohorror: plant life is often figured as a concealing mass, ominous only until it is revealed that the animals, humans, or monsters that lurk within constitute the real threat. At one moment in 1980's *Friday the 13th*, for instance, one nervous girl asks another as the campers are swimming, "Did you see something?" The camera pans the thick woods bordering the lake—and the "something" that causes fear is, for a moment, the implacable menace of the woods themselves.[7] It soon becomes clear, though, that what is to be feared is not the woods but what the woods hide. While foregrounded visually, the woods are backgrounded thematically. Plant life becomes terrifying only to the extent that it hides the dangerous predator. If revenge-of-nature narratives represent nature (usually animals) as a mirror of human motives, vegetation is an opaque screen. Whereas revenge-of-nature narratives are rooted in the human drive to dominate nature and the consequent guilt such domination engenders, films that feature obscuring vegetation, as Mathias Clasen has pointed out, originate in the equally long-standing, adaptive human fear of predators hiding in jungles and forests.[8] Plants and trees fade in the face of what we have long been hardwired to fear—that which is concealed in their midst.

Nature is subordinated to the human in both of these dominant formations of ecohorror—the animal-oriented revenge-of-nature narrative and the vegetation-dominated plot of the concealing mass. In these variants of ecohorror, nature stands either as a blank backdrop upon which human motivation is imposed or as the inert landscape concealing a human drama. In the latter category especially, though, there is often the seed of something else—the moment when nature *refuses* to stay in the background. Evan Calder Williams has brilliantly described how nature comes "monstrously to the fore" in *The Texas Chain Saw Massacre* (1974).[9] He points to scenes in which even the "life-and-death ordeal" of the protagonist—Sally chased by a chainsaw-wielding Leatherface—"becomes a distant signal obscured by wheat waving gently in the breeze."[10] These junctures when nature refuses its place within the human mapping of the world gesture to a third category of ecohorror—a *tentacular ecohorror*, which describes the terrifying encounter with a nonhuman nature that reaches out to grab and entangle the human.[11] Tentacular ecohorror is structured first by an encounter with a recalcitrantly alien form of life and second by a character's becoming enmeshed with that life. Nature comes truly to the fore here, as it starts to do in films like *The Texas Chain Saw Massacre* or 1999's *The Blair Witch Project*. But, unlike in those films, nature doesn't stop, doesn't give way to a concealed human, animal, or supernatural entity. Nature itself *keeps coming*. Its more ineffable threat doesn't fade away to be replaced by the human or the monster. In its relentless coming, moreover, nature's motives (if it has any) are inscrutable: it is not clearly propelled by revenge or by any recognizably human impulsion. Nature simply comes to the fore in all its irreducible alterity.

A story and a film published more than a century apart illuminate tentacular ecohorror via their characters' horrifying encounters with trees. In Algernon Blackwood's 1912 story "The Man Whom the Trees Loved," David Bittacy, who has always felt a strange kinship with trees, is drawn toward the deep forest that borders his house. The attraction grows throughout the story, and after one particularly stormy might, as the trees and wind roar, Bittacy vanishes into the forest. The 2016 Irish film *Without Name*, directed by Lorcan Finnegan and written by Garret Shanley, has an eerily similar plot. It follows a man named Eric (Alan McKenna) who travels from a dead, gray Dublin to a rich, green forested region in order to survey it for development. Like Blackwood's David Bittacy, Eric finds himself drawn to the uncannily alive woods, and, at the end of the film, he too has disappeared into them. In both texts, the forest has an agential power. And by the end of both story and film, the protagonists resemble the trees that have drawn them in as much as they do anything human.

What is crucial about both story and film is that the forests that absorb each man are no more or less than just forests. They contain no predators, fairies, witches, monsters, or ghosts. The horror is not humans' encounter with what is *in* the trees; the horror is the humans' encounter *with* the trees. And it is a transformative encounter. In this way, "The Man Whom the Trees Loved" and *Without Name* shape a new variant of ecohorror within an emerging taxonomy of the subgenre, a variant that is about the vegetal (rather than animal) threat but that also refuses the more familiar drama of nature's attack across fixed boundaries (e.g., shark versus human), staging instead the dissolution of those fixed boundaries. As Christy Tidwell's chapter 2 in this collection similarly demonstrates, one of ecohorror's impulses is to obscure the difference between human and nonhuman.[12] There is horror in this blurring but also the prospect of a new kind of being.

Encountering Alien Nature

The first movement of tentacular ecohorror is the encounter with nature as an absolute form of alterity, a form of life that escapes our grasp.[13] Numerous theorists have argued that horror involves the confrontation with that which is unmapped. Noël Carroll writes that the monsters of horror are "unnatural relative to a culture's conceptual scheme of nature" and that horror itself is a "literalization of the notion that what horrifies is that which lies *outside* cultural categories and is, perforce, unknown."[14] Maria Beville similarly claims that horror is defined by the encounter with the "unnameable monster," which "defies all attempts to constrain it in naming" and which "exists enigmatically" and "autonomously."[15] Paul Santilli has usefully demarcated horror from evil by arguing that while evil is "defined within a cultural matrix," horror "evokes elements of the real that *have not been assimilated into a culture*."[16] The horrifying encounter, in other words, is an encounter with what Santilli calls "the undefined other of a culture." Both Blackwood's "The Man Whom the Trees Loved" and Finnegan's *Without Name* derive their horror precisely from this encounter with the utterly unassimilable. What is unusual in both cases is that what is unassimilable is trees—just trees.[17]

Blackwood's "The Man Whom the Trees Loved" tells the story of David and Sophia Bittacy, a married couple who live on the edge of the New Forest in Kent. David, now retired, has worked with trees his whole life, learning to love them passionately.[18] As the story progresses, though, his wife realizes with dread that the forest is actively pulling him in. His distinctive identity as human begins to dissolve, and David becomes more treelike until, at the end of the story, he disappears altogether. The last line of the story tells us that Sophia "heard the roaring of the Forest further out. Her husband's voice was in it."[19] The story is told largely from Sophia's perspective, although we certainly learn much about David from his conversations with her and with Sanderson, an artist who visits them early in the story and who, like David, understands trees.

It is through Sophia, avatar of normality, that we experience the real horror of the trees. Carroll has argued that works of horror encode instructions for readers "in the responses of the positive, human characters" that show readers, by example, how to react to the monster. The power of the utterly alien monster is thus amplified by the reader's identification with the "normative" response of the characters themselves.[20] In Blackwood's story, the conventional Sophia can only regard with horror the increasingly animate trees that surround her, challenging her unimaginative worldview. Her dread, terror, and horror[21] at the trees punctuate the story. It is only because the story is told from her perspective that it is a *horror* story—or, indeed, a story at all. For David, not only are the trees not horrifying, but as he merges with them, he becomes unable to tell a recognizable narrative.[22]

As the story progresses, the trees become more "alien,"[23] heightening Sophia's dread; in this way, the story explicitly aligns the monstrous with everything that lies beyond what is categorized and known. The "great encircling mass of gloom that was the Forest" lay as a "sleeping monster,"[24] and Sophia is unable to articulate the reason for the dread the trees inspire: "It lies otherwise beyond all explanation, this mysterious emanation of big woods." The trees stir emotions that are "nameless."[25] And, later, Blackwood tells us that "this tree-and-forest business was so vague and horrible. It terrified her."[26] While Sophia "would not even name" the thing that terrified her, "it was waiting," inducing a "dread" that was "vague and incoherent." And although it remained "so ill-explained and formless, the thing yet lay in her consciousness."[27] Still later, we are told that "things" came to Sophia, "formless, wordless."[28] In the latter part of the story, trees become "things" and the forest becomes "it," no longer able to be named. As much as the forest terrifies Sophia, however, she does come to realize that it is not evil, reinforcing Santilli's distinction between that which is evil and that which induces horror. Sofia thinks that there was "no positive evil at work [here], but only something that usually stands away from humankind, something alien and not commonly recognized."[29] She nonetheless resists this unknowable mass, desiring only that the trees stay where they are, consigned to be passive and explicable vegetation in the background of the known life she wants for herself and her husband.

Perhaps even more so than "The Man Whom the Trees Loved," Lorcan Finnegan's *Without Name* literalizes what Santilli calls the inexplicable "*horror with no name*" that "haunts the edges of a culture, as an indeterminate menace and potential violation of the established norm."[30] Eric leaves Dublin to survey a stretch of forested land for a mysterious developer who tells Eric to keep what he is doing secret.[31] Out in the woods, trying to map the land, Eric finds his instruments won't work, and he has strange experiences, becoming disoriented and lost—overwhelmed by nothing but the trees themselves. One night when Eric is at the local pub, a man named Gus (James Browne) adds to the mystery by telling Eric that the locals call the region "Gan Ainm" (Without Name) and that no one has ever been able to map the region: in its recalcitrant namelessness, it refuses ownership.[32] Baffled by what is happening to him, Eric scours the house he is renting in Gan Ainm, poring over the possessions of the previous owner, William Devoy, who disappeared into the woods one day and whose comatose body now lies in a hospital room. Discovering a manuscript Devoy wrote called "Knowledge of Trees," Eric stops at a page titled "Everywhere Nowhere" and reads Devoy's attempts to describe the forest around him. "I must stop thinking of it as a place, a location. It is not," Devoy writes. "There are no words for what it is.... It has to be understood on its own terms, but I don't understand those terms." Devoy articulates what Eric experiences; he feels he is in a familiar place, but then that place swims out of his grasp, stubbornly refusing to be measured and catalogued. The woods will not remain either familiar or mere background. They assert an unassimilated and undefined life, striking both Eric and, before him, William, with an ineffable horror.[33] And despite *Without Name*'s brief nod to fairies, it is only the trees that haunt the film.[34]

Although both "The Man Whom the Trees Loved" and *Without Name* represent trees as, in Santilli's words, an "indeterminate menace,"[35] they do not only embody an ineffable external threat. In both texts, the trees' eeriness comes from the way they assert an animate nonhuman life that is not separate from but imbricated with human life. As Michael Marder has put it, we can "discern the constitutive vegetal otherness in ourselves."[36] Sophia is particularly unnerved by a conversation between her husband and the artist Sanderson, for instance, because it "brought the whole vegetable kingdom nearer to that of man."[37] The nature of this encounter with an element of the nonhuman that is revealed to be also indwelling is brilliantly articulated in Emmanuel Levinas's *Existence and Existents*. Levinas describes an "anonymous current of being" that "invades, submerges every subject, person or thing," dissolving the subject-object distinction.[38] Levinas identifies this anonymous life as the "there is," since it "resists a personal form" and is "being in general."[39] "There is" is impersonal and, Levinas argues, aligned especially with darkness. Darkness does not terrify because it shrouds daylight objects, he claims, but because it "reduces them to undetermined, anonymous being, which they exude."[40] And darkness not only reduces *objects* to "undetermined, anonymous being" but also reduces us—we who think we inhabit the darkness as subjects. Indeed, in an essay that unexpectedly turns into a primer for horror, Levinas defines the encounter with impersonal life *as horror*: "In horror, a subject is stripped of his subjectivity, of his power to have private existence. The subject is depersonalized." Horror, Levinas claims, is "a participation in the *there is*."[41] This Levinasian definition of horror as a "participation in the *there is*"—as a recognition of the anonymity of *all* life—is different from the horror of the human's confrontation with an ineffable menace (as Carroll, Beville, and Santilli describe). It suggests an encounter in which the subject dissolves too, becoming as ineffable as the menace it confronts. Both subject and object disappear, then, in an encounter that lays bare the impersonal life that pervades *both*; impersonal life razes subjects, persons, and identities.

Blackwood's story and Finnegan's film depict this impersonal life in ways that startlingly evoke Levinas. At a key moment in his essay, Levinas writes, "The rustling of the *there is* . . . is horror."[42] "Rustling" is a way for Levinas to signal a life that—because it resists subjectivity, because it is not confined to the human, because it "submerges every subject, person or thing" (including plants, trees, and forests)—also resists human language. And this "invading, inevitable, and anonymous rustling of existence," Levinas writes, the "anonymous rustling of the *there is*," always marks a moment of horror.[43] In "The Man Whom the Trees Loved," the *rustling* of the trees repeatedly intrudes into the lives of David and Sophia: Blackwood uses the word six times.[44] In each instance, the rustling of the trees marks the presence of an unassimilable reality, the menace that is not only the trees but also the impersonal life that inheres in the trees. This menace drives the story, and David finally succumbs to it. Just as Levinas associates the rustling of the "there is" with darkness and sleep,[45] so too Sophia is woken on one occasion by "a rushing noise" from across her lawn: "Just above her face while she slept had passed this murmur as of rustling branches in the very room, a sound of foliage whispering."[46] On a later night, she wakes to see "the green, spread bulk" of "wet and shimmering presences" grouped around the bed: "They shifted to and fro, massed yet translucent, mild yet thick, moving and turning within themselves to a hushed noise of multitudinous soft rustling."[47] The "massed" and "impersonal"[48] life of the trees, utterly alien to Sophia, who holds on to her

Fig. 1.1 *Without Name* (2016): Eric standing wordlessly in front of the trees

identity with desperate tenacity, arrives with an inchoate rustling that strikes her with a dread commensurate with its dissolutive effects on that identity. David does not resist, though, and is drawn further into the trees; he speaks less, his voice less human. When Sophia wakes him on one occasion, in terror at the rustling trees, his voice when he replies contains "a sighing sound, like wind in pine boughs."[49] His dissolution into the impersonal life of the "there is" is marked, then, not only by his increasing silence but also by the increasing depersonalization and even dehumanization of his speech.

In *Without Name*, too, Eric repeatedly confronts the rustling of trees. He thinks there's someone outside one night, but when he goes looking, he finds only the trees blowing violently in the wind. And in a powerful later scene, after Eric has started changing, dissolving, he goes and stands at the edge of the woods and, for a strikingly long time, stands wordlessly staring at the trees. The only sound is that of the trees blowing. In this moment (figure 1.1), Eric is still distinct from the forest, still on a threshold, which Blackwood also notes repeatedly in his story. Although his smallness within the frame augurs his imminent subsuming, Eric is still recognizably human—a line of distinction still drawn. He will soon cross this line, however.

Tentacular Ecohorror

If the first movement of tentacular ecohorror is the encounter with an impersonal nature that asserts its own life with rustling insistence, the second

Expanding Ecohorror

Fig. 1.2 *Without Name* (2016): Eric framed by the trees, as if they are reaching out to him

movement is the human's entanglement with this nature. Nature reaches out its tentacles, rendered all the more alien in their startling agency. Eugene Thacker has described this moment as "the sudden realization of a stark, 'tentacular' alienation from the world in which one is enmeshed."[50] Thacker refers here to the cephalopods of the Lovecraftian supernatural horror tradition, whose tentacles "envelop human beings in their unhuman embrace" and thus signify the vast unknowability of the sea they inhabit.[51] Tentacles are, however, everywhere in nature: the twining branches of a tree can evoke the irreducibly strange, the "unhuman embrace," as much as a kraken from the depths of the ocean. In Blackwood's story, Sophia thinks at one point that "like a rising sea, the Forest had surged a moment in their direction through the covering darkness, and this visible movement was its first wave." Sophia opposes this "outward surge" because "it threatened her and hers."[52] In *Without Name*, too, there are numerous scenes of wind-blown trees reaching out to Eric, their branches accruing an uncanny agency as they stretch toward him, entangling him (figure 1.2). Trees in both narratives are far from inert: they draw humans into the realm of alterity, into the terrain of "no name," irrevocably changing them in the process.

It is central to the tentacular ecohorror of "The Man Whom the Trees Loved" and *Without Name*, then, that the trees are mobile, driving the entanglement of human and tree integral to each text's conclusion. In a much-quoted claim, Stacy Alaimo has argued that human corporeality should be imagined as "trans-corporeality, in which the human is always intermeshed with the more-than-human world."[53] It is much less frequently noted, however, that her theory is grounded in motion. Alaimo writes of the "transits" between human bodies and nonhuman natures and stresses the "movement across bodies" and the "movement across different sites."[54] This itinerant trans-corporeality is not framed as particularly horrifying in *Bodily Natures*, but in an earlier essay Alaimo describes a kind of cross-bodily transit that *is* horrifying. Films about "monstrous natures," she argues, typically include "muddled middles" that depict a "horrific but pleasurable sense of the 'melting of corporeal boundaries'" (she quotes Elizabeth Grosz here); viewers may experience, Alaimo writes, "a sort of visceral identification in which the boundaries of their own bodies seem to dissolve."[55] In her claim about viewers' "corporeal identification" with "monstrous natures," Alaimo is writing about the horrifying but perhaps also pleasurable merging of human and *animal*, specifically.[56] There can, however, be an equally terrifying and yet also transformative merging of the human and *vegetal*—an even more terrifying encounter, perhaps, because of our long-standing certainty of plant life's inert immobility and because of the greater (relative to animals) alienness of plant life.

In her 2016 book, *Staying with the Trouble: Making Kin in the Chthulucene*, Donna J. Haraway articulates this kind of itinerant trans-corporeal entanglement not only with the animal but with the vegetal (and even the fungal and microbial). Haraway frames this trans-corporeal entanglement as monstrous, in the sense of opening up new realities and ways of being. What she calls "chthonic [ku-thinic] ones" or the "tentacular" are "replete with tentacles, feelers, digits, cords, whiptails, spider legs, and very unruly hair." They "writhe and luxuriate."[57] Far from being "disembodied figures," the "tentacular" are "matted and felted microbial and fungal tangles, probing creepers, swelling roots, reaching and climbing tendrilled ones."[58] Tentacularity is, Haraway writes, "wound with abyssal and dreadful graspings, frayings, and weavings, passing relays again and again, in the generative recursions that make up living and dying."[59] Although she does not herself take it up, Haraway frames a theory that can usefully explicate horror; indeed, the very visual nature of her language is anticipated in Blackwood's story and rendered on-screen in *Without Name*.

In the human encounter with palpably alien nature that is at the heart of tentacular ecohorror, nature reaches out in its tendriled life, entangling and fundamentally changing the human. This is horror—the encounter with the impersonal other and with its transformation of human nature. Early in the story, Blackwood reminds us that the vegetable kingdom covers "a third of the world with its wonderful tangled network of roots and branches,"[60] and it is soon clear that this "tangled network" is far from inert. Sophia thinks that the forest "was ever ready to encroach. All the branches, she sometimes fancied, stretched one way—towards their tiny cottage and garden, as though it sought to draw them in and merge them in itself."[61] Later in the story, when Sophia is in the forest, she feels its force and asks herself, "Could this be what [my] husband felt—this sense of thick entanglement with stems, boughs, roots, and foliage?"[62] She feels as if the "terrible soft enchantment" of the trees "branched all through her, climbing to the brain."[63] And near the conclusion, when she realizes how her husband is being entangled and absorbed, Sophia has a realization about plant life that strikingly anticipates Haraway's description of pervasive tentacularity. She remembers having seen "the world of seaweed rising from the bottom of the sea like a forest of dense green—long, sinuous stems, immense thick branches, millions of feelers spreading through the darkened watery depths the power of their ocean foliage." Sophia suddenly comprehends that the "Vegetable Kingdom was even in the sea. It was everywhere. Earth, air, and water helped it, way of escape there was none."[64]

While Sophia learns throughout the story to understand the power of trees, it is David they want. David inexorably becomes more treelike as the roots twine, the tendrils reach, the creepers stretch and feel. Blackwood describes David in ways that suggest trees, insinuating from the beginning that humans and trees share a "life" and anticipating the later amalgamating, blending, merging, engulfing—all words Blackwood uses to describe the exchange between David and the forest.[65] As David talks to his wife, for instance, the foliage was "rustling all about his quiet words as they went."[66] He tells his wife his life is "deeply rooted in this place."[67] He starts to move "with a restless, swaying motion" that reminds his wife of trees.[68] Near the end of the story, she sees David moving among the trees, "a man, like a tree, walking,"[69] and he responds to her alarmed questions as a "garden tree the wind attacks too suddenly, bending it over when it does not want to bend—the mild unwillingness with which it yields. She often saw him this way now, in the terms of trees."[70] The story ends with Sophia hearing "the roaring of the Forest further out," beyond their little house, and "her husband's voice was in it."[71] He has become a part of the woods, absorbed by the branches, tendrils, creepers, and roots—absorbed because he bridged the gulf to an alien life that the story discloses is not in fact all that alien.[72]

Without Name represents visually what Blackwood describes—the persistent movement of the trees and their reaching out to Eric in moments of tentacular ecohorror. What Blackwood calls the "thick entanglement"[73] of human and nonhuman life, however, involves not only trees in the film but also fungi, dramatizing Haraway's "fungal tangles, probing creepers, swelling roots, reaching and climbing tendrilled ones."[74] Science has begun to describe the vast networks of fungi that lie under the ground and that, in their multiple connections with tree roots, help transmit chemical signals—help trees communicate.[75] Fungi, Peter Wohlleben writes, thus form "something like the forest Internet."[76] If trees are entangled with fungi, we see both become entangled with humans in *Without Name* as first William Devoy and then Eric drink a brew of local wild mushrooms and are drawn still further into a mesh of human and nonhuman—trees, mushrooms, men.

Without Name represents what Jane Bennett has called an assemblage—that is, "ad hoc groupings of diverse elements, of vibrant materials of all sorts" that attenuate anything resembling human agency and form instead a distributed agency, dispersed among human, nonhuman, and thing.[77] Indeed, the trajectory of both Eric and Devoy is toward an amalgamation with the fungi and trees of Gan Ainm in a process that transforms individual free will into the agency of the human/nonhuman assemblage. Finnegan offers one powerful image of this new form of life in a strange picture Devoy took of himself in which his head incorporates a fungus, an image of the interconnectedness of humans and plants (figure 1.3). This image strikingly depicts Sophia's sense that the trees "branched all through her, climbing to the brain."[78] In the film, this shot is intercut with shots of the trees waving and rustling around the small house. At the same time, Eric's assistant and lover, Olivia (Niamh Algar), reads from Devoy's book: "Everything is involved in a kind of choreography. Light, wind, organic matter, all dance to a silent tune." After Eric takes the mushrooms, he, like Devoy before him, wanders into the woods, losing human language and distinctiveness; as the fungus dissolves within him, he dissolves among the trees.

Levinas argues that in the encounter with the pure impersonal of the "there is," an encounter that is at the heart of horror, it is impossible to remain as one was. Before the "obscure invasion" of impersonal life, Levinas

Fig. 1.3 *Without Name* (2016): Images of an embedded human and fungus

writes, "it is impossible to take shelter in oneself, *to withdraw into one's shell. One is exposed. The whole is open upon us.*"[79] Both "The Man Whom the Trees Loved" and *Without Name* represent their protagonists—or part of their protagonists—becoming shells in the process of their transformative encounter with trees. Sophia thinks, near the conclusion of the story, that as her husband "amalgamates" with the forest, the "body lolling in that armchair before her eyes contained the merest fragment of his actual self. It was little better than a corpse. It was an empty shell."[80] In *Without Name*, too, first William Devoy and then Eric are reduced to shells, lying catatonic in hospital beds. But in neither story nor film does this shell represent who they are at the end of the story. This corporeal shell is the mere discarded corpse of their former known, human selves. And they are not, as Levinas wrote, taking shelter in this shell anymore. Their lives, their beings, are entangled with the irreducibly nonhuman and are now elsewhere. Both David and Eric are (in) the trees.

Jeffrey Jerome Cohen has written that monsters "can be pushed to the farthest margins of geography and discourse, hidden away at the edges of the world and in the forbidden recesses of our mind, but they always return. And when they come back, they bring not just a fuller knowledge of our place in history and the history of knowing our place, but they bear self-knowledge, *human* knowledge—and a discourse all the more sacred as it arises from the Outside."[81] Blackwood's "The Man Whom the Trees Loved" and Finnegan's *Without Name* show that the vegetal world—trees in this case—can act as "monsters." Indeed, we make them into monsters by pushing them from the

Tentacular Ecohorror and the Agency of Trees

center of our world "to the furthest margins of geography and discourse." But they come back—their branches, tendrils, and roots reaching toward us, forming a radical tentacular ecohorror in which uncanny alien nature entangles the human and ushers in new forms of life. Algernon Blackwood's story and Lorcan Finnegan's film offer a horror that allows us to hear the "rustle" of a being we don't (yet) understand, to experience its dreadful reach out to us, and to see its creation of a new hybrid life beyond the borders of the known.

Notes

1. In his foundational study of horror and repression, Robin Wood includes "the revenge of Nature" as one of the recurrent motifs dominating horror since the 1960s (83). Critics who discuss the "revenge of nature" include Lee Gambin, whose *Massacred by Mother Nature* makes the case for a "natural horror film," beginning in the 1950s, that depicts nature as "the real evil that will ultimately destroy us" (18). See also Joseph Foy, who defines ecohorror as "fright flicks in which nature turns against humankind due to environmental degradation, pollution, encroachment, nuclear disaster, or a host of other reasons" (167); Brian Merchant, who argues that in ecohorror, "man tampers with nature—or worse ruins nature—and nature kicks man's ass"; Bernice M. Murphy, who discusses the "revenge-of-nature" horror film (178–213); and Robin L. Murray and Joseph K. Heumann's *Monstrous Nature*, which argues throughout that nature will have its revenge on the humans who are the real monsters.

2. Bernice M. Murphy, *The Rural Gothic in American Popular Culture: Backwoods Horror and Terror in the Wilderness* (New York: Palgrave Macmillan, 2013), 181. Murphy is building on what Simon C. Estok famously calls "ecophobia"—an "irrational and groundless hatred of the natural world," Estok, "Theorizing," 204.

3. Murphy, *Rural Gothic*, 182.

4. Not all films that show nature attacking humans offer a ready explanation. Carter Soles has argued of Alfred Hitchcock's *The Birds* (1963), for instance, that it "presents its attacking birds as an inexplicable force of nature, whose motivations and specific origins are never made clear" (527). Sometimes, even when a film leaves nature's motives unstated, critics nonetheless read the film anthropocentrically. One reading of M. Night Shyamalan's 2008 film *The Happening*, for instance, insists that "nature, after having had enough of man's pollution and overpopulation, has apparently . . . *made the decision to attack* highly populated areas of humans" (Morgart, "Deleuzians of Ecohorror," 121; emphasis mine). This explanation illuminates nonhuman nature by the ready light of explanations that are familiar to us, even though *The Happening* actually leaves nature's motives unclear.

5. Christy Tidwell, "Monstrous Natures Within: Posthuman and New Materialist Ecohorror in Mira Grant's *Parasite*," *ISLE: Interdisciplinary Studies in Literature and Environment* 21, no. 3 (2014): 539.

6. For two interesting essays that address revenge enacted by plants, see Elizabeth Parker, "Just a Piece of Wood"; and T. S. Miller, "Lives of the Monster Plants."

7. This dynamic also occurs in *The Blair Witch Project* (1999), although the sub-

stitution of a monstrous predator for the threat to humans is not as complete as it is in *Friday the 13th*, since it remains unclear through the end of the film whether there actually *is* something in the woods.

8. Mathias Clasen, *Why Horror Seduces* (New York: Oxford University Press, 2017), 42.

9. Evan Calder Williams, "Sunset with Chainsaw," *Film Quarterly* 64, no. 4 (Summer 2011): 33.

10. Ibid., 32.

11. This theory draws from the work of Stacy Alaimo, China Miéville, Eugene Thacker, Donna J. Haraway, Agnes Scherer, and Randy Laist.

12. Tidwell builds on the work of Stephen A. Rust and Carter Soles, who also argue for a variant of ecohorror that dramatizes the mutation of characters from human to nonhuman. See Rust and Soles, "Ecohorror Special Cluster," 509.

13. See Dawn Keetley, "Introduction," 6–9.

14. Noël Carroll, *The Philosophy of Horror; or, Paradoxes of the Heart* (New York: Routledge, 1990), 34–35.

15. Maria Beville, *The Unnameable Monster in Literature and Film* (New York: Routledge, 2013), 1–2. See Stephen Prince's essay on *The Thing* (dir. John Carpenter, 1982), in which he describes the "Thing" as exactly this kind of boundary-dissolving entity. Its very existence, he writes, "challenges the ontology separating human from nonhuman, solid from liquid, edible from inedible. It threatens to erase the distinctions and, in so doing, to erase the bounded human world" (126).

16. Paul Santilli, "Culture, Evil, and Horror," *American Journal of Economics and Sociology* 66, no. 1 (January 2007): 174.

17. See Randy Laist for an excellent discussion of the horror of the chestnut tree in Jean-Paul Sartre's *Nausea*. See Christy Tidwell, chapter 2 in this volume, for a discussion of Junji Ito's manga *Uzumaki*, which includes proliferating spirals merging with humans in a way, Tidwell argues, that likens the weird spirals to plants.

18. For critical discussion of Blackwood's story, see Sharon Healy, "Algernon Blackwood's Gentle Gothic"; Greg Conley, "The Uncrossable Evolutionary Gulfs"; David Punter, "Algernon Blackwood"; and Michelle Poland, "Walking with the Goat-God." Although he takes up Blackwood's "The Willows" (not "The Man Whom the Trees Loved"), Anthony Camara's "Nature Unbound" is an excellent discussion of the role of nature in Blackwood's fiction generally.

19. Algernon Blackwood, "The Man Whom the Trees Loved," in *Ancient Sorceries and Other Weird Stories* (New York: Penguin, 2002), 274.

20. Carroll, *Philosophy of Horror*, 31.

21. Blackwood, "Man Whom the Trees Loved," 217, 220, 221, 232, 235, 243, 244.

22. In depicting David Bittacy's increasing speechlessness as he merges with the trees around him, Blackwood offers glimmers of what Greg Garrard has called a "disanthropic world" (51), which Keri Stevenson takes up in chapter 4 in this volume, discussing landscapes markedly absent of humans.

23. Blackwood, "Man Whom the Trees Loved," 265.

24. Ibid., 214.

25. Ibid., 231.

26. Ibid., 235.

27. Ibid., 243.

28. Ibid., 254.

29. Ibid., 265.

30. Santilli, "Culture, Evil, and Horror," 175–76.

31. *Without Name* enters a contested history about Ireland's forests, which had been depleted by human agriculture by the ninth century (Hall 53) and experienced some regrowth but generally were so exploited there was "little left by the eighteenth century" (O'Carroll and Joyce 6). Throughout the twentieth and twenty-first centuries, the Irish government has engaged in systematic reforestation, which is controversial because of its emphasis on nonnative trees, notably the Sitka spruce, which predominates in Wicklow County (Gilligan).

32. See Carter Soles, chapter 12 in this volume, for a related exploration of the implication of naming—and not naming—in colonial projects. In his discussion of the 2016 shark horror film *The Shallows*, Soles points out the refusal of the native Mexicans in the film to tell white US visitor Nancy (Blake Lively) the name of the beach to which she's traveling. This refusal constitutes a striking denial of Nancy's attempt to "own" a beach to which she clearly has no claim, just as the locals in *Without Name* implicitly refuse Eric's efforts to measure and "own" the land around them by telling him it is "Without Name."

33. Like Blackwood, the director of *Without Name*, Lorcan Finnegan, discounts "evil" as the preoccupation of his film about the ineffable horror of trees. He has said in an interview that he hopes people don't come away from his film thinking "that nature's evil. It's more like it's something just powerful and not necessarily understood." This short interview from September 14, 2016, is on YouTube at https://youtu.be/HbReBVlbEOM.

34. It's interesting in this regard to compare *Without Name* to the similar Irish film *The Hallow* (dir. Corin Hardy, 2015). Like *Without Name*, *The Hallow* succeeds early on in making the woods appear menacing, but then, as happens in almost all horror films set in the woods, the threat of the woods gives way to the monsters hidden in their midst.

35. Santilli, "Culture, Evil, and Horror," 175.

36. Michael Marder, *Plant-Thinking: A Philosophy of Vegetal Life* (New York: Columbia University Press, 2013), 136. See Keetley, "Introduction," specifically Thesis 4: "The Human Harbors an Uncanny Constitutive Vegetal" (16–19).

37. Blackwood, "Man Whom the Trees Loved," 225.

38. Emmanuel Levinas, *Existence and Existents*, trans. Alphonso Lingis (Pittsburgh: Duquesne University Press, 2001), 52.

39. Ibid., 52.

40. Ibid., 54.

41. Ibid., 56.

42. Ibid., 55.

43. Ibid., 61, 88.

44. Blackwood, "Man Whom the Trees Loved," 211, 234 (twice), 237, 243, 268.

45. Levinas makes it clear that the "there is" becomes more apparent at night "when the forms of things are dissolved" (52). Indeed, both "The Man Whom the Trees Loved" and *Without Name* highlight the menacing rustling of trees during the night.

46. Blackwood, "Man Whom the Trees Loved," 237.

47. Ibid., 268.

48. Ibid., 254, 255.

49. Ibid., 269.

50. Eugene Thacker, *Horror of Philosophy*, vol. 3, *Tentacles Longer Than Night* (Winchester, UK: Zero Books, 2015), 153.

51. Ibid., 150. Despite the title of his book, Thacker does not say much about "tentacles," which are discussed only in a short section on China Miéville's 2010 novel *Kraken* (150–53).

52. Blackwood, "Man Whom the Trees Loved," 233.

53. Stacy Alaimo, *Bodily Natures: Science, Environment, and the Material Self* (Bloomington: Indiana University Press, 2010), 2.

54. Ibid.

55. Stacy Alaimo, "Discomforting Creatures: Monstrous Natures in Recent Film," in *Beyond Nature Writing: Expanding the Boundaries of Ecocriticism*, ed. Karla Armbruster and Kathleen Wallace (Charlottesville: University of Virginia Press, 2001), 294.

56. Ibid.

57. Donna J. Haraway, *Staying with the Trouble: Making Kin in the Chthulucene* (Durham, NC: Duke University Press, 2016), 2.

58. Ibid., 32.

59. Ibid., 33. See Agnes Scherer's important discussion of the tendril motif in early modern art and contemporary horror film, specifically the tendriled monsters in *A Sound of Thunder* (2005), *The Thing* (1982), and *The Ruins* (2008).

60. Blackwood, "Man Whom the Trees Loved," 220.
61. Ibid., 246–47.
62. Ibid., 258.
63. Ibid., 259.
64. Ibid., 270–71.
65. Ibid., 226, 230.
66. Ibid., 243.
67. Ibid., 248.
68. Ibid., 256.
69. Ibid., 260.
70. Ibid., 263.
71. Ibid., 274.
72. Poland also points out that Bittacy "becomes one with the trees" (61), as does Punter, who reads the story through Gilles Deleuze and Félix Guattari as about "becoming-forest" (47).
73. Blackwood, "Man Whom the Trees Loved," 258.
74. Haraway, *Staying with the Trouble*, 32.
75. See Ed Young, "The Wood Wide Web"; Stefano Mancuso and Alessandro Viola, *Brilliant Green*, 95–96; and Peter Wohlleben, *The Hidden Life of Trees*, 49–55.
76. Wohlleben, *Hidden Life of Trees*, 51.
77. Jane Bennett, *Vibrant Matter: A Political Ecology of Things* (Durham, NC: Duke University Press, 2010), 23.
78. Blackwood, "Man Whom the Trees Loved," 259.
79. Levinas, *Existence and Existents*, 31. Emphasis added.
80. Blackwood, "Man Whom the Trees Loved," 267.
81. Jeffrey Jerome Cohen, "Monster Culture (Seven Theses)," in *Monster Theory: Reading Culture*, ed. Jeffrey Jerome Cohen (Minneapolis: University of Minnesota Press, 1996), 20.

References

Alaimo, Stacy. *Bodily Natures: Science, Environment, and the Material Self*. Bloomington: Indiana University Press, 2010.

———. "Discomforting Creatures: Monstrous Natures in Recent Film." In *Beyond Nature Writing: Expanding the Boundaries of Ecocriticism*, edited by Karla Armbruster and Kathleen Wallace, 279–96. Charlottesville: University of Virginia Press, 2001.

Bennett, Jane. *Vibrant Matter: A Political Ecology of Things*. Durham, NC: Duke University Press, 2010.

Beville, Maria. *The Unnameable Monster in Literature and Film*. New York: Routledge, 2013.

Blackwood, Algernon. "The Man Whom the Trees Loved." In *Ancient Sorceries and Other Weird Stories*, 211–74. New York: Penguin, 2002.

Camara, Anthony. "Nature Unbound: Cosmic Horror in Algernon Blackwood's 'The Willows.'" *Horror Studies* 4, no. 1 (2013): 43–62.

Carroll, Noël. *The Philosophy of Horror; or, Paradoxes of the Heart*. New York: Routledge, 1990.

Clasen, Mathias. *Why Horror Seduces*. New York: Oxford University Press, 2017.

Cohen, Jeffrey Jerome. "Monster Culture (Seven Theses)." In *Monster Theory: Reading Culture*, edited by Jeffrey Jerome Cohen, 3–25. Minneapolis: University of Minnesota Press, 1996.

Conley, Greg. "The Uncrossable Evolutionary Gulfs of Algernon Blackwood." *Journal of the Fantastic in the Arts* 24, no. 3 (2013): 426–45.

Estok, Simon C. "Theorizing in a Space of Ambivalent Openness: Ecocriticism and Ecophobia." *ISLE: Interdisciplinary Studies in Literature and Environment* 16, no. 2 (Spring 2009): 203–25.

Foy, Joseph J. "It Came from Planet Earth: Eco-Horror and the Politics of Postenvironmentalism in *The Happening*." In *Homer Simpson Marches on Washington: Dissent Through American Popular Culture*, edited by Timothy M. Dale and Joseph J. Foy, 167–88. Lexington: University Press of Kentucky, 2010.

Gambin, Lee. *Massacred by Mother Nature: Exploring the Natural Horror Film*. Baltimore: Midnight Marquee Books, 2012.

Garrard, Greg. "Worlds Without Us: Some Types of Disanthropy." *SubStance* 41, no. 1, issue 127 (2012): 40–60.

Gilligan, Cecily. "Sitka Spruce Mars the Wicklow Way." *Irish Times*, August 24, 2018. https://www.irishtimes.com/opinion/letters/sitka-spruce-mars-the-wicklow-way-1.3605579.

Hall, Valerie. "The History of Irish Forests Since the Ice Age." *Irish Forestry* 54, no. 1 (1997): 49–54.

Haraway, Donna J. *Staying with the Trouble: Making Kin in the Chthulucene*. Durham, NC: Duke University Press, 2016.

Healy, Sharon. "Algernon Blackwood's Gentle Gothic." *The Romantist* 9–10 (1985): 61–64.

Keetley, Dawn. "Introduction: Six Theses on Plant Horror; or, Why Are Plants Horrifying?" In *Plant Horror: Approaches to the Monstrous Vegetal in Fiction and Film*, edited by Dawn Keetley and Angela Tenga, 1–30. New York: Palgrave Macmillan, 2016.

Laist, Randy. "Sartre and the Roots of Plant Horror." In *Plant Horror: Approaches to the Monstrous Vegetal in Fiction and Film*, edited by Dawn Keetley and Angela Tenga, 163–78. New York: Palgrave Macmillan, 2016.

Levinas, Emmanuel. *Existence and Existents*. Translated by Alphonso Lingis. Pittsburgh: Duquesne University Press, 2001.

Mancuso, Stefano, and Alessandra Viola. *Brilliant Green: The Surprising History and Science of Plant Intelligence*. Translated by Joan Benham. Washington, DC: Island Press, 2015.

Marder, Michael. *Plant-Thinking: A Philosophy of Vegetal Life*. New York: Columbia University Press, 2013.

Merchant, Brian. "The Evolution of Ecohorror, from Godzilla to Global Warming." *Motherboard*, November 14, 2012. https://motherboard.vice.com/en_us/article/xyy473/the-evolution-of-eco-horror-from-godzilla-to-global-warming.

Miéville, China. "M. R. James and the Quantum Vampire." *Weird Fiction Review*, November 29, 2011. https://weirdfictionreview.com/2011/11/m-r-james-and-the-quantum-vampire-by-china-mieville/.

Miller, T. S. "Lives of the Monster Plants: The Revenge of the Vegetable in the Age of Animal Studies." *Journal of the Fantastic in the Arts* 23, no. 3 (2012): 460–79.

Morgart, James. "Deleuzians of Ecohorror: Weighing Al Gore's Ecostrategy Against *The Day After Tomorrow*." *Horror Studies* 8, no. 1 (2017): 115–30.

Murphy, Bernice M. *The Rural Gothic in American Popular Culture: Backwoods Horror and Terror in the Wilderness*. New York: Palgrave Macmillan, 2013.

Murray, Robin L., and Joseph K. Heumann. *Monstrous Nature: Environment and Horror on the Big Screen*. Lincoln: University of Nebraska Press, 2016.

O'Carroll, Niall, and Padraic M. Joyce. "A Forest Centenary." *Irish Forestry* 61, no. 2 (2004): 6–19.

Parker, Elizabeth. "'Just a Piece of Wood': Jan Švankmajer's *Otesánek* and the EcoGothic." In *Plant Horror: Approaches to the Monstrous Vegetal in Fiction and Film*, edited by Dawn Keetley and Angela Tenga, 215–25. New York: Palgrave Macmillan, 2016.

Poland, Michelle. "Walking with the Goat-God: Gothic Ecology in Algernon Blackwood's *Pan's Garden: A Volume of Nature Stories*." *Critical Survey* 29, no. 1 (Spring 2017): 53–69.

Prince, Stephen. "Dread, Taboo, and *The Thing*: Toward a Social Theory of the Horror Film." In *The Horror Film*, edited by Stephen Prince, 118–30. New Brunswick, NJ: Rutgers University Press, 2004.

Punter, David. "Algernon Blackwood: Nature and Spirit." In *EcoGothic*, edited by Andrew Smith and William Hughes, 44–57. New York: Manchester University Press, 2013.

Rust, Stephen A., and Carter Soles. "Ecohorror Special Cluster: 'Living in Fear, Living in Dread, Pretty Soon We'll All Be Dead.'" *ISLE: Interdisciplinary Studies in Literature and Environment* 21, no. 3 (Summer 2014): 509–12.

Santilli, Paul. "Culture, Evil, and Horror." *American Journal of Economics and Sociology* 66, no. 1 (January 2007): 173–93.

Scherer, Agnes. "The Pre-cosmic Squiggle: Tendril Excesses in Early Modern Art and Science Fiction Cinema." In *Plant Horror: Approaches to the Monstrous Vegetal in Fiction and Film*, edited by Dawn Keetley and Angela Tenga, 31–53. New York: Palgrave Macmillan, 2016.

Soles, Carter. "'And No Birds Sing': Discourses of Environmental Apocalypse in *The Birds* and *Night of the Living Dead*." *ISLE: Interdisciplinary Studies in Literature and Environment* 21, no. 3 (Summer 2014): 526–37.

Thacker, Eugene. *Horror of Philosophy*. Vol. 3, *Tentacles Longer Than Night*. Winchester, UK: Zero Books, 2015.

Tidwell, Christy. "Monstrous Natures Within: Posthuman and New Materialist Ecohorror in Mira Grant's *Parasite*." *ISLE: Interdisciplinary Studies in Literature and Environment* 21, no. 3 (2014): 538–49.

Williams, Evan Calder. "Sunset with Chainsaw." *Film Quarterly* 64, no. 4 (Summer 2011): 28–33.

Wohlleben, Peter. *The Hidden Life of Trees: What They Feel, How They Communicate*. Vancouver, BC: Greystone Books, 2015.

Wood, Robin. *Hollywood from Vietnam to Reagan*. New York: Columbia University Press, 1986.

Young, Ed. "The Wood Wide Web." *The Atlantic*, April 14, 2016. https://www.theatlantic.com/science/archive/2016/04/the-wood-wide-web/478224/.

2.
Spiraling Inward and Outward
Junji Ito's *Uzumaki* and the Scope of Ecohorror

Christy Tidwell

The work of ecohorror scholars to this point has been to define and delimit: What is *ecohorror*? What does this term include—or exclude? This scholarship has made a strong case for the term and the concept and has shown its value to both ecocriticism and horror studies, often by beginning with animal attack narratives and what's known as natural horror—nature strikes back. As Stephen A. Rust and Carter Soles argue, however, ecohorror can include a wide range of approaches: "Horrific texts and tropes are used to promote ecological awareness, represent ecological crises, or blur human/non-human distinctions more broadly."[1] Many discussions of ecohorror focus on the first two ideas outlined by Rust and Soles, but I am drawn to that third point—blurring distinctions between human and nonhuman.

Similarly, here I want to blur distinctions between subgenres. Ecohorror doesn't truly stand alone but reaches out into and works with other kinds of horror, including body horror and cosmic horror. As I have argued elsewhere,[2] it is often difficult to separate a focus on nature and environment from issues related to the body; as a result, the lines between ecohorror and body horror are not always clear. Body horror focuses on mutations, mutilations, and (often violent) transformations of the human body. The transformation of Seth Brundle to Brundlefly in David Cronenberg's *The Fly* (1986) or the alien mutations of John Carpenter's *The Thing* (1982) are classic examples of the subgenre. These bodily mutations or transformations often blur the line between human and nonhuman—as in *The Fly*—and thereby connect with a central ecohorror concept.[3] While body horror is typically focused on individual bodily transformations, cosmic horror works on a larger scale and is centrally concerned with the way the human is overwhelmed by the alien, the ancient, the unfathomable. Jason Colavito defines cosmic horror as representing "the individual's fear of losing himself in the face of larger forces beyond his control."[4] This definition certainly can reflect environmental fears, but it is most often associated with alien life-forms or "the truly weird"—elements that "[shatter the individual's] understanding of the way the world works."[5] H. P. Lovecraft's Great Old Ones (e.g., Cthulhu) are well-known examples of "larger forces" that overwhelm the human.

Considering these subgenres together reveals that ecohorror is more central to horror as a genre than has previously been acknowledged—it cannot fully be separated from body horror or cosmic horror, and it appears in many other kinds of horror too.[6] How could it not, given how fundamentally we humans are connected to the rest of the natural world? I argue therefore that there is value in expanding the definition of *ecohorror* even further than Rust and Soles's already expansive definition. Incorporating the concerns of other horror subgenres into ecohorror analyses strengthens ecohorror by acknowledging the ways in which environmental concerns are not isolated from concerns such as health and disability or from existential crises.

Junji Ito's manga *Uzumaki*, the tale of a town "contaminated with spirals,"[7] illustrates the power of combining—or contaminating—ecohorror with body horror and cosmic horror. *Uzumaki*, although not as familiar to US audiences as other ecohorror texts, is globally well regarded and well known within horror manga circles.[8] The text was originally published in three volumes (1998–99) and was published as an omnibus edition in 2000. *Uzumaki* was translated into English in 2002, rereleased in English in 2007–8, and republished in a deluxe omnibus edition in 2010.[9] It was also adapted into two video games and a Japanese live-action film. Finally, it was nominated for an Eisner Award in 2003, and in 2009 it was listed as one of the Top 10 Graphic Novels for Teens by the Young Adult Library Services Association. Although it is classified as YA in the United States, it is marketed to adults in Japan. Japanese manga are published within several categories, each clearly targeting different genders or age groups. *Uzumaki* is a *seinen* manga, geared toward adult male readers (in their twenties and older) and distinguished from manga for younger readers or for women. This audience is what enables the graphic and upsetting imagery throughout.

The plot of *Uzumaki* is seemingly very simple: the town of Kurouzu-cho is contaminated by spirals. Spirals begin to appear all around town, observed primarily by Shuichi (the young adult male protagonist) and Kirie (the teenage female protagonist). Spirals appear in the stream water, the pottery created by Shuichi's father becomes dominated by spiral shapes, and the smoke from the crematorium begins to display distinct spirals in the air. All of this is odd but does not seem dangerous. Only Shuichi, in fact, expresses any concern about the spirals. No logical explanation is ever provided for their arrival, and, as in much horror, it doesn't matter why or how the horrific is happening.

What matters are people's responses to the spirals as they become more invasive and more sinister. For instance, Shuichi's father becomes obsessed with spirals and forces his body into a spiral shape. He begins by rolling his eyes independently of each other; then he creates a spiral with his tongue; and, finally, he twists his entire body into a spiral inside a large tub and dies in this form.[10] After this death, Shuichi's mother, rather than embracing them, "develop[s] an extreme phobia of spirals," which leads to her death as well.[11] She shaves her head to eliminate any curling in her hair, cuts the skin from her fingers and toes to remove the spirals in her fingerprints, and finally, realizing that there are spirals in her ears (the cochlea), stabs herself in the ears. Ironically, "by stabbing her ears, she destroyed not only her hearing but her sense of balance. As a result, she was in a constant state of vertigo."[12] She spends her last days feeling as if she is spinning and exclaims, "I don't want to become a spiral!"[13] The inexplicable spirals have power, whether characters embrace or reject them.

Beyond such individual transformations, the town itself is reshaped by the invading spirals. Eventually, typhoons and cyclones (spiral storms) destroy much of the town, and even a quick movement or loud noise can trigger a whirlwind, causing even more destruction. The small spiral eddies seen earlier in the stream take on much larger and more dangerous forms too: the pond in the center of town becomes a whirlpool, and any boats that try to escape the town or ships that attempt to come to their rescue are sucked into huge ocean whirlpools. In the end, the entire town—including both geography and built elements—becomes a giant spiral, from which no humans can escape.

Ito's *Uzumaki* incorporates a wide range of stories and fears. Its episodic structure allows it to jump from one story of spirals in the town of Kurouzu-cho to another, sometimes with little connection between these stories beyond the centrality of spirals, the town setting, and the witness of

Shuichi and/or Kirie. *Uzumaki*'s length—over six hundred pages—provides space for the text to draw upon a variety of horror subgenres (and includes far more subplots than I am able to address here). Therefore, *Uzumaki* illustrates ecohorror's ability (and need) to attend not only to nature and the environment but also to the body and a more-than-human scale. In drawing upon elements of ecohorror, body horror, and cosmic horror, *Uzumaki* indicates the inseparability of these subgenres and demonstrates that the issues raised within ecohorror require a willingness to move from one scale to another—spatially, we must be able to move from ecosystem to individual bodies; temporally, we must be able to move from the life-span of a human to the life-span of the planet.

Ecohorror: *Uzumaki* Spirals Across Species Lines

Reading *Uzumaki* as ecohorror provides a clear illustration of Rust and Soles's definition. To begin with, *Uzumaki* clearly works "to promote ecological awareness" and "represent ecological crises."[14] It addresses the natural world by representing major spiral effects in the air and water that mirror real-world natural disasters (e.g., hurricanes, typhoons, and earthquakes) and reflect human fears of nature's power. This both promotes awareness of these kinds of disasters and provides a dramatic—though fantastic—representation of their power. *Uzumaki* also illustrates Rust and Soles's third element of ecohorror, focusing on the transformation of characters from human to nonhuman. The slipperiness between categories here evokes Noël Carroll's argument that "horrific creatures are also impure. . . . Impurity involves a conflict between two or more standing cultural categories."[15] In *Uzumaki,* Ito calls attention to the perceived impurity of human/animal hybrids, which grows out of a conflict between our cultural definitions of human and nonhuman. Although we know that humans are animals, we often avoid classifying ourselves with other animals and define ourselves and our humanity in contrast to their animality.

One of *Uzumaki*'s central plot points features humans transforming into snails, highlighting human anxieties about our nearness to other species and the possible loss of our humanity. The process of becoming-snail begins with a spiral on the character's back. This happens to a boy named Katayama, who is bullied by other kids at school for being slow and damp (constantly sweating, it seems), both snail-like qualities. Katayama falls to the ground and begins to crawl; he grows a shell on his back and develops eyestalks; his damp sweatiness becomes slime; and he loses the ability to speak. Because his family rejects him and refuses to take him home (reflecting his loss of both social and species status), Katayama is held in a pen at school, where another boy, Tsumura, torments him. Before too long, however, Tsumura also turns into a snail and enters the pen with Katayama. Their perceived shift away from humanity is sealed when they mate, having become hermaphroditic, like many snails. The humans around them largely see them as no longer human at all and are disgusted by them. Mr. Yokota, their teacher, says, "These two boys are no longer remotely human. They're . . . mollusk people."[16] This naming of them as "mollusk people" formalizes the sense of them as impure and highlights the way this boundary-crossing forfeits their humanity (which must be pure). After they mate, Mr. Yokota crushes the eggs laid by one of them in the forest, saying, "It's disgusting, unnatural! These creatures mustn't breed!"[17] This disgust seems to be provoked by their transformation, their perceived sexual deviance,[18] and their bizarre appearance. The change in scale (the boys become human-sized snails) highlights the disgusting and horrific elements of their animality; things we would normally interpret as cute are read as grotesque instead. It also draws upon a familiar creature-feature trope in which animals are made monstrous by becoming oversized (e.g., *Them!* [1954], *Night of the Lepus* [1972], and *Eight Legged Freaks* [2002]).[19]

Uzumaki does not just rely on the monstrosity of animals for its horrific effect; it also finds horror in the way animals are treated by humans.[20] As the situation becomes more desperate, the dehumanization of the snail-people leads to some humans cooking and eating them. This practice is clearly represented as horrific and cannibalistic. In one scene, relatively large images of the snail shells cooking are accompanied by sound effects ("crackle crackle") but little dialogue. These details combine with Kirie's horrified viewpoint to instruct us in reading the scene, and then (after a page turn, for extra dramatic effect) we see an image of the broken-open snail shell with burned human remains and a charred, skeletal human face inside it, making it impossible to ignore the truth that Kirie insists upon: "But that's not escargot. . . . They're *human*. . . ."[21] To further underscore the horror of these acts of cannibalism, one group is later seen keeping a person on a leash as he slowly becomes a snail so that when he fully transforms, they can eat him. As if this enslavement is not enough, when their captive finally turns, one man says that he doesn't want to cook him: "I'd like to try one raw."[22] The snail-person slips out of the leash and tries to hide inside his shell, reminding the reader (if not the man who wishes to eat him, who seems only angered by this) of his desire to live and ability to act with intent. In a detailed two-page sequence, the man crawls inside the shell after him and eats him alive. The other men in the group see this not as a cannibalistic and monstrous act but as merely selfish: "Y-you bastard! Don't eat all of it! Come out!"[23] Kirie and her friends, however, are sickened by this and use the distraction to slip away from these men, who are dangerous because, as Shuichi says, "the spiral has them."[24]

These scenes illustrate the horrors not only in becoming nonhuman but also in being *treated* as nonhuman by others. This connects the text's eco-horrific blurring of lines between human and nonhuman to Rust and Soles's other elements of ecohorror—promoting ecological awareness and highlighting ecological crises—through explicit attention to the ethics of eating others, both human and animal. Val Plumwood identifies the strong desire of many cultures "to deny that we humans are also animals positioned in the food chain," noting that "horror movies and stories also reflect this deep-seated dread of becoming food for other forms of life. . . . Even being nibbled by leeches, sand flies, and mosquitoes can stir various levels of hysteria."[25] Here, *Uzumaki* evokes these fears. We are horrified when the snail-people are eaten because they still retain some of their human traits (e.g., largely human faces), their individual human histories, and their ability to resist and make choices.

Significantly, however, the snail-people are human-animal hybrids, so the horror of seeing them eaten is more complex than that of seeing humans treated as food. This is best illustrated by a later sequence featuring Kirie's younger brother, Mitsuo. As he begins to transform into a snail, Kirie tries to protect him by helping him hide his growing shell and carrying him so that he does not fall behind. This works until he completes his metamorphosis, but then the men who ate the snail-person—who have since caught up with them—see his change and want to eat him too. Here, primed by the previous scenes of snail-people consumption, the audience is ready to respond with horror at the idea of Mitsuo—a person, after all—being eaten. Fortunately, Mitsuo is spared this fate. Kirie, Mitsuo, and Shuichi flee from the men but quickly reach a dead end, a cliff looking over the ocean. Mitsuo indicates that he can climb down the cliff, but he does not want to leave his sister and their friends, so Kirie has to threaten to hurt him to make him leave. This scene resonates with animal narratives in which humans try to chase away a loved animal for its own good,[26] which suggests a shift in perception, a move from thinking of Mitsuo as a person to thinking of him as a sympathetic animal. *Uzumaki* thus engages with animal studies critiques of a system that would place humans above nonhuman animals. Just as Plumwood is critical of a system in which humans can be "predators but never prey,"[27] *Uzumaki* is critical of the assumption that humans have the right to be predators but remains uncomfortable with the idea of humans being prey. As Plumwood writes, "We act as if we live in a separate realm of culture in which we are never food, while other animals inhabit a different world of nature in which they are no more than food, and their lives can be utterly distorted in the service of this end."[28] *Uzumaki* refuses to let Mitsuo become food, providing a powerful response to this cultural narrative and locating the horror of this scene not just in the threat of a human becoming food but also in the threat of an *animal* becoming food.

This desire to eat Mitsuo does not just threaten him individually; it also harms the men who wish to eat him. Although Mitsuo escapes, the men who have been chasing him imagine climbing inside and eating Mitsuo raw: "That sensation of being inside his shell, chewing on the soft parts of his face . . . Fitting your whole body into those wet, wonderful curves . . . That magical space . . . made me feel like *my* body was becoming a spiral! Just thinking about it makes me feel like I'm going to . . ."[29] In the midst of this violent and weirdly sexual vision, one man transforms, but not into a snail—into a deformed spiral. His mutilation into a spiral and subsequent death rather than transformation into a living snail-person indicates just how deeply degrading and dehumanizing the embrace of the horrific action of eating another living and feeling being is. Mitsuo, as a snail-person, is still an individual worth saving (whether human, animal, or hybrid). These men are not. They are, instead, serial cannibals and abusers of nonhuman Others, and they face horrific consequences as a result.[30]

Uzumaki's approach to crossing species lines therefore combines horror and sympathy, a technique common to horror narratives, which rarely, as Robin Wood argues, "have totally unsympathetic Monsters."[31] Furthermore, Rajyashree Pandey writes, "The Japanese context, unlike that of the Christian West, offers a much greater fluidity between man and beast, which mitigates against the monstrous animal's merely being demonized as 'the other.'"[32] *Uzumaki*'s snail-people illustrate this fluidity by allowing readers to acknowledge the frightening nature of such transformations without simply demonizing the transformed. They are nonhuman and look like monsters, but they are also our friends and family. By representing the snail-people as monstrous and acknowledging the horror of losing one's humanity while simultaneously defending the snail-people as sympathetic hybrids, *Uzumaki*'s ecohorror narrative provides a vision of how we might respond to animals that threaten or frighten humanity without necessarily destroying them.

The form of *Uzumaki* also lends itself to the blurring of boundaries between human and animal. As Christine L. Marran writes, "Graphic novels, for their capacity to allow for the bending and stretching of morphologies and lines, can generate visually a sense of corporeal possibility."[33] The image of Shuichi's father contorting himself into a spiral, for instance, can be convincingly presented in this medium. The style is realistic, paying attention to details of skin and bone and transmitting a sense of the pain of his body's contortion as it curves backward into a tightly wound spiral, but the human body is not realistically able to bend like this. This general corporeal possibility is applied specifically to the nonhuman by Thomas LaMarre as he discusses "plasmaticity" in animation (and manga), which refers to "the deformation and reformation of characters—stretching, bending, flattening, inflating, shattering."[34] He argues that plasmaticity provides vitalism and force to animated animals, linking them to traits we typically reserve for the human.

These linkages are complex, however. The snail-people have largely human faces (despite the eyestalks) and human teeth, and many retain human hair; at the same time, they move like snails, are damp like snails, and have snail shells. They are neither snails made more human (like anthropomorphized Disney cartoon animals) nor humans with one or two snail traits. They are true hybrids, and the manga form allows this to be convincing. The snail-people are believable on the page, and this believability itself leads to a strong emotional response. As LaMarre writes, "Animation delights in constructing zones where human and animal become indiscernible, where the animal opens into the human, and the human into the animal. . . . This is not necessarily a comfortable situation."[35] *Uzumaki* asks readers to accept its convincingly created human-animal hybrids, but as a horror manga it also traffics in readers' discomfort with these blurred boundaries. Ultimately, manga's ability to construct "zones where human and animal become indiscernible" helps to create a middle ground for interpretation, one that aligns with ecohorror's tendency to blur human/nonhuman boundaries.

Body Horror: *Uzumaki* Spirals Inward

Body horror also draws upon the "corporeal possibility" that Marran and LaMarre describe. Jay McRoy writes that body horror films "contribute to a discourse of boundary and body invasion, graphically enacting, in the process, perhaps the most dreadful apocalypse of all—the perpetual intimate apocalypse of the human body."[36] *Uzumaki* enacts this bodily apocalypse over and over again, thereby "disallow[ing] for illusions of corporeal integrity or for ideologies privileging the sovereignty of the human form."[37]

A horrific approach to the body is not new in Japanese art and culture. As Pandey notes, "Depictions of the disintegration of the body or grotesque caricatures" are common in medieval picture scrolls and in seventeenth- and eighteenth-century wood-block prints, and later Japanese art is influenced by these works.[38] For instance, Tsukioka Yoshitoshi's "Reizei Hangan Takatoyo" (1868), a graphic image of the warrior Reizei Takatoyo dying from *seppuku* (ritual disembowelment), highlights the destruction of the body, showing the warrior's guts falling out of his body. Utagawa Kuniyoshi's "Hito katamatte hito ni naru" (People joining together to form another person) (c. 1847) shows, true to its title, a person made of many smaller people molded together.[39] Spirals even appear in some Japanese horror art: Katsushika Hokusai's 1831–32 "The Mansion of the Plates" (also sometimes listed as "Okiku the Well Ghost" or "A Woman Ghost Appeared from a Well") depicts the ghost of a woman rising in a spiral shape from a well, her long black hair streaming behind her. Although contemporary horror manga do not have the same didactic purpose as many of the earlier image texts, their visual language is, Pandey argues, quite similar.

Thanks perhaps in part to this long history of body horror within Japanese art, such imagery appears in much of Junji Ito's work, and body horror is the subgenre that he is most often associated with.[40] One of *Uzumaki*'s best-known images provides a dramatic instance of body horror. The image focuses on a girl, Azami, who has the power to attract the attention of any boy she likes. When Shuichi meets her, he describes seeing her as "like looking down from a high place . . . like vertigo . . . It's like looking into a spi-

Fig. 2.1 *Uzumaki*, p. 100: Azami becoming a spiral

ral!"[41] Already paranoid about spirals, he warns others of her, saying, "You have to watch out. She's a spiral!" and "She's contaminated by the spiral!"[42] Ultimately, her entire head becomes a spiral, which sucks in a boy, and then she is drawn into her own spiral, "devoured from head to toe . . . without leaving a trace behind."[43] The central, memorable image from this narrative (figure 2.1) shows her face partially taken over by the spiral.[44] One half-page image shows the spiral growing on one side of her face, around her eye. Her eyes are bloodshot, and the eye surrounded by the spiral is grotesque and bulbous. Following this image (to the left, because manga are read from right

Spiraling Inward and Outward

to left), there is a vertical sequence showing the further progression of the spiral. Her eyeball is sucked down into the spiral, and the spiral takes up more and more of the image. In the next image of Azami, both her eyes are gone and the spiral covers most of her face, leaving just her sinister, laughing mouth.

This is a clear instance of body horror—the destruction and distortion of the human body—and not necessarily of ecohorror. The emphasis here is on Azami's physical destruction, not on any connection between this spiral and environmental issues or the blurring of boundaries between human and nonhuman. This set of images not only illustrates the powerful body horror within *Uzumaki* but also serves as a reminder that although body horror and ecohorror both appear within *Uzumaki* and can productively speak to each other, the two subgenres bring different issues and questions to bear. Body horror emphasizes the human body and its destruction; ecohorror emphasizes the other-than-human and its relationship to the human.

Other examples of body horror within *Uzumaki* connect more directly to ecohorror, however, showing how the two approaches can work together. For instance, the transformations into animalized forms discussed in the previous section can be read as body horror. Those scenes are not simply about the horror of losing one's humanity and becoming animal but also about the horror of bodily mutation. Ito's attention to the slow growth of eyestalks and shells emphasizes this, asking the audience to consider how it might *feel* to grow eyestalks, just as body horror frequently asks the audience to identify with characters undergoing horrific transformations. In Cronenberg's *The Fly*, for instance, as Seth Brundle (Jeff Goldblum) gradually becomes a fly, the film explores the transformations in his body by focusing on the loss of specific human characteristics and body parts. In one striking scene, he stands before his bathroom mirror and tears off a fingernail. The film—through our identification with Brundle, through our human sensitivity about such body parts, and through effective sound design—makes us flinch and squirm as he peels off his fingernail and loses another part of his human body. This is classic body horror, but (in contrast with the scene featuring Azami) it is not clearly separable from ecohorror because it is not just about the destruction of his human body but also about becoming-animal.

Bodies and environments come together even more clearly in the language used to describe the encroaching spirals, which echoes the rhetoric of environmental justice and illness narratives. For instance, Shuichi repeatedly describes the town as "contaminated with spirals."[45] This language of contamination points to real-world issues raised by environmentalist and public health movements. One instance appears early in *Uzumaki*. The spirals from the crematorium repeatedly fall into Dragonfly Pond, at the center of town, "as if . . . the pond is sucking [them] in."[46] Afterward, Kirie's father's pottery becomes deformed and covered in spirals. It is also covered in faces of the dead. It turns out that the clay was taken from Dragonfly Pond, carrying the contamination from the crematorium through the pond and into Kirie's home and her father's art. The spirals function as a pollutant. They move through the air, through the water, and into human bodies, poisoning the community. Later on, individuals' transformations into snail-people might also be read as the result of such poisoning, a kind of illness. Even the fact that the man who ate a snail-person raw was so violently transformed into a spiral could be read as the effects of eating poisoned meat and taking on a high load of the contaminant. Furthermore, the entire town is transformed because the elements of everyday life they have taken for granted—clean air and water, food to eat, and safe spaces in which to live—are removed.

Notably, Shuichi describes Dragonfly Pond not only as contaminated but also as "infested with spirals."[47] With this language, the spirals are more like an invasive species, something that doesn't belong and that threatens the ecosystem. Therefore, they are both natural and unnatural. The invasive spirals change the dynamic, and humans are not able to adapt effectively. Although *Uzumaki* does not use a consistent and coherent metaphor for the environmental effects of the spirals—relying sometimes on contamination, sometimes on invasion—it repeatedly emphasizes the dangers of the spirals, both for individuals' health and for the health of the environment. This rhetorical messiness strengthens the connection between the focus on the damaged and/or contaminated body (a form of body horror) and on the dangers of an imbalance in the ecosystem (a form of ecohorror).

These concerns with environmental health connect in meaningful ways to Japan's recent history. In *Toxic Archipelago: A History of Industrial Disease in Japan*, Brett L. Walker describes several instances of environmental pollution in Japan that have had significant impacts on human lives and human health (e.g., Minamata disease). These recurrences of environmental pollution mean that "the victims of industrial disease and environmental pollution became subversive symbols of Japan's (and, at a certain level, everybody else's) everlasting enslavement to nature,"[48] reminders that human health and the health of the natural world cannot be separated. These victims, Walker writes, are "antimodern ghosts shrieking from the modern industrial landscape" whose "cries tell us that true modernity, for all its lofty promise, is a cruel fantasy."[49] Such victims haunt Japanese culture in much the same way that spirals haunt Kurouzu-cho. And both the real-world stories of pollution and disease and *Uzumaki*'s fantastic stories of spiral contamination serve as reminders that, as opposed to the idea of pure nature unsullied by humans, "in Japan the 'living environment' comprises those landscapes and organisms most closely associated with human habitation. It is the place where we, and our allied organisms, are present."[50]

Similarly, the horrific bodily transformations of *Uzumaki* cannot be disentangled from the environment in which they take place and the contamination of that environment. Stacy Alaimo's concept of trans-corporeality, "in which the human is always intermeshed with the more-than-human world," illuminates this further.[51] Trans-corporeality, Alaimo writes,

> underlines the extent to which the substance of the human is ultimately inseparable from "the environment." It makes it difficult to pose nature as mere background, as Val Plumwood would put it, for the exploits of the human since "nature" is always as close as one's own skin—perhaps even closer.[52]

External environments, therefore, are not necessarily even external. As I have argued elsewhere, "It is important . . . to note ecohorror narratives that challenge this division of human and nonhuman, internal and external. . . . If [as Brian Merchant argues] we have everything to fear, then even our own bodies—not to mention what lives in our bodies—are not safe."[53] *Uzumaki* not only accepts this blurring of boundaries between—or, to stick with the theme, this spiraling together of—ecohorror and body horror, environment and health, nature and human, but it *relies upon* it for its effect.

Cosmic Horror: *Uzumaki* Spirals Outward, Beyond the Human

Uzumaki also approaches the more-than-human through cosmic horror in the tradition of H. P. Lovecraft. According to Lovecraft, in "the true weird tale" (which is what he aimed to write), "a certain atmosphere of breathless and unexplainable dread of outer, unknown forces must be present" as well as "a malign and particular suspension or defeat of those fixed laws of Nature which are our only safeguard against the assaults of chaos and the daemons of unplumbed space."[54] Lovecraftian tales often focus on non-Euclidean geometries and spaces or shapes that are difficult to comprehend (and impossible to describe). They frequently feature Elder Things or creatures from beyond the stars, beings greater and older than us. Lovecraft has been a major influence on horror in Anglophone literature and in Japan, as Raechel Dumas notes: "In recent decades Japan has witnessed an explosion of evolutionary science fiction inspired largely by the Western tradition of cosmic horror, and especially the mythos fiction of H. P. Lovecraft."[55] In addition, Ito himself has said that "the different stages of the spiral (in 'Uzumaki') were definitely inspired from the mysterious novels of H. P. Lovecraft."[56]

This influence can be seen most clearly in the conclusion of *Uzumaki*. The text ends with the town itself becoming a spiral of row houses and Kirie and Shuichi descending into a "city of spirals" beneath the town (figure 2.2).[57] Kirie describes the city as "unlike anything I'd ever seen. The ancient ruins emitted a mesmerizing light. The floor was made of everyone who had poured in from Kurouzu-cho. They were all staring at the light."[58] Shuichi also describes the ruins as "like a living thing . . . with a will of its own."[59] This description of the city highlights its more-than-human qualities—it is living, like a part of the natural world, but it also has a will of its own, something beyond human control or understanding. Further, Shuichi says that he feels like the city is "permeating" him,[60] echoing his earlier statements about spirals contaminating the town—now the city too is invading him.

Significantly, the spiral city's purpose and its creators are mysterious. Shuichi says, "I don't know who . . . or *what* . . . built all this, or why . . . but every few hundred, or thousands, or tens of thousands of years . . . it can reach the people above ground. And though its builders are gone . . . *maybe it's still building itself*."[61] The spiral city exceeds the understanding of the mere humans affected by it; it exists on a much grander timescale than they do and for reasons they cannot grasp. The story ends very quickly after this moment. Kirie and Shuichi lie down in each other's arms, and the spiral completes itself. Then, Kirie notes, "a strange thing happened. Just as time sped up when we were on the outskirts, in the center of the spiral it stood still. So the curse was over the same moment it began, the endless frozen moment I spent in Shuichi's arms. And it will be the same moment when it ends again . . . When the next Kurouzu-cho is built amidst the ruins of the old one

Fig. 2.2 *Uzumaki*, pp. 600–601: City of spirals

... When the eternal spiral awakes once more."[62] This eternal spiral is reminiscent of Lovecraft's Elder Gods or Great Old Ones, and it dwarfs Kirie and Shuichi (and the reader) with its scale and power. It overwhelms the human, revealing our insignificance in the face of a larger, ineffable cosmic threat.

Placing *Uzumaki* in the larger context of Japanese manga further illustrates the relationship between its spirals and cosmic horror. Notably, the work of Osamu Tezuka (often called the "god of manga") exhibits an "insistence on circles and spheres" that "combines evolution and reincarnation, tending graphically and narratively toward the ideal of the Circle of Life that overarches and underlies the generation and regeneration of all circles and cycles."[63] Tezuka's circles, LaMarre argues, "[stand] in contrast to divisions, segregations, and hierarchies, which are imagined in rectilinear and angular terms (and evoke violence and death)."[64] Given Tezuka's reputation, Ito almost certainly read and was influenced by his work, and, in *Uzumaki*, Ito also moves away from "rectilinear and angular terms" and seems to combine evolution and reincarnation in his use of spirals. However, where Tezuka turned to circles and spheres as positive symbols, Ito does not. His spirals are not neatly closed or contained spheres but remain open and more obviously reflect Lovecraft's "monstrous perversions of geometrical laws" than they do Tezuka's circles.[65] Instead of the closure provided by circles, Ito's spirals remain open, refusing closure.

This lack of closure marks *Uzumaki* as an instance of what Andrew Tudor calls "paranoid horror," which is defined in contrast to "secure horror."[66] Secure horror features an external threat that is defeated in the end; the narrative provides closure, and normalcy prevails. Paranoid horror features a threat that cannot be conquered by humans; the narrative remains open, and not only normalcy but reality itself may be called into question.[67] This lack of closure—and the remaining threat—is also, Dumas argues, typical of "an apocalyptic mode that has ... long governed Japanese science fiction."[68] This apocalyptic mode, Dumas notes, "also intimates the possibility of future catastrophe,"[69] which she interprets as reflecting fears of further war but which could also be related to the possibility of environmental apocalypse. Whatever the referent, apocalypticism and lack of closure define *Uzumaki*'s conclusion. Our protagonists are left in the horrific spiral city, knowing that this may all happen again and that there's nothing they can do to stop it.

The spiral city's imagery not only resonates with cosmic horror but also echoes the concerns of plant horror; both cosmic and plant horror move beyond the human, to different scales and temporalities. Dawn Keetley writes, in her introduction to *Plant Horror*, that "plants embody an inscrutable silence, an implacable strangeness"[70] and that we often fear "being overrun, overcome, by vegetation—harbinger not only of death itself but of the ruin of culture, of our hard-built world."[71] This destruction of human worlds is made possible by what she describes as "the perennial and terrifying ability of vegetable life to swallow, engulf, overrun, and outlive humans."[72] The spiral city, too, is inscrutable and strange and even *looks* like vegetation. It spirals upward in the way leaves or vines do, reaching toward the light, and both plants and the spiral city "menace with their wild, purposeless growth."[73]

In its refusal to be mere background to human drama, the spiral also takes on elements of Keetley's "tentacular ecohorror."[74] Tentacular ecohorror, she writes, "is structured first by an encounter with a recalcitrantly alien form of life and second by a character's becoming enmeshed with that life."[75] Ito's spirals function similarly to the trees Keetley analyzes and are, if nothing else, "recalcitrantly alien." Furthermore, *Uzumaki* concludes with a scene in which "uncanny alien nature entangles the human and ushers in new forms of life,"[76] in which Kirie and Shuichi (and the rest of the people of Kurouzucho) become part of the spiral city, literally entangled and enmeshed with it. This scene promises future destruction "when the eternal spiral awakes once more,"[77] and the spiral city echoes human fears of plants as "harbinger not only of death itself but of the ruin of culture"[78] as well as fears of plants' abilities to *outlive* humans. The new form of life ushered in here has no room for Kirie, Shuichi, and their fellow humans, yet the spiral city will continue and will return. Like plants, it moves and grows in cycles, and it will once again reach out toward the town at some undetermined future time.

These cycles—and the apocalypticism of this conclusion—point to one final way of reading *Uzumaki*'s cosmic horror in relation to ecohorror: as climate change fiction. Although Lovecraft—and his contemporaries and imitators—may not have often directly addressed environmental issues or the natural world,[79] the concerns of cosmic horror are readily applicable to climate change and the Anthropocene. In fact, as Brian Attebery notes, cosmic horror has a long history in American writing, but Lovecraft's cosmic horror

> took rather a new form under the influence of twentieth-century scientific exploration. Discoveries in astronomy and physic [*sic*] made the earth seem small and terribly vulnerable to physical forces or (if one had a good imagination) alien invasion.

Advances in biology increased our awareness of grotesque life forms here on earth and led to speculation about hitherto inconceivable monstrosities elsewhere.[80]

Lovecraft's cosmic horror was shaped by scientific discoveries and fears of what those discoveries revealed; Ito's cosmic horror may reflect newer discoveries and contemporary concerns such as climate change.

The cycles of the spiral city happen on a timescale well beyond the human, as does climate change. In the short story "Nine Last Days on Planet Earth," Daryl Gregory writes, "Plant speed, and *planet* speed, that's just a hard timescale for us mammals to keep our attention on,"[81] and *Uzumaki* illustrates this difficulty. We may know climate change is occurring, but because it has been so hard to *see* it happening—because it unfolds at a pace much slower than the human, on a scale much larger than a human life—it is difficult to fully understand. In fact, many people feel there is nothing they can do about it, that it is on such a huge scale that it dwarfs their human abilities.

Both the alien and the planetary operate on scales and in modes that exceed our human understanding. Bringing the two together opens a new set of ecohorror conversations. The attempt to bridge these scales is unique to ecohorror: body horror does not typically do this, remaining focused on the individual; and although cosmic horror addresses two distinct scales of experience—the alien gods and the human—it does not do much beyond overwhelming the human with the gap between them. Ecohorror—because environmental issues are never just individual and never just right now—requires such attention to scale.

Conclusion: Intertwined Spirals

The combination of subgenres in *Uzumaki* highlights the ways in which ecohorror is—and must be—concerned not only with the environment, narrowly defined, but also with human bodies (always implicated in and impacted by ecological issues) as well as with large-scale threats, such as climate change, that are not easily grasped by the single human mind or experience. Ecohorror, like the issues it addresses, is often messy. As *Uzumaki* illustrates, it can spiral inward (into the human body, considering the microscopic scale, health, and illness), it can spiral across (toward other species, muddling lines between human and nonhuman), and it can spiral outward (to the larger planetary system and into a cosmic scale).

Perhaps because of this messiness, *Uzumaki* is one of the most effective works of ecohorror I know. Those spirals ensnare me and won't let me go. The text's argument is perhaps less obvious or direct than something like *Jaws* or *The Happening*, but its openness is its strength. It's not a sermon. It's a nightmare, one that draws on as many elements of environmental fear and as many elements of horror as possible to create its effect and provide a memorable story. *Uzumaki* therefore meets Lovecraft's "one test of the really weird," which is "whether or not there be excited in the reader a profound sense of dread, and of contact with unknown spheres and powers; a subtle attitude of awed listening, as if for the beating of black wings or the scratching of outside shapes and entities on the known universe's utmost rim."[82]

Because of its emphasis on something beyond the human, it also provides a model for what Jeffrey Jerome Cohen calls disanthropocentric thought.[83] Cohen writes, "Only in admitting that the inhuman is not ours to control, possesses desires and even will, can we apprehend the environment disanthropocentrically, in a teetering mode that renders human centrality a problem rather than a starting point."[84] *Uzumaki* asks us to face this reality, reminding us that the inhuman (the spiral, but also what it represents) is not ours to control, that it possesses its own desires. As a horror text, it also allows us to feel the fear that accompanies this reality, a crucial element in thinking differently about humanity's place in the world. After all, such a significant change to the way we are accustomed to seeing the world is frightening; pretending it's not is only another form of denial, one that can get in the way of creating the very changes we wish to see.

And denial is a powerful force preventing us from addressing climate change. As Naomi Klein writes in *This Changes Everything: Climate Change vs. Capitalism*, it is far too easy for us to "look for a split second" and then look away, joke about it, "tell ourselves comforting stories about how humans are clever," and so on.[85] It is far too easy to look and then forget: "Climate change is like that; it's hard to keep it in your head for very long."[86] She writes, "All we have to do is *not* react as if this is a full-blown crisis. All we have to do is keep on denying how frightened we actually are. And then, bit by bit, we will have arrived at the place we most fear, the thing from which we have been averting our eyes. No additional effort required."[87] Through its fantastic premise, *Uzumaki* shows what might happen if we fail to grapple with these larger issues, and it pushes us toward a direct response to them that is harder to defer.

It accomplishes this by refusing to allow its narrative to resolve into one clear type of horror. *Uzumaki* is a tangle of fears around the environment, the body, and our place in the universe. This messiness does not undo the distinctions between subgenres, but it does challenge the firm lines we often try to establish between them. Cosmic horror is not simply another type of ecohorror, but the two speak to each other. Body horror is not subsumed by ecohorror, but it makes little sense to ignore the ways in which our bodies and the environments we live in are materially connected. Stacy Alaimo writes about the "muddled middles" of monster movies, describing how viewers may pleasurably identify with monsters in the middle of a monster movie, even if that identification is accompanied by fear and does not last through the closure provided by the end of the film.[88] *Uzumaki*'s generic hybridity indicates that it's not only the middles of monster movies that are muddled—it's horror itself.

Notes

1. Stephen A. Rust and Carter Soles, "Ecohorror Special Cluster: 'Living in Fear, Living in Dread, Pretty Soon We'll All Be Dead,'" *ISLE: Interdisciplinary Studies in Literature and Environment* 21, no. 3 (Summer 2014): 509–10.

2. See both "Ecohorror" and "Monstrous Natures Within: Posthuman and New Materialist Ecohorror in Mira Grant's *Parasite*."

3. Body horror need not work so closely with ecohorror, however. Another example from David Cronenberg, *Videodrome* (1983), underscores this—it features dramatic and disturbing distortions of the body that are oriented toward technology rather than toward nonhuman animals or the natural world. Clive Barker's corpus provides even more examples of body horror not directly related to the natural world; *Hellraiser* (1987), for instance, anchors its body horror in the supernatural, featuring Cenobites and a portal to hell.

4. Jason Colavito, *Knowing Fear: Science, Knowledge and the Development of the Horror Genre* (Jefferson, NC: McFarland, 2008), 161.

5. Ibid.

6. Carter Soles reads rural slasher films like *The Texas Chain Saw Massacre* (1974) and *The Hills Have Eyes* (1977) as well as zombie films like *Night of the Living Dead* (1968) in ecocritical terms. Found-footage films like *The Blair Witch Project* (1999) or *The Bay* (2012) have also been read ecocritically. See Soles's "Sympathy for the Devil" and "And No Birds Sing"; see also Dawn Keetley's "Ecohorror" and Robin L. Murray and Joseph K. Heumann's *Monstrous Nature*.

7. Junji Ito, *Uzumaki*, trans. Yuji Oniki (San Francisco: VIZ Media, 2010), 17, 91, 174.

8. The lack of familiarity with Ito's work in the United States may result from a history of not taking graphic texts seriously. See Nicole Seymour's *Bad Environmental-*

ism for a discussion of the ecocritical value of "bad" forms like animation and comic books: "Animation may be a means of bringing large and diverse audiences, and greater flexibility, to environmental discourse" (214).

9. I refer to the 2010 omnibus edition throughout.

10. Ito, *Uzumaki*, 40–41.

11. Ibid., 51.

12. Ibid., 74.

13. Ibid.

14. Rust and Soles, "Ecohorror Special Cluster," 509.

15. Noël Carroll, *The Philosophy of Horror: Or, Paradoxes of the Heart* (New York: Routledge, 1990), 43.

16. Ito, *Uzumaki*, 264. *Uzumaki* includes ellipses within lines and when lines break between speech bubbles. All ellipses in quotations are in the original.

17. Ibid., 265.

18. In "Fecund Snails," Noah Berlatsky provides a reading of the snail-people in terms of sex and reproduction, although not from an ecocritical perspective. The heteronormativity of this scene is worth exploring, especially in light of recent work on queer ecologies and queer animals. See Catriona Mortimer-Sandilands and Bruce Erickson's *Queer Ecologies* (2010); and Nicole Seymour's *Strange Natures* (2013).

19. See Bridgitte Barclay, chapter 6 in this volume, for another discussion of mollusks, reproduction, and heteronormativity.

20. See Kristen Angierski, chapter 10 in this volume, and Sharon Sharp, chapter 11 in this volume, for more on the politics and horror of eating animals. See also Brittany R. Roberts, chapter 8 in this volume, for more on our ethical responsibilities toward nonhumans.

21. Ito, *Uzumaki*, 481.

22. Ibid., 537.

23. Ibid., 540.

24. Ibid., 541.

25. Val Plumwood, "Surviving a Crocodile Attack," *Utne Reader*, July–August 2000, www.utne.com/arts/being-prey.

26. Two familiar stories of this type (called "Shoo the Dog" by TV Tropes) are *The Fox and the Hound* (1981) and *Harry and the Hendersons* (1987), both of which rely heavily on sympathy for the animal.

27. Plumwood, "Surviving a Crocodile Attack."

28. Ibid.

29. Ito, *Uzumaki*, 553.

30. A disability studies critique of such dehumanization is valuable but outside the scope of this chapter. See Sunaura Taylor's *Beasts of Burden* (2017); and Eli Clare's *Brilliant Imperfection* (2017) for more on the complicated relationships between disability studies and animal studies and/or environmental studies.

31. Robin Wood, "An Introduction to the American Horror Film," in *Planks of Reason: Essays on the Horror Film*, ed. Barry Keith Grant and Christopher Sharrett (Lanham, MD: Scarecrow Press, 2004), 119.

32. Rajyashree Pandey, "Medieval Genealogies of Manga and Anime Horror," in *Japanese Visual Culture: Explorations in the World of Manga and Anime*, ed. Mark W. MacWilliams (New York: Routledge, 2015), 249.

33. Christine L. Marran, "The Metamorphic and Microscopic in Tezuka Osamu's Graphic Novels," in *Mechademia 8: Tezuka's Manga Life*, ed. Frenchy Lunning (Minneapolis: University of Minnesota Press, 2013), 76.

34. Thomas LaMarre, "Speciesism, Part I: Translating Races into Animals in Wartime Animation," in *Mechademia 3: Limits of the Human*, ed. Frenchy Lunning (Minneapolis: University of Minnesota Press, 2008), 79.

35. Ibid., 83.

36. Jay McRoy, *Nightmare Japan: Contemporary Japanese Horror Cinema* (New York: Rodopi, 2008), 139.

37. Ibid.

38. Pandey, "Medieval Genealogies," 247.

39. Clive Barker's "In the Hills, the Cities" (1984) develops this concept even more explicitly and horrifically.

40. Ito's *Gyo* (Fish; first serialized 2001–2) also functions as body horror with elements of ecohorror. It features mutated fish walking out of the ocean and attacking humans, including one scene in which a shark

on legs chases someone through an apartment building. The fish combine with machines in grotesque ways, and ultimately human bodies are incorporated into these machine assemblages. Ito has said that *Gyo* was inspired by Spielberg's *Jaws*: "He masterfully captured the essence of fear in the form of a man-eating shark. I thought it would be even greater to capture that fear in a man-eating shark that goes on land as well as sea" ("Into the Spiral").

41. Ito, *Uzumaki*, 87.
42. Ibid., 87, 88.
43. Ibid., 106.
44. Ibid., 100.
45. Ibid., 17, 91.
46. Ibid., 109.
47. Ibid., 119.
48. Brett L. Walker, *Toxic Archipelago: A History of Industrial Disease in Japan* (Seattle: University of Washington Press, 2010), 26.
49. Ibid.
50. Ibid., 217.
51. Stacy Alaimo, *Bodily Natures: Science, Environment, and the Material Self* (Bloomington: Indiana University Press, 2010), 2.
52. Ibid.
53. Christy Tidwell, "Monstrous Natures Within: Posthuman & New Materialist Ecohorror in Mira Grant's *Parasite*," *ISLE: Interdisciplinary Studies in Literature and Environment* 21, no. 3 (Summer 2014): 539.
54. H. P. Lovecraft, "Supernatural Horror in Literature," in *At the Mountains of Madness: The Definitive Edition* (New York: Modern Library, 2005), 107.
55. Raechel Dumas, "Monstrous Motherhood and Evolutionary Horror in Contemporary Japanese Science Fiction," *Science Fiction Studies* 45 (2018): 30.
56. Junji Ito, "Into the Spiral: A Conversation with Japanese Horror Maestro Junji Ito," by Mira Bai Winsby, trans. Miyako Takano, *78 Magazine*, February–March 2006, www.78magazine.com/issues/03-01/arts/junji.shtml.
57. Ito, *Uzumaki*, 600–601.
58. Ibid., 602.
59. Ibid., 605.
60. Ibid., 606.
61. Ibid.
62. Ibid., 610.
63. Thomas LaMarre, "Speciesism, Part III: Neoteny and the Politics of Life," in *Mechademia 6: User Enhanced*, ed. Frenchy Lunning (Minneapolis: University of Minnesota Press, 2011), 130.
64. Ibid.
65. H. P. Lovecraft, *At the Mountains of Madness: The Definitive Edition* (New York: Modern Library, 2005), 29. In his typical verbose style, Lovecraft provides multiple descriptions of such geometries. Here is just one: "The effect was that of a Cyclopean city of no architecture known to man or to human imagination, with vast aggregations of night-black masonry embodying monstrous perversions of geometrical laws and attaining the most grotesque extremes of sinister bizarrerie" (29).
66. Andrew Tudor, *Monsters and Mad Scientists: A Cultural History of the Horror Movie* (Oxford, UK: Blackwell, 1989).
67. Isabel Cristina Pinedo's analysis of postmodern horror applies here too: "Narratives are apt to end apocalyptically, with the defeat of the protagonists or with incipient signs of a new unleashing" (32).
68. Dumas, "Monstrous Motherhood," 43.
69. Ibid.
70. Dawn Keetley, "Introduction: Six Theses on Plant Horror; or, Why Are Plants Horrifying?," in *Plant Horror: Approaches to the Monstrous Vegetal in Fiction and Film*, ed. Dawn Keetley and Angela Tenga (New York: Palgrave Macmillan, 2016), 1.
71. Ibid., 5.
72. Ibid.
73. Ibid., 13.
74. See Keetley, chapter 1 of this volume.
75. Keetley, chapter 1 in this volume, 25.
76. Ibid., 36.
77. Ito, *Uzumaki*, 610.
78. Keetley, "Introduction," 5.
79. Algernon Blackwood is an exception to this, as Keetley's reading of "The Man Whom the Trees Loved" in chapter 1 of this volume illustrates. See also Blackwood's "The Willows."

80. Brian Attebery, *The Fantasy Tradition in American Literature: From Irving to Le Guin* (Bloomington: Indiana University Press, 1980), 129.

81. Daryl Gregory, "Nine Last Days on Planet Earth," *Tor*, September 19, 2018, www.tor.com/2018/09/19/nine-last-days-on-planet-earth-daryl-gregory/.

82. Lovecraft, "Supernatural Horror in Literature," 108.

83. Similarly, Keri Stevenson discusses Greg Garrard's concept of the disanthropic in chapter 4 of this volume.

84. Jeffrey Jerome Cohen, "Introduction: Ecology's Rainbow," in *Prismatic Ecology: Ecotheory Beyond Green*, ed. Jeffrey Jerome Cohen (Minneapolis: University of Minnesota Press, 2013), xxiv.

85. Naomi Klein, *This Changes Everything: Capitalism vs. the Climate* (New York: Simon and Schuster, 2014), 3.

86. Ibid., 4.

87. Ibid.

88. Stacy Alaimo, "Discomforting Creatures: Monstrous Natures in Recent Films," in *Beyond Nature Writing: Expanding the Boundaries of Ecocriticism*, ed. Karla Armbruster and Kathleen R. Wallace (Charlottesville: University Press of Virginia, 2001), 294.

References

Alaimo, Stacy. *Bodily Natures: Science, Environment, and the Material Self*. Bloomington: Indiana University Press, 2010.

———. "Discomforting Creatures: Monstrous Natures in Recent Films." In *Beyond Nature Writing: Expanding the Boundaries of Ecocriticism*, edited by Karla Armbruster and Kathleen R. Wallace, 279–96. Charlottesville: University Press of Virginia, 2001.

Attebery, Brian. *The Fantasy Tradition in American Literature: From Irving to Le Guin*. Bloomington: Indiana University Press, 1980.

Berlatsky, Noah. "Fecund Snails." *The Hooded Utilitarian*, October 31, 2011. www.hoodedutilitarian.com/2011/10/fecund-snails/.

Carroll, Noël. *The Philosophy of Horror: Or, Paradoxes of the Heart*. New York: Routledge, 1990.

Clare, Eli. *Brilliant Imperfection: Grappling with Cure*. Durham, NC: Duke University Press, 2017.

Cohen, Jeffrey Jerome. "Introduction: Ecology's Rainbow." In *Prismatic Ecology: Ecotheory Beyond Green*, edited by Jeffrey Jerome Cohen, xv–xxxvi. Minneapolis: University of Minnesota Press, 2013.

Colavito, Jason. *Knowing Fear: Science, Knowledge and the Development of the Horror Genre*. Jefferson, NC: McFarland, 2008.

Dumas, Raechel. "Monstrous Motherhood and Evolutionary Horror in Contemporary Japanese Science Fiction." *Science Fiction Studies* 45 (2018): 24–47.

The Fly. Directed by David Cronenberg, performances by Jeff Goldblum and Geena Davis. 20th Century Fox, 1986.

Gregory, Daryl. "Nine Last Days on Planet Earth." *Tor*, September 19, 2018. www.tor.com/2018/09/19/nine-last-days-on-planet-earth-daryl-gregory/.

Ito, Junji. *Gyo*. 2002. Translated by Yuji Oniki. San Francisco: VIZ Media, 2015.

———. "Into the Spiral: A Conversation with Japanese Horror Maestro Junji Ito." By Mira Bai Winsby. Translated by Miyako Takano. *78 Magazine*, February–March 2006. www.78magazine.com/issues/03-01/arts/junji.shtml.

———. *Uzumaki*. 2002. Translated by Yuji Oniki. San Francisco: VIZ Media, 2010.

Keetley, Dawn. "Ecohorror: The Nature of Horror." *Horror Homeroom*, April 22, 2018. www.horrorhomeroom.com/ecohorror-the-nature-of-horror/.

———. "Introduction: Six Theses on Plant Horror; or, Why Are Plants Horrifying?" In *Plant Horror: Approaches to the Monstrous Vegetal in Fiction and Film*, edited by Dawn Keetley and Angela Tenga, 1–30. New York: Palgrave Macmillan, 2016.

Klein, Naomi. *This Changes Everything: Capitalism vs. the Climate*. New York: Simon and Schuster, 2014.

LaMarre, Thomas. "Speciesism, Part I: Translating Races into Animals in Wartime Animation." In *Mechademia 3: Limits of the Human*, edited by Frenchy Lunning, 75–95. Minneapolis: University of Minnesota Press, 2008.

———. "Speciesism, Part III: Neoteny and the Politics of Life." In *Mechademia 6: User Enhanced*, edited by Frenchy Lunning, 110–36. Minneapolis: University of Minnesota Press, 2011.

Lovecraft, H. P. *At the Mountains of Madness: The Definitive Edition*. New York: Modern Library, 2005. First published in 1936.

———. "Supernatural Horror in Literature." In *At the Mountains of Madness: The Definitive Edition*, 103–82. New York: Modern Library, 2005. First published in 1927.

Marran, Christine L. "The Metamorphic and Microscopic in Tezuka Osamu's Graphic Novels." In *Mechademia 8: Tezuka's Manga Life*, edited by Frenchy Lunning, 73–85. Minneapolis: University of Minnesota Press, 2013.

McRoy, Jay. *Nightmare Japan: Contemporary Japanese Horror Cinema*. New York: Rodopi, 2008.

Mortimer-Sandilands, Catriona, and Bruce Erickson, eds. *Queer Ecologies: Sex, Nature, Politics, Desire*. Bloomington: Indiana University Press, 2010.

Murray, Robin L., and Joseph K. Heumann. *Monstrous Nature: Environment and Horror on the Big Screen*. Lincoln: University of Nebraska Press, 2016.

Pandey, Rajyashree. "Medieval Genealogies of Manga and Anime Horror." In *Japanese Visual Culture: Explorations in the World of Manga and Anime*, edited by Mark W. MacWilliams, 244–60. New York: Routledge, 2015.

Pinedo, Isabel Cristina. *Recreational Terror: Women and the Pleasures of Horror Film Viewing*. Albany: SUNY Press, 1997.

Plumwood, Val. "Surviving a Crocodile Attack." *Utne Reader*, July–August 2000. www.utne.com/arts/being-prey.

Rust, Stephen A., and Carter Soles. "Ecohorror Special Cluster: 'Living in Fear, Living in Dread, Pretty Soon We'll All Be Dead.'" *ISLE: Interdisciplinary Studies in Literature and Environment* 21, no. 3 (Summer 2014): 509–12.

Seymour, Nicole. *Bad Environmentalism: Irony and Irreverence in the Ecological Age*. Minneapolis: University of Minnesota Press, 2018.

———. *Strange Natures: Futurity, Empathy, and the Queer Ecological Imagination*. Urbana: University of Illinois Press, 2013.

Soles, Carter. "'And No Birds Sing': Discourses of Environmental Apocalypse in *The Birds* and *Night of the Living Dead*." *ISLE: Interdisciplinary Studies in Literature and Environment* 21, no. 3 (Summer 2014): 526–37.

———. "Sympathy for the Devil: The Cannibalistic Hillbilly in 1970s Rural Slasher Films." In *Ecocinema Theory and Practice*, edited by Stephen A. Rust, Salma Monani, and Sean Cubitt, 233–50. New York: Routledge, 2013.

Taylor, Sunaura. *Beasts of Burden: Animal and Disability Liberation*. New York: New Press, 2017.

Tidwell, Christy. "Ecohorror." In *Posthuman Glossary*, edited by Rosi Braidotti and Maria Hlavajova, 115–17. London: Bloomsbury Academic, 2018.

———. "Monstrous Natures Within: Posthuman and New Materialist Ecohorror in Mira Grant's *Parasite*." *ISLE: Interdisciplinary Studies in Literature and Environment* 21, no. 3 (Summer 2014): 538–49.

Tudor, Andrew. *Monsters and Mad Scientists: A Cultural History of the Horror Movie*. Oxford, UK: Blackwell, 1989.

TV Tropes. "Shoo the Dog." Accessed May 16, 2019. tvtropes.org/pmwiki/pmwiki.php/Main/ShooTheDog.

Walker, Brett L. *Toxic Archipelago: A History of Industrial Disease in Japan*. Seattle: University of Washington Press, 2010.

Wood, Robin. "An Introduction to the American Horror Film." In *Planks of Reason: Essays on the Horror Film*, edited by Barry Keith Grant and Christopher Sharrett, 107–41. Lanham, MD: Scarecrow Press, 2004.

3.
"The Hand of Deadly Decay"
The Rotting Corpse, America's Religious Tradition, and the Ethics of Green Burial in Poe's "The Colloquy of Monos and Una"

Ashley Kniss

Rot, decay, decomposition. All three words conjure visceral feelings of loathing, disgust, even horror. Daily television lineups are evidence enough that the corpse both repulses and fascinates. From *CSI* to the *Walking Dead*, the rotting corpse haunts terror narratives, even though the corpse is a natural and essential component of human life. As a necessary part of biological communities, ecosystems, and the environment, the corpse also holds particular importance for ecohorror, a genre defined by "those instances in texts when nature strikes back against humans as punishment for environmental disruption."[1] Extending the definition further, the corpse becomes particularly significant in narratives that "blur human/non-human distinctions" and plot lines in which humans are "attacked by natural forces."[2] Rot and decomposition are processes within ecosystems that benefit countless organisms, and yet the corpse, specifically the gruesome appearance and antagonistic characterization of the rotting corpse, remains a figure of horror that ecocritics have mostly overlooked. Because it is no longer entirely human as the environment reclaims it, the corpse represents an uncanny blurring of the familiar human form and what is alien, frightening, and inhuman in nature. Nature as represented by the corpse thus takes on the qualities of the Other, a characterization that Neil Evernden captures in his definition of nature as "that great mass of otherness that encloaks the planet."[3] This characterization of nature as Other lies at the heart of society's fear of the natural world.

Whereas critics such as Julia Kristeva in *The Powers of Horror* (1982) have explored the otherness of the corpse at great length, ecocritics have yet to examine how the corpse, representing nature as Other, might help further define the parameters of ecohorror by recognizing the corpse as a primary source of horror in the genre. One of Edgar Allan Poe's lesser-known works, "The Colloquy of Monos and Una" (1841), is an example of early American literature that highlights the critical potential of the corpse as a source of ecohorror. "The Colloquy" provides a firsthand account of death and its gruesome biological processes. The still-conscious narrator, Monos, describes his death and the process of decay as his body fuses with the environment and transforms his consciousness and his human identity. In addition to this monstrous mingling of the human and the nonhuman, for ecocritics the corpse represents the human body at its most permeable. At no other point in the life cycle of a body is it more evident that humankind is inseparable from the nonhuman world than at the first signs of decomposition. As a body begins to decompose, a horde of microbes that aid in human digestion begin to feast on their host, releasing gases that alert an array of insects, such as flies, maggots, beetles, and other invertebrates, of human food.[4] This process in which nature turns the body into food forces humankind to confront what Val Plumwood calls its own "foodiness."[5] Without the intervention of modern embalming practices, this process would be unavoidable, making the corpse the site of nature's final and irrevocable claim on the human body. Poe's text provides a powerful example for ecocritics of how the dead body is both a site and source of ecohorror as well as a physical link between the human and nonhuman worlds.

One of the primary disrupting forces between the human and nonhuman worlds is the religious belief in a mind/body split in which the body is a temporary dwelling place for the soul with little value of its own. Poe's colloquy disrupts this notion. "The Colloquy" is both a postapocalyptic conversation between two spirits and a Gothic tale of live burial, though it differs from similar tales of the time by omitting both the resurrection of the biblical apocalypse and the terror usually inherent in tales of live burial.[6] Monos, the primary narrator, relates the tale of his death and continued consciousness after death to his beloved Una. Monos describes his loss of physical senses, the loss of human sentiment, and the acquisition of additional senses that provide him with an awareness of cosmic time. The most jarring aspect of his account is his awareness of his body's decay: "All of what man has termed

"The Hand of Deadly Decay"

sense was merged in the sole consciousness of entity, and in the one abiding sentiment of duration. The mortal body had been at length stricken with the hand of the deadly *Decay*. Yet had not all of sentience departed."[7] Rather than adhering to typical resurrection narratives of his time, Monos relates the neutral observations of a disinterested observer as Monos's body slowly becomes its surrounding environment through the process of decay: "The narrow space immediately surrounding what had been the body, was now growing to be the body itself."[8] Monos never experiences terror from within the confines of the grave, which also departs from the sensational narratives of live burial. Although Monos does experience a loss of individual identity, he describes his experience neutrally without horror as he fuses with his surrounding environment. While "The Colloquy" contains similarities to other Gothic tales featuring a grisly corpse, live burial, and the horrors of the charnel house, it is markedly different from others of its kind. By depicting death and decay as a neutral rather than terrifying fusion of the human body with the nonhuman world of nature, Poe's tale subverts the religious notions of the afterlife that have negatively affected humanity's relationship with the environment and aligns instead with current environmental ethics, specifically those of green burial.

Texts such as "The Colloquy" that describe humanity's relationship with nature often explore one of two dichotomous, problematic ways of interacting with nature. The first is specific to ecohorror. In 2009, Simon C. Estok used the term *ecophobia* in an essay that calls for a clearer theoretical system of discourse within ecocriticism, one that would acknowledge that "contempt for the natural world is a definable and recognizable discourse."[9] Estok defines *ecophobia* as "an irrational and groundless hatred of the natural world, as present and subtle in our daily lives and literature as homophobia and racism and sexism."[10] Matthew Taylor describes the opposing side of this dichotomy—the equally problematic *ecophilia*. According to Taylor, ecophilia is an extension of the same problem as ecophobia. For Taylor, British and American Romantics advocate union with the natural world in reaction to the "Enlightenment's radical estrangement" between humankind and the environment.[11] But Taylor notes that this union with the natural world represents a "vampiric logic" wherein "wildness, the lifeblood of self-becoming, is not a renewable resource but we cannot preserve it without starving ourselves."[12] Both paradigms highlight humankind's harmful inclination to either fear or exploit the more-than-human.

Taylor suggests that Poe's texts might contain a third viewpoint: a mediation of the binary tension between ecophobia and ecophilia. According to Taylor, Poe's texts "foreclose both the idea that human selves are inherently distinct from or superior to their nonhuman environments and the seemingly antithetical (but actually coextensive) notion that we can self-constructively lose ourselves to the world."[13] Instead, Poe explores a radical and "irresolvable fear" of the blurred distinction between the human and nonhuman worlds.[14] This lack of a border between the human and nonhuman, according to Taylor, does not offer a "promise of reconciliation."[15] Instead, "Poe's cosmos . . . whispers, awfully, that something other than 'us' might be."[16] Supporting Taylor's claim, "The Colloquy" does explore how "something other than 'us' might be," dislocating the "border between 'us' and the 'world,'" but Taylor's assertion that Poe explores a radical and irresolvable fear due to the lack of distinction between us and the world is overstated. Poe certainly recruits the conventions of Gothic horror in his tale, but the narrator's sentiments are largely neutral regarding his transformation as decay takes hold.

Sara L. Crosby also approaches Poe's texts in search of a solution to the ecophobia/ecophilia dichotomy. In response to Taylor, Crosby argues that the problem with his critical stance is its lack of a "pro-active course of action or ethical model of identity."[17] Crosby argues for a "positive Poe" found in his detective stories, in which the detective, with his "ratiocinative method . . . insists upon a nonviolent reading of surfaces and . . . is restricted to parsing the human traces on the landscape. This method responds to the nonhuman world as an opaque other."[18] Crosby argues that Poe's detective tales provide an alternative to the dual problems of ecophobia and ecophilia in which humankind need not "embrace nature" but need not give in to an "irrational hatred of nature" either.[19] This approach, however, seeks a "positive Poe" outside of Poe's texts that most clearly contain elements of ecohorror. Poe's Gothic texts, as opposed to Poe's detective fiction, thrive on liminality and introduce spaces that transcend otherwise seemingly inescapable dichotomies. Rather than adhering to the nature-as-savior versus nature-as-monster dichotomy, Poe's Gothic texts provide a third option wherein the body and consciousness rejoin the environment through a loss of human identity while gaining a more-than-human sense of time and location. This fusion with nature is not what Crosby would call "bad love," a "pretended merger with the other."[20] Rather, it is an actual physical merger with the nonhuman Other. Crosby notes that only when nature is viewed as an "opaque other" is it possible to escape the ecophobia/ecophilia problem. In "The Colloquy," though, nature is not necessarily opaque or unknowable; instead, nature can be known, but only once the body and human identity have been surrendered to the environment, even destroyed, by the biological process of decomposition.

This loss of human identity positions Poe's text firmly within the genre of horror, a positioning that becomes even more pronounced in light of the tale's religious content. The religious context of Poe's tale is essential to a complete understanding of the text and of the way American society views both the corpse and, by extension, nature as malevolent. Typical nineteenth-century religious narratives about the process of death were mostly sentimental, primarily depicting the soul flying directly to heaven, followed by joyous reunions with already deceased loved ones. Poe's depiction of a conscious soul in a dead body represented a fringe belief that the soul remained conscious and active within the dead body until the Second Coming. By undermining mainstream conceptions of death and the afterlife with the alternative in "The Colloquy," Poe explores a radical reimagining of the corpse's narrative. Eschewing the typical depictions of the corpse in which the body is at best a mere by-product of death and at worst a representation of sin, Poe gives the corpse a narrative of its own that provides a new way of imagining it after death—not as an object of fear but as a new organism fully integrated with its surrounding environment. Poe undermines religious narratives of death and resurrection in favor of an earth-centered ethic that is neither ecophilic nor ecophobic and makes space for a mutually beneficial fusion between humanity and nature. Thus, the earth-centered ethic of "The Colloquy" offers a solution to the dual problems of ecophobia and ecophilia, especially considering the way Poe abandons his society's contemporary religious beliefs in favor of an ethic of decay.

Poe's subversion of conventional narratives of death and resurrection builds on America's Puritan heritage, which began by carving out a clearing amid what William Bradford notoriously described as a "hideous and desolate wilderness."[21] This attitude toward the wilderness offers an important parallel to American attitudes toward death and the accompanying fear of the corpse. The grave shares specific aspects of the Puritan characterization of the wilderness and can be viewed as a microcosm of or metaphor for the natural world, a world beyond human control that we enter at our own peril. Early Puritan settlers identified themselves as God's chosen people, carving out a new Eden amid the wilderness. Sacvan Bercovitch claims that this narrative would become "the foundational national story."[22] This foundational story, however, would establish an essential binary in American history and identity: the contrast between civilization and the wilderness. As Bernice M. Murphy states, "The forest beyond the settlement is the place where the representatives of 'civilization' are pitched against forces that embody 'savagery' and order—moral, psychological, and geographical—as opposed to 'chaos.'"[23] More important, "whilst the Puritans feared the Indians, there was one thing that they were even more afraid of—and that was *becoming* like them."[24] Murphy's study traces this fear of the wilderness, claiming that it continues in popular horror narratives today. The prevailing message remains: "The further the characters stray from 'civilization' and towards the intangible *something* that lurks at the heart of the American forest, the further they stray from their daylight, or rational *'original'* selves."[25] The same is true of the grave. The longer the corpse remains in the grave, the more it merges with its environment through the process of decomposition. The grave, like the wilderness, has the power to transform the human into the monstrous.

In this way, the grave is an extension of the Puritan conception of the wilderness and is therefore representative of nature itself. Both the wilderness and the grave are locations that represent a lack of control and where malevolent forces may be at work. Just as the Puritans believed that contact with the wilderness risked contamination and transformation, the grave carries equal risk. To enter the grave is to enter the alien world of the wilderness and come into contact with nature as Other—the inhuman, frightening not-me. The grave is where humanity not only comes into contact with this form of monstrous nature but also *becomes* monstrous and othered through the process of decomposition. That said, Poe interrogates this old Puritan narrative. Monos does transform within the grave, but his transformation is not terrifying or monstrous, which contradicts previous narratives and asserts the primacy of the body rather than of the soul.

Popular poetry of Poe's time also highlights Poe's divergence from an anthropocentric narrative of death and provides insight into society's continued aversion to decay. Nineteenth-century consolation verse, poetry that provides comfort for the bereaved, exemplifies the dominant religious narrative surrounding death and illustrates the prevailing anthropocentric dualism of religious culture that rejects the corporeal body after death and glosses over the inevitable decay of the body. The primary emphasis in this mainstream narrative is on the immediate resurrection of the soul, while the body is characterized as a burdensome afterthought or, worse, a representation of sin. Lydia Huntley Sigourney's collection of poems, *The Weeping Willow* (1847), is perhaps the best-known example of consolation verse in the nineteenth century. Sigourney's poetry depicts happy souls flying to heaven after death. These departed souls enjoy the glories of the Future Life, and the bereaved are assured of an inevitable spiritual reunion with loved ones who have passed away. Focusing primarily on the spiritual rather than the physical, these poems depict the body as a burden to be cast off at the time of death. One such example from *The Weeping Willow* is "The Mother's Departure":

> On a high arm, —and strong,
> The soul its burden cast,
> Till soaring free and high
> The weakness of mortality
> Fled like a wither'd leaf before the rushing blast,
> And with a conqueror's song
> Heaven's gate she pass'd.[26]

This poem is one among many that reveal the dominant view of the corpse in the nineteenth century. Upon death, souls achieve "soaring" freedom, released from the "weakness" and "burden" of the physical body. These poems also relegate the body to a representation of human weakness—the "weakness of mortality"— that the soul must escape before resurrection is possible. This view of the body is harmful and persists today. The body, belonging to the earth rather than to heaven, is inherently sinful; it is both a metaphorical and literal representation of sin and evil that the soul escapes through death. By extension, this evil also applies to the earth, creation, and nature itself as the body is returned to the earth when placed in the grave. Neither the body nor the earth is redeemed.

Today, these attitudes surrounding body and soul continue to widen the conceptual rift between the human and the nonhuman, imbuing Poe's tale with a significance both timely and subversive. Val Plumwood explores these attitudes in "Cemetery Wars: Cemeteries, Biodiversity and the Sacred" and argues that the prevailing notion of "mind/body splits" is harmful.[27] The belief that the mind is separate from the body reinforces the sentiment that "the earth is at best a temporary lodging; the true human home is beyond the earth, in heaven."[28] As Plumwood later notes, this system of belief comes at a cost: "Its comfort, the prospect of meeting again in the hereafter, is bought at the price of alienation from the earth, animals and the world of embodied life."[29] In "The Colloquy," Poe rejects this alienation. Monos's consciousness remains with his body throughout the tale. Even the tale's exposition—with its two speakers who have presumably been resurrected from the grave—refers to Monos and Una as "immortal . . . but still . . . *material*."[30] Although his body decays, Monos's consciousness remains tied to his material self, illustrating a total departure from typical religious narratives of the body and prioritizing an embodied humanity not so different from the rest of the nonhuman world.

Similar to consolation verse, popular nineteenth-century hymns serve as evidence of a harmful religious narrative that has separated body and soul and engendered disregard, loathing, and even fear of the material world. As in consolation verse, in hymns, the body has no intrinsic value of its own; it remains a subject of grisly terror—food for worms—that must undergo destruction in order for the soul to enter heavenly paradise, a burden to be cast off. Older hymns, such as those of Isaac Watts, further emphasized the divide between body and soul, relegating the body and its decay to a form of punishment for sin. In *The Psalms, Hymns, and Spiritual Songs of the Reverend Isaac Watts* and *Christian Psalmody in Four Parts*, the narrative feature of comfort and reassurance for believers remains present, but the older hymns often emphasize that the destruction of the body was to be desired, that only through the annihilation of the corrupt flesh could the refined soul enter paradise. Thus, the body, as a representation of sin and an object of loathing, *deserves* the punishment of corruption and decay. One example in particular illustrates decay as both justified and desired:

Great God, I own the sentence just,
And nature must decay
I yield my body to the dust
To dwell with fellow clay.
Yet faith may triumph o'er the grave,
And trample on the tombs;
My Jesus, my Redeemer, lives,
My God, my Saviour comes.
The mighty conqu'ror shall appear,

> High on a royal seat;
> And death, the last of all his foes,
> Lie vanquish'd at his feet.
> Though greedy worms devour my skin,
> And gnaw my wasting flesh;
> When God shall build my bones again,
> He'll clothe them all afresh.
> Then Shall I see thy lovely face,
> With strong, immortal eyes;
> And feast upon thy unknown grace,
> With pleasure and surprise.[31]

The speaker of the hymn admits that the "sentence" of death and corruption is "just," and he willingly "yield[s]" his body to the "dust." Yet, despite the horror of having "greedy worms devour [his] skin, / And gnaw [his] wasting flesh," he speaks of death and decay as an instrument of the resurrection, when God will "build [his] bones again." Despite the promise of renewal at the moment of resurrection, this vision of the body is one that devalues human flesh while lionizing the soul.

This attitude persists today, particularly in the problematic practices found in modern-day funerals and burials that seek to preserve the body in chemicals and vaults. Plumwood describes these practices as being "human-centered and anti-ecological, demonizing materiality, hyper-separating the human body from the earth and preventing its decay from benefitting other forms of life."[32] Poe's text, again, departs from these harmful religious notions of death and decay. Although Poe was certainly not ecologically motivated, his narrative nevertheless puts forth a compelling account of death from the corpse's perspective that eschews a heavenly afterlife in favor of material continuity in the form of a consciousness that remains linked to the material body and the nonhuman world. Within the context of ecocriticism, these religious attitudes are problematic because they separate humankind from the environment, and, as Plumwood argues, they are particularly evident in modern burial practices that prevent the material fusion of the body with the environment. Building on Plumwood's argument, Suzanne Kelly argues in *Greening Death: Reclaiming Burial Practices and Restoring Our Tie to the Earth* that the dead body matters. It is a sacred object, "not because the dead are tied to religion," but because "it evokes in us feelings of apprehension and dread, feelings that surface from its mysteriousness."[33] However, religious narratives such as those seen in consolation verse and hymns have capitalized on both the sense of dread that accompanies a corpse and its mysteriousness in order to venerate the soul at the expense of the body.

At first, Poe appears to endorse these harmful attitudes about the body in "The Colloquy," when he incorporates the hopeful rhetoric of contemporary religious discourse in the tale's opening scene. For example, Monos alludes to the New Testament (John 3:3) with the phrase "Born again," echoing the words of the biblical text: "Jesus answered and said unto him, Verily, verily I say unto thee, Except a man be born again, he cannot see the kingdom of God."[34] Other allusions include references to "the Life Eternal," borrowed from John 17:3, which states, "This is life eternal, that they might know thee the only true God." And finally, Poe references the Psalms when Monos describes the time between death and resurrection as "the Valley of the Shadow" (Psalms 23:4). Poe's allusions to these biblical passages frame the tale within the same narrative trajectory as consolation verse. As a result, Poe establishes a set of expectations for the tale's conclusion that he will later deny by ending the tale in darkness rather than resurrection or a return to the tale's initial location in paradise.

One of the ways Poe undermines these sentimental narratives of death in "The Colloquy" is by blending the religious framework of his tale with the popular Gothic tale of live burial, thus denying his audience's expectations of a resurrection that immediately follows death. In popular tales of live burial such as the two examples that follow, the prematurely interred express a variety of terrors, and, significantly, many of these tales have their roots in religious notions of the afterlife and the lack of theological consensus regarding the fate of the soul after death. While many of Poe's contemporaries would have subscribed to the belief that upon death the soul flies immediately to heaven, others would have believed the soul slept, waiting for the general resurrection on the Last Day; this space of time between death and resurrection was referred to as the "intermediate state." Others would have believed that the soul remained conscious within the grave as it awaited the final resurrection. Given the frequency of live and/or conscious burials in Poe's works, it appears that Poe was particularly influenced by this latter possibility, which essentially posits that all burials are live burials regardless of whether the person is buried alive or not. Along these lines, tales of live burial serve as a nightmarish metaphor for the state of the dead, wherein all souls go conscious to the grave to await eventual resurrection in darkness and isolation rather than acquiring new life immediately after death. Within the context of ecohorror, this narrative takes on further significance. If tales that include corpses are, in fact, staples of ecohorror, then they are not merely lurid Gothic tales that feature live burial for sensational reasons. Instead, live burial becomes analogous to the monstrous merger with the nonhuman world frequently found in ecohorror.

One example of a tale of live burial is an anonymous submission to *The Casket* in 1826 titled "The Buried Alive." The narrator finds himself dead in a darkened world, where he could yet "hear, and feel, and suffer," not unlike Monos in "The Colloquy" (257). The narrator hears those around him speaking of the "smell of corruption" emanating from the narrator's own body. He is conscious of being prepared unceremoniously for the grave, placed in a coffin, and buried. The author writes,

> This is death, thought I, and I am doomed to remain in the earth, until the Resurrection. Presently the body will fall into corruption, and the epicurean worm, that is only satisfied with man's flesh, will come to partake of the banquet that has been prepared for him.[35]

This particular account is remarkable due to its specific reference to the resurrection and the narrator's realization of the state of the body as it falls into corruption and is consumed by the "epicurean worm." Later, when grave robbers exhume the narrator's body, looking for medical cadavers, the narrator describes himself being "carried swiftly away, I thought to judgment, perhaps to perdition."[36] The author, like Poe, blends the sensational, Gothic tale of live burial with religious beliefs through his specific reference to the bar of judgment and hell. Although the title of this particular tale is "The Buried Alive," the narrator states that he is truly dead upon arriving at the medical school where he is to be dissected. Despite being subjected to "galvanic experiments," the narrator states, "still I was dead," emphasizing the Gothic elements in the tale.[37] Even though the tale contains elements of religious belief, specifically references to resurrection, judgment, and perdition, its intent is to terrify. The tale's horror is evident in the speaker's terror as he characterizes his "doomed" fate to remain in the grave while being consumed by worms. It is the tale's conspicuous omission of resurrection, however, that subverts typical notions of the afterlife and forms the bedrock of the tale's terror.

The same is true in a second tale of live burial, "Post Mortem Recollections of a Medical Lecturer" (1837), by an anonymous author. The dead but conscious narrator conveys a fear of bodily decomposition, a terrifying paralysis, an inability to communicate with the living, and a horror at the prospect of an afterlife where a soul goes to the grave trapped within its own dead body:

> I now knew well that I had died, and for my interment was intended the awful preparations about me. Was this then death? Could it be, that though coldness wrapped the suffering clay, passion and sense would soon survive—and that while every external trace of life had fled, consciousness should still cling to the cold corpse destined for the earth. —Oh! How horrible, how more than horrible! The terror of that thought.[38]

In addition to the immediate horror of conscious death is the terrifying realization concerning the nature of the afterlife: "Was this then death?" The narrative implies not only that heavenly paradise is absent but that the consciousness would survive within its now rotting body. The intention of both tales is terror: terror of the grave, of the corpse, and of decomposition, all essential components of the American conception of the wilderness and, by extension, the environment, placing this tale of live burial within the realm not only of horror but also of ecohorror.

Poe's tale functions within the realm of ecohorror due to the conspicuous merging of Monos's body with the earth of the grave, but Poe also conceptualizes a space in which this mingling of the human and the nonhuman need not be terrifying. Poe accomplishes this divergent possibility through Monos's state of mind after death: unlike victims of live burial, Monos never expresses terror. Instead, his tone is largely objective, verging on inhuman. Upon death, Monos ceases to experience emotions that are often identified as essential to being human—empathy, compassion, terror, sadness—aligning him more closely with the benign indifference of the nonhuman. When those around Monos determine him dead, he compares his state of consciousness to slowly waking up from an afternoon slumber: "It appeared to me not greatly dissimilar to the extreme quiescence of him, who, having slumbered long and profoundly, lying motionless and fully prostrate in a midsummer noon, begins to steal slowly back into consciousness."[39] Although Monos "breathed no longer" and his "heart had ceased to beat," he declares that his "condition did not deprive him of sentience" even though he is unable to move or speak: "Volition had not departed, but was powerless."[40] When Poe blends the Gothic elements of live burial with a familiar religious lexicon that includes specific biblical allusions, he recalibrates conventional religious narratives in the service of an alternative vision of death and the afterlife. This countervision resituates the body into more neutral territory than that of the popular religious rhetoric of the era and suggests an alternative model for humanity's relationship to the environment.

This alternative model rejects nineteenth-century religious paradigms as well as depictions of nature as contaminating and inherently malevolent. Instead, the body's decay and subsequent fusion with its environment provide a kind of physical immortality made possible by the process of decay rather than occurring in spite of it. From the moment Monos dies, he begins a gradual transformation from human to nonhuman that seems to confirm the puritanical fear that to come into contact with the wilderness, here embodied by the environment within the grave, is not merely to risk contamination but to guarantee it. As the tale progresses, however, Monos's transformation receives increased emphasis, and his story simultaneously contradicts the preeminence of the human soul and generates a new narrative for the physical body that reconceptualizes the afterlife to make room for the nonhuman world of nature, a world that also encompasses the body. Indeed, for Monos, the afterlife consists of physical union with nature that amounts not to a vampiric exploitation of nature but instead to a physical continuity between human and nonhuman. When Monos states, "I breathed no longer," his next observation refers to the physical senses: the "senses were unusually active, although eccentrically so—assuming often each other's functions at random. The taste and the smell were inextricably confounded, and became one sentiment, abnormal and intense."[41] Later, Monos observes that

> *all* my perceptions were purely sensual. . . . Of pain there was some little; of pleasure there was much; but of moral pain or pleasure none at all. Thus [Una's] wild sobs floated into my ear with all their mournful cadences, and were appreciated in their every variation of sad tone; but they were soft musical sounds and no more; they conveyed to the extinct reason no intimation of the sorrows which gave them birth; while the large and constant tears which fell upon my face, telling the bystanders of a heart which broke, thrilled every fibre of my frame with ecstasy alone.[42]

While Monos's indifference to Una's tears makes him appear inhuman, unfeeling, even othered, his indifference is nevertheless a benign indifference, not unlike that of the nonhuman world. As the elevation of Monos's physical senses foregrounds a narrative of the physical corpse rather than of the soul, it also neuters the concept of a monstrous mingling between human and nonhuman. Monos's human conceptions of morality and reason fall away, and he merges with the expansive universe of nature that surrounds him. In this reconceptualization of the afterlife, death is not an end but the beginning of an existence that is alien yet also timeless and anything but monstrous.

This reconceptualization is most evident when, despite his loss of essential human characteristics, Monos becomes privy to the timeless perspective of nature itself. While the process of Monos's transformation into "that great mass of otherness that encloaks the planet" entails Monos becoming increasingly alien in death, it also precipitates the experience of an entirely new, sixth sense. Monos describes the experience of this new sense as something impossible to communicate to the "merely human intelligence":

> There seemed to have sprung up in the brain, *that* of which no words could convey to the merely human intelligence even an indistinct conception. Let me term it a mental pendulous pulsation. It was the moral embodiment of man's abstract idea of *Time*. By the absolute equalization of this movement—or of such as this—had the cycles of the firmamental orbs themselves, been adjusted.[43]

With his new understanding of time, Monos becomes irritated with the inaccuracies of the clocks in his vicinity and describes this new understanding as a "step of the intemporal soul upon the threshold of the temporal Eternity."[44] Moreover, Monos gains access to this more-than-human sense of time only through the process of death, decay, and subsequent fusion with the environment, suggesting that a transformative journey into the wilderness—a synthesis with nature through death—provides ontological continuity outside typical religious narratives. The process of decay within nature is ultimately responsible for this perpetuation of being by generating the process of human-nature synthesis. Whereas Taylor argues that this transformation into the "something other than us" represents a radical and "irresolvable fear," Monos expresses no such fear, describing his experience dispassionately for the most part and occasionally with something akin to awe. Readers may, nevertheless, remain repulsed and horrified by Monos's inhuman indifference, dispassion, and the loss of what makes him essentially human. Poe, after all, is a master of horror and draws on any number of Gothic conventions that enhance the effect of horror within the tale. But whether intentionally or unintentionally, Poe puts forth in "The Colloquy" a timely alternative to the still-pervasive anthropocentric vision of death and the afterlife that ignores the significance of the body and how it might benefit the earth's ecosystems.

This rendering of death as a physical process rather than a spiritual one seems as though it would compound the tale's Gothic leanings. Poe does retain some of the language of conventional religious narratives in "The Colloquy," but he omits the beatific vision of heaven entirely and glosses over the typical horrors of the grave as Monos begins to experience the decomposition of his body:

> A dull shock like that of electricity pervaded my frame, and was followed by total loss of the idea of contact. All of what man has termed sense was merged in the sole consciousness of entity, and in the one abiding sentiment of duration. The mortal body had been at length stricken with the hand of the deadly *Decay*. Yet had not all of sentience departed.[45]

Monos then lapses into the typical rhetoric of Christian hymns and poems, speaking of "the direful change now in operation upon the flesh" and describing death and the grave as "sad and solemn slumbers with the worm" and a "prison-house."[46] This would appear an appropriate narrative moment to return to the initial frame of the story, with two souls speaking in paradise after the apocalypse and resurrection. But this is not what Poe provides. Instead, he describes how Monos literally *becomes* his environment:

> A year passed. The consciousness of *being* had grown hourly more indistinct, and that of mere *locality* had, in great measure, usurped its position. The idea of entity was becoming merged in that of *place*. The narrow space immediately surrounding what had been the body, was now growing to be the body itself. . . . Dust had returned to dust. The worm had food no more. The sense of being had at length utterly departed, and there reigned in its stead—instead of all things—dominant and perpetual—the autocrats *Place* and *Time*. For *that* which *was not*—for that which had no form—for that which had no thought—for that which had no sentience—for that which was soulless, yet of which matter formed no portion—for all this noth-

ingness, yet for all this immortality, the grave was still a home, and the corrosive hours, co-mates.[47]

The tale ends with a complete transformation. Monos, once human, is now completely devoid of human consciousness and being. Other than a sense of locality and time, Monos is no longer capable of human sentiment, the culmination of the process that began at the moment of death. But the tale is not the horrific narrative, seen so often in Gothic tales such as Nathaniel Hawthorne's "Young Goodman Brown," in which the individual comes into contact with a dark and malevolent environment and then reveals *himself* to be the "chief horror of the scene" as a consequence of leaving the safe haven of human contact.[48] Rather, Poe offers a new narrative in which Monos's contact with nature as Other *does* result in the loss of the self, but that loss is conveyed as inconsequential in the face of Monos's new experience of physicality and eternity. Poe again neutralizes the dire religious depictions of the grave. In his rendering of death, "the solemn slumbers with the worm" and the "prison-house" of the grave are inconsequential features of Monos's transformation, in which identity transgresses human definitions and fuses with the nonhuman concepts of locality and duration.[49]

While Monos's transformation from human to nonhuman does contain elements of terror, Poe's tale nevertheless advances an earth-centered attitude toward death that aligns with the modern green burial movement. According to Kelly, green burial, or *natural burial*, "aims to care for the dead with minimal impact to the environment. Where conventional burial typically includes embalming and caskets, often sealed, and manufactured from finished hardwoods and metals and sometimes non-plant-based materials as well as use of reinforced concrete vaults or liners, whole-body green interment steers clear of all of them."[50] These burials use biodegradable coffin material of cardboard, wicker, or sometimes merely a simple shroud. This means a complete abandonment of techniques such as embalming that attempt to eradicate human contact with decay and that eventually leach chemicals into the soil and watershed. In many ways, traditional burial treats the human body as waste, a contaminant that must be held at a distance. When Marisol Cortez describes human waste disposal as a harmful process that widens the divide between humans and nature, she reveals a striking similarity between the treatment of human waste and the treatment of the corpse.[51] Both human waste and the corpse are treated as othered subjects rather than as essential components of human identity and biology. Rather than viewing human bodies (or waste for that matter) as distinct from ecosystems, the ethics of green burial sees the body as *part* of the environment. According to Suzanne Kelly, embracing the practice of green burial by removing the physical separation between human and environment at death helps achieve integration. In addition, instead of viewing human decay as contaminating, polluting, or otherwise unhealthy, green burial embraces it as "good and valuable, as microbes and insects descend to feed on the dead. As food and nourishment for other creatures, the corpse is of consequence to the land and to the species of mammals, birds, amphibians, plants, and insects that inhabit it. In essence, the corpse is of consequence to the planet."[52] Thus, green burial offers a new ethic regarding the relationship between humankind and the environment by restoring the value of the corpse and reestablishing the mutual belonging of body and earth.

Poe's tale reinforces this ethic in which the body facilitates a mutually beneficial union between humankind and nature. Kelly argues for the necessity of green burial in order to "change . . . the way people see themselves in terms of being a part of, and not apart from, nature," and Poe's text offers a glimpse of an afterlife that envisions this continuity between humans and nature.[53] The biblical rhetoric surrounding death and burial provides religious precedent for this connection as well—upon death "thou return unto the ground; for out of it wast thou taken: for dust thou art, and unto dust shalt thou return" (Genesis 3:19). The gulf between humankind and the environment narrows, when, as Genesis 3:19 implies, the body becomes part of nature rather than separate from and superior to it. Add to this sentiment the modern ethics of green burial. Through the practice of green burial, the body becomes the site on which modern society might generate a tangible connection with the earth by allowing the body to benefit the earth's ecosystems. Such a practice might help remove death's terror, replacing it with a neutral acceptance of death at the body's inevitable return to the earth that is not unlike the neutral sentiments Monos expresses in "The Colloquy." Although Poe's tale does not go so far as to assert the value of the corpse to its environment, it does provide a narrative of human transformation and integration into the environment that supersedes a narrative of salvation and resurrection.

Replacing resurrection with material continuity, itself a form of immortality, Poe also provides the twenty-first-century reader a glimpse of how humankind might find comfort rather than horror in the physical continuity of decay as the body decomposes into the surrounding environment. While Monos's transformation entails a loss of what makes him human as well as a monstrous mingling with the more-than-human world of nature, Poe's text is most remarkable for its preservation of the concept of human immortality upon death. Although Monos's "consciousness of *being* had grown hourly more indistinct" as his body merged with its environment, Poe is clear that despite all the "direful" changes wrought on Monos, he remains immortal, privy in death to the eternal.[54] Poe's final passage in the tale is halting as he attempts to describe this new way of being. Monos "*was not*"; he has "no form . . . no thought . . . no sentience," and Poe describes him as "soulless" yet still in possession of immortality.[55] At several points, Kelly argues that the dead body "belongs to the planet,"[56] that green burial has the potential to rectify "our severance from the natural world in both symbolic and literal ways,"[57] and that our "severance from nature has had us running from decay" instead of recognizing that "we do, indeed, belong to the earth."[58] While halting and incomplete, Poe's final passage offers a vision of what Kelly's recognition might look like. Rather than "running from decay," Poe's tale depicts the process as integrative, and, rather than being horrifying, it articulates what that integration with the earth offers: a vision of ecological immortality in which the body, made from dust, returns to the dust, heralding not a heavenly reunion but an earthly reunion with the material world of the more-than-human.

Although Poe wrote well over a century before the green burial movement, his tale offers a narrative that does not shy away from the physicality of death and the reality of rot. Moreover, he offers a vision of death that denies the preeminence of the soul, envisioning instead a physical union with the environment that requires neither a total annihilation of the self nor an exploitative union with nature. Rather than serving merely sensational purposes, Poe's use of Gothic elements in "The Colloquy" both highlights and undermines religious narratives of death and the afterlife. These same narratives that lionize the soul and relegate the body to a mere burden that deserves destruction are the same narratives that today perpetuate the myth of humankind as separate from the natural world. While Poe capitalizes on the sensationalism of the corpse—its grisly demise that both fascinates and repels—his narrative focuses more on the conceptualization of Monos's transformation, which includes decay (as well as enhanced senses), an expanded understanding of time and eternity, and a sense of *being* that fuses with location and environment. Kelly writes that "we are, en masse, a culture terrified of human rot. And we've done our best to shun it. As green burial offers back to us a relationship with nature that's long overdue, it demands a rethinking of human decay" so that "we can find our way back to union with the earth."[59] This cultural shunning of decay has its roots in American religious traditions that focus only on a narrative of the soul while denying the body a narrative. Spurning these traditions, Monos's recognition of his body's decay does not result in the desperate pleas of a prisoner longing for Puritan-inspired resurrection. Instead, the rotting body is one facet of death's transformation, a transformation that offers a glimpse of what Kelly calls "union with the earth." This transformation may entail contact with nature as Other, as alien, or as a malevolent force beyond human control, but it also provides a glimpse of how we might reconceptualize our relationship with the environment, not as two diametrically opposed forces but as equal components of an ecosystem, each essential to the other.

Notes

1. Stephen A. Rust and Carter Soles, "Ecohorror Special Cluster: 'Living in Fear, Living in Dread, Pretty Soon We'll All Be Dead,'" *ISLE: Interdisciplinary Studies in Literature and Environment* 21, no. 3 (Summer 2014): 509.

2. Ibid., 510.

3. Neil Evernden, *The Social Creation of Nature* (Baltimore: Johns Hopkins University Press, 1992), xi.

4. Part of what makes the corpse an essential facet of ecohorror is that it is a primary site of trans-corporeality as microbes and macroinvertebrates such as maggots enter and exit the corpse and facilitate the body's integration with the environment. See chapters 1, 2, 6, and 7 by Dawn Keetley, Christy Tidwell, Bridgitte Barclay, and Marisol Cortez, respectively, for further discussion and for the definition of Stacy Alaimo's concept of trans-corporeality.

5. Val Plumwood, *The Eye of the Crocodile* (Canberra: ANU E Press, 2012), 91.

6. Although this chapter does not address apocalypse directly, "The Colloquy" does contain a detailed description of the apocalyptic destruction of the earth and its inhabitants—a significant subject for environmental writers, including Rachel Carson, as well as for ecocritics. For further exploration in this volume of apocalypse and a world without humans, see chapter 2 by Christy Tidwell and chapter 4 by Keri Stevenson.

7. Edgar Allan Poe, *Edgar Allan Poe: Tales and Sketches*, ed. Thomas Ollive Mabbott, vols. I and II (Champaign: University of Illinois Press, 2000), 615–16.

8. Ibid., 616.

9. Simon C. Estok, "Theorizing in a Space of Ambivalent Openness: Ecocriticism and Ecophobia," *ISLE: Interdisciplinary Studies in Literature and Environment* 16, no. 2 (Spring 2009): 2.

10. Ibid., 6. Responding to Estok's article in the same year, Tom J. Hillard asserts

that perhaps "'fear' might be a more accurate word than 'hatred' (for doesn't most hatred arise from some deep-seated fear?)" (686). Hillard argues that "we need look no further than the rich and varied vein of critical approaches used to investigate fear in literature. That is, what happens when we bring the critical tools associated with gothic fiction to bear on writing about nature?" (688). In this study in particular, both Freud's theory of the uncanny and Kristeva's theory of abjection could provide useful frameworks for the role of the corpse in ecohorror, especially given that Poe's tale provides narration from the perspective of such an abject and uncanny object of horror: the corpse.

11. Matthew Taylor, "The Nature of Fear: Edgar Allan Poe and Posthuman Ecology," *American Literature* 84, no. 2 (2012): 354.

12. Ibid., 357.

13. Ibid., 369.

14. Ibid., 370.

15. Ibid.

16. Ibid.

17. Sara L. Crosby, "Beyond Ecophilia: Edgar Allan Poe and the American Tradition of Ecohorror," *ISLE: Interdisciplinary Studies in Literature and Environment* 21, no. 3 (Summer 2014): 514.

18. Ibid., 515.

19. Ibid., 523.

20. Ibid.

21. William Bradford, *Of Plymouth Plantation: 1620–1647* (Boston: Massachusetts Historical Society, 1856), 78.

22. Sacvan Bercovitch, *The American Jeremiad* (Madison: University of Wisconsin Press, 2012), xiii.

23. Bernice M. Murphy, *The Rural Gothic in American Popular Culture: Backwoods Horror and Terror in the Wilderness* (London: Palgrave MacMillan, 2013), 16.

24. Ibid., 36.

25. Ibid., 1.

26. Lydia Huntley Sigourney, *The Weeping Willow* (Hartford, CT: Henry S. Parsons, 1847), 118.

27. Val Plumwood, "Cemetery Wars: Cemeteries, Biodiversity and the Sacred," *Local-Global: Identity, Security, Community* 3 (2007): 56.

28. Ibid.

29. Ibid.

30. Poe, *Tales and Sketches*, 612. Italics in original.

31. Samuel M. Worcester, *The Psalms, Hymns, and Spiritual Songs, of the Rev. Isaac Watts, D.D. to which are added Select Hymns, from other Authors and Directions for Musical Expression* (Boston: Crocker and Brewster, 1834), 294.

32. Plumwood, "Cemetery Wars," 56.

33. Suzanne Kelly, *Greening Death: Reclaiming Burial Practices and Restoring Our Tie to the Earth* (London: Rowman and Littlefield, 2015), 23–24.

34. The King James Version is used throughout.

35. "The Buried Alive," *The Casket, or, Flowers of Literature, Wit and Sentiment* 1, no. 9 (1826): 257–58, American Periodicals, Proquest.

36. Ibid., 258.

37. Ibid.

38. "Post Mortem Recollections of a Medical Lecturer," *Atkinson's Casket* 3 (1837): 118, American Periodicals, Proquest.

39. Poe, *Tales and Sketches*, 612.

40. Ibid.

41. Ibid., 612–13.

42. Ibid., 613.

43. Ibid., 615.

44. Ibid.

45. Ibid., 615–16.

46. Ibid., 616.

47. Ibid., 616–17.

48. Nathaniel Hawthorne, *Mosses from an Old Manse*, ed. William Charvat, Roy Harvey Pearce, and Claude M. Simpson, (Columbus: Ohio State University Press, 1974), 83.

49. See chapter 5 in this volume, by Chelsea Davis, on Ambrose Bierce's "A Tough Tussle" for further consideration of the horror and fascination the grave worm, or maggot, held for nineteenth-century audiences.

50. Kelly, *Greening Death*, 4.

51. Marisol Cortez, chapter 7 in this volume.

52. Kelly, *Greening Death*, 4.
53. Ibid., 66.
54. Poe, *Tales and Sketches*, 616.
55. Ibid., 617.
56. Kelly, *Greening Death*, 5.
57. Ibid., 6.
58. Ibid., 10.
59. Ibid., 33.

References

Bercovitch, Sacvan. *The American Jeremiad*. Madison: University of Wisconsin Press, 2012.

Bradford, William. *Of Plymouth Plantation: 1620–1647*. Boston: Massachusetts Historical Society, 1856.

"The Buried Alive." *The Casket, or, Flowers of Literature, Wit and Sentiment* 1, no. 9 (1826): 257–58. American Periodicals, Proquest.

Crosby, Sara L. "Beyond Ecophilia: Edgar Allan Poe and the American Tradition of Ecohorror." *ISLE: Interdisciplinary Studies in Literature and Environment* 21, no. 3 (Summer 2014): 513–25.

Estok, Simon C. "Theorizing in a Space of Ambivalent Openness: Ecocriticism and Ecophobia." *ISLE: Interdisciplinary Studies in Literature and Environment* 16, no. 2 (Spring 2009): 2–23.

Evernden, Neil. *The Social Creation of Nature*. Baltimore: Johns Hopkins University Press, 1992.

Hawthorne, Nathaniel. *Mosses from an Old Manse*, edited by William Charvat, Roy Harvey Pearce, and Claude M. Simpson. Columbus: Ohio State University Press, 1974.

Hillard, Tom J. "'Deep into That Darkness Peering': An Essay on Gothic Nature." *ISLE: Interdisciplinary Studies in Literature and Environment* 16, no. 4 (Autumn 2009): 685–95.

Kelly, Suzanne. *Greening Death: Reclaiming Burial Practices and Restoring Our Tie to the Earth*. London: Rowman and Littlefield, 2015.

Murphy, Bernice M. *The Rural Gothic in American Popular Culture: Backwoods Horror and Terror in the Wilderness*. London: Palgrave MacMillan, 2013.

Plumwood, Val. "Cemetery Wars: Cemeteries, Biodiversity and the Sacred." *Local-Global: Identity, Security, Community* 3 (2007): 54–71.

———. *The Eye of the Crocodile*. Canberra: ANU E Press, 2012.

Poe, Edgar Allan. *Edgar Allan Poe: Tales and Sketches*, edited by Thomas Ollive Mabbott. Vols. I and II. Champaign: University of Illinois Press, 2000.

"Post Mortem Recollections of a Medical Lecturer." *Atkinson's Casket* 3 (1837): 117–19. American Periodicals, Proquest.

Rust, Stephen A., and Carter Soles. "Ecohorror Special Cluster: 'Living in Fear, Living in Dread, Pretty Soon We'll All Be Dead.'" *ISLE: Interdisciplinary Studies in Literature and Environment* 21, no. 3 (Summer 2014): 509–12.

Sigourney, Lydia Huntley. *The Weeping Willow*. Hartford, CT: Henry S. Parsons, 1847.

Taylor, Matthew. "The Nature of Fear: Edgar Allan Poe and Posthuman Ecology." *American Literature* 84, no. 2 (2012): 353–79.

Worcester, Samuel M. *The Psalms, Hymns, and Spiritual Songs, of the Rev. Isaac Watts, D.D. to which are added Select Hymns, from other Authors and Directions for Musical Expression*. Boston: Crocker and Brewster, 1834.

Part 2
Haunted and Unhaunted Landscapes

4.
The Death of Birdsong, the Birdsong of Death
Algernon Charles Swinburne and the Horror of Erosion

Keri Stevenson

With the creation by climate change of rising oceans and their inevitable impact on coastal ecosystems, erosion looms as a modern source of ecohorror. In a study of erosion impacts in Europe, P. C. Roebeling and colleagues note that many ecosystems have deteriorated as a result of increasing sea levels, storm surges, and human transformation of coasts.[1] In addition, Rodolfo Silva and his collaborators point out that 10 percent of the world's human population lives in areas forecast to be affected by oceanic erosion.[2] Loss of seashore will obliterate habitat as well as cities, hotels, and villages, and it will compromise human subsistence activities such as fishing as well as the subsistence activities of animals like horseshoe crabs and shorebirds that come ashore to perform vital tasks—for example, laying eggs. The "disastrous repercussions for the world's coastal zones, the people who occupy them, and the historical and archaeological resources they contain"[3] include literally erasing the past through the loss of archaeological sites that could teach us about how our ancestors coped with erosion. The sea in this figuration of death and disaster is the monster of one kind of ecological horror, swallowing up the world with a radical ability to conquer time and space, feeding on the earth with no satiation of its appetite possible.

Yet while the cause of this kind of horror—climate change as well as increased awareness of human impacts on coastal habitats—is new, the figuration itself is not. In particular, it occurs in several poems by the Victorian poet Algernon Charles Swinburne (1837–1909), with a twist not usually found in modern approaches to coastal erosion as a disaster: Swinburne's poetic voice is on the sea's side.

Swinburne is a poet of the sterile and the desolate. "His greatest love poetry," says his anthologist, John D. Rosenberg, "is addressed . . . to his bitter, salt mother the sea, and to those bleakly beautiful, ravaged margins of earth that yield their substance to her."[4] Swinburne creates landscapes that outlive humanity and do so with gleeful grace, both in association with and represented by sea-birds. But he does so partially by invoking what Greg Garrard calls the disanthropic, a world "completely and finally *without people*."[5] The landscapes of Swinburne's poetry—usually seashores or on the margin of the sea—are shed of humanity, pictured in some stanzas at the moment when humans are dead and no longer walk the earth. This does not end their artifacts; such poems as "By the North Sea," which I later consider in detail, portray the lingering of monuments that the sea inevitably takes. But Swinburne paints an ultimately bleaker and more convincing image than the greening of the world shown by disanthropic thought experiments such as Alan Weisman's *The World Without Us*, which, while imagining the disappearance of humanity and how "nature's revenge for our smug, mechanized superiority arrives waterborne,"[6] also pictures the "banished natural foliage that was still hovering on the subdivision's fringes, awaiting the chance to retake its territory."[7] Weisman's world is green and quiet—regenerating, not eroded. Swinburne's world is not beautiful because humanity has abandoned it. His poetry's world is beautiful because of the gleeful indifference of the animals that continue to inhabit the bleak, even polluted landscapes that Swinburne raises to the level of the sublime.

Among these animals, birds of the seashore are especially important, partially for their adaptation to an environment that humans must leave behind and partially for their voices. These voices are usually referred to as "songs," the name that Swinburne most frequently used for poetry. (Swinburne used the word in such poetic collection titles as *Songs Before Sunrise* [1871], *Songs of Two Nations* [1875], and *Songs of the Springtides* and *Studies in Song* [1880].) Swinburne's still-human narrative voice circumvents one of the major questions of the disanthropic—how can humans convincingly portray a landscape devoid of humanity?—by hailing the spoiled and ugly as what endures, as mockingly beautiful, and the world without us as in no need of any salvation because it has the birds to sing of it; erosion itself is part of what makes the sea's power horrifying and glorious. Two of Swinburne's seashore poems, "A Forsaken Garden" and "By the North Sea," are emblems of this horror and portray particularly well the disanthropic ethos that underpins much of Swinburne's writing.

The Disanthropic

Greg Garrard defines the disanthropic as "inspired, in part, by ordinary misanthropic hatred of 'the crowd,' but [as] distinguished by [man's] *absence* from the future he envisages."[8] It is a challenging genre: it tries both to represent geological deep time and to "paradoxically [be] . . . often momentary or microcosmic." It is also caught up in the inevitable problem of a human narrator proposing a world in which humans are extinct. As Garrard writes, "The helpless allegiance of written genres to narrative voice and anthropomorphic characterization makes disanthropic literature . . . probably impossible."[9] Therefore, disanthropic literature is rare. Garrard identifies several moments in modernist texts, including the second section of Virginia Woolf's *To the Lighthouse*, that provide him with the definitions for disanthropy, and he then discusses a few films, two based on Weisman's *The World Without Us*, that manage to achieve something close to the absence of the human narrator. Yet these remain human artifacts, their construction something the audience can be coaxed to forget only for small flashes of time. Garrard describes the experience of watching these films as at first mesmerizing, but he notes that eventually the movies begin to seem "interminable."[10] The audience's attention span, then, conditioned as it is to associate a narrative with a human narrator and a human-filled world, cannot take three hours of a truly disanthropic piece, no matter how marvelously mediated.

These combined definitions suggest that disanthropic literature is, by its nature, constructed in flashing glimpses, fighting constantly against the viewpoint of its human narrator, since that narrator's presence implies that at least one human is left alive in a landscape that is supposed to be devoid of all *Homo sapiens*. A story that contains more than a glimpse or series of glimpses bores its readers or viewers, and one that attempts to ignore its narrator seems ignorant of its own nature. Garrard's prescription that disanthropic literature is impossible by definition seems truer the more one looks at it.

Yet this loop of complicated paradoxes renders disanthropy a good fit for Swinburne's poetry. Sarah Eron argues for the importance of paradox in Swinburne's writing, especially when focused on landscape: "In most of Swinburne's landscape poetry, images are at once drawn and thereupon erased, observations asserted and thereupon rejected."[11] This comfort with Swinburne's paradoxes is in stark contrast to the irritation exhibited by critics such as T. S. Eliot, who complained of Swinburne's "diffuseness" that ripples out and embraces many other ideas.[12]

In truth, Swinburne tends more to alternation between specifics and generalities. When using birds and their voices in his horrific poems that depict the erosion of humanity, for example, he sometimes uses specific common names, such as "nightingale" and "swallow," and sometimes uses more general terms—"bird" or "sea-bird," for example. The alternations make the lens of the writing more drifting and detached and also give the audience something to cling to that is not horrifying monotony. Swinburne's alliteration, complex syntax, and changes of meter and rhyme pattern between different sections in poems such as "By the North Sea" force the reader to pay more attention to his desolate poetic landscapes and mockingly singing birds. Swinburne has found one possible solution to the problem of our short attention span in disanthropic works: if readers look, and look, and look again, they meet the conditions of seeing that landscape in flashing glimpses and of returning intermittent attention to it. We can confront the nightmare of erosion—including, in Swinburne's case, erosion of our own gods and monuments—without needing to *constantly* confront it.

"A Forsaken Garden": Love and E-rose-sion

Although Swinburne wrote more than two poems about the collapsing seashore, he wrote two in particular that bring his vision of coastal erosion and the voices of birds within it to horrifying life. "A Forsaken Garden," from *Poems and Ballads, Third Series* (1878), portrays the ruined garden by the sea as a source of apparently humanized desolation. Still, this is one of Swinburne's most disanthropic poems, as it creates the *illusion* of human life and love persisting in the garden where all plants have died, only to brutally reveal it as false. The "lovers none ever will know, / Whose eyes went seaward a hundred sleeping / Years ago,"[13] are described in one stanza as standing in the garden and rejoicing in what seems to be the eternity not only of the human species but also of their love. The male lover prophesies the future, which in the poem is the modern garden when there will "never [be] a rose to reply" to a nonexistent nightingale,[14] and, by inference, he forecasts death for everyone except him and the woman at his side, implying that everyone else loves lightly. Human extinction is a delightful fate to mull over when it will spare you and your lover and is therefore not "real" extinction. So far, so far from horrific.

But then Swinburne's narrator introduces the first wrenching change, using the omniscient point of view to indicate that extinction was the fate of the lovers even as they assumed eternity. "Love was dead" for the lovers "and or ever the garden's last petals were shed."[15] Either that "or they loved their life through, and then went whither? / And were one to the end—but what end who knows? . . . They are loveless now as the grass above them / Or the wave."[16] The lovers did not exist *as* lovers for that eternity, either because their love died even before the roses of the garden did or because they are now dead. Like the roses, like other flowers of the garden, like every other human being who at one point stood here, the lovers are gone. The poem relentlessly points the way to extinction for humans as individuals, for humans as a species on this particular plot of land, and for the force—love—that is supposed to outlast all of them. Neither human bodies nor human relationships last as long as we assume they will.

Instead, it is the sea that lives, "loveless" and intent on devouring the garden in a distant someday when "the slow sea [will] rise and the sheer cliff crumble."[17] This will be the time when "terrace and meadow the deep gulfs drink, / [And] the strength of the waves of the high tides humble / The fields that lessen, the rocks that shrink."[18] As is common in the poetry of Swinburne, who "deployed language with more precision [and] awareness" than any "poet before him,"[19] a pun shows up here: "shrink" in line 76 refers both to the literal diminishment of the rocks and to their flinching back in terror. Earth and humans are allied in "A Forsaken Garden" because, as Pauline Fletcher argues, "life belongs to the land and to the 'meadows that blossom and wither' [here Fletcher cites Swinburne's poem]; its chief characteristic is that it is subject to time, change, and mortality. Eternity belongs to the sea."[20] The sea inflicts endless change on the land without changing in its own essential nature; if it expands, it is, for Swinburne's narrators, still "a fluid and formless mass given structure by the rhythms of the waves and the tides and the coast's outlines."[21] The coast's outline can only ever yield to the sea. Despite being Victorian, this poem portrays a thoroughly modern world that's haunted by the prospect of the earth's inevitable collapse into water. Human lives and loves vanish into extinction, and the land follows them; it is the sea, which the lovers contemplated in smug assurance of their own immortality,[22] that outlasts and feeds on them all.

"A Forsaken Garden" ends with this stunning image: "Here now in his triumph where all things falter, / Stretched out on the spoils that his own hand spread, / As a god self-slain on his own strange altar, / Death lies dead."[23] Eron argues that "this imagined future, in which death may 'deal not again' and change may 'come not till all change end' is something of a visionary apocalypse, [in which] we must distinguish between this fantasy of stasis and the reality of time."[24] What makes "A Forsaken Garden" disanthropic instead of postapocalyptic, however, is how flashing glimpses show that something of the garden *does* survive—but nothing human. In the same stanza that mentions the deaths of nightingales and roses, it becomes clear that not all life here is dead. But the survivors are not birds or flowers with strong symbolic ties to human notions of romance. The nightingale, with her symbolism of "an intense doomed love" and "her associations with the natural, the erotic and the feminine,"[25] dies with her song; in her place, "Over the meadows that blossom and wither / Rings but the note of a sea-bird's song."[26] The sea-bird is a symbolic bird in Swinburne, but not of romance; it is far more symbolic of the sea—the "bitter, salt mother" of Rosenberg's praise—and of death and drowning. In a landscape where humans, roses, and nightingales are nonexistent, where the cliffs of the garden are crumbling, and where, finally, "Death lies dead,"[27] the sea-bird survives, the only present and real animal life in the poem.

The sea-bird is also singing, an unusual description for its call. The landscape and the narrator have shed common human symbolic associations and human names. This is one place where the diffuseness Eliot praised and damned in Swinburne works to the latter's advantage. A "sea-bird" ties together the important nouns, the sea that eats the land and the bird that survives it, without specifying further that the bird is a gull or a sandpiper. Such a bird is appropriate for this garden, where "love [is] dead,"[28] with "not a flower to be pressed of the foot that falls not"[29] and "never a rose to reply"[30] to "the nightingale [that] calls not."[31] It is fitting that human knowledge, the specificity of a human glancing at a bird and divining its species, should join the other casualties, leaving the birds free to be themselves and to sing, without humans to decide the musicality of their voices.

But this view, though bleak, might not seem horrific. Why should a single sea-bird "singing" amid a desolate landscape be so? In this case, because of the horror of continuation. Despite the majority of the poem being laden with negative adjectives and adverbs—"never," "not," "dead," "ghost,"[32] "guestless,"[33] "no life but the sea-wind's"[34]—there is this shocking moment of existence. The sea-bird still sings, and later in the poem it is made clear that thorns survive as well: "the thorns that are touched not of time"[35] and "the weeds wind-shaken, / These remain."[36] The poem appears contradictory, as sea-birds, thorns, and weeds *are* life. But the audience can understand the apparent contradiction as a disjunction between destruction and disanthropy.

Even though the sea has destroyed the garden and killed those who might once have laughed and wept there,[37] in truth, time and the sea have destroyed only the *human* portions of the garden. The weeds that gardeners battle now thrive. The birds that humans have less romanticized notions of still sing. The thorns that humans would find useless as decorations or food appear several times. Although less noticeable than the surface portion of the poem that portrays death and destruction for everything extant, the disanthropic future shimmers under the surface, realizable only in glimpses of life in which humans and their thoughts die. Swinburne's forsaken garden is free of the colonization of human minds and needs. There is nothing here humans can use, want, name, or eat. The poem looks into the future of the garden crumbling into the sea and Death slaying himself, but the important moment is the present one, in which the diffusion of general words—"weeds," "sea-birds," "thorns"—pulls apart the concept of a garden and sets the landscape free, even if in a reduced, fragmented manner, from the human. The diffuseness and fragmentation make sense, since there is the illusion of no human mind to comprehend or grasp the landscape. Since the reader remains to self-narrate the poem, this is not the impossibility of a disanthropic landscape set completely free from the human that Garrard describes.

But the poem pushes our thoughts as close to the void as possible, confronting us not with our own death but with our own *nothingness*. The end of humans with the world going on is a special form of horror, as is Swinburne's rejection of the redemptive green fantasy that restores the landscape to a pastoral idyll. This landscape will never brighten with trees or flourish with clear streams reclaiming their own, the way Weisman pictures the streams under New York City rising with no humans to control them.[38] But neither is the garden irredeemably dead, devastated forever the way that words such as "disaster" in modern accounts of coastal erosion imply the ecosystem will be. This landscape remains triumphant over human thoughts of hope *and* eternity, turning the green and rose-laden garden into a dead landscape pocked here and there with unbeautiful life.

That unbeautiful life contrasts sharply with D. H. Lawrence's representation of the disanthropic future as "a beautiful clean thought, a world empty of people, just uninterrupted grass, and a hare sitting up."[39] There are no verdant thoughts in Swinburne's garden, even among the life that he portrays as flourishing there when the flowers die. Instead, this is "where the weeds that grew green from the graves of its roses / Now lie dead."[40] The only weeds that can exist now are those not described as green. Likewise, the "rose-red seaweed that mocks the rose . . . must wither."[41] The only color in Swinburne's garden is grey, mentioned only once, in a reference to the "grey bare walks"[42] that human strangers would find *if* they were to force themselves into the garden. "If" is used twice in this stanza, emphasizing the unlikeliness of this event. There is no human here but the detached narrative voice and the reader, and the reader is pushed to reconsider his or her own presence not only by the poem as a whole but also by lines such as "a track none turn to climb."[43] The narrative voice has no interest in creating an imaginative journey for the reader; the stanzas of the poem are not arranged to give a physical tour of the garden but to press forward all at once the bleakness and death and ongoing life free of humans. Readers do not poetically walk around in the garden, because they are not there to walk around in it. "A Forsaken Garden" forces the erosion of the reader's own existence on them while leaving them alive to comprehend their own nothingness.

"By the North Sea": The Dis-burial of the Dead

In contrast, "By the North Sea," Swinburne's poem of a wild and hungry seashore from *Studies in Song* (1880), does proclaim the presence of humans and their relics but also proclaims the destruction of eternity and the salvation they depended on. Kerry McSweeney accurately declares, "In no other poem of Swinburne's is the natural setting so unrelievedly desolate and inimical to man."[44] This land does have life, but not the life that makes for a comfortable love poem landscape or a pastoral idyll, being "far fields that a rose never blew in"[45] and "pastures [that] are herdless and sheepless."[46] But here, where human minds do not rest in easy genre conventions, are birds: "Far flickers the flight of the swallows ... And restless and songless [are] the birds; / Their cries from afar fall breathless, / Their wings are as lightnings that flee."[47] They are creatures of the wind, which is always blowing in this poem, able to thrive where humans cannot in these "fruitless"[48] fields. Humans, by contrast, interact with the sea and the wind only as the dead, and specifically as eroded groves and putrefying flesh.

The central image of humanity in "By the North Sea" comes from the graveyard that Swinburne's narrator initially portrays as a rest in peace. The sailors among the dead no longer have to struggle to come back to the land from the ocean: "The wind is divested of danger / And scatheless the sea."[49] They have "rest from the wind as it passes,"[50] which the birds still flying do not have, and "the souls of the dead men [are] disburdened / And clean of the sins that they sinned."[51] But this is another of Swinburne's illusions—in fact, "By the North Sea" is a powerful blow aimed at what Ashley Kniss, in chapter 3 of this volume, identifies as a theological soul/body split that drives a wedge between humanity and the natural world. If human bodies are objects of terror and loathing to be left behind by the pure soul, as Kniss sees portrayed in nineteenth-century American hymns and consolation verse, Swinburne's poem shows a natural world emptied of purity and with no hope of transcendence beyond its putridity. Here, human voices and lives are rendered meaningless once finished; God is dead and unable to rescue the soul; and preserved bodies wash out of the coffins in a graveyard built too close to the sea, becoming food for waves instead of for worms.

Swinburne's narrator seems to set up the expectation of traditional Christian peace and transcendence when first describing the graves. After all, "the roar of the banks they breasted / Is hurtless as bellowing of herds."[52] This statement, however, ought to give the alert reader pause, since the narrator earlier proclaimed the lack of herds and fodder for them around this seashore. Given that, it will be less of a surprise that the peace for the dead is illusory and reversed quickly, the first of several reversals in these lines. Swinburne likewise creates and then dismisses an idea of enduring human strength, as if part of each of the sailors lives on to be noticed and remembered in a landscape that is in fact occupied only by still-living birds. The idea of human strength is conveyed by the waves that the sailors "breasted" in life. The humans' fight against the wind is compared to a living bird's and found wanting: "And the strength of his wings that invested / The wind, as the strength of a bird's; / As the sea-mew's might or the swallow's / That cry to him back if he cries."[53] A first reading of these lines might make it sound as though it is the *bird* who is weak, or that the bird and the human are equal in strength. But a closer reading shows how neatly these lines undercut human exceptionalism, placing humans and birds on an equal footing instead. The birds fly as well as the sailors do; they master the wind as well as the sailors do; they speak back to the sailors. The human voice is made as nonsensical as a bird's cry is usually assumed to be and, unlike the bird's, does not endure.

The lines also begin to strip meaning from the language—one of the characteristics often assumed to separate humans and animals. For the reader to continue to value the humans' voices in Swinburne's poem, the voices of the birds must be invested with significance—a power that Swinburne's poetic narrator is eager to lend them. The repetition of "as" in lines 76–78 emphasizes the equal comparison. Indeed, this repetition forces the reader to see communication between humans and an avian species in a new light, since the most famous talking avian species is usually seen as simply "parroting" nonsense. Swinburne insists that the chance to listen to birds is present but that humans typically ignore it, caught up in an assumption of superiority that says parrots *must* be mimicking humans, that the sea-birds' cries back to the sailor's cry *must* be meaningless. Swinburne challenges this belief in human superiority by letting the birds speak in this world where the dead sailors will never speak again.

Swinburne then pulls yet another reversal to return the birds to prominence. A closer reading of the lines in stanza 11 that speak of "disburdened" souls "clean" from sins reveals that these lines do not refer to dead humans. Instead, the living birds—who in the theological tradition that divides soul and body are usually considered bodies alone—are truly disburdened and clean, and it is they who enjoy the sun, the waves, and the wind:

> As the souls of the dead men disburdened
>   And clean of the sins that they sinned,
> With a lovelier than man's life guerdoned
>   And delight as a wave's in the wind,
> And delight as the wind's in the billow,
>   Birds pass, and deride with their glee
> The flesh that has dust for its pillow
>   As wrecks have the sea.[54]

At the beginning of the stanza, the first "As" of equal comparison persists here, but by the third line, it is the humans who have been found wanting. Birds have "a lovelier than man's life"[55] and an interlocking "delight" flowing back and forth between air and water.[56] They also mock the dead, breaking the sacredness possibly expected to prevail in a graveyard. And while the dead, as living humans, anticipated rest after burial, the world outside their graves "derides" them. Significantly, it is birds, so strongly allied with sailors in the previous stanza, who do so. They have more freedom than the confined sailors, and they understand nature better, being as capable of understanding the elements as the wave is the wind and the wind is the billow. Humans are no longer the equals of birds; instead, birds are the equals of the elements. Swinburne's poem has twisted to isolate dead humans in their graves from the rest of the natural world that can still speak and signify and, finally, to give only as much dignity to "Ashes to ashes, dust to dust" as the sea does to shipwrecks. Human constructions, meant to rule the waves and to dominate nature by sailing the seas and by being built of cut wood from forests, are drowned by the water that the birds, being its equals, have no reason to fear. The natural world that humans once thought to master jeers at them, and, once again, humans are subject to the horror of continuation; there is no immortality of human thought, voice, or body. The world carries on without them.

The next stanza exalts the superiority of living birds by taking their point of view and making them a source of light, with human graves losing any sense of sacredness and becoming a bird perch. "Wings flash through the dusk like beams"[57] even at sunset, and "as the clouds in the lit sky glimmer, / The bird in the graveyard gleams,"[58] while "the graves that the bird's note brightens / Grow bright for the bird."[59] This linking of song and light is common in Swinburne's poetry, but here it is notable that it is not a lovestruck narrator who is able to see the graves brighten but the bird alone. The disanthropic moment of the poem gives the bird the priority in this vision. It is possible to see the birds as connected to the sailors, as they were two stanzas before, but at this moment the birds are the source and the union of light, of song, and of movement; the birds experience a moment of joy in triumph over the human dead. There is no longer a living human who can tend the graves or keep up the proper mood of reverence that this place would usually demand. Swinburne's poem creates its horror by centering the birds who laugh at the dead and continue on.

The final and most horrific destruction and subsequent triumph, of course, come from the sea, along with another of Swinburne's reversals that mocks immortality and religion. As McSweeney notes, "In the first section of 'By the North Sea,' the speaker had derived some comfort from the thought that to be dead was to be free from nature's cruel assaults. This assumption is now revealed to have been mistaken."[60] The sea, in the later sections of the poem, breaks in on the graves and sweeps the coffins into the water, and time desecrates the small church that still stands there. Humanity's monuments, which have endured here as they did not in "A Forsaken Garden," mourn for their missing masters, only to be answered with word of an even deeper loss: "'Where is man?' the cloister murmurs wailing; / Back the mute shrine thunders—'Where is God?'"[61] In the horror of erosion, time and water can destroy even God. God shares his dead worshippers' fate, reduced to less than dust and disconnected from the elemental forces that the living animals rejoice in, for "less than clouds across the sea-line sailing, / Lies he, stricken by his master's rod."[62] The natural world, far less than pure by human standards, nevertheless has the life that the dead humans now lack and that their God, in Swinburne's cosmology, never had.

This might read as childish blasphemy, turning God's immortality inside out, reflected in part by using "he" rather than "He" and elevating clouds above him. But that God, like his worshippers, is meant to be contrasted with the life the poet values is shown in stanza 7 of section IV, which places the now-crumbled city, described in past tense, next to the present-tense invocation of the place "where sharp the sea-bird shrills his ditty, / Flickering flame-wise through the clear live calm."[63] A bird reigns over the death of God as it does over the death of the shoreline, of immortality, and of any comfort or hope in the landscape. And again, as in "The Forsaken Garden," where it is "the note of a sea-bird's *song*"[64] that serenades the thorns and the weeds, here the sea-bird is presented as singing a "ditty." Human notions of relevance and specificity are again rejected. The sea-bird, presiding genius of the eroded shoreline, flies over this shore as it does over the garden, establishing the continuity of the horror of continuation.

Again, the sea-bird is at home in an environment that desecrates the human dead. It sings in a place where "Tomb from tomb the waves devouring sever, / Dust from dust as years relapse along; / Graves where men made sure to rest, and never / Lie dismantled by the seasons' wrong."[65] Human surety in the physical world suffers erosion this time, as the graves give way to the devouring sea. The assurance of one modern version of *The Book of Common Prayer* that "All of us go down to the dust; yet even at the grave we make our song: Alleluia, alleluia, alleluia" is utterly destroyed, dust and grave and song; the word "dismantled" provides a graphic image of the condition of the bodies in the coffins as the ocean washes in on them. The bodies' spiritual dignity is degraded into horror along with their physical condition:

> Naked, shamed, cast out of consecration,
>   Corpse and coffin, yea the very graves,
> Scoffed at, scattered, shaken from their station,
>   Spurned and scourged of wind and sea like slaves,
> Desolate beyond man's desolation,
>   Shrink and sink into the waste of waves.[66]

The wind and the sea, acting together as attackers on the graves the way they act together as forces of erosion, "spurn" and "scourge" the human bodies, indicating once and for all that even the very forces of nature hold humans in contempt, rather like the birds who cry out in "glee" at their deaths. The bodies "shrink" and are "scattered," and any "station" they imagined they held, as humans above nature or as consecrated Christians, is gone. The "waste of waves" both recalls a wasteland and hints at the transformation of corpse, coffin, and tomb into so much garbage. Sean Ireton, defining "dirty nature" that needs to be represented in contrast to "pure" or idealized nature, includes "such matter [as] dirt, waste, bodies, and food."[67] Swinburne's innovation is merely to transform bodies into all the rest.

In triumph at this transformation, more specific visual images abruptly appear, forcing the reader to envision what the previous stanza hinted at. Now the destruction of bodies is tied forcefully to the decay of the earth: the graveyard was built too close to the sea. "Tombs, with bare white piteous bones protruded," wash "down the loose collapsing banks" and "crumble" into "the sea [that] devours and gives not thanks."[68] The destruction is explicitly of human hopes as well as physical grave sites. "They that thought for all time through to be"[69] become "scarce a stone whereon a child might stumble."[70] And the final lines of section VI make the scene a grim pastoral idyll for the real gods of this shore: "Earth, and man, and all their gods wax humble / Here, where Time brings pasture to the sea."[71] The earlier field that had "no pasture . . . for herds" is in fact, according to McSweeney, "fodder to feed the sea's destructive appetite. We are reminded by this spectacular description . . . [that] we are not to think that after burial we shall be absorbed into and become part of the living and verdant natural world, and survive as part of the perpetually renewed cycle of the seasons."[72] Human bodies are just more food in the ultimate marine food chain, and graves, being made of dust and ashes, wash down into the waves like the rest.

The full scope of Swinburne's ecohorror vision has not yet been expressed, however. This is a vision of both erosion and global warming, and Swinburne's narrator presents this vision with the same terrifying joy that accompanies the earlier collapse of graveyards and the songs of sea-birds. The one god that Swinburne's narrator salutes is the sun, and the whole of section VII is a hymn to him, showing what happens to the same seashore when the sun is shining on it. "Where the horn of the headland is sharper,"[73] likely due to the crumbling of the banks, "The sea has the sun for a harper."[74] He is "Our father, the God,"[75] to whom the narrator presents as a gift the landscape he has constructed in part by revealing its erosion. The lines "O Sun, whereof all is beholden, / Behold now the shadow of this death"[76] place the sun literally above the crumbling graves and emphasize that the sun will continue rising and the elemental forces will continue to move no matter how devastated human bodies or dreams are. This is a world that can encompass climate change and the rising of the ocean and laugh at human fears concerning them, a world that in fact *celebrates* the rising of the ocean to consume the earth and portrays the land left behind when human dwellings and systems are gone as better, because those beliefs were themselves already dead and decaying. The "sun as deity is, from one point of view, a response of the organism to a set of conditions of which the physical sun is one,"[77] and Swinburne's lines ally the sun to these other conditions: the crumbled landscape, the glee of the sea-birds, and the death of God.

Swinburne reinforces this ugly-beautiful landscape in the penultimate stanza of the poem, demonstrating that the vision of the sun's beauty in section VII depends on, rather than contrasts with, the ugliness of the rising ocean. The narrator honors the sun's heat and light and combines them with references to music that recall the earlier parts of the poem in which singing birds mocked humans:

> The hills and the sands and the beaches,
> > The waters adrift and afar,

> The banks and the creeks and the reaches,
>> How glad of thee all these are!
> The flowers, overflowing, overcrowded,
>> Are drunk with the mad wind's mirth:
> The delight of thy coming unclouded
>> Makes music of earth.[78]

Swinburne's pun on "delight" / "the light" in line 515 recalls the connection between brightness and birdsong in lines 95–96, in which the bird sings in the graveyard and watches the graves brighten for itself. The "mad wind," the gladness of the earth to welcome the sun, and the half-drowned seashore paint a ghastly, cheerful picture for modern audiences of a postwarming world in which windstorms rage and the oceans grow larger with their meals of earth as well as of the ice melt that the "unclouded" sun has inspired. That this particular climatic resonance would have been invisible for Victorian audiences does not lessen the ability of a twenty-first-century reader of Swinburne to shiver at it. And, indeed, at the time Swinburne still captured a terror associated with the sun because "by associating Apollo's appearance with terror . . . , Swinburne manipulates Judeo-Christian conventions in order to define his own conception of Apollonian divinity. Terror becomes, then, an indication of Apollonian presence."[79] Where the sun walks, so does the ocean, whose "waters are haggard and yellow / And crass with the scurf of the beach."[80] Thus, light and water are united in terrorizing the human reader rather than in closing the poem with an uplifting denial of that ugliness. Swinburne might indeed be said to "re-divinize" the landscape that he has cleansed of God, but only with a deity that increases that ecological horror.

Yisrael Levin, in his analysis of "By the North Sea," concludes that it does not matter that Swinburne describes the sea farther away from shore as "pure" and "clean." He writes that the cleansing cycle does happen: "Once cleansed, however, the waves will bring the sea back to the shore where she will kill and snatch the dead from their graves once again, thereby maintaining a perpetual cycle of degeneration and regeneration, destruction and creation. . . . Nature itself functions as . . . creator and the thing created."[81] Nature exists without humanity and without a God that maintains a heaven for their souls and responsibility for creation, and the voices left are the voices of sea-birds that can soar over the collapsing earth and breast the wind that is also a force of erosion on the coastal outline. Levin adds that "the result of the sea's hunger for the dead [in "By the North Sea"] is no less than horrifying."[82] Swinburne is a poet of ecohorror *because* he is the poet of the crumbling landscape, the bitter salt sea, and the death of Christianity and immortality. His poetic voices are those of joyful doom, gleefully celebrating the eroding earth, horrifying the human reader, and granting us glimpses of the ultimate disanthropic landscape, in which so many things we fear, including human extinction, have come to pass—and the sea and its birds are glad.

Notes

1. P. C. Roebeling et al., "Ecosystem Service Value Losses from Coastal Erosion in Europe: Historical Trends and Future Projections," *Journal of Coastal Conservation* 17, no. 3 (September 2013): 389, www.jstor.org/stable/42657031.

2. Rodolfo Silva et al., "Present and Future Challenges of Coastal Erosion in Latin America," *Journal of Coastal Research* 71, Coastal Erosion and Management Along Developing Coasts (Fall 2014): 3, www.jstor.org/stable/43290026.

3. Jon McVey Erlandson, "As the World Warms: Rising Seas, Coastal Archaeology, and the Erosion of Maritime History," *Journal of Coastal Conservation* 16, no. 2, Archaeology and Coastal Conservation (June 2012): 138, www.jstor.org/stable/41506561.

4. John D. Rosenberg, introduction to *Swinburne: Selected Poetry and Prose* (New York: Modern Library, 1968), xv.

5. Greg Garrard, "Worlds Without Us: Some Types of Disanthropy," *SubStance* 41, no. 1, issue 127 (2012): 40. Emphasis in original.

6. Alan Weisman, *The World Without Us* (New York: St. Martin's Press, 2007), 14.

7. Ibid., 16.

8. Garrard, "Worlds Without Us," 41.

9. Ibid., 43.

10. Ibid., 46.

11. Sarah Eron, "Circles and the In-Between: Shaping Time, Space, and Paradox in Swinburnian Verse," *Victorian Poetry* 44, no. 3 (Fall 2006): 293, www.jstor.org/stable/40002834.

12. T. S. Eliot, "Swinburne as Poet," in *The Sacred Wood: Essays on Poetry and Criticism* (North Chelmsford, MA: Courier Corporation, 1997), 95.

13. Algernon Charles Swinburne, "A Forsaken Garden," in *Algernon Charles Swinburne: Major Poems and Selected Prose*, ed. Jerome McGann and Charles L. Sligh (New Haven, CT: Yale University Press, 2004), lines 38–40.

14. Ibid., line 28.

15. Ibid., lines 48, 46.

16. Ibid., lines 49–50, 55–56.

17. Ibid., 73.

18. Ibid., lines 73–76.

19. Cecil Y. Lang, ed., *The Pre-Raphaelites and Their Circle* (Chicago: University of Chicago Press, 1975), 523.

20. Pauline Fletcher, "Romantic and Anti-Romantic Gardens in Tennyson and Swinburne," *Studies in Romanticism* 18, no. 1, Victorian Romanticism II (Spring 1979): 93–94, www.jstor.org/stable/25600169.

21. John A. Walsh, "'Quivering Webs of Living Thought': Conceptual Networks in Swinburne's *Songs of the Springtides*," in *A. C. Swinburne and the Singing Word: New Perspectives on the Mature Work*, ed. Yisrael Levin (Burlington, VT: Ashgate, 2010), 51.

22. Swinburne, "Forsaken Garden," lines 42–44.
23. Ibid., lines 77–80.
24. Eron, "Circles and the In-Between," 307.
25. Jeni Williams, *Interpreting Nightingales: Gender, Class, and Histories* (Sheffield, UK: Sheffield Academic Press, 1997), 61.
26. Swinburne, "Forsaken Garden," lines 29–30.
27. Ibid., line 80.
28. Ibid., line 56.
29. Ibid., line 25.
30. Ibid., line 28.
31. Ibid., line 27.
32. Ibid., line 4.
33. Ibid., line 13.
34. Ibid., line 15.
35. Ibid., line 20.
36. Ibid., lines 23–24.
37. Ibid., lines 37–40.
38. Weisman, *World Without Us*, 24.
39. D. H. Lawrence, quoted in Garrard, "Worlds Without Us," 41.
40. Swinburne, "Forsaken Garden," lines 7–8.
41. Ibid., lines 52, 51.
42. Ibid., line 13.
43. Ibid., line 18.
44. Kerry McSweeney, "Swinburne's 'By the North Sea,'" *The Yearbook of English Studies* 3 (1973): 223, www.jstor.org/stable/3506872.
45. Algernon Charles Swinburne, "By the North Sea," in *Algernon Charles Swinburne: Major Poems and Selected Prose*, ed. Jerome McGann and Charles L. Sligh (New Haven, CT: Yale University Press, 2004), line 3.
46. Ibid., line 17.
47. Ibid., lines 9, 20–22.
48. Ibid., line 6.
49. Ibid., lines 71–72.
50. Ibid., line 61.
51. Ibid., lines 81–82.
52. Ibid., lines 73–74.
53. Ibid., lines 75–78.
54. Ibid., lines 81–88.
55. Ibid., line 83.
56. Ibid., lines 84–85.
57. Ibid., line 90.
58. Ibid., lines 91–92.
59. Ibid., lines 95–96.
60. McSweeney, "Swinburne's 'By the North Sea,'" 229.
61. Swinburne, "By the North Sea," lines 431–32.
62. Ibid., lines 427–30.
63. Ibid., lines 415–16.
64. Swinburne, "Forsaken Garden," line 30. Emphasis added.
65. Swinburne, "By the North Sea," lines 441–44.
66. Ibid., lines 451–56.
67. Sean Ireton, "Between Dirty and Disruptive Nature: Adalbert Stifter in the Context of Nineteenth-Century American Environmental Literature," *Colloquia Germanica* 44, no. 2 (2011): 150, www.jstor.org/stable/43551604.
68. Swinburne, "By the North Sea," lines 457–60.
69. Ibid., line 463.
70. Ibid., line 465.
71. Ibid., lines 467–68.
72. McSweeney, "Swinburne's 'By the North Sea,'" 229–30.
73. Swinburne, "By the North Sea," line 477.
74. Ibid., line 479.
75. Ibid., line 484.
76. Ibid., lines 493–94.
77. George M. Ridenour, "Time and Eternity in Swinburne: Minute Particulars in Five Poems," *ELH* 45, no. 1 (Spring 1978): 114, www.jstor.org/stable/2872454.
78. Swinburne, "By the North Sea," lines 509–16.
79. Yisrael Levin, "The Terror of Divine Revelation and Apollo's Incorporation into Song: Swinburne's Apollonian Myth," *Victorian Review* 34, no. 2 (Fall 2008): 133, www.jstor.org/stable/27793673.
80. Swinburne, "By the North Sea," lines 27–28.
81. Yisrael Levin, "Solar Erotica: Swinburne's Myth of Creation," in *A. C. Swinburne and the Singing Word: New Perspectives on the Mature Work*, ed. Yisrael Levin (Burlington, VT: Ashgate, 2010), 69.
82. Ibid., 68.

References

Eliot, T. S. "Swinburne as Poet." In *The Sacred Wood: Essays on Poetry and Criticism*, 93–97. North Chelmsford, MA: Courier Corporation, 1997.

Erlandson, Jon McVey. "As the World Warms: Rising Seas, Coastal Archaeology, and the Erosion of Maritime History." *Journal of Coastal Conservation* 16, no. 2, Archaeology and Coastal Conservation (June 2012): 137–42. www.jstor.org/stable/41506561.

Eron, Sarah. "Circles and the In-Between: Shaping Time, Space, and Paradox in Swinburnian Verse." *Victorian Poetry* 44, no. 3 (Fall 2006): 293–309. www.jstor.org/stable/40002834.

Fletcher, Pauline. "Romantic and Anti-Romantic Gardens in Tennyson and Swinburne." *Studies in Romanticism* 18, no. 1, Victorian Romanticism II (Spring 1979): 81–97. www.jstor.org/stable/25600169.

Garrard, Greg. "Worlds Without Us: Some Types of Disanthropy." *SubStance* 41, no. 1, issue 127 (2012): 40–60.

Ireton, Sean. "Between Dirty and Disruptive Nature: Adalbert Stifter in the Context of Nineteenth-Century American Environmental Literature." *Colloquia Germanica* 44, no. 2 (2011): 149–71. www.jstor.org/stable/43551604.

Lang, Cecil Y., ed. *The Pre-Raphaelites and Their Circle*. Chicago: University of Chicago Press, 1975.

Levin, Yisrael. "Solar Erotica: Swinburne's Myth of Creation." In *A. C. Swinburne and the Singing Word: New Perspectives on the Mature Work*, edited by Yisrael Levin, 54–71. Burlington, VT: Ashgate, 2010.

———. "The Terror of Divine Revelation and Apollo's Incorporation into Song: Swinburne's Apollonian Myth." *Victorian Review* 34, no. 2 (Fall 2008): 129–48. www.jstor.org/stable/27793673.

McSweeney, Kerry. "Swinburne's 'By the North Sea.'" *The Yearbook of English Studies* 3 (1973): 222–31. www.jstor.org/stable/3506872.

The (Online) Book of Common Prayer and Administration of the Sacraments and Other Rites and Ceremonies of the Church, Together with the Psalter or Psalms of David. New York: Church Hymnal Corporation. Accessed May 13, 2018. www.bcponline.org.

Ridenour, George M. "Time and Eternity in Swinburne: Minute Particulars in Five Poems." *ELH* 45, no. 1 (Spring 1978): 107–30. www.jstor.org/stable/2872454.

Roebeling, P. C., L. Costa, L. Magalhães, and V. Tekken. "Ecosystem Service Value Losses from Coastal Erosion in Europe: Historical Trends and Future Projections." *Journal of Coastal Conservation* 17, no. 3 (September 2013): 389–95. www.jstor.org/stable/42657031.

Rosenberg, John D. Introduction to *Swinburne: Selected Poetry and Prose*. New York: Modern Library, 1968.

Silva, Rodolfo, M. Luisa Martinez, Patrick A. Hesp, Patricio Catalan, Andres F. Osorio, Raul Martell, Monica Fossati, et al. "Present and Future Challenges of Coastal Erosion in Latin America." *Journal of Coastal Research* 71, Coastal Erosion and Management Along Developing Coasts (Fall 2014): 1–16. www.jstor.org/stable/43290026.

Swinburne, Algernon Charles. "By the North Sea." In *Algernon Charles Swinburne: Major Poems and Selected Prose*, edited by Jerome McGann and Charles L. Sligh, 189–202. New Haven, CT: Yale University Press, 2004.

———. "A Forsaken Garden." In *Algernon Charles Swinburne: Major Poems and Selected Prose*, edited by Jerome McGann and Charles L. Sligh, 158–60. New Haven, CT: Yale University Press, 2004.

Walsh, John A. "'Quivering Webs of Living Thought': Conceptual Networks in Swinburne's *Songs of the Spring-*

tides." In *A. C. Swinburne and the Singing Word: New Perspectives on the Mature Work*, edited by Yisrael Levin, 28–52. Burlington, VT: Ashgate, 2010.

Weisman, Alan. *The World Without Us.* New York: St. Martin's Press, 2007.

Williams, Jeni. *Interpreting Nightingales: Gender, Class, and Histories.* Sheffield, UK: Sheffield Academic Press, 1997.

5.
An Unhaunted Landscape
The Anti-Gothic Impulse in Ambrose Bierce's "A Tough Tussle"

Chelsea Davis

When we deem a certain place to be haunted, we are engaging in anthropomorphism. As Paul Manning notes, to imagine a building or a forest as harboring ghosts is to "'breath[e] life' into" that locale's inanimate materials—to make its stones, its wood, and the air in its rooms collude or even merge physically with the spirits of those who once walked upon and in them.[1] But it is not just any kind of animating life-form that can perform this alchemy: in both fiction and folklore, the spectral entities that bring settings to life are overwhelmingly of the human variety. As anthropologist Péter Berta observes, people across cultures and epochs consistently "project . . . their anthropomorphic categories and relations" onto the afterlife.[2] While it is therefore typical for a nonhuman object or creature to absorb the residue of a human (a haunted house, a cursed mirror, a possessed tree), the inverse event (a person being haunted by a building, object, or plant) very rarely occurs, especially in Anglophone literature—in part due to ghosts' original association with the human soul in those traditions.[3]

Given that human traits and history are thus implicitly folded into our notions of "haunting," telling stories about ghosts in the woods (or in any natural setting) implies a certain degree of imaginary imperialism on our part, a spectral extension of the human into a nonhuman setting. Thus far, much scholarship on ecohorror—the subgenre of fiction defined by Christy Tidwell as any narrative whose plot or mood centers on "our fears and anxieties about the environment"—has dedicated itself to investigating the contours of this imperialism.[4] Critics such as Matthew Wynn Sivils and Tom J. Hillard have effectively illuminated the ways in which the vengeful forests of ecogothic literature and film respond to our species in the style of our species, absorbing our unhappy ghosts and traits in order to frighten, mutilate, and kill us as a human adversary might.[5] Conversely, other scholars have attended to the botanical world's potentially frightening dissimilarity from and indifference toward humanity in ecohorror narratives and to that world's passive abdication from any figurative or physical connection to our species.[6] But some fictional landscapes more actively refuse to absorb, echo, or respond to us in the first place—in other words, they explicitly reject our hauntings. Such rejections might take the form of a parody, a hoax, or an empiricist dismissal of ghosts in the wilderness. If the particular subset of horror literature that we call the Gothic is, as Paul Manning has suggested, fundamentally invested in linking place to human history through the vehicle of haunting,[7] we might then characterize an ecohorror narrative that aggressively cleaves natural setting from human histories and haunting as "anti-Gothic." I do not mean to suggest that when anti-Gothic works thus exorcise humans from plants they are also marking themselves as anti-*horror* narratives. Instead, this chapter proposes that such texts cohere into what we should conceptualize as a particular subset of ecohorror—one that terrifies precisely because it overtly declines to engage with human hauntings, traits, and history.

The profusion of such unhaunted landscapes at particular moments on the literary timeline indicates that certain human events and cultural contexts render us particularly anxious about our species' ephemerality, about our collective inability to leave a lasting historical imprint on the aloof and abiding nonhuman world. The American Civil War was one such context that catastrophically severed the presumed connection between natural memory and human event.[8] This chapter illustrates the nature and magnitude of this schism by examining Ambrose Bierce's "A Tough Tussle" (1888), an anti-Gothic short story set during the war. Bierce's tale initially presents a scene of comforting anthropomorphism: a soldier keeps watch overnight in a forest so invested in the human battles unfolding within it that the natural landscape itself becomes more human, mimicking our species in the form of hauntings, a reanimated corpse (a dead object imbued once more with a human soul), and personified vegetal and animal life. But the story's final act violently retracts each of these supernatural possibilities, making clear that these apparent extensions of the human were generated only by the protagonist's superstition and fright.

Although scholarship on the American and European Gothic has tended to emphasize the traumatic and undesirable qualities of hauntings, "Tough Tussle" primarily figures its late-stage exorcism not as a source of relief but as a disappointment—a rude awakening that "br[eaks] the spell of th[e] enchanted [protagonist]."[9] Bierce's choice to frame the loss of these ghosts as a form of disenchantment hints that writers and readers of ecohorror literature (and of the Gothic more broadly) might actually *hope* to encounter ghosts in the woods at least as much as we fear to find them there. As Judith Richardson argues, there are certain "consolations . . . of being haunted."[10] This chapter proposes that one such consolation is the apparent proof that ghosts provide that human history has successfully left its mark on a given place over the course of the centuries. It is the desire for such proof, for instance, that spurs Jenny, the protagonist of Charlotte Perkins Gilman's conventionally ecogothic short story "The Giant Wistaria [sic]" (1891), to remark joyfully that her new vacation home is "a lovely house! I am sure it's haunted! . . . I'm convinced there is a story [attached to the house], if we could only find it."[11] Unlike Bierce's unhaunted soldier, Jenny is rewarded with a lasting supernatural presence, the truly haunted Wistaria of the story's title (which comes with an attendant tragic "story"—the more important payoff, for her as for most admirers of spooky buildings). But the persistence of Wistaria's haunting is contingent on the tale's setting outside the context of war, the force that, as this chapter will reveal, swiftly erases human accomplishments in "Tough Tussle." It is only because of continuous peacetime that Wistaria's mansion-like home has been able to uninterruptedly house several generations of Americans and to consequently produce spectral presences that bleed over into its vegetal surroundings. This is exactly the paranormal echo of the human in the natural world that the protagonist of Bierce's "Tough Tussle" so longs for and whose dissolution in the story's eventual anti-Gothic turn so devastates the reader. It would seem that the most distressing landscape for nineteenth-century Americans was the one *un*haunted by human events. This was precisely the self-renewing natural landscape, and the associated threat that human cataclysm would be forgotten, to which the Civil War exposed its participants.

We can better understand the dreadful implications of this earthly amnesia by considering the emotional charge that place-based memory held for antebellum Americans. In the 1700s and 1800s, European historians and art critics contended that a rich national heritage could blossom only in physical settings infused with "ruins and traditions, . . . the remains of architecture, the traces of battlefields, and the precursorship of eventful history," as English writer John Ruskin phrased it.[12] This reification of the usable physical past presented a conundrum for American intellectuals throughout the late eighteenth and nineteenth centuries because their newly minted nation allegedly lacked the visibly ancient buildings that populated the European countryside. This "almost total deficiency in those local associations produced by history" worried American writers such as Washington Irving who yearned to establish a coherent cultural heritage for their country.[13]

Because of this supposed shortcoming in the arena of built antiquity, Americans zealously fixed their sights on their country's wilderness as the potential source material for their own national heritage. Thus, as the 1800s wore on, old trees were "increasingly celebrated for their age and associations alone . . . as part of a larger quest for cultural validation" in the United States, according to historian Thomas J. Campanella; writers and landscape painters exalted natural landmarks associated with America's oldest European settlements and Revolutionary War battles, such as Lake George and the lower Hudson River; and travelers reverently recorded the "natural ruins" produced by floods, rockslides, and forest fires in the wilderness, finding in them, as author Theodore Dwight wrote of floodplains along the Ammonoosuc River, a "general desolation" akin to a wasted "Gothic edifice."[14]

Dwight's allusion to the Gothic is telling. As a genre preoccupied with place and with the past, Gothic literature was the crucible in which Americans' national anxieties regarding geographically manifest history came to a boil. Like the historians of their region, European authors in the Gothic tradition had found in ruined fortresses, mansions, and monasteries ready emblems for old institutions and events. But where was the American writer of supernatural fiction to find such castles in his own ruin-poor country? A small subset of Gothic writers in the early republic chose to conjure American castles out of thin air,[15] but a more common strategy was to turn to the country's rugged natural environment as a source of site-specific terror and mystery. In the preface to his 1799 novel *Edgar Huntly; Or, Memoirs of a Sleepwalker*, American Gothic pioneer Charles Brockden Brown defiantly asserted the superiority of the New World's geographical lexicon: "Puerile superstition and exploded manners; Gothic castles and chimeras, are the materials usually employed" in European literature as a means "of calling forth the passions and engaging the sympathy of the reader. . . . [But] the perils of the western wilderness, are far more suitable . . . for a native of America."[16] Throughout the 1800s, myriad American Gothic authors would follow Brown's example in shifting the settings of their historicized hauntings from buildings to forests, swamps, mountains, and rivers.

This transfer was made possible in part by early Anglo-Americans' wishful perception of the natural environment as always already haunted by the human past and even by human traits.[17] Puritan colonists viewed the natural landscape of the New World as a typological analog to the Old Testament's desert wilderness: it was in this harsh physical environment that they, as God's chosen people, would be tested by distinctly anthropomorphic incarnations of evil—Satan (the "Black Man") and his demons. The American wilderness therefore did not terrify settlers because of its utter *in*humanity per se, because of its radical difference from or apathy toward our species. Rather, Anglo-Americans perceived the wild landscape as terrifying in ways simultaneously anthropomorphized and anthropocentric. As Tom J. Hillard argues, this Puritan "way of reading nature symbolically" fed directly into American Gothic authors' treatment of the landscape as infused with portentous meaning.[18]

But this tendency to inscribe human memory and meaning onto the slate of the nonhuman eventually met with a profound challenge: the Civil War. In two respects, this conflict significantly eroded Americans' confidence that nature was at all invested in human affairs and that therefore it would ever deign to be haunted. First, as Union and Confederate soldiers marched through and waged battle in remote natural regions such as swamps, woods, mountains, and fields, many men were thrust into relatively untrammeled nature for the first time. Generations had passed since Americans had been forced to grapple en masse with the raw wilderness, and what they found now was a far cry from the well-farmed vistas to which nineteenth-century agrarian life had accustomed them. As Kathryn S. Meier observes, these "new environments, sometimes astoundingly foreign," unnerved many of the soldiers passing through them.[19] "The dark forests of cypress that live by both banks may be very inviting to beasts and reptiles, but they have very little attraction for the human eye," mused John Quincy Adams Campbell, a second lieutenant from Iowa passing south of the Mason-Dixon Line for the first time.[20] Second, the Civil War saw the revival of a brutal land-clearing practice, known as *chevauchée*, in which soldiers burned Southern crops, trampled fences, and destroyed agricultural structures, reducing Confederate farmlands to a state of uncultivated chaos. *Chevauchée* sweeps quickly transformed many civilians' living environments into wildernesses that bore ominously little evidence that humans had ever dwelled there; besieged Southerners frequently compared their ruined fields to a biblical "wasteland" and a "desert."[21] During the Civil War, therefore, soldiers and civilians alike experienced an unsettlingly intimate encounter with a physical environment apparently "devoid of human influence," as historian Lisa Brady writes.[22]

These novel encounters with untamed natural settings forced many Americans to reckon with the apparent indifference of those settings to the human violence unfolding within them. For although some Civil War historians have emphasized the enormity of the conflict's ecological destruction—the extent to which guns, cannons, fire, and camp clearings flattened wide swathes of woods and meadows[23]—actually that destruction was largely ephemeral. In fact, the vegetation at battle sites grew back so rapidly that soldiers and civilians observed its regeneration even as the war still raged. During a battlefield tour immediately after the Confederate surrender at Appomattox in 1865, writer J. T. Trowbridge remarked that the "old fields" of Virginia were already filling again with "thick growth[s] of infant pines coming up like grass. . . . [In] much of the land devastated by the war . . . , in two or three years, these young pines shoot up their green plumes five or six feet high. In ten years there is a young forest."[24]

While some took an optimistic view of this regrowth, others feared that the landscape's regeneration amid widespread human death threatened to dissolve the anthropomorphic tether between man and nature. In 1864, as he walked through a Georgia forest that the Union Army had recently razed, a correspondent for the *Natchez Weekly Courier* channeled a widespread sense of bewilderment at nature's speedy return to its prewar robustness:

> The utter loneliness, the want of human life, strikes one with a feeling of desolation. . . . The bubbling spring by the road side shows no happy child drinking or

paddling in its waters. . . . When the wild bird of the forest carols a note, you look around surprised that amid such loneliness any living being should be happy.[25]

This reporter twice mentions the landscape's "loneliness," a term that asserts humankind's centrality by representing the nonhuman world as deficient without us. Yet the passage immediately gives the lie to the notion that the earth even notices, let alone mourns, our absence: the article notes with "surprise" the careless spring and bird that carry on their activities as though a civilization has not fallen around them. The particular "feeling of desolation" that the reporter experiences in the face of the animals' and landscape's chipper perseverance embodies what Keri Stevenson calls, in chapter 4 of this volume, "the horror of continuation"—the existential dread that humans feel in imagining the natural world indifferently outliving our species.[26] As the natural environment steadily regrew toward status quo antebellum, evidently unmarred by and unaware of the nation-shaping warfare that had so recently raged within its bounds, it was humankind, rather than the trees or birds, that began to seem the "lonel[y]" species.

Bierce, Disenchanted

Nature's amnesiac temporality, as registered in regrowing forests and self-healing battlefields, radically disrupted the mainstream American conception of human history as forward moving in its progress—a conception that had been essential to most justifications of the war's appalling bloodshed. Throughout both the propagandistic self-importance of the war years themselves and the age of reinvigorated nostalgia that was the 1890s, there were few Americans more cynical about the nobility and significance of human events than Ambrose Bierce. Initially roused by the abolitionist cause, a nineteen-year-old Bierce eagerly enlisted in the Union army in 1861 and went on to fight in more major battles than any other published Civil War author.[27] But direct exposure to mass slaughter on the front lines, especially at the brutal Battle of Shiloh in 1862, swiftly eroded the teenager's military enthusiasm. When he wrote home from the field in 1864 that he no longer wished to witness or experience death "for my country—for a cause which may be right and may be wrong," Bierce evinced a distrust not only in the violent form that the war was taking but also in its basic motivations and teleology.[28] Subsequent battles would further transmute his ambivalence into an active disgust for the combination of religious rhetoric and jingoism that Northerners and Southerners alike leveraged to argue that the war's effects would be positive, substantial, and permanent.

Bierce's post-Shiloh contempt for romanticized notions of the Civil War is widely recognized by critics as a trait that distinguished him from his contemporaries and shaped the remainder of his literary output. But we can refine our understanding of the particular vector of that contempt by attending to the anti-Gothic moves of his war tales. One of Bierce's biographers, Roy Morris Jr., remarks that Shiloh brought to a blunt end Bierce's conception of war as "fairy-tale fighting in Virginia."[29] Although Morris's turn to the vocabulary of speculative fiction is idiomatic, I want to take seriously the possibility that the supernatural mode itself becomes a target of Bierce's criticism in the context of the Civil War. For while Bierce enthusiastically populated many of his nonmilitary tales with spirits whose objective existence within the fabula goes undisputed, his war stories engage with the supernatural almost exclusively in order to debunk it.[30] Critics have tended to focus on the continuities, rather than the divergences, between the seemingly Gothic elements of Bierce's war stories and those of his peacetime ghost stories. Russell Duncan and David J. Klooster, for instance, posit that military works such as "An Occurrence at Owl Creek Bridge," "A Horseman in the Sky," "The Mocking-Bird," "Chickamauga," "A Tough Tussle," and "On a Mountain" routinely enact "an examination of paranormal experience, supernatural events and fantastic occurrences."[31] Yet what bears closer scrutiny is the final outcome of the "examination[s]" that these tales conduct, for a story's engagement with the mere possibility of the supernatural does not de facto enter that story into the supernatural genre. On the contrary, Bierce's war stories often teasingly introduce glimpses of spectral soldiers and ominously animate landscapes but in each case eventually reveal the distinctly nonmagical origins of these phenomena, aggressively genre-shifting away from their earnestly paranormal beginnings into the realm of the explained supernatural. If the haunted forests of ecogothic literature presuppose that the environments in which human events unfold both are marked lastingly by those events and possess a humanlike investment in them, then Bierce's anti-Gothic plot shifts definitively denounce that presupposition. In other words, his war tales repudiate both anthropomorphism and anthropocentrism.

Among the most explicit in this denunciation is "A Tough Tussle," a story that recounts a Union officer's horrific encounter with a corpse during an all-night guard shift near the Confederate line in a West Virginia forest. The work's spatial and temporal settings seem to signal initially that this will play out as a routine, even hackneyed, nineteenth-century tale of haunted place. "Tough Tussle" unfolds on a dark night, lit only and occasionally by the moon. The protagonist, Brainerd Byring, sits alone in a forest that seethes with potentially spectral noise and motion ("half-heard whispers" and "forms without substance"), and he soon notices a dead soldier's body on the ground nearby—a body that seems to be inching slowly toward him.[32] This third element—the apparently reanimated cadaver—simultaneously evokes both ecohorror and the ecogothic. As Ashley Kniss notes in chapter 3 of this volume, because the human body is most permeable during the process of decomposition, a corpse decaying into the soil represents a quite literal merging of the human with the natural world. It is because of this species category violation that human bodies rotting into the earth constitute a common and uniquely disturbing trope in ecohorror. But so too does the ostensible revivification of the corpse in the early stages of "Tough Tussle" imply that both this earthen corpse and the land that houses it have become animated with human spirit once more, a development aligned with the eco*gothic* as I have defined it in this chapter.

Lest the reader miss these none-too-subtle clues about the genre in which we are operating, Bierce's narrator supplements his description of the physical elements of this Gothic setting with a piece of metacommentary on the making of a Gothic setting. Closely echoing the "Custom-House" section of Nathaniel Hawthorne's *The Scarlet Letter*, which describes moonlight's unique capacity to inspire eerie Romance fiction, "Tough Tussle" develops an origin story for the Gothic:

> From the vast, invisible ocean of moonlight overhead fell, here and there, a slender, broken stream. . . . He to whom the portentous conspiracy of night and solitude and silence in the heart of a great forest is not an unknown experience needs not to be told what another world it all is—how even the most commonplace and familiar objects take on another character. The trees group themselves differently; they draw closer together, as if in fear. The very silence has another quality than the silence of the day. And it is full of half-heard whispers . . . , ghosts of sounds long dead . . . , the cries of small animals in sudden encounters with stealthy foes, or

in their dreams, a rustling in the dead leaves. . . . What [caused] the low, alarmed twittering in that bushful of birds?³³

In casually transplanting the moonlit locus of the spectral imagination from Hawthorne's decidedly human domestic space (the "Custom-House" passage unfolds in "a familiar room") to the wilderness, the early pages of Bierce's story colonize even these remote woods with human traits, therefore delineating a classically anthropocentric understanding of the paranormal. Thus, Bierce describes a natural setting that appears not only to reflect and participate in the production of supernatural events but also to confirm the human quality of those events. Flora seem to assume human agency and affect when "the trees group themselves differently; they draw closer together, as if in fear"; fauna assume apparently interpersonal relationships when Byring takes the "cries of small animals" as evidence of their "sudden encounters with stealthy foes, or in their dreams"; anthropoid emotion haunts his description of the birds' "alarmed twittering"; and a nonliving abstraction, noise itself, even transforms into the "ghosts of sounds long dead." The forest here becomes a blank canvas onto which the human mind triumphantly reinscribes itself via Gothic anthropomorphization. Moreover, the fact that a lone human subject (our protagonist) suffices to fill the forest with humanity drives home the omnipresence and omnipotence of the human.

In this way, Bierce at first crafts a setting with geographic and sensory features that seem pulled from a standard nineteenth-century ecogothic tale, particularly evoking the haunted or hyperanimate forests of works such as Hawthorne's "Young Goodman Brown" (1835) and Harriet Elizabeth Prescot Spofford's "Circumstance" (1860). So too does "Tough Tussle" align the unfortunate occupant of its own neutral territory—Brainerd Byring—with an archetypal character found throughout the nineteenth-century Gothic more broadly: the arrogant rationalist who is converted to belief in the supernatural through a distinctively otherworldly experience.³⁴ We are told at the outset of "Tough Tussle" that Second Lieutenant Byring "[does] not at all believe" in the supernatural. As one tenet of this firm commitment to the real, Byring resolutely regards the dead he has encountered throughout the war strictly as objects "with . . . clay faces, blank eyes and stiff bodies," as inanimate matter devoid of spiritual residue, emotional charge, or other traces of the human. Marveling smugly at the tendency of superstitious people to attribute these otherworldly qualities to the dead, Byring wonders aloud,

"Where and when did [these beliefs] originate? Away back, probably, in what is called the cradle of the human race—the plains of Central Asia. . . . [Those ancient cultures] th[ought] a dead body a malign thing endowed with some strange power of mischief, with perhaps a will and a purpose to exert it. Possibly they [taught this] as our [priests] teach the immortality of the soul. As the Aryans moved slowly on, to and through the Caucasus passes, and spread over Europe, . . . the old belief in the malevolence of the dead body was lost from the creeds. . . ."[35]

In claiming that it is specifically an object's apparent possession of "will" and "purpose" that, to the naïve mind, affords that object "strange powers," Byring establishes the barometer by which "Tough Tussle" will measure the paranormal: the supernatural is figured throughout as the presence of human intention and thought—humankind's cognitive traits—in the nonhuman world. As Dawn Keetley observes, "intent and purpose" are key elements of "human subjectivity" that distinguish our species from other forms of life, particularly plants.[36] So too does Byring's forename of "Brainerd" nod toward this cognitive metric of enchantment, in that his tendency to attribute a "brain" or mind to the corpse, to plants, and to animals grows more marked as the setting grows increasingly haunted. Thus, the human is again registered as the essential ingredient of the supernatural.

But the nonhuman is not the only topic from Byring's monologue on cultural history that prefigures the story's later events. The officer's confident disbelief in the supernatural potential of the natural world is scaffolded here by a second rationalist conviction: a teleological view of human intellectual history. He tracks death beliefs from the superstitions of ancient Asia to the later, allegedly more sophisticated credos of Europe (a genealogy that implicitly frames North America as the most recent and therefore most advanced site of Caucasian thought). Byring's side-by-side presentation of the possibility of enchantment and the certainty of the West's past and future moral growth anticipates the gradual convergence of these concepts that will unfold over the course of "Tough Tussle." By the story's conclusion, the tripartite fairy tales that enable the Civil War—the interdependent fantasies of the natural world's anthropocentrism, of the persistence of individual and collective human history, and of civilizational progress—will be uniformly dismantled and recoded as foolish superstitions that overlook nature's indifference to human action.

By so heavy-handedly enumerating Byring's rationalisms, this first third of "Tough Tussle" primes any reader familiar with ghost story formulas to expect the middle section of the tale to follow a well-trodden Gothic path: the eventual conversion of a skeptic to a believer in the supernatural. In this expectation we are not disappointed—at least not at first. About halfway through the story, the corpse seems to begin to slowly make its way toward Byring, "mov[ing] a trifle nearer" each time the light shifts, and eventually "visibly moving."[37] (We will later learn that the corpse's apparent motions are caused by maggots squirming around inside the cadaver.) Unsettled by these apparent signs of supernatural human life, Byring ascribes to the body a mounting litany of anthropomorphic traits as his conviction that the dead are mere things, "stiff bodies," gradually weakens. When Byring remarks, upon his second glimpse of the corpse, "Damn the thing! . . . What does it want?," he imbues the corpse with desire and, in so doing, begins to graft subjectivity onto an entity that minutes ago had avowedly been only an object in his eyes.[38]

The corpse's apparent transformation into a living man only accelerates as another shaft of moonlight gives the officer a glimpse of the body in full and its "whole posture impresse[s] Byring as having been studied with a view to the horrible. 'Bah!' [Byring] exclaim[s]; 'he was an actor—he knows how to be dead.'"[39] Several elements of this remark reveal that Byring is now distinctly anthropomorphizing the cadaver, mentally transforming it from dead thing to living man. First of all, it is telling that Byring finds it necessary to voice his thoughts aloud even though he is in a glen devoid of other living men; the corpse is as much Byring's audience as Byring is the audience of the "actor" corpse. Furthermore, in alluding to acting, Byring adds performativity to the corpse's human attribute of desire ("What does it want?"), imbuing the cadaver's previously random movements with social intention and a conjectured personal past. And grammatically speaking, Byring's shift from "it" to "he" in referring to the body and his use of the present tense in his quip that the corpse "knows how to be dead" drive home his growing suspicion that the corpse is more living person than inanimate thing. A few paragraphs later, Byring reinforces this vocabulary of personhood when he reflects to himself that he is "crouching like a gladiator ready to spring at the *throat of an antagonist*" and that he'd "better go away from this *chap.*"[40]

Ecocritics Andrew Bennett and Nicholas Royle have observed that anthropomorphic "figurations of the apparently non-human lead inexorably to anthropocentrism."[41] Inexorable indeed is the momentum that propels Byring toward further acts of anthropomorphism after he imaginatively animates the corpse from material object back into human subject. As Byring glimpses the body apparently moving a third time, "an incalculable host of [Byring's] own ancestors shriek into the ear of his spirit their coward counsel [and] sing their doleful death-songs in his heart," insisting to Byring that the corpse is alive and dangerous.[42] Other elements of the natural landscape soon follow suit, apparently also becoming infected with humanity. A "breath of cold air str[i]k[es] Byring full in the face": Bierce's phrasing here draws an anthropomorphic parallel between the exhaling mouth of the wind and the mouth of the man that it hits. The plant world achieves animacy when "the branches of trees above [Byring] stir ... and moan." Even the darkness itself seems to assume mischievous agency when, as if in direct response to Byring's panicked observation that the corpse moves most when it is not in the light, a "strongly defined shadow passe[s] across the face of the dead, le[aves] it luminous, passe[s] back upon it and le[aves] it half obscured."[43] These humanlike descriptions of the wind, the tree, and the shadow might in other contexts be interpretable merely as figurative language—realist stories, like paranormal ones, abound in anthropomorphic metaphors. But this passage, coming as it does immediately after the supernatural reanimation of the corpse, primes both Byring and the reader to suspect that a very real supernatural takeover of the landscape is also underway. The natural world becomes Gothic precisely when it becomes actually, rather than metaphorically, human.

To be sure, the story initially presents these paranormal occurrences as more horrifying than comforting. Byring's abject terror and "violent ... trembling" at the apparent resurrection betray no obvious pleasure in the spectral.[44] Yet during Byring's final seconds with the corpse, the narrator intimates that some form of pleasure has very much entered into this encounter between man and zombie. Byring emerges at last from his tussle with the supernatural when a gunshot rings through the air, a sound that the narrator describes as "br[eaking] the spell of that enchanted man."[45] The vocabulary of magic here hints that Byring's brush with the undead has not been unequivocally dreadful. Rather, the multivalent terms "spell" and "enchanted" imply that the soldier has derived a distinct thrill from his paranormal experience in nature, just as Jenny of "Giant Wistaria" becomes excited over her "lovely house" specifically because she is "sure it's haunted!" The forest has become enchanted for Byring because it has staged the fantasy that the human will be reflected back in every corner of the natural world to which the Civil War soldier on the edges of civilization turns his gaze.

This anthropocentric fantasy takes three forms throughout the story, embodying a trio of "consolations . . . of being haunted," to recall Judith Richardson's phrase. First, the apparent preservation of the corpse's mind—the survival of the human ghost despite the decay of its body's meat back into the natural landscape—implies the endurance (however ghastly) of the individual human soul after death. Much like a ghost, a cadaver that retains elements of its human character provides an alternative to what Matthew Wynn Sivils has called "the ecogrotesque" understanding of bodily decomposition, the insight that the human "self . . . will eventually become re-assimilated into the nutrient flow of the amoral macroorganism of the natural environment."[46] An everlasting spirit and personal history are among the few traits that might distinguish a human corpse from the inanimate landscape in which it is buried. As such, the undead soldier represents the comforting possibility that our legacies and individual identities are not destined to be swallowed up by nature after our deaths.

Second, the zombie fantasy in which Byring has indulged is also the fantasy that the march of human historical events can effect lasting change more broadly, both in the natural and the cultural realms. During the Civil War, many Americans regarded the military's visible destruction of forests and fields in battle as evidence of humankind's awesome power to transform the physical world—and, by extension, as symbolic evidence that the war could also bring about permanent transformations of the nation's political and social problems.[47] This hope for enduring change—for abolition and the preservation of the union in the North and for perpetual slavery and states' rights in the South—was a desperately necessary narrative for Americans struggling to cope with the war's staggering losses.[48] Propagandistic songs, sermons, and political speeches about battlefield death framed the fallen as martyrs who would live on in the immortal ideals and communities for which they had fought.[49] What Byring seems to be witnessing in the forest, then, is the literal immortalization of a combatant, an incarnation (albeit an unsettling one) of the nationalist conviction that soldiers live on eternally through their sacrifice. If, however, the social causes for which the Union and Confederate troops fought achieved no lasting purchase after the war, then the actions of those slain soldiers would seem as insubstantial as their bodies, decaying into the soil of battlefields and cemeteries. To hope for the endurance of human bodies and spirits in the natural landscape was, therefore, to hope for the endurance of human political ideals.

Third, Byring is charmed by the revivified corpse because its apparent interaction with him suggests that the nonhuman wilderness is responding to him in some fashion, even if the tenor of that response is malicious. Lawrence Buell has argued that nineteenth-century American culture was predominantly anthropocentric, characterized by a collective narcissism that conceived of the natural landscape as having no meaning outside of the human frame of reference.[50] Therefore, the most intolerable prospect of all was that of a natural world "indifferent to [our] will and struggle, to [our] life or death," as Val Plumwood phrases it.[51] It thus comes as a kind of existential relief that the cadaver and the forest in "Tough Tussle" are not apathetic toward Byring; on the contrary, the corpse *moves toward* him and the trees and wind go out of their way to attack him. The natural world wants this man, whether for purposes malevolent or benign, and in wanting him, it becomes more like him. The perplexing allure of the supernatural, for Byring, hinges on the fulcrum of our species' mixed feelings toward anthropomorphism. The story figures human cognitive and corporeal traits as uncanny when they appear in nature because such transfers violate traditional distinctions between the human and the nonhuman; yet such violations are also exhilarating because they confirm humankind's ubiquity. The ecological paranormal disturbs us, but not nearly as much as the possibility of a disenchanted world that lacks it.

Yet the latter vision is precisely the anti-Gothic world that the Civil War laid bare in all its truth to soldiers witnessing, in real time, the swift return of battlefields to antebellum lushness. Accordingly, "Tough Tussle" does not permit the comforts of the seemingly enchanted corpse to linger long. Whereas the first two-thirds of the story transforms Byring's skepticism to faith in the supernatural, its third and final act—from the spell-breaking gunshot onward—doubles back, once more undermining and ridiculing such belief. The sound of the rifle "disperse[s] the hindering host [of ghostly ancestors] from Central Asia" that has been whispering into Byring's ear about the magical undead, and Byring rushes forward to attack the carcass.[52] Meanwhile, the skirmishing Confederate and Federal soldiers who issued the gunshot pass by this macabre duel without noticing it. The next morning, a Union captain and surgeon discover Byring's dead body lying alongside the Confederate soldier's: Byring has unintentionally stabbed himself with his own sword in the heat of his fight with the corpse. The surgeon attempts to move the two cadavers and discovers that the Confederate one is in a state of advanced decay, confirming that the corpse has indeed been deceased for days—and that Byring therefore waged his final battle against an already dead and decidedly unsupernatural soldier.

In interrupting Byring's fairy-tale daydream with the outbreak of battle, Bierce juxtaposes two kinds of horror: the enchantments of the Gothic (as a literary genre and as a way of reading the natural world) are dispelled by the modern, disenchanted event of warfare. By reneging on a scene of miraculous resurrection and an anthropomorphic landscape, the story ultimately reduces the horror of war to the stark materiality of its merely human violence. Although we must take care not to oversimplify Bierce's views on the Civil War by reducing them to a straightforwardly pacifist polemic,[53] this surreal final snapshot of a soldier accidentally killing himself while fighting a dead man certainly deflates any romanticism that the reader may have attached to the supernatural promises of the story's early scenes and to the war itself. Stuart C. Woodruff asserts that what "remains at the end [of 'Tough Tussle'] is the meaninglessness of it all,"[54] but we might further elaborate that this meaninglessness is specifically rooted in the story's renunciation of anthropocentric histories, both individual and public. An initially Ruskinian landscape that is absorbed by (i.e., fascinated with) the affairs of men is eventually revealed to be an ecogrotesque landscape that itself absorbs men's corpses and events indifferently.

Yet Bierce was not universally allergic to the optimistic possibility that certain kinds of human history might endure, as his ample output of civilian ghost tales demonstrates; it is only in the context of war that he insists on the environment's disinterest in retaining traces of human events. Indeed, Bierce's definition of the word *war* in *The Devil's Dictionary* (1911) explicitly short-circuits the notion that the cataclysmic violence of armed conflict can bring about permanent material or social change:

> WAR, n. A by-product of the arts of peace. . . . "In time of peace prepare for war" . . . means, not merely that all things earthly have an end—that change is the one immutable and eternal law—but that the soil of peace is thickly sown with the seeds of war and singularly suited to their germination and growth. It was when

Kubla Khan had decreed his "stately pleasure dome"—when, that is to say, there were peace and fat feasting in Xanadu—that he "heard from far / Ancestral voices prophesying war."[55]

If recruiting the public to the bloody cause of the Civil War entailed convincing Americans both that the conflict's violence was temporary and that its resultant improvements and peace were everlasting, then Bierce's demoralizing intervention here is to invert these assumptions, implying that the social progress for which soldiers of the Civil War perished in droves is fleeting, whereas war itself is perpetual. More specifically, Bierce suggests, the eternal recurrence of war demonstrates the eternal primitivism of man: the atavistic practice of large-scale violence has persisted throughout the span of our species' history, from the earliest "ancest[ors]" of Kubla Khan, to Khan himself, to Samuel Taylor Coleridge (the author of the poem about Kubla Khan that Bierce quotes), to the 1911 reader of *The Devil's Dictionary*. Tellingly, the passage metaphorically positions the natural world as the epitome of a particular kind of organic eternity—a temporality whose processes are immortal but whose individual iterations of those processes (single lives or generations, and whatever systemic changes they might bring about) are ephemeral. "Soil," "seeds," "germination," "growth," and the eventual decay and repetition of the latter two processes embody "the one immutable and eternal law" of change.[56] Above all, the vegetal realm embodies a state of forgetting: it retains memories neither of its own constituent organisms nor of man.

An uncomfortable analogy likewise emerges along the axis of *the natural*: like plants who live out their short and brutish existences without substantially advancing their species, humans who wage war exist in a state of amoral, nonadvancing anarchy—both kinds of life-forms seek only to survive rather than to develop. It is this form of cyclical forgetting via decomposition and regrowth (and its human counterpart, humanity's inevitable backsliding from social evolution into primeval violence) that has already begun to rot away and subsume the bodies, defining characteristics, and personal histories of Byring and his nameless Confederate adversary by the final lines of "Tough Tussle." To dis- and misremember our own proclivity for violence is our nature, Bierce intimates, and the earth's own numb repetitions painfully remind us of this trait. Humanity's amnesia on this front and the natural world's amnesia toward the histories that humanity has tried to carve into its wildernesses lie at the indifferent heart of ecohorror.

Notes

1. Paul Manning, "No Ruins. No Ghosts," *Preternature: Critical and Historical Studies on the Preternatural* 6, no. 1 (2017): 70.

2. Péter Berta, "Afterlife in Cross-Cultural Perspective," in *Macmillan Encyclopedia of Death and Dying I–II*, ed. Robert Kastenbaum, vol. I (New York: Macmillan, 2003), 14.

3. The Anglophone literary tradition contains more stories about animal ghosts than about object ghosts. But even spectral beasts are, for the most part, "few and far between," as Maud Ellmann writes ("Cold Noses at the Pearly Gates," 707).

4. Christy Tidwell, "Ecohorror," in *Posthuman Glossary*, ed. Rosi Braidotti and Maria Hlavajova (London: Bloomsbury Academic, 2018), 115.

5. In chapter 1 of this anthology, Dawn Keetley also highlights the degree to which "revenge-of-nature" narratives project a specifically human agency onto plants and/or animals. My distinction between "ecohorror" and "ecogothic" works follows the distinction between "horror" and "Gothic" that I lay out slightly later in this chapter—namely, that the ecogothic is a subset of ecohorror that specifically features hauntings and takes them seriously. Critical works that focus on botanical anthropomorphism in ecohorror include Matthew Wynn Sivils's "The Herbage of Death" (2012), Tom J. Hillard's "From Salem Witch to Blair Witch" (2015), and Monika Elbert and Wendy Ryden's "EcoGothic Disjunctions" (2017).

6. See, for instance, David Mogen's "Wilderness, Metamorphosis, and Millennium" (1993), Andrew Smith and William Hughes's "Introduction" (2013), Christy Tidwell's "Monstrous Natures Within" (2014), and Dawn Keetley's "Introduction: Six Theses on Plant Horror" (2016).

7. Manning, "No Ruins. No Ghosts," 64.

8. Other examples of anti-Gothic landscapes in Civil War literature include John William De Forest's short story "Lieutenant Barker's Ghost Story" (1869); Walt Whitman's *Specimen Days and Collect* (1882); Ambrose Bierce's "Chickamauga" (1889), "An Occurrence at Owl Creek Bridge" (1890), and "The Mocking-Bird" (1891); and Stephen Crane's *The Red Badge of Courage* (1895).

9. Ambrose Bierce, "A Tough Tussle," in *Tales of Soldiers and Civilians and Other Stories*, ed. Tom Quirk (New York: Penguin, 2000), 141.

10. Judith Richardson, *Possessions: The History and Uses of Haunting in the Hudson Valley* (Cambridge, MA: Harvard University Press, 2003), 139.

11. Charlotte Perkins Gilman, "The Giant Wistaria," in *Frontier Gothic: Terror and Wonder at the Frontier in American Literature*, ed. David Mogen, Scott Patrick Sanders, and Joanne B. Karpinski (Vancouver, BC: Fairleigh Dickinson University Press, 1993), 167–68.

12. John Ruskin, *Modern Painters*, vol. 4 (London, 1843), 310.

13. Washington Irving, "A Biographical Sketch of Thomas Campbell, Author of The Pleasures of Hope, Gertrude of Wyoming, Lochiel's Warning, &c. &c. &c," in *The Poetical Works of Thomas Campbell* (Baltimore: Philip N. Nicklin, 1811), 36–37. Irving's grievances evince decidedly Eurocentric conceptions of "ruins" and "history," as Indigenous peoples had lived and constructed buildings on the American continent for millennia before the arrival of English colonists.

14. Thomas J. Campanella, *Republic of Shade: New England and the American Elm* (New Haven, CT: Yale University Press, 2003), 45; Paul Shepard, *Man in the Landscape: A Historic View of the Esthetics of Nature* (Athens: University of Georgia Press, 2002), 183; Theodore Dwight, *Sketches of Scenery and Manners in the United States* (New York: A. T. Goodrich, 1829), 75–76.

15. See Cathy Davidson's *Revolution and the Word* (221) on these "Costume Gothics."

16. Charles Brockden Brown, *Edgar Huntly; Or, Memoirs of a Sleep-Walker: With*

Related Texts (1799; Indianapolis: Hackett, 2006), 4.

17. Roderick Frazier Nash, *Wilderness and the American Mind* (New Haven, CT: Yale University Press, 2001), 36.

18. Tom J. Hillard, "From Salem Witch to Blair Witch: The Puritan Influence on American Gothic Nature," in *EcoGothic*, ed. Andrew Smith and William Hughes (Oxford: Oxford University Press, 2015), 106.

19. Kathryn S. Meier, "'No Place for the Sick': Nature's War on Civil War Soldier Mental and Physical Health in the 1862 Peninsula and Shenandoah Valley Campaigns," *Journal of the Civil War Era* 1, no. 2 (June 2011): 183, https://doi.org/10.1353/cwe.2011.0033.

20. John Quincy Adams Campbell, "March 4, 1863," in *The Union Must Stand: The Civil War Diary of John Quincy Adams Campbell, Fifth Iowa Volunteer Infantry*, ed. Mark Grimsley and Todd D. Miller (1863; Knoxville: University of Tennessee Press, 2016), 82.

21. Lisa M. Brady, "The Wilderness of War: Nature and Strategy in the American Civil War," *Environmental History* 10, no. 3 (July 2005): 423, https://doi.org/10.1093/envhis/10.3.421.

22. Ibid., 425.

23. See, for example, Kevin C. Armitage's *This Green and Growing Land* (2017).

24. J. T. Trowbridge, *The South: A Tour of Its Battle-Fields and Ruined Cities . . .* (Hartford, CT: L. Stebbins, 1866), 225.

25. "The Desolation of War," *Natchez Weekly Courier*, November 15, 1864, Library of Congress National Periodicals Room. Veterans were similarly shocked at the grotesque misalignment between the verdant regrowth of the natural world and the human suffering to which it had recently borne witness. Surveying a site where he had recently fought in the Battle of Chancellorsville, Abner Small, a major in the Sixteenth Maine Infantry, observed a countryside "shaggy with forest and thicket. . . . I saw it green and smiling with spring. . . . The vast green covert of the Wilderness . . . was lovely with the careless innocence of nature; yet I remembered that in lonely hollows under those trees lay horrors of charred bones and rotting flesh. Only last spring we were at Chancellorsville" (*Road to Richmond*, 129).

26. Keri Stevenson, "The Death of Birdsong, the Birdsong of Death" (chapter 4 of this volume), 97.

27. Daniel Aaron, *The Unwritten War: American Writers and the Civil War* (Tuscaloosa: University of Alabama Press, 2003), 183.

28. Ambrose Bierce, "Ackworth, Ga., June 8th, 1864," in *A Much Misunderstood Man: Selected Letters of Ambrose Bierce*, ed. S. T. Joshi and David E. Schultz (Columbus: Ohio State University Press, 2003), 1. For an account of Bierce's transformation at Shiloh, see Roy Morris Jr., *Ambrose Bierce: Alone in Bad Company* (Oxford: Oxford University Press, 1998), 38.

29. Morris, *Ambrose Bierce*, 38.

30. Bierce stories that feature spectral elements that are not eventually explained away include "An Inhabitant of Carcosa" (1886), "The Middle Toe of the Right Foot" (1890), "Haïta the Shepherd" (1891), "At Old Man Eckert's" (1901), and "The Moonlit Road" (1907). This tension between the naturalistic and the paranormal Gothic is on full display in Bierce's collection *Tales of Soldiers and Civilians* (1892), whose title and internal organization imply a fundamental dichotomy between its military stories (which are all nonsupernatural) and its nonmilitary ones (many of which are supernatural). A rare exception to this distinction is "Three and One Are One," a Civil War story by Bierce that is unabashedly paranormal.

31. Russell Duncan and David J. Klooster, "Introduction: Fighting and Writing the Civil War," in *Phantoms of a Blood-Stained Period: The Complete Civil War Writings of Ambrose Bierce*, ed. Russell Duncan and David J. Klooster (Amherst: University of Massachusetts Press, 2002), 22.

32. Bierce, "Tough Tussle," 138.

33. Ibid. Compare to Hawthorne's *The Scarlet Letter*, 29.

34. This same brand of self-righteously skeptical protagonist appears in several of the Gothic tales that Bierce published alongside "A Tough Tussle" in the "civilian" half of *Tales of Soldiers and Civilians*: Mr. Jarette of "A Watcher by the Dead," Willard Marsh of "The Suitable Surroundings," and Harker Brayton of "The Man and the Snake."

35. Bierce, "Tough Tussle," 139.

36. Dawn Keetley, "Introduction: Six Theses on Plant Horror; or, Why Are Plants Horrifying?," in *Plant Horror: Approaches to the Monstrous Vegetal in Fiction and Film*, ed. Dawn Keetley and Angela Tenga (New York: Palgrave Macmillan, 2016), 9.

37. Bierce, "Tough Tussle," 139, 141.

38. Ibid., 139.

39. Ibid., 140.

40. Ibid. Emphases added.

41. Andrew Bennett and Nicholas Royle, *An Introduction to Literature, Criticism and Theory*, 5th ed. (New York: Routledge, 2016), 168.

42. Bierce, "Tough Tussle," 141.

43. Ibid.

44. Ibid.

45. Ibid.

46. Matthew Wynn Sivils, "'The Base, Cursed Thing': Panther Attacks and Ecotones in Antebellum American Fiction," *Journal of Ecocriticism* 2, no. 1 (January 2010): 30.

47. Megan Kate Nelson, *Ruin Nation: Destruction and the American Civil War* (Athens: University of Georgia Press, 2012), 104.

48. Harry S. Stout, *Upon the Altar of the Nation: A Moral History of the Civil War* (New York: Penguin, 2007), 10, 82.

49. Franny Nudelman, "'The Blood of Millions': John Brown's Body, Public Violence, and Political Community," in *The Afterlife of John Brown*, ed. Andrew Taylor and Eldrid Herrington (New York: Palgrave Macmillan, 2005), 27–29.

50. Lawrence Buell, *The Environmental Imagination: Thoreau, Nature Writing, and the Formation of American Culture* (Cambridge, MA: Harvard University Press, 1995), 56.

51. Val Plumwood, "Being Prey," in *The New Earth Reader: The Best of Terra Nova*, ed. David Rothenberg and Marta Ulvaeus (Cambridge, MA: MIT University Press, 1999), 79.

52. Bierce, "Tough Tussle," 141.

53. As Jonathan Elmer has observed, Bierce "despised cheap patriotism . . . but also despised many of the positions from which one might oppose the war" ("American Idiot: Ambrose Bierce's Warrior," 446).

54. Stuart C. Woodruff, *The Short Stories of Ambrose Bierce: A Study in Polarity* (Pittsburgh: University of Pittsburgh Press, 1964), 139.

55. Ambrose Bierce, *The Devil's Dictionary* (New York: World Publishing, 1911), 361.

56. For further discussion of ecohorror's terrifying juxtaposition of human and earthly timescales, see Christy Tidwell, chapter 2 in this volume.

References

Aaron, Daniel. *The Unwritten War: American Writers and the Civil War*. Tuscaloosa: University of Alabama Press, 2003.

Armitage, Kevin C. *This Green and Growing Land: Environmental Activism in American History*. Lanham, MD: Rowman and Littlefield, 2017.

Bennett, Andrew, and Nicholas Royle. *An Introduction to Literature, Criticism and Theory*. 5th ed. New York: Routledge, 2016.

Berta, Péter. "Afterlife in Cross-Cultural Perspective." In *Macmillan Encyclopedia of Death and Dying I–II*, edited by Robert Kastenbaum, vol. I, 13–16. New York: Macmillan, 2003.

Bierce, Ambrose. "Ackworth, Ga., June 8th, 1864." In *A Much Misunderstood Man:*

Selected Letters of Ambrose Bierce, edited by S. T. Joshi and David E. Schultz, 1–2. Columbus: Ohio State University Press, 2003.

———. "Chickamauga." In Quirk, *Tales of Soldiers*, 20–25.

———. *The Devil's Dictionary*. New York: World Publishing, 1911.

———. "Haïta the Shepherd." In Quirk, *Tales of Soldiers*, 172–76.

———. "An Inhabitant of Carcosa." In Quirk, *Tales of Soldiers*, 241–47.

———. "The Man and the Snake." In Quirk, *Tales of Soldiers*, 187–99.

———. "The Middle Toe of the Right Foot." In Quirk, *Tales of Soldiers*, 259–75.

———. "The Mocking-Bird." In Quirk, *Tales of Soldiers*, 95–100.

———. "The Moonlit Road." *Cosmopolitan*, January 1907: 334–39.

———. "An Occurrence at Owl Creek Bridge." In Quirk, *Tales of Soldiers*, 11–19.

———. "At Old Man Eckert's." *San Francisco Examiner*, November 17, 1901.

———. "The Suitable Surroundings." In Quirk, *Tales of Soldiers*, 227–40.

———. "Three and One Are One." In Quirk, *Tales of Soldiers*, 185–87.

———. "A Tough Tussle." In Quirk, *Tales of Soldiers*, 136–42.

———. "A Watcher by the Dead." In Quirk, *Tales of Soldiers*, 165–85.

Brady, Lisa M. "The Wilderness of War: Nature and Strategy in the American Civil War." *Environmental History* 10, no. 3 (July 2005): 421–47. https://doi.org/10.1093/envhis/10.3.421.

Brown, Charles Brockden. *Edgar Huntly; Or, Memoirs of a Sleep-Walker: With Related Texts*. Indianapolis: Hackett, 2006. First published 1799.

Buell, Lawrence. *The Environmental Imagination: Thoreau, Nature Writing, and the Formation of American Culture*. Cambridge, MA: Harvard University Press, 1995.

Campanella, Thomas J. *Republic of Shade: New England and the American Elm*. New Haven, CT: Yale University Press, 2003.

Campbell, John Quincy Adams. "March 4, 1863." In *The Union Must Stand: The Civil War Diary of John Quincy Adams Campbell, Fifth Iowa Volunteer Infantry*, edited by Mark Grimsley and Todd D. Miller, 82. Knoxville: University of Tennessee Press, 2016. First published 1863.

Crane, Stephen. *The Red Badge of Courage: An Episode of the American Civil War*. New York, 1895.

Davidson, Cathy N. *Revolution and the Word: The Rise of the Novel in America*. Oxford: Oxford University Press, 1986.

De Forest, John William. "Lieutenant Barker's Ghost Story." *Harper's Magazine*, October 1869, 713–20.

"The Desolation of War." *Natchez Weekly Courier*, November 15, 1864. Library of Congress National Periodicals Room.

Duncan, Russell, and David J. Klooster. "Introduction: Fighting and Writing the Civil War." In *Phantoms of a Blood-Stained Period: The Complete Civil War Writings of Ambrose Bierce*, edited by Russell Duncan and David J. Klooster, 5–30. Amherst: University of Massachusetts Press, 2002.

Dwight, Theodore. *Sketches of Scenery and Manners in the United States*. New York: A. T. Goodrich, 1829.

Elbert, Monika, and Wendy Ryden. "EcoGothic Disjunctions: Natural and Supernatural Liminality in Sarah Orne Jewett's Haunted Landscapes." *ISLE: Interdisciplinary Studies in Literature and Environment* 24, no. 3 (Summer 2017): 496–513. https://doi.org/10.1093/isle/isx042.

Ellmann, Maud. "Cold Noses at the Pearly Gates." *Textual Practice* 24, no. 4 (August 2010): 707–24. https://doi.org/10.1080/0950236X.2010.499659.

Elmer, Jonathan. "American Idiot: Ambrose Bierce's Warrior." *American Literary History* 27, no. 3 (September 2015): 446–60. https://doi.org/10.1093/alh/ajv025.

Gilman, Charlotte Perkins. "The Giant Wistaria." In *Frontier Gothic: Terror and Wonder at the Frontier in American*

Literature, edited by David Mogen, Scott Patrick Sanders, and Joanne B. Karpinski, 165–73. Vancouver, BC: Fairleigh Dickinson University Press, 1993.

Hawthorne, Nathaniel. *The Scarlet Letter and Other Writings*. Edited by Leland S. Person. New York: W. W. Norton, 2005.

———. "Young Goodman Brown." *New England Magazine*, April 1835, 249–60.

Hillard, Tom J. "From Salem Witch to Blair Witch: The Puritan Influence on American Gothic Nature." In *EcoGothic*, edited by Andrew Smith and William Hughes, 103–19. Oxford: Oxford University Press, 2015.

Irving, Washington. "A Biographical Sketch of Thomas Campbell, Author of *The Pleasures of Hope, Gertrude of Wyoming, Lochiel's Warning*, &c. &c. &c." In *The Poetical Works of Thomas Campbell*, 7–46. Baltimore: Philip N. Nicklin, 1811.

Keetley, Dawn. "Introduction: Six Theses on Plant Horror; or, Why Are Plants Horrifying?" In *Plant Horror: Approaches to the Monstrous Vegetal in Fiction and Film*, edited by Dawn Keetley and Angela Tenga, 1–30. New York: Palgrave Macmillan, 2016.

Manning, Paul. "No Ruins. No Ghosts." *Preternature: Critical and Historical Studies on the Preternatural* 6, no. 1 (2017): 63–92.

Meier, Kathryn S. "'No Place for the Sick': Nature's War on Civil War Soldier Mental and Physical Health in the 1862 Peninsula and Shenandoah Valley Campaigns." *Journal of the Civil War Era* 1, no. 2 (June 2011): 176–206. https://doi.org/10.1353/cwe.2011.0033.

Mogen, David. "Wilderness, Metamorphosis, and Millennium: Gothic Apocalypse from the Puritans to the Cyberpunks." In *Frontier Gothic: Terror and Wonder at the Frontier in American Literature*, edited by David Mogen, Scott P. Sanders, and Joanne B. Karpinski, 94–108. Vancouver,

CA: Fairleigh Dickinson University Press, 1993.

Morris, Roy, Jr. *Ambrose Bierce: Alone in Bad Company*. Oxford: Oxford University Press, 1998.

Nash, Roderick Frazier. *Wilderness and the American Mind*. New Haven, CT: Yale University Press, 2001.

Nelson, Megan Kate. *Ruin Nation: Destruction and the American Civil War*. Athens: University of Georgia Press, 2012.

Nudelman, Franny. "'The Blood of Millions': John Brown's Body, Public Violence, and Political Community." In *The Afterlife of John Brown*, edited by Andrew Taylor and Eldrid Herrington, 27–55. New York: Palgrave Macmillan, 2005.

Plumwood, Val. "Being Prey." In *The New Earth Reader: The Best of Terra Nova*, edited by David Rothenberg and Marta Ulvaeus, 76–91. Cambridge, MA: MIT Press, 1999.

Quirk, Tom, ed. *Tales of Soldiers and Civilians and Other Stories*. New York: Penguin, 2000.

Richardson, Judith. *Possessions: The History and Uses of Haunting in the Hudson Valley*. Cambridge, MA: Harvard University Press, 2003.

Ruskin, John. *Modern Painters*. Vol. 4. London, 1843.

Shepard, Paul. *Man in the Landscape: A Historic View of the Esthetics of Nature*. Athens: University of Georgia Press, 2002.

Sivils, Matthew Wynn. "'The Base, Cursed Thing': Panther Attacks and Ecotones in Antebellum American Fiction." *Journal of Ecocriticism* 2, no. 1 (January 2010): 19–32.

———. "'The Herbage of Death': Haunted Environments in John Neal and James Fenimore Cooper." In *John Neal and Nineteenth-Century American Literature and Culture*, edited by Edward Watts and David J. Carlson, 39–56. Lewisburg, PA: Bucknell University Press, 2012.

Small, Abner Ralph. *The Road to Richmond: The Civil War Memoirs of Major*

Abner R. Small of the Sixteenth Maine Volunteers, Together with the Diary That He Kept When He Was a Prisoner of War. Edited by Harold Adams Small. New York: Fordham University Press, 2000.

Smith, Andrew, and William Hughes. "Introduction: Defining the EcoGothic." In *EcoGothic*, edited by Andrew Smith and William Hughes, 1–14. New York: Palgrave Macmillan, 2013.

Spofford, Harriet Elizabeth Prescot. "Circumstance." *Atlantic Monthly*, May 1860, 558–65.

Stout, Harry S. *Upon the Altar of the Nation: A Moral History of the Civil War*. New York: Penguin, 2007.

Tidwell, Christy. "Ecohorror." In *Posthuman Glossary*, edited by Rosi Braidotti and Maria Hlavajova, 115–17. London: Bloomsbury Academic, 2018.

———. "Monstrous Natures Within: Posthuman and New Materialist Ecohorror in Mira Grant's *Parasite*." *ISLE: Interdisciplinary Studies in Literature and Environment* 21, no. 3 (Summer 2014): 538–49.

Trowbridge, J. T. *The South: A Tour of Its Battle-Fields and Ruined Cities . . .* Hartford, CT: L. Stebbins, 1866.

Whitman, Walt. *Specimen Days and Collect*. Philadelphia, 1882.

Woodruff, Stuart C. *The Short Stories of Ambrose Bierce: A Study in Polarity*. Pittsburgh: University of Pittsburgh Press, 1964.

6.
The Extinction-Haunted Salton Sea in *The Monster That Challenged the World*

Bridgitte Barclay

While the krakens in the creature feature *The Monster That Challenged the World* (1957) are pleasantly frightening, as far as giant mollusks go,[1] the real horror of the film is the Salton Sea setting and its human-made environmental apocalypse. Written by Pat Fielder, one of the few female science fiction/horror screenwriters of the era, the film opens with a shot of California's Salton Sea, a sea "formed in 1905 when an irrigation canal ruptured, diverting the Colorado River into the Salton Basin."[2] Today the sea is contaminated with agricultural runoff. The voiceover for *The Monster That Challenged the World* explains this setting as "a strange phenomenon in which nature has placed four hundred square miles of salt water in the middle of an arid desert" and where "top secret atomic experiments are carried out under rigid security control." Nature did not, in fact, place the salt water there. Instead, the sea—really a lake—was a human-caused accident with long-lasting repercussions.

The film's plot is based in mid-twentieth-century science news of dormant creatures coming to life and of institutionalized science disasters, including those involving radiation. The creatures in this film have been dormant since prehistoric times, but an earthquake in the irradiated Salton Sea revives the eggs, and krakens begin attacking humans. Fielder based the film's premise on a *Life* magazine article about millions of shrimp hatching from centuries-dormant eggs in a dry lake bed after a flash flood hydrated them, an article the film's scientist, Dr. Jess Rogers (Hans Conried), cites.[3] After several military personnel die during a training exercise and strange excretions found on the scene are discovered to be irradiated, hero Lieutenant

Commander John Twillinger (Tim Holt) and his team discover the initial creature and its eggs. Although the film title uses the singular *monster*, part of the horror is the proliferation of the threat, with multiple hatchlings invading waterways. This plot utilizes growing midcentury scientific knowledge about the nonhuman world being outside of human control (dormant creatures coming to life) to critique science run amok (radiation). Perhaps unintentionally, this plot also applies to the Salton Sea itself, an engineering feat and nightmare that was hailed as both a success and a disaster and that decades later we can see as a product of scientific hubris.

The Monster That Challenged the World is part of a de-extinction subgenre of mid-twentieth-century science fiction/horror films featuring attacks by prehistoric creatures, often dinosaurs or dinosaur-like creatures rather than mollusks.[4] These films often address unexplored spaces—ocean depths, lost islands, the Arctic, or other planets. Some of these de-extinct creatures are revived from dormancy (Godzilla, Gamera, and the monsters in this film, for example), and some are assumed extinct only to be discovered in earthly or extraplanetary frontiers (as in films like *Unknown Island* [1948], *Lost Continent* [1951], and *King Dinosaur* [1955]). Revisiting this subgenre of 1950s creature features with a material-ecocritical perspective illuminates midcentury attitudes toward extinction, institutional science, and environmental toxicity; in *The Monster That Challenged the World*, a material-ecocritical frame re-horrors the film, both emphasizing the ways that the film's extinction fears have been realized and foreshadowing the growing ecological horrors in and around the Salton Sea.

The extinction narratives in *The Monster That Challenged the World* and films like it are entangled with mid-twentieth-century extinction narratives of past Western-frontier extinctions, a new understanding of the prehistoric earth and its extinctions, and concerns about atomic-caused human extinction. By the 1950s when the film was made, the western frontier was already an extinction-haunted space, something in American cultural memory that impacted new landscapes with "declensionist" narratives, as Ursula K. Heise defines them—narratives that are "intimately linked to a foreboding sense of . . . looming destruction."[5] This midcentury era was decades after the West was officially declared closed by Frederick Jackson Turner at the 1893 World's Columbian Exposition in Chicago, a declaration that was part of what prompted museums to begin collecting species for habitat dioramas, a way of preserving endangered species for later generations. Museum collectors understood the human impact on the American West. At the turn of the century, William Hornaday, the chief taxidermist at the Smithsonian's National Museum of Natural History, and Theodore Roosevelt, among many others, worked in some capacity (and in deeply flawed ways) to preserve western land and animals and to educate the public to prevent further extinctions. By the mid-twentieth century, extinction caused by human impact on American land and animals was well established. And midcentury pop culture was still deeply tied to nostalgia for the American West, so horror at its loss is part of an extinction narrative of the time. We see that horror reflected and reworked in *The Monster That Challenged the World*. By 1957, this nostalgia and horror was intensified by a growing understanding of evolution and extinction and by postwar fears of human extinction.

Additionally, extinct prehistoric life was also a popular science narrative by the mid-twentieth century, meaning both evolution and extinction impacted horror. At the beginning of the twentieth century, museum excavations and displays of full prehistoric skeletons affected cultural knowledge of evolution, extinction, and the age of the earth. As John Bruni writes, according to *Scientific American* and *Popular Science Monthly* articles at the time, "Scientific practice became deeply enmeshed in an early-twentieth-century shifting worldview," of which evolution was one of the "dynamic components."[6] Paul D. Brinkman notes that the turn-of-the century dinosaur rush had a huge impact "on science and society," as "the status of dinosaurs soared from prehistoric relic to cultural phenomenon" and "household word."[7] The dinosaur rushes brought on a paradigm shift with an understanding that the earth hosted life well before humans. As Jeremy Vetter points out, the second dinosaur rush, which extended into the early twentieth century, was driven by museums that invested in paleontological digs to secure dinosaur skeletons.[8] So by midcentury, the American public could visit museums in metropolitan areas and see dinosaur skeletons up close, which affected how people thought and talked about evolution, extinction, and the place of the human among the nonhuman. This shift was fodder for horror. Emily Alder asserts that discoveries in various scientific fields led to the narratives of animals and humans being rewritten, noting that understanding "common ancestry" in the "evolution of species, and the ecological entanglement of life on earth set out in Darwin's *Origin of Species* (1859)[,] challenged humanity's position as divinely created masters in the world, separate from other animals."[9] This material entanglement possibly foreshadows later toxic fears, with evolution as the ultimate trans-corporeal horror in an era grounded in human uniqueness. If prehuman life had existed, anthropocentric notions of earth and Edenic creation narratives were flawed, and our understanding of the human place in the cosmos thus necessarily shifted. These discoveries haunt our own extinctions and influence this subgenre of films that make prehistoric creatures the monsters.

Institutionalized Science as Mad Scientist: Extinction and De-extinction

The Monster That Challenged the World evidences a distrust of institutionalized and militarized science, a distrust that began in the mid-twentieth century and has been magnified in the twenty-first century. De-extinction is an ethical question of our era in which we imagine ourselves in control. But *The Monster That Challenged the World* and films like it imagine de-extinction as *out* of our control, as an unintended consequence of institutionalized science, a difference from the archetypal lone mad scientists in science fiction/horror. De-extinction, intended or not (as in this movie), can be understood as Frankenstein institutionalized. In these films, it is not a mad scientist acting alone that creates the single anomaly but scientific institutions (often aligned with the military) that have a hand in awakening or creating gargantuan creatures. In *The Monster That Challenged the World*, the Frankensteinian creatures are both large and multiple, with eggs hatching and creatures invading waterways.

The amorphous monsters that challenge the world in this film are a stand-in for these de-extinction fears. Jason Colavito writes that such creatures consistently symbolize "knowledge, whether forbidden or achieved."[10] The specific horror of atomic knowledge is apparent in *The Monster That Challenged the World*, a less-than-subtle title for atomic horror.[11] The film's promotional posters point to science gone awry. One shows a monster over a supine female and reads, "Crawling up from the depths . . . to terrify and torture!" and "A new kind of terror to numb the nerves!" A crustacean is not an inherently frightening creature, but one that towers over humans is, and a multitude of them invading waterways is even more so.[12] Additionally, on the movie posters, the monster echoes the look and shape of a mushroom cloud. Its head is wider than its body; it is framed in fiery red; and it has short appendages curled in to create a mushroom silhouette looming over the humans. The monster's quickly spreading damage is the result of uncontrolled science and *uncontrollable* nature colliding. ("Uncontrollable nature" is also the way the Salton Sea crisis was referred to in 1907, as I will discuss later.) Like radiation and toxicity, the monsters are in the waterways, and both the scientists and military are unable to protect citizens.

A material-ecocritical frame—with its focus on material agency, emphasis on human/nonhuman entanglements, and critique of scientific power structures—highlights institutionalized science as an antagonist in *The Monster*. The film is based in part on the prehistoric mollusk being irradiated, echoing the origins of Godzilla and other *kaiju* as noted in the opening voiceover's focus on the fact that "top secret atomic experiments are carried out under rigid security control." Fairly early in the film, some excretions discovered at the site of the first attacks are found to be irradiated. Shortly before this, when Lt. Cdr. Twillinger asks Dr. Rogers whether the radiation in the Salton Sea could be the source of the strange excretion, Dr. Rogers responds, "I find that people are always jumping to conclusions about nuclear reaction. Science fact and science fiction are not the same thing, not the same thing at all." It turns out, of course, that radiation is at least in part the cause, and the scientific hubris and lack of control of the radiation and of the natural world (the dormant mollusks awakened by the earthquake) are major conflicts in the film. In fact, scientific hubris and ignorance are so great that Dr. Rogers brings a kraken egg back to the lab to study. He assures the military and government personnel that there is no way the egg can hatch because he is keeping the water temperature cool enough to prevent it. This bad decision becomes even worse when a child plays with the controls in this supposedly top secret, highly secure atomic lab. As she is playing with lab rabbits, Sandy (Mimi Gibson), daughter of female lead Gail MacKenzie (Audrey Dalton), turns up the heat, setting the perfect conditions for the kraken to hatch. In the end, it is science that creates the issue—through the engineering failure of the Salton Sea, its irradiated water, the certainty that the radiation is not harmful, and the hubris of bringing an egg back to the lab (and letting a child run around in an atomic lab).

This critique of science also echoes the fears brought on by atomic devastation and other midcentury industrial environmental health disasters, making human extinction fears palpable. An editorial titled "Is Our Age Lop-Sided?" in the September 1937 issue of *Scientific American* warned against unchecked scientific advancement like that of the atomic bomb, declaring,

"Possibly... it is time to call a halt on the discovery of new forces such as the too-much-hoped-for energy within the atom..., until man has grown up and learned to control himself."[13] In 1956, after the atomic bombings of Nagasaki and Hiroshima, an article in *Scientific American* titled "Science and the Citizen" warned that "as the atomic age advances at an accelerating pace, man must learn how best to cope with the inherently dangerous radioactivity he is releasing in ever increasing quantities," pointing to genetic mutations in children and of concentrating radioactive substances in marine life.[14] By the mid- to late 1950s, the effects of the radiation from the bombings in Japan were well known. In the foreword to Brett L. Walker's *Toxic Archipelago*, William Cronon notes that by the 1950s, there were global concerns about radiation's effects.[15] Other industrial environmental and health disasters were also bubbling up in this era. As Walker documents, the first cases of Minamata disease, caused by mercury pollution from the Chisso fertilizer and plastics factory in Japan's Minamata Bay, had been reported by 1957.[16]

Interestingly, in addition to fears of institutionalized science and its consequences, fears of uncontrollable nature are also apparent in the film, with female reproduction reflected in that of the kraken and showing fears of toxicity. There are a number of reproductive patterns that align with the monster's swift procreation. In addition to Sandy's care for the rabbits—symbols of fecundity—and the role her concern for them plays in the kraken egg hatching, her single mother, Gail, is an interesting choice for a female romantic lead. Gail is a military widow, an "unnatural" role, pointing to one of the negative consequences of the war machine for families: women are left without men, and children are left without fathers (a mutation of the heteropatriarchal family system). Additionally, one of the only other female characters, Connie Blake (Marjorie Stapp), is near the end of her pregnancy when her scientist husband, Dr. George Blake (Dennis McCarthy), is killed by the monster, leaving another widowed mother-to-be. Within a material-ecocritical frame, viewers could interpret this pattern in the film as aligning single, reproducing women with the reproducing kraken—females as vectors spreading disaster. Reproduction happens outside of the rules; the "unnatural" is naturally possible.

The dangers of such female vectors emphasize trans-corporeal toxicity as well. Trans-corporeality, according to Stacy Alaimo, is "the time-space where human corporeality, in all its material fleshiness, is inseparable from 'nature' or 'environment.'"[17] If anything emphasizes the entanglement of bodies, a pregnant woman does—two creatures in one. The figures of a pregnant woman, fetus, and child also call to mind midcentury mutations and toxic vulnerability based on knowledge of the permeability of the human body that radiation and other environmental catastrophes have produced. In "Comfortably Numb: Material Ecocriticism and the Postmodern Horror Film," Stephen A. Rust notes the impact of real-world atrocities on viewers, writing that, in postmodern horror, "bodies figure as the site of individual, social, and ecological disruption."[18] His assertion sheds light on trans-corporeal fears in this earlier era of films as well. Images and articles on the horrors of radiation poisoning, Minamata disease, and other toxicities emphasized the horror of the trans-corporeal at midcentury, and those horrors are reflected in *The Monster*. Rust writes, "Horrific images penetrate the body."[19] Those penetrating images of toxically penetrated bodies are inevitably called to mind in a creature feature about radiation's creations and destructions.

The lone female reproducing, then, may echo not just the dangers of uncontrolled krakens in the film but also a fear of losing the future if we consider the fetus and child as resources to protect. Rebekah Sheldon writes in *The Child to Come: Life After the Human Catastrophe* that the child figure "in an age riven between unprecedented technoscientific control and equally unprecedented ecological disaster . . . is freighted with expectations and anxieties about the future."[20] This women-and-children argument critiquing institutionalized science and monstrous toxicity relies on heteropatriarchal norms that must be reestablished. By the end of the film, with all the monsters defeated, single mother Gail is coupled with Twill, women and children are safe, and the "natural" order is reinstated.

To midcentury viewers and contemporary viewers, then, these horrific environmental health fears reflected in *The Monster That Challenged the World* are part of the tension. Having seen the first creature attack, viewers know of the monstrous danger even as Dr. Rogers denies the possibility of it, noting that there are only normal levels of radiation in the Salton Sea—that is, normal for the ongoing radiation testing done in the area. Dr. Rogers is dismissive of any possibility of something out of his scientific control, counting on a static nature. The dynamic, unpredictable natural world, though— the earthquake and the dormant kraken eggs—are pieces of the horror puzzle that the audience fits into place, and neither the military nor the scientific community seems able to stop the monstrous offspring slipping through the waterways. So, the horror of *The Monster* is in the danger of the de-extinct creature but also in scientific hubris and the material agency of the natural world. Addressing those horrors refocuses the film away from the monster itself and onto the world it is challenging. This is important in a material-ecocritical reading of the film not only for understanding how monster films were subversive in their own era, despite their saccharine endings, but also for showing how re-horroring the films changes monstrosity. The monstrous is the violence of institutional conformity.

Midcentury monster films were often already subversive, aiming for a teenage audience disenchanted with postwar institutionalized scientific militarism and Cleaver-like homogeneity. After World War II, science fiction/horror tended to be more critical of uses of science, especially the science fiction/horror aimed at teens, such as *The Monster That Challenged the World* and other creature features. Mark Jancovich utilizes Brian Murphy's claim that "the state and its authorities are usually associated with 'military-scientific types' or more precisely, 'scientists working in "full co-operation" . . . with the military.'"[21] Jason Colavito also notes this, calling the midcentury era of horror "Psycho-Atomic Horror," writing that "following World War II, science became institutionalized and gradually infiltrated most aspects of life," resulting "in a rash of 1950s mutant monster movies."[22] That institutionalization of science—often by the military—created a distrust of science and the military in some audiences, notably in the teenage audiences these monster films were aimed at. As Jancovich writes, some "horror texts of the period used aliens [or monsters] as an image of difference through which they investigated, problematised and even rejected the notions of 'normality' prevalent in 1950s America," and the creature "was used to criticize . . . conformity."[23] Institutionalized science was part of what was being criticized—the "mad scientist" of the first half of the twentieth century.

The Salton Sea is one of the monstrous creations of such mad science. At the time the film was released, the Salton Sea was a resort area, evidencing the victory of science over nature. Today, we see the long-term environmental devastation that results from such a view—I will discuss this devastation in the next section. As I noted earlier, the monsters are the result of scientific hubris and uncontrollable nature colliding. The Salton Sea was such a monster as well—an engineering wonder with the unintended consequences of flooding and agricultural runoff that continues to wreak environmental havoc. In a 1907 *Scientific American* article on the diversion of the Colorado River to the Imperial Valley, W. D. H. Washington writes, "Seldom has a greater victory been won over rebellious nature."[24] Washington explains the "feat" of engineering that tamed the "obstreperous" river to flow to the seemingly "uninviting" soil of the valley, bringing "marvelous fertility" and "productivity," enabling two thousand farms to open and twelve thousand people to move to the area.[25] And he ends the article by congratulating Colonel Epes Randolph and the Southern Pacific Railroad for which he worked, noting that "the people of Mexico, California, and Arizona, if not of the nation, owe many thanks" to them for "furnishing men, money, and physical equipment and saving such large and important vested and property interests."[26] By midcentury, though, even the editors of *Scientific American* critiqued militarized and corporatized science.

This critique carried over to the convergence of horror and science fiction in midcentury monster movies. Brian Murphy notes that 1950s monster movies were uniquely both genres,[27] and Jason Colavito points out the blurred boundaries between the two genres, especially in such films in which "horror is often found in dark works of science fiction, and science fiction trappings are often used in horror stories."[28] Likewise, Steve Neale argues that creature-feature fiction and films defy boundaries, much like the creatures they feature do.[29] The focus on science-based horror is important to the material-ecocritical reading of the film because it emphasizes fear of science damaging the natural world and fear of science not fully demystifying the natural world, calling knowledge itself into question, as Colavito argues. In *The Monster*, this is certainly the case, as multiple scientific and technological issues, including understanding the real science of extinction, lead to the tension in the film.

To understand institutionalized science as flawed, as perhaps the real monster in these creature features, we must appreciate early feminist science critiques that inform current material-ecocritical perspectives as well.[30] Serpil Oppermann argues that feminist science studies helped to emphasize the political and ethical implications of science ideologies and to lay the groundwork for material ecocriticism, which emphasizes the intermingling of culture and matter. Like Alaimo, Oppermann and other ecocritics note the importance of feminist science in breaking down hierarchies and understanding material exchanges (for instance, in understanding environmental toxicity and toxic bodies)—important concepts in current material ecocriticism. Oppermann writes that material ecocriticism emerged in part from "the radical revisions of our ideas about the description of physical entities, chemical and biological processes, and their ethical, political, and cultural implications represented in recent discourses of feminist science studies, posthumanism, and environmental humanities."[31] Feminist science scholars, such as Anne Balsamo, Sandra Harding, and Evelyn Fox Keller, interrogate the gendered and other power structures of institutionalized science and the ways in which ethics and politics interact with science. Balsamo, for instance, writes that feminist science studies seeks to show "the process whereby science, technology and medicine accrue cultural authority so that [we] may be better equipped ... to recognize abuses of this authority" and "to intervene in the ongoing reproduction of the misuse of such authority in the future."[32] Recognizing the historic and potential continued abuses of scientific authority, such as the abuses of war technologies and lingering environmental toxicity, is an important premise in material-ecocritical scholarship today. As Donna J. Haraway asks, "How might inhabitable narratives about science and nature be told, without denying the ravages of the dedication of techno-science to militarized and systematically unjust relations of knowledge and power?"[33] Ecocritical framing of creature features such as *The Monster That Challenged the World* emphasizes the power structures and negative consequences of institutionalized science.

Additionally, the unintended consequences of institutionalized science also foreshadow current de-extinction or resurrection science narratives, the science of reviving extinct species with gene technology. Peter B. Banks and Dieter F. Hochuli write, "Given that extinction is such a profoundly bad thing, de-extinction would seem to be a logical solution to this problem."[34] But, of course, the ethics and safety of deliberate de-extinction are major concerns. M. R. O'Connor addresses the ethical questions in *Resurrection Science: Conservation, De-extinction and the Precarious Future of Wild Things*, writing, "The looming ethical question is now whether or not humans, recognizing our evolutionary impact on species, should begin to consciously direct or engineer evolution in the direction we want it to go," including using the technologies of de-extinction or resurrection science.[35] As with any new science (such as the radiation that creates the environment for *The Monster That Challenged the World*), we cannot now know the full impact of resurrection science. Lucia Martinelli, Markku Oksanen, and Helena Siipi write, "Some fear that the re-created species may become vectors or reservoirs for viruses that can be harmful for other animals [or] human beings," and they then give the example of "*Pithovirus sibericum*, the 30,000-year-old ancestral amoeba-infecting virus" that was found "recently revived from Siberian permafrost."[36] In a contemporary ecocritical viewing of *The Monster That Challenged the World*, such de-extinction fears—fears of the unintended consequences of science—resonate as the science of de-extinction progresses. This Frankensteinian resurrection was scientifically implausible at the time the films were made but certainly calls to the contemporary viewer's mind the ethical and environmental dilemmas in the *Jurassic Park* film series. At this point in the Anthropocene, material-ecocritical scholars have established how problems of unfettered technoscience and the dynamism of the natural world mean that we cannot fully hypothesize negative environmental consequences. Revisiting *The Monster* using this frame engages the film with new types of horror even as the film remains haunted by midcentury fears.

Re-horroring *The Monster That Challenged the World*

A material-ecocritical viewing of *The Monster* emphasizes midcentury critiques of institutionalized science and its unintended consequences, re-horroring the film with over half a century of new monstrosities and the festering of those old fears. The most horrifying part of viewing the film in the midst of the sixth extinction is the film's setting—the Salton Sea. The Salton Sea is an ecological disaster: a lake (the biggest in California) formed in a Colorado River canal breach at the beginning of the twentieth century that caused nearly two years of flooding into the desert. The flooded area that resulted from this mistake was then made into a resort area but quickly slid into apocalypse. According to NASA, "agricultural runoff from the Imperial, Coachella, and Mexicali valleys supplies 90 percent of the inflow to the Sea," killing off large numbers of fish and making the lake level fluctuate unpredictably.[37] Tyler Hayden writes, "Just a half-century ago the Salton Sea supported a thriving economy, . . . but nobody wants to sunbathe beside algal blooms or amid the stench of rotting fish."[38] The old resorts and communities that formed along the lake are now landscapes of extinction. We see the validity of midcentury fears of institutional science more clearly in the twenty-first century.

More than just resort turned horrorscape, though, the Salton Sea is dangerous for both humans and animals. In Franck Tabouring's documentary *The Useless Sea*, narrator Leila Symington explains that since the resort-like boom on the Salton Sea in the early to mid-twentieth century, "increasing salinity, a steady inflow of waste, and the inevitable arrival of toxic dust have pushed the fragile ecosystem of the Salton Sea to the brink of collapse. What's left today is an advanced environmental catastrophe." Tilapia populations have dwindled, impacting the four hundred species of migratory birds that feed on them, and as the agricultural wastewater recedes, it leaves behind dust laced with large amounts of mercury, arsenic, and selenium.[39] The crisis is ongoing for the surrounding communities of humans and nonhumans, and the sea is a crumbling home to those left behind, marked by abandoned houses with family portraits still hanging, by skeletons of resort structures, and by dead palm trees. Films and photographs of the Salton Sea resemble those of Chernobyl.

In addition to *visually* resembling Chernobyl, the Salton Sea is similar in its toxicity and is thus also an example of trans-corporeal slow violence. As the Salton Sea shrinks, the chemical runoff remains in the dirt, making toxic dust. Louis Sahagun writes in the *Los Angeles Times* that scientists note that the dust from receding waters contains "heavy metals, agricultural chemicals and powdery-fine particulates" that are "linked to asthma, respiratory diseases and cancer . . . , affecting the health of thousands of nearby residents."[40] The macabre poetry of this toxic trans-corporeality—residents breathing in the very land-sea agrichemical by-product of technoscientific disasters and environmental disregard—is an example of what Rob Nixon defines as slow violence, "a violence of delayed destruction" that "is neither spectacular nor instantaneous, but rather incremental and accretive."[41] The toxicity of the lake fed by agricultural runoff not only has killed fish but also is becoming a greater issue as it recedes, exposing harmful agents that move more freely. John R. Marshall of UC Irvine's Department of Emergency Medicine writes that the "greater exposed lakebed" will "create dust storms, increasing the particulate burden in the atmosphere as well as releasing toxic chemicals" in the Salton Sea area where "the particulate matter in the atmosphere surrounding the lake exceeds California and National Ambient Air quality standards."[42] The slow and steady evaporation of the lake exposing the toxic particulates locally and already causing "high incidence of chronic lung disease in the area" is the definition of trans-corporeal slow violence.[43] And the violence may well spread to nearby Los Angeles and San Diego, according to Marshall, as more of the dust is exposed.[44]

As such, the Salton Sea functions as a vision of a localized apocalypse that emphasizes environmental decay and also points to a future extinction landscape, decrying the horrors of ecological disasters and serving as a sort of ghost of past landscapes.[45] There are a number of films about the Salton Sea showing the images of extinction, including *Plagues and Pleasures on the Salton Sea* (2004), *The Salton Sea: A Desert Saga* (2009), *Breaking Point: The Disappearing Salton Sea* (2015), and *The Jewels of the Salton Sea* (2018). In the short documentary *The Accidental Sea* (2011), writer and director Ransom Riggs notes that the Salton Sea is "where Sublime landscapes . . . are framed against scenes of the apocalypse come early." Riggs continues: "Today, what remains is a landscape out of science fiction. . . . Beaches made not of shell or sand but of the pulverized skeletons of uncountable millions of fish. Houses half tumbled into toxic-looking pits. I go there to catch glimpses of what the world will look like without us."

These images of the Salton Sea's ruin are more haunting than the irradiated prehistoric creature emerging from its depths in *The Monster That Challenged the World*. And to a modern viewer, they offer a glimpse of a past, current, and future collapse all at once in a complexly extinction-haunted space, what Connor Pitetti calls the postapocalyptic trend in end-time narratives. Pitetti defines these narratives as those that, in contrast to the distinct era-dividing catastrophes of apocalyptic narratives, "draw attention to the necessarily indeterminate nature of a future that is constantly in the process of emerging from the past."[46] The Salton Sea is haunted by past scientific hubris, attempts to control the natural world, and disregard for the health of human and nonhuman communities. And this toxic sea haunts the future with omens of global toxicity and human and nonhuman extinctions.

Conclusion

Part of what re-horrors *The Monster That Challenged the World* is that the safe, saccharine ending and the silliness of a 1950s creature feature are undone by the real environmental toxicity of the Salton Sea today. The danger is not removed or far off but even more tangible than perhaps originally intended. The horror is real. Philip J. Nickel cites Annette Baier in explaining how horror can make us question what we might otherwise trust, writing that "trust is like the air we breathe in that we only notice it when it disappears or goes bad."[47] This rings especially true in *The Monster That Challenged the World*. If a resort can become a horrorscape, water can kill even the fish in it, and the evaporation of that water can create toxic dust, then nothing seems safe. Everything is haunted.

The Salton Sea setting, then, is a strange convergence of extinctions—an old lake bed revived by accident, communities ruined by environmental catastrophe, and a localized picture of global environmental apocalypse. While the film's narratives in the 1950s may have been haunted by the extinctions that era was just coming to terms with, the film's narratives today are more horrifying. The apocalyptic landscape calls to mind a larger human and nonhuman extinction as well as the slow violence of environmental toxicity.

In the closing scene of the film, Lieutenant Commander Twillinger tells Sandy she can go swimming again, that the beaches are open—a tidy ending with the krakens dead and all back to normal. This saccharine ending is part of the horror, though, when viewing the film through a modern material-ecocritical lens. The monster of the Salton Sea's environmental damage is not defeated and has multiplied to, as Dr. Rogers says in the film, "threaten the entire world," devouring all life—a haunting forecast of our present extinctions.

Stephen A. Rust and Carter Soles note that ecohorror "assumes that environmental disruption is haunting humanity's relationship to the non-human world," and they call for an expansion of what we consider ecohorror.[48] Rereading creature features such as *The Monster That Challenged the World* with a material-ecocritical framework answers that call and re-horrors the films. This resonates with Ursula K. Heise's notion that the Anthropocene itself can be understood as speculative fiction, "an already if incompletely materialized future that makes palpable the obsolescence of the present" by "focus[ing] on the reality of a terraformed planet that . . . has already arrived."[49] The monster has not been contained, has seeped into water systems, and is still challenging the world.

Notes

1. Part of what makes this film so interesting is how nonthreatening a mollusk is under normal circumstances. See chapter 1 by Dawn Keetley in this collection for more on presumably nonthreatening species, specifically trees, as ecohorror.

2. NASA, "Algal Bloom in the Salton Sea, California," *Visible Earth*, October 21, 2003, https://visibleearth.nasa.gov/view.php?id=69091.

3. Tom Weaver, *I Talked with a Zombie* (Jefferson, NC: McFarland, 2009), 122.

4. *Kaiju* such as Godzilla and Gamera, for instance, have received a good deal of attention as symbols for atomic destruction. See Sean Rhoads and Brooke McCorkle's *Japan's Green Monsters* (2018). *The Beast from 20,000 Fathoms* (1953) and *The Creature from the Black Lagoon* (1954) are two other notable examples of this extinction creature feature subgenre.

5. Ursula K. Heise, *Imagining Extinction: The Cultural Meanings of Endangered Species* (Chicago: University of Chicago Press, 2016), 7.

6. John Bruni, *Scientific Americans: The Making of Popular Science and Evolution in Early-Twentieth-Century U.S. Literature and Culture* (Cardiff: University of Wales Press, 2014), 2.

7. Paul Brinkman, *The Second Jurassic Dinosaur Rush Museums and Paleontology in America at the Turn of the Twentieth Century* (Chicago: University of Chicago Press, 2010), 1–2.

8. Jeremy Vetter, "Cowboys, Scientists, and Fossils," *ISIS* 99, no. 2 (2008): 273–303.

9. Emily Alder, "(Re)encountering Monsters: Animals in Early-Twentieth-Century Weird Fiction," *Textual Practice* 31, no. 6 (2017): 1085, https://doi.org/10.1080/0950236X.2017.1358686.

10. Jason Colavito, *Knowing Fear: Science, Knowledge and the Development of the Horror Genre* (Jefferson, NC: McFarland, 2008), 6.

11. See chapter 9 by Robin L. Murray and Joseph K. Heumann in this collection for more on the trope of critiquing militarized science in midcentury horror films.

12. See chapter 2 by Christy Tidwell in this collection for a discussion of other creepy mollusks.

13. Orson D. Munn, "Is Our Age Lop-Sided?," *Scientific American* 157, no. 3, "Our Point of View" (1937): 137. Science fiction authors such as Judith Merril, Carol Emshwiller, and Leigh Brackett, among many others, took up such critical views, writing about atomic apocalypse and human and nonhuman extinctions.

14. "Science and the Citizen," *Scientific American*, 1956, 46–47.

15. William Cronon, foreword to *Toxic Archipelago*, by Brett L. Walker (Seattle: University of Washington Press, 2010), ix.

16. Brett L. Walker, *Toxic Archipelago: A History of Industrial Disease in Japan* (Seattle: University of Washington Press, 2010), 139.

17. Stacy Alaimo, "Trans-corporeal Feminisms and the Ethical Space of Nature," in *Material Feminisms*, eds. Stacy Alaimo and Susan Hekman (Bloomington: Indiana University Press, 2008), 238.

18. Stephen A. Rust, "Comfortably Numb: Material Ecocriticism and the Postmodern Horror Film," *ISLE: Interdisciplinary Studies in Literature and Environment* 21, no. 3 (Summer 2014): 552.

19. Ibid., 551.

20. Rebekah Sheldon, *The Child to Come: Life After the Human Catastrophe* (Minneapolis: University of Minnesota Press, 2016), 3.

21. Mark Jancovich, *Rational Fears: American Horror in the 1950s* (New York: Manchester University Press, 1996), 15.

22. Colavito, *Knowing Fear*, 18.

23. Jancovich, *Rational Fears*, 82.

24. W. D. H. Washington, "The Colorado River Closure," *Scientific American* 96, no. 18 (1907): 374.

25. Ibid., 376–77.

26. Ibid., 377.

27. Brian Murphy, "Monster Movies," *Journal of Popular Film* 1, no. 1 (1972): 31, https://doi.org/10.1080/00472719.1972.10661638.

28. Colavito, *Knowing Fear*, 14–15.

29. See Steve Neale, *Genre and Hollywood* (New York: Routledge, 2000).

30. In "An Introduction to the American Horror Film," Robin Wood writes, "Few horror films have totally unsympathetic monsters . . . ; in many . . . the Monster is clearly the emotional center, and much more human than the cardboard representatives

of normality," noting that a film's progressiveness can be measured by how monstrous the monster is (119, 134).

31. Serpil Oppermann, "From Ecological Postmodernism to Material Ecocriticism: Creative Materiality and Narrative Agency," in *Material Ecocriticism*, ed. Serenella Iovino and Serpil Oppermann (Bloomington: Indiana University Press, 2014), 21.

32. Anne Balsamo, "Teaching in the Belly of the Beast," in *Wild Science: Reading Feminism, Medicine and the Media*, ed. Janine Marchessault and Kim Sawchuk (New York: Routledge, 2000), 186.

33. Donna J. Haraway, "Otherworldly Conversations; Terran Topics; Local Terms," in *The Haraway Reader* (New York: Routledge, 2004), 134.

34. Peter B. Banks and Dieter F. Hochuli, "Extinction, De-extinction and Conservation: A Dangerous Mix of Ideas," *Australian Zoologist* 38, no. 3 (2006), 390, https://www.ncbi.nlm.nih.gov/pmc/articles/PMC6265789/.

35. M. R. O'Connor, *Resurrection Science: Conservation, De-extinction and the Precarious Future of Wild Things* (South Melbourne, AU: Affirm Press, 2015), 7. Helen Pilcher notes in *Bring Back the King: The New Science of De-extinction* that one of the terms for resurrection science used before *de-extinction* became the norm was *undead* but that it was "too 'zombie apocalypse,' so the term 'de-extinction' stuck" instead (15). This is interesting for the process of framing the de-extinction narratives as horror in these films.

36. Lucia Martinelli, Markku Oksanen, and Helena Siipi, "De-extinction: A Novel and Remarkable Case of Bio-objectification," *Croatian Medical Journal* 55, no. 4 (2014): 426.

37. NASA, "Algal Bloom."

38. Tyler Hayden, "Sea Change," *Audubon* 118, no. 4 (Summer 2016): 36.

39. *The Useless Sea*, directed by Franck Tabouring, 2016.

40. Louis Sahagun, "As Salinity Grows and Toxic Dust Spreads, Patience Wears Thin at Salton Sea," *Los Angeles Times*, May 17, 2018, https://www.latimes.com/local/california/la-me-salton-sea-20180517-story.html.

41. Rob Nixon, *Slow Violence and the Environmentalism of the Poor* (Cambridge, MA: Harvard University Press, 2011), 2.

42. John R. Marshall, "Why Emergency Physicians Should Care About the Salton Sea," *Western Journal of Emergency Medicine* 18, no. 6 (2018): 1008.

43. Ibid.

44. The horrific complication is that the Salton Sea is also home to the new ecosystem that grew around it, despite its unintentional creation and toxicity. Lake evaporation impacts the fish and wildlife around the sea but also migratory birds that depend on them.

45. This extinction-haunted locale is unique in the midcentury extinction subgenre of science fiction/horror. Many of the other films are set on pastoral undiscovered islands or planets or in largely unexplored or uninhabited spaces (such as the Arctic or the ocean floor) and are not necessarily tied to environmental toxicity.

46. Connor Pitetti, "Uses of the End of the World: Apocalypse and Postapocalypse as Narrative Modes," *Science Fiction Studies* 44, no. 3 (November 2017): 438. Such trans-corporeal slow violence as evidence of the ills of institutionalized science also calls to mind Rachel Carson's midcentury warnings and later feminist science studies. In 1962, just five years after *The Monster*, Carson's *Silent Spring* emphasized the environmental damage of pesticides.

47. Philip J. Nickel, "Horror and the Idea of Everyday Life: On Skeptical Threats in *Psycho* and *The Birds*," in *The Philosophy of Horror*, ed. Thomas Fahy (Lexington: University Press of Kentucky, 2010), 27.

48. Stephen A. Rust and Carter Soles, "Ecohorror Special Cluster: 'Living in Fear, Living in Dread, Pretty Soon We'll All Be Dead,'" *ISLE: Interdisciplinary Studies in Literature and Environment* 21, no. 3 (Summer 2014): 510.

49. Heise, *Imagining Extinction*, 219.

References

The Accidental Sea. Directed by Ransom Riggs, 2011. https://www.imdb.com/title/tt2317143/.

Alaimo, Stacy. "Trans-corporeal Feminisms and the Ethical Space of Nature." In *Material Feminisms,* edited by Stacy Alaimo and Susan Hekman, 237–64. Bloomington: Indiana University Press, 2008.

Alder, Emily. "(Re)encountering Monsters: Animals in Early-Twentieth-Century Weird Fiction." *Textual Practice* 31, no. 6 (2017): 1083–1100. https://doi.org/10.1080/0950236X.2017.1358686.

Balsamo, Anne. "Teaching in the Belly of the Beast." In *Wild Science: Reading Feminism, Medicine and the Media,* edited by Janine Marchessault and Kim Sawchuk, 185–214. New York: Routledge, 2000.

Banks, Peter B., and Dieter F. Hochuli. "Extinction, De-extinction and Conservation: A Dangerous Mix of Ideas." *Australian Zoologist* 38, no. 3 (2006). https://www.ncbi.nlm.nih.gov/pmc/articles/PMC6265789/.

Brinkman, Paul. *The Second Jurassic Dinosaur Rush Museums and Paleontology in America at the Turn of the Twentieth Century.* Chicago: University of Chicago Press, 2010.

Bruni, John. *Scientific Americans: The Making of Popular Science and Evolution in Early-Twentieth-Century U.S. Literature and Culture.* Cardiff: University of Wales Press, 2014.

Colavito, Jason. *Knowing Fear: Science, Knowledge and the Development of the Horror Genre.* Jefferson, NC: McFarland, 2008.

Cronon, William. Foreword to *Toxic Archipelago,* by Brett L. Walker, ix–xii. Seattle: University of Washington Press, 2010.

Haraway, Donna J. "Otherworldly Conversations; Terran Topics; Local Terms." In *The Haraway Reader,* 125–50. New York: Routledge, 2004.

Hayden, Tyler. "Sea Change." *Audubon* 118, no. 4 (Summer 2016): 36.

Heise, Ursula K. *Imagining Extinction: The Cultural Meanings of Endangered Species.* Chicago: University of Chicago Press, 2016.

Jancovich, Mark. *Rational Fears: American Horror in the 1950s.* New York: Manchester University Press, 1996.

Marshall, John R. "Why Emergency Physicians Should Care About the Salton Sea." *Western Journal of Emergency Medicine* 18, no. 6 (2018): 1008–9.

Martinelli, Lucia, Markku Oksanen, and Helena Siipi. "De-extinction: A Novel and Remarkable Case of Bio-objectification." *Croatian Medical Journal* 55, no. 4 (2014): 423–27.

The Monster That Challenged the World. Directed by Arnold Laven, performances by Tim Holt and Audrey Dalton. Gramercy Pictures, 1957.

Munn, Orson D. "Is Our Age Lop-Sided?" *Scientific American* 157, no. 3, "Our Point of View" (1937): 137.

Murphy, Brian. "Monster Movies." *Journal of Popular Film* 1, no. 1 (1972): 31–44. https://doi.org/10.1080/00472719.1972.10661638.

NASA. "Algal Bloom in the Salton Sea, California." *Visible Earth,* October 21, 2003. https://visibleearth.nasa.gov/view.php?id=69091.

Neale, Steve. *Genre and Hollywood.* New York: Routledge, 2000.

Nickel, Philip J. "Horror and the Idea of Everyday Life: On Skeptical Threats in *Psycho* and *The Birds.*" In *The Philosophy of Horror,* edited by Thomas Fahy, 14–32. Lexington: University Press of Kentucky, 2010.

Nixon, Rob. *Slow Violence and the Environmentalism of the Poor.* Cambridge, MA: Harvard University Press, 2011.

O'Connor, M. R. *Resurrection Science: Conservation, De-extinction and the Precarious Future of Wild Things.* South Melbourne, AU: Affirm Press, 2015.

Oppermann, Serpil. "From Ecological Postmodernism to Material Ecocriticism: Creative Materiality and Narrative Agency." In *Material Ecocriticism*, edited by Serenella Iovino and Serpil Oppermann, 21–36. Bloomington: Indiana University Press, 2014.

Pilcher, Helen. *Bring Back the King: The New Science of De-extinction*. New York: Bloomsbury, 2016.

Pitetti, Connor. "Uses of the End of the World: Apocalypse and Postapocalypse as Narrative Modes." *Science Fiction Studies* 44, no. 3 (November 2017): 437–54.

Rhoads, Sean, and Brooke McCorkle. *Japan's Green Monsters: Environmental Commentary in Kaiju Cinema*. Jefferson, NC: McFarland, 2018.

Rust, Stephen A. "Comfortably Numb: Material Ecocriticism and the Postmodern Horror Film." *ISLE: Interdisciplinary Studies in Literature and Environment* 21, no. 3 (Summer 2014): 550–61.

Rust, Stephen A., and Carter Soles. "Ecohorror Special Cluster: 'Living in Fear, Living in Dread, Pretty Soon We'll All Be Dead,' *ISLE: Interdisciplinary Studies in Literature and Environment* 21, no. 3 (Summer 2014): 509–12.

Sahagun, Louis. "As Salinity Grows and Toxic Dust Spreads, Patience Wears Thin at Salton Sea." *Los Angeles Times*, May 17, 2018. https://www.latimes.com/local/california/la-me-salton-sea-20180517-story.html.

"Science and the Citizen." *Scientific American*, 1956, 46–47.

Sheldon, Rebekah. *The Child to Come: Life After the Human Catastrophe*. Minneapolis: University of Minnesota Press, 2016.

The Useless Sea. Directed by Franck Tabouring, 2016. https://www.imdb.com/title/tt5508996/.

Vetter, Jeremy. "Cowboys, Scientists, and Fossils." *ISIS* 99, no. 2 (2008): 273–303.

Walker, Brett L. *Toxic Archipelago: A History of Industrial Disease in Japan*. Seattle: University of Washington Press, 2010.

Washington, W. D. H. "The Colorado River Closure." *Scientific American* 96, no. 18 (1907): 374–77.

Weaver, Tom. *I Talked with a Zombie*. Jefferson, NC: McFarland, 2009.

Wood, Robin. "An Introduction to the American Horror Film." In *Planks of Reason: Essays on the Horror Film*, edited by Barry Keith Grant and Christopher Sharrett, 107–41. Lanham, MD: Scarecrow Press, 2004.

Part 3
The Ecohorror of Intimacy

7.

From the Bedroom to the Bathroom
Stephen King's Scatology and the Emergence of an Urban Environmental Gothic

Marisol Cortez

Horror critic Tony Magistrale has argued that the future of the horror genre lies in the direction of disembodiment—away from the "body horror" of the 1980s and toward a "techno-horror" that collapses generic boundaries between science fiction and horror. "As we enter into a new century of terror on celluloid," he writes, "the body has become increasingly mechanized; ... the monsters of the future appear to be less about flesh and blood and more about machinery and computer chips."[1] Magistrale is right in some ways, I think, but not in others. For at the same time that we see an emphasis on the technological structures that increasingly mediate and threaten social life, we also see an emphasis on the bodies that these technologies regulate, manage, and render socially invisible. I am thinking particularly of an offhand observation I made some years ago while watching *Boogeyman* (2005): "Why," I wondered aloud, "do so many of these films have bathroom scenes?" And in fact, a content analysis of the most commercially successful horror films from the 1960s to 2010 reveals that over half feature significant bathroom scenes. Moreover, within the past twenty-five years, the locus of anxiety in these scenes has shifted such that we should consider them in relation to ecohorror and ecocritical analyses.[2]

The trend toward bathroom horror undoubtedly begins with *Psycho*'s infamous shower scene, in which the private but ordinary domestic space of the bathroom suddenly becomes the site of inexplicable violence. This emphasis coincides with what film scholar Andrew Tudor calls the "paranoid" tendency of modern horror, where open-ended narratives imagine a monstrous threat that is increasingly internal and immanent to social normality.[3] In the paranoid turn, the monstrous is no longer easily recognizable—any one of us could be Norman Bates; any ordinary shower could turn out to be our last. But we can also read the recent turn to the bathroom simply as a contemporary extrapolation of the "closed space" that has served as Gothic mise-en-scène for the genre since its eighteenth-century inception.[4] Within the imaginary of modern horror, the bathroom has become, according to Magistrale, the most Gothic space in the house,[5] a space where the structuring oppositions of capitalist modernity (public/private, outer/inner, culture/nature) both meet and diverge. From *Psycho* onward, then, horror has repeatedly returned to the bathroom as a means of commenting on how the horrific possesses the ability to invade the commonplace and suggest that "no one is safe anywhere."[6] And since the late 1980s, these bathroom scenes have increasingly centered on toilets, plumbing, and "dark water" to present a threat that is ambient and "nonpoint source"[7]—environmental, in a word.

Visual artist and art historian Margaret Morgan has considered this trend toward bathroom horror in an installation piece called *Toilet Training* (2001), which seamlessly stitches together bathroom scenes from twenty different popular films (largely horror) to highlight how, "in a body-phobic, misogynistic culture, plumbing stands in for the very bodily stuff that it allows us to flush away—the wastes and fluids we'd rather not ponder, lest we be reminded of just how porous and permeable we really are."[8] She comes to similar conclusions in "The Plumbing of Modern Life" (2002), which examines the toilet as a cultural icon (in art and architecture as much as in horror films) and draws a connection between the white porcelain "revered and reviled" by industrial culture and the white women whose bodies are rendered both abject and desirable, targeted for mutilation in the tubs and showers of horror cinema. In life and in culture, Morgan argues, plumbing encodes a fear of the body and particularly of female sexuality, the perceived excessiveness of which is to be controlled just as sewers and toilets control the flow and flooding of rivers and watersheds within the urban environment.

But as with Magistrale, Morgan is only partially right in her account of this trend, largely because, as suggested earlier, so much recent bathroom horror is concerned with an all-pervasive sense of environmental risk more than with the threat of sexual violence. Moving beyond a psychoanalytic framework of abjection, I would locate these scenes as part of an emergent urban environmental Gothic that focuses on the technologies, services, and infrastructures that manage the body within urban industrial landscapes, rendering it "out of sight, out of mind." Not only has the body not gone away in horror, but the technologies of its routinized disappearance have become hypervisible and "deroutinized," to use environmental sociologist Elizabeth Shove's term, in a way that calls attention to the "inconspicuous consumption" that drives much environmental destruction.[9]

The trend toward bathroom horror is thus more productively engaged via literary critic Simon C. Estok's concept of ecophobia, defined as "modernity's *irrational* fear of nature" or "antagonism between humans and their environments[,] in which humans sometimes view nature as an opponent."[10] Critically, Estok includes cultural disgust for "bodily processes and products (microbes, bodily odors, menstruation, defecation)" as a subset of ecophobia, situating what feminist theorist Elizabeth Grosz originally identified as "somatophobia" in relation to its environmental origins and effects.[11]

Using Estok's concept of ecophobia as a theoretical touchstone, this chapter examines two key texts in the literary subconscious of what I have presented so far as a mostly cinematic trajectory—Stephen King's *It* (1986) and his science fiction/horror hybrid *Dreamcatcher* (2001). Bathrooms and plumbing are front and center in both novels, and King is well known for his scatological bent. As one critic commented in a 1987 review of *It*, King's fiction contains so much "blood, mud, slime, sewage, vomit, urine, feces, and oozing flesh" that it almost exceeds the classification of horror: "[his] spendthrift elaboration and gargantuan iteration are more appropriate to the genius of comedy than to the spirit of horror, which is anal and claustrophiliac."[12] But as much as these scatological sensibilities reflect an ecophobic abjection of the body and nature, they also stage a confrontation with the ecological embeddedness denied by ecophobia. Per Morgan, *It* does use plumbing to figure social processes of abjection, and in some ways it is female sexuality that is abjected (in the novel's final horrific revelation that the monster is not only female but pregnant, or in the famous scene of menstrual horror in which It appears to Beverly as a "gout of blood"[13] spewing from her bathroom sink). These dynamics are absent, however, in later, equally scatological King novels such as *Dreamcatcher* (2001), whose excretory bodies are exclusively male and whose bathroom scenes reflect anxieties around not sexuality but the vulnerability of the body to environmental contamination within a modernity variously described as a "risk society,"[14] a "piped society,"[15] and a "network society."[16] When the two texts are read together, we see that King's deployment of the bathroom in *It* initiates a confrontation with ecophobic relations to embodiment that culminates in *Dreamcatcher*, drawing attention to the infrastructural, technological, and historical ecophobia that has *produced*, rather than simply affirmed, this construction of the body. As such, the urban environmental Gothic ultimately recasts in more materialist and ecological terms the traditional textual and psychic dynamics of repression and return that Morgan emphasizes, underscoring the need for an ecocritical approach to horror.

The Most Gothic Room in the House

In an interview featured on the DVD for the film version of *Dreamcatcher*, King comments on his rationale for writing so frequently from the bathroom, stating that while horror's "taboo zone" used to be the bedroom, "eventually the movies got beyond the bedroom door. And I thought to myself, well, is there a door that's still closed anymore? And the answer was, yes, it's true—the bathroom door is a place that we don't go anymore.... You can say I wrote the whole book in order to have the scene where he sits on the toilet and he can't get off because the thing is inside.... That scene that became the driving force of the book. It's gonna do for the toilet what *Psycho* did for the shower."[17] Yet more than the taboo shock of the excretory body, plumbing—or more specifically, the bathroom—is the real focus of King's Gothic impulses in both *Dreamcatcher* and *It*. In both novels, the bathroom is a space for making spectacularly visible what ordinarily remains hidden: the body but also the banal secret of the body's insertion into the technological systems (utilities provision, waste disposal, communications, transportation) that make up what environmental historians Joel Tarr and Gabriel Dupuy have called "the networked city."[18]

Before addressing these elements of King's novels, however, it is important to take a brief look at the cultural histories that have rendered the bathroom a particularly Gothic space—a "taboo zone," in King's words. Although a private domestic space for the elimination of bodily wastes is today taken for granted, the bathroom's normalization as marker of modernity and minimum standard of living in the West is a fairly recent development. According to David Eveleigh in *Bogs, Baths, and Basins: The Story of Domestic Sanitation* (2002), throughout much of the 1800s, people bathed and took care of bodily functions in separate parts of the house using portable technologies—tubs for bathing in the kitchen and chamber pots in bedrooms, which were then taken outside to privies or outhouses. Private bathrooms were a status symbol—only the wealthiest had them. Likewise, ideas about bodily routine reflected technological access; given its difficulty, bathing was believed less necessary and even unhealthy. Yet by the beginning of the 1900s, certain ways of organizing everyday domestic experience and everyday relations to bodily functioning became standard, as did ideas about the relationship of cleanliness to health, such that the bathroom became an essential part of everyone's minimum standard of living.

These changes in the normality of the modern bathroom and its associated cultural meanings lie in the transformations wrought by urbanization and industrialization, chiefly the development of systems for bringing water into homes and removing it again. At the same time, the late 1800s saw significant scientific changes in what environmental historian Martin Melosi calls "environmental paradigms."[19] Although we assume sewers were built because of new understandings that germs caused illness, the first sewer systems in the modern West were built *before* the wide acceptance of germ theory, in the era of miasma theory, which maintained that the cause of illness was bad odors and that the solution was to neutralize them, using water to flush away household wastes. Germ theory thus only retroactively provided the authority of a rational, scientific justification for a technological solution that had, by virtue of its scale and centralization, already become entrenched. Germ theory linked sewers within the cultural imagination to public health arguments about the necessity of disease control, so that the practice of making excrement (and the excretory body) disappear became a hallmark of scientific progress, civilization, cleanliness, rationality, and control over nature—what Jonas Hallström refers to as "the sanitary idea."[20] Conversely, bodily functions became stigmatized as contaminating, impure, primitive, and improper—something to be relegated to the realm of the "private" bathroom.

As germ theory tied cleanliness to notions of health as control over potentially dangerous, contaminating bodies, in particular the collective embodiment of the poor, the state came to require greater vigilance over body, home, and city in the form of building codes ensuring a higher universal standard of living for all. Once a distinction strategy used to mark those of high social position, the bathroom became a basic condition of social acceptance, an index of civilization and modernity.[21] Yet from an environmental standpoint, the triumphalism baked into our understanding of sewers, flush toilets, and the private bathroom also institutionalizes a distancing from nature that has had destructive ecological effects. Until the passage of the Clean Water Act in the 1970s, most of the United States released its partially treated sewage into waterways, leading to widespread pollution of rivers and oceans. This occurred in large part because the meaning of *shit* as something to get rid of is embedded in the technologies designed to allow us not to think about shit (or waterways). As philosopher Gay Hawkins has pointed out in *The Ethics of Waste* (2006), the meaning of the bathroom as a *private* place where we get rid of dirt (on or in bodies) displaces an awareness of how we actually use nature in the process, as a set of *public* decisions. The bathroom mediates our relation to nature—it's where we're trained to lose track of how we are actually physically embedded in local ecological and hydrological systems. In horror, then, as we will see in both *It* and *Dreamcatcher,* the bathroom becomes a place for that relationship—at once familiar and distant, uncanny and Gothic—to resurface to consciousness. But King's bathroom scenes do not simply express and reproduce environmental anxieties about the threatening return of hazards that urban technologies are supposed to keep away from bodies; they also destabilize and problematize that anxiety, drawing critical attention to the structures and spaces that have trained us to abject the body and not think about how we are in fact embedded within natural systems.

It: Scatology as Ethical Refusal of the Refusal

Published in the mid-1980s, *It* finalizes the early part of King's career, which focused more traditionally on supernatural horror; in King's words, *It* is his final work concerned with "children and monsters."[22] The novel tells the story of the Losers Club, a group of preadolescent friends drawn together by shared experiences of marginalization to confront the monster It. There's the Jewish kid, the fat kid, the Black kid, the working-class girl from an abusive home, the wimpy (and thus queer-coded) asthmatic, the nerdy wiseass with Coke-bottle glasses, and protagonist Stuttering Bill, who, appropriately, later grows up to be a horror novelist. The monster they face is a glamour—a shapeshifter that appears to its victims in the guise of their worst fears, allowing King to bring together in one novel all the classic monsters of the Western literary and cinematic unconscious (the Mummy, the Creature from the Black Lagoon, Rodan, the Werewolf, a giant crawling eye, and a giant spider—the final form, revealed to be female and pregnant). Yet even this monster story, read ecocritically, suggests a wider concern with the psychic and temporal production of ecophobia, primarily in the way its bathroom scenes reverse a logic of forgetting central to what Rob Nixon calls "slow violence."[23] With its sewer settings and scatological focus, *It* remembers what an ecophobic culture would prefer to forget.

The story of the Losers' confrontation with It unfolds in Derry, a fictional small town in King's home state of Maine where It lives and sleeps, awakening generationally in twenty-seven-year cycles to prey on Derry's most vulnerable residents. The act of violence that signals It's return, for instance, involves an incident during the town festival in which a homophobic mob throws a gay man into the canal that runs through the middle of Derry; later in the book we learn that, several generations before, a catastrophic fire at a Black soldiers' nightclub announced It's return. And yet It's primary (and largely unseen) victims are Derry's children, who are uniquely attuned to the monster's presence in their town. By contrast, adults are actively oblivious to the mysterious cycles of violence that recur with each successive generation. King in fact presents adulthood as the assumption of a willful ignorance of historical violence, a purposeful forgetting that allows It's predations to repeat. King positions this violent compulsion to repeat against the transformative circularity embodied by the Losers' collective journey as adults. As they physically return to Derry to confront the monster they battled as children, they must also psychically move from willful disavowal to willful remembrance—an act of radical recursivity on the part of the excluded against the rituals of sacrificial violence that renew social relations of exclusion.

The setting for these acts of radical remembering is the Derry municipal sewer system where It lives, transporting itself via the system of drains that link the private domestic sphere to the surrounding watershed. Consequently, many scenes in the novel take place in the bathroom, given that sinks, tubs, and toilets serve as portals between the surface world of domestic normality and the subterranean sewer world of It. At the outset of the novel, Bill Denbrough's younger brother George is killed by It, his arm ripped off at the shoulder at the mouth of a storm drain, and throughout the novel multiple characters hear the voices of other dead children, murdered in or near the sewers, talking and laughing from bathroom sinks that spout fresh blood visible only to children.

Likewise, half the vignettes that introduce us to the Losers as adults unfold in the bathroom. After receiving Mike Hanlon's call that It has returned to Derry, Eddie Kaspbrak packs his entire medicine cabinet in preparation for his pending journey; Richie Tozier pukes his guts out as memories of It begin to surface; and Stan Uris commits suicide in the bathtub. In all these scenes, the bathroom figures as a space that recalls what we want to disavow. As a space that links the surfaces of urban domestic normality with the largely invisible systems that manage the by-products of capitalist production and consumption—its garbage and sewage—the bathroom is where we flush what we want to forget and where what we want to forget sometimes returns to memory, with visceral, even emetic, consequences.

Much of the novel's literary criticism has understood the sewer setting as part of a moral geography of good and evil, according to which the town's appearance is negated by what lies beneath and It embodies the violence visited by the townsfolk on those already marginalized. For example, Tony Magistrale views the novel's topographical organization—aboveground/belowground, city/sewer—as reflective of King's critique of Derry's social corruption and decay: "The sewer system of any city contains the wastes of its populace; Derry's accumulative moral wastes coalesce into Pennywise [It]."[24] In Magistrale's reading, town and sewer symbolically conceal what is "within" and "below," which reduces the meaning of *scatological* in the novel to its purely negative aspect, equating shit with sin.

But King's project is arguably far more complex and radical than a moral framework can account for. First, it is apparent that the city/sewer and adulthood/childhood distinctions that organize the novel spatially and temporally chart more of a *psychic* landscape than a moral one. A traditional psychoanalytic reading might view these distinctions as a dramatization of the split subject rather than as a battle between good and evil; the sewer and the hydraulic logic of modern wastewater disposal are models both for the "clean and proper" adult subject constituted through its repressions and for an official history constituted by what it actively erases, excludes, or forgets. This would place us on the familiar terrain of much classic horror theory, which locates its narrative fulcrum in psychoanalytic dynamics of repression and return.[25]

It actually offers an ecomaterialist theory of the split subject, however, linking its formation to the modern privileging of rationality that disenchants nature and thus deprives it of agency. The novel in fact both dramatizes *and* problematizes the social and psychic orders of capitalist modernity, suggesting their historical formation in Enlightenment views of nature and the body as inanimate and innately subject to rational/technological domination. Through the story of children who descend into the sewers to defeat forces of exclusion and purification, then, *It* challenges the forces of disenchantment that produce the rationalist split subject. In doing so, the novel reverses the logics of spatial and temporal displacement—forgetting—that ecocritic Rob Nixon sees as central to the slow violence of much environmental destruction, which "occurs gradually and out of sight, . . . dispersed across time and space, an attritional violence that is typically not viewed as violence at all."[26]

We see both nature's disenchantment and the slow violence that results in King's extended discussion of Derry's political ecology. For the sewers in *It* are not simply symbols of a repressed corporeality but also the technological means for Derry residents to use local waterways as a dumping ground for this despised embodiment. As was true for much of the United States from the widespread adoption of municipal sewers in the late 1800s until the formation of the EPA in the 1970s, Derry uses local waterways as the repository for all raw sewage and gray water; the result is that the Kenduskeag is "polluted to drop dead levels."[27] Whereas "once there had probably been fish in [the] river[,] [n]ow your chances of catching a trout wouldn't be so hot. Your chances of catching a used wad of toilet paper would be better."[28] This is as clear an example as any of how somatophobia is integral to a broader ecophobia.

Released downstream of downtown, Derry's wastewater flows into an undeveloped area of town called the Barrens, where the Losers Club plays and where all of Derry's environmental ills converge (right next to the poor part of town, as Nixon's emphasis on environmental justice would corroborate). Like the bathroom, the Barrens are a liminal space where opposing distinctions between culture and nature are both erased and reaffirmed, a place within the city where, uncannily, "the only vestiges of the city . . . were Derry Pumphouse #3 (the municipal sewage-pumping station) and the City Dump."[29] Its waterways full of sewage, its air smoky from the adjacent dump's incinerator, and its landscape covered with "trash plants," the Barrens are what geographer Kevin Anderson has called "marginal nature":[30] a space of danger and disuse but equally of enchantment, where a repressed nature returns and whose exclusion from economic productivity makes it a safe haven for those excluded socially. The entire novel, in fact, is a tour of such marginal spaces, of Derry's industrial back spaces and ruins—not just sewers and dumps but gravel pits, abandoned houses, train yards, and alleyways behind stores where trucks offload their cargo.

King presents pollution and the domination over nature it represents as the "dark side" of Derry's economic success, which also centers on the Kenduskeag, enclosed in a concrete canal as it passes through town: "It had been the Canal which had fully opened Derry to the lumber trade in the years 1884 to 1910; it had been the Canal which had birthed Derry's boom years."[31] And it is the Canal where Derry dumps its shit and where It resides. When the Losers finally defeat It at the end of the novel, Derry crumbles as well due to the total disintegration of its invisible infrastructures. Flooding overwhelms its sewers, and its streets collapse, as does the Standpipe, the water tower that houses Derry's water supply. Bridges give way, power transformers explode, and the office building of Bangor Hydroelectric Company sinks into the ground. Inside the houses of Derry, drains back up catastrophically, with "every toilet on Merit Street suddenly explod[ing] in a geyser of shit and raw sewage as some unimaginable reversal took place in the pipes."[32]

This "unimaginable reversal" is arguably a confrontation with the ecophobic disavowal that the sewer represents through its embodiment of the rationalist imperative to master nature and the body. As Estok writes, modern waste-removal regimes produce an imagined "awayness" that "signifies a core element of ecophobia: indifference."[33] This indifference is apparent not only in the instrumentalization of nature as a waste sink for dumping but also in human unconcern for nature's own agency. The Losers, by contrast, refuse the sewer's logic of awayness and indifference as they confront what Derry wants only to forget; the novel does the same in meditating, at great length, on the excretory body and the spaces that contain it. In this respect, the floods that bookend the novel can be seen as a revenge of the urbanized environment on the slow violence of river taming and waste dumping: "You couldn't drop that much shit into a raging body of water without causing a lot of trouble," says one of Derry's residents as he flees the rising water.[34] This complicates Morgan's argument that horror only reaffirms the desire to master (female) flooding; in *It*, flooding is also an ethical refusal of the refusal that plumbing symbolizes. It is a reminder of the impossibility of an "awayness" that strips both waste and nature of agency, a reminder that "far from having dominion over waste [and nature], we are subject to the vagaries, often unforeseen and unpredictable, of the things we want to be rid of."[35]

Thus, what a moral framework would read as forces of evil might instead be read ecocritically as the logic of domination arising from an Enlightenment privileging of instrumental rationalism—a logic of purification and disenchantment that justifies the exploitation of nature alongside the marginalization of social others, represented by the novel's seven Losers. Similarly, children are not "innocents" to morally fallen adults; rather, children represent the political possibilities of reenchantment against the forces of disenchanted modernity. From the beginning, King contrasts adults' fatal inability to believe in the extrahuman (to see the blood that spouts from the sinks) with kids' "faith" in monsters. But this is not faith in a religious or theistic sense as much as it is an openness to the autonomy of more-than-human otherness. This capacity allows children to coexist with the horrific/inexplicable, whereas adults, King suggests, cannot cope:

> [Ben Hanscom] remembered that the day after he had seen the Mummy on the iced-up Canal, his life had gone on as usual. He had known that whatever it had been had come very close to getting him, but his life had gone on. . . . He had simply *incorporated* the thing he had seen on the Canal into his life, and if he had almost been killed by it . . . , well, kids were always almost getting killed. . . . But when you grew up, all that changed. . . . When something *did* happen, something beyond rational explanation, the circuits overloaded. . . . You couldn't just incorporate what had happened into your life experience. It didn't digest.[36]

King's corporeal language here is interesting, suggesting that the rationalist symbolic and social order dramatized by the novel can abide neither the inexplicable nor the ordinary embodied experience. In fact, what escapes rational explanations is equated with bodily functioning: the adult/modern subject casts off the inexplicable like shit or vomit rather than "digesting" it. This childhood tolerance for both irrationality and corporeal porousness ("Shit washes off," Stan reassures the others as they descend into the sewers) animates Bill's adult encounter with a skater kid upon his return to Derry. Without thinking, he advises the kid to be careful—the standard adult directive—to which the kid replies, "You can't be careful on a skateboard."[37] In this response we hear an ethical imperative to accept the risks inherent in mortality, the uncertainty and unpredictability of embodied existence, as a child does.

This childlike "digestion" of monsters is ultimately what allows the Losers, even as adults, to defeat the monster (that is, to undo the logic of sacrificial violence the monster represents). This is reflected in the talisman Bill uses against It, an expression originally learned to help him overcome his stutter: "He thrusts his fists against the posts and still insists he sees the ghosts."[38] This mantra suggests that if It, that which lies outside a rationalist symbolic order, thrives on a refusal to accept the inexplicable, the key to It's undoing lies in a radical affirmation, or *insistence*, despite social and historical disavowal, that one "sees the ghosts."

As a mode of sustained reflection on what we don't want to confront, the horror novel similarly engages in a kind of "unimaginable reversal," insisting against ecophobic logics of purification and disenchantment that it "sees the ghosts." This evokes an important point from Nixon's analysis, which is the representational crisis posed by slow violence and the critical role of "imaginative writing" in "help[ing] make the unapparent appear."[39] If, as Nixon argues, environmental injustice is characterized by a temporal and geographic scale that makes it largely invisible—a "temporal as well as spatial denial through a literal concretizing of out of sight out of mind"[40]—then the crisis of slow violence is equally a crisis of representation. "How can we convert into image and narrative," Nixon asks, "the disasters that are slow moving and long in the making, disasters that are anonymous and that star nobody . . . ?"[41]

In this regard, it is interesting that of the seven Losers, Bill Denbrough and Mike Hanlon are the characters most central to the novel. A horror novelist and a librarian, respectively, Bill and Mike represent the writer of tales and their collector and archivist; through these characters, King presents writing and archiving as modes of radical *remembering*, against the violence of forgetting and erasure that It and Derry represent. While it would be a stretch to place King into the category of the "environmental writer-activist" whose work Nixon highlights—writers who explicitly ally themselves with environmental justice movements—Nixon's point has some elasticity to it. Arguably, we can add the urban environmental Gothic to those representational forms capable of intervening in "the politics of the visible and the invisible" that characterize slow violence and, in the process, of "pushing back against the forces of temporal inattention that compound injustices of class, gender, race, and region."[42] Through its focus on bathrooms and plumbing, the horror novel engages in an act of "socioenvironmental memory,"[43] an ethical act of reenchantment similar to the Losers' battle against the monster.

Dreamcatcher: Scatology as Trans-corporeality

Like *It*, *Dreamcatcher* (2001) is an intensely corporeal novel, full of flatulence, shit, blood, and vomit; gluttonous urges and bodies pushed beyond exhaustion; and cancer and illness. Much of this emphasis reflects the fact that King wrote the novel by hand during six and a half months of convalescence following a near-fatal accident in which he was hit by a car during a walk; a preoccupation with the body's fragility and vulnerability consequently permeates the text (originally titled *Cancer*).

But *Dreamcatcher* conceptualizes embodiment differently than in *It*, evoking Stacy Alaimo's notion of trans-corporeality—the zone of contact and transit between "human corporeality and [the] more-than-human world." Trans-corporeality acknowledges "the often unpredictable and always interconnected actions of environmental systems, toxic substances, and biological bodies"—in short, the agency of the "bodily natures" that form the substance of the material/social world.[44] Instead of charting a subject organized around axes of up/down and in/out, *Dreamcatcher* presents a psychic topography in which relations to the body are not the constitutive exterior to consciousness but rather part of an intermediary realm between conscious and unconscious—the realm of "practical consciousness" described by sociologist Anthony Giddens in *The Constitution of Society*.[45] And rather than a subject modeled on the relationship between city and sewer, *Dreamcatcher* suggests a subject shaped laterally, by a diffuse landscape of infrastructures, technologies, and services that condition norms of embodiment in urban industrial cultures. King's vision of urban industrial subjectivity here is one structured less by the abject body as absolutely exterior negativity and more by those mundane daily activities that ordinarily position the body below the threshold of social perception, even as they create "the often invisibly hazardous landscapes of the risk society" whose impact on bodies remains unknown and unknowable.[46] Although the excretory body remains wildly spectacular and carnivalesque/abject in *Dreamcatcher*'s key bathroom scene, this scene opens onto a more persistent (even paranoid) focus on water infrastructures in the novel.

As in *It*, *Dreamcatcher* is set in and around Derry, Maine, and centers on the relationship between childhood friends who share a quasi-mythical bond that leads them to reunite as adults to defeat a continuing threat. Temporally, the story moves between the late 1970s and early 1980s of the protagonists' adolescence and their adulthood. Compared to the convoluted narrative and metaphysical universe of *It*, however, *Dreamcatcher* is a fairly straightforward tale of alien invasion, set largely in a cabin in the Maine woods where Jonesy, Henry, Pete, and Beaver meet for their annual hunting trip. This particular trip happens to take place during an alien invasion by the byrus, an inanimate fungus that reproduces by infecting its hosts via spore or, in more serious cases, voracious parasites that grow in human bowels and erupt from human asses—a carnivalesque inversion of *Alien*'s famous chest-bursting scene.

This sets the stage for what is arguably one of the most graphically scatological bathroom scenes in the genre. This scene opens during what will be the final annual gathering of the four protagonists, when Jonesy nearly shoots a man who wanders in front of his hunting blind, appearing lost and disoriented. On returning to the cabin with Jonesy, the man reveals that his name is Richard McCarthy, a reference to "Kevin McCarthy in that old horror movie [*Invasion of the Body Snatchers*] about the pods from space that made themselves look like people."[47] Shortly thereafter, McCarthy begins to exhibit increasingly bizarre behavior. Not only is he oblivious to several freshly missing teeth and mysterious red patches on his face, but he also complains of a stomachache and emits several volcanic belches and farts before locking himself inside the bathroom, trailing blood. From behind the bathroom door Jonesy and Beaver can hear McCarthy continue to fart, "sounds . . . brutal and meaty, like ripping flesh," while a horrible stench hangs in the air, "the smell of something contaminated and dying badly."[48] Disturbed, the two friends knock on the door, but McCarthy shrieks, "Get away from me! . . . I have to shit, that's all, I HAVE TO SHIT! If I can shit I'll be all right!"[49] Breaking down the bathroom door, Jonesy and Beaver discover McCarthy sitting naked on a toilet running over with blood; when Beaver shakes him, he topples off the toilet and into the tub, and the two friends scream: "McCarthy's ass was a lopsided full moon with a giant bloody crater in its center, the site of some terrible impact.... It seemed to Jonesy that the hole was a foot across."[50]

But the horror (or comedy) is not yet over, for they soon notice that the thing once inside McCarthy (later dubbed a shit weasel) is now splashing around in the toilet. Quickly Beaver sits on top of the lid to trap it, but the creature headbutts its way out of the toilet and attaches itself to Beaver's back, biting his neck with its needle-sharp teeth and wrapping itself around his waist to attack his face. Thus, like McCarthy, Beaver dies on the toilet. After his death, Jonesy tries to bar the bathroom door against the shit weasel, but the creature proves too strong for him. Just when Jonesy's demise seems inevitable, another figure appears, the novel's introduction of the grays that, along with the byrus and the weasels, comprise the various manifestations of the invading alien presence. A moment later Mr. Gray explodes and the detritus enters Jonesy, snatching his body and leaving his human consciousness a mere "kernel in a cloud, a bit of undigested food in an alien gut."[51]

As in *It*, the bathroom in *Dreamcatcher* functions to expose and make starkly, even spectacularly, visible what ordinarily remains hidden: like the flash of a camera at a crime scene, the "harsh fluorescent light" of the bathroom "kept no secrets but blabbed everything in a droning monotone."[52] But the secret the bathroom reveals in *Dreamcatcher* is of a different nature than that revealed in *It*. In the latter novel, the discovery of Stan Uris's mutilated body in the bathtub—Stan having committed suicide rather than confront It as an adult—bespeaks a subject constituted by the history it rejects, just as the appearance of urban order is ensured through the purifying logic of the sewer. But in *Dreamcatcher*, the very graphic bathroom scene that opens the novel reveals the secret of the body's insertion into the technological systems that make up Joel Tarr's "piped" or "network" city. Thus we have a subject constituted not through repression but via a routinized distance from a trans-corporeal embeddedness within landscapes of risk that remain equally displaced from view. Here King equates the body (particularly its excretory and alimentary capacities) with water delivery/disposal infrastructure, discussing the former in terms of the latter (as when he refers to the intestines of a shit weasel–infected soldier as his "sewage treatment plant") and vice versa (as when he describes the Quabbin Reservoir aqueduct that supplies Boston's water, and where Mr. Gray plans to unload a shit weasel, as "an intestine sixty-five miles long" with "Shaft 12 . . . the throat").[53]

The novel's first use of the body to figure an invisibilized infrastructure occurs when, having commandeered Jonesy's body, Mr. Gray drives to Derry expecting to find the Standpipe, the water tower that collapsed at the end of *It*. All he finds in its place, however, is a pedestal memorializing those killed in the flood, a direct allusion to *It* that implies both novels occupy the same narrative universe. After this unsuccessful trip, Mr. Gray probes Jonesy's memories of where Derry's water came from postflood, but, like most urban residents, Jonesy truly doesn't know: "The water came, you drank it. You didn't worry about where it came from as long as it didn't give you the heaves or the squitters."[54] Finally, Mr. Gray is able to access knowledge of the nearest water source via an urban legend in Jonesy's memories, according to which a woman committed suicide by jumping down a shaft at Quabbin Reservoir outside Boston. Gradually, the novel reveals a bioterrorism subplot: Mr. Gray is in search of large water-storage facilities because they provide an effective means of propagating his species. Because neither the grays nor the byrus can survive the earth's environment and the weasels grow only inside human intestines, the hijacking of Jonesy's body after Mr. Gray's physical death is one of the only ways Mr. Gray can reach a place like Quabbin Reservoir, where water "starts on its way to the taps and faucets and fountains and backyard hoses of Boston,"[55] ultimately reaching the innards of urban residents oblivious to their own critical relationship to this infrastructure.

As in *It*, then, the bathroom scene at the beginning of *Dreamcatcher* crucially opens onto a larger preoccupation with the systems and services that link bodies to ecosystems, remaining largely imperceptible even as these technologies structure subjectivity within urban industrial modernity. But unlike *It*, *Dreamcatcher* presents a different psychic topography, one concerned primarily with the trans-corporeal porosity of bodily boundaries to invasion and toxicity (as captured in the novel's original title). And yet these anxieties over alien invasion and bioterrorism do not straightforwardly pathologize otherness as much as critique this view via King's portrayal of the military characters in the novel—primarily the aptly named Colonel Kurtz—charged with exterminating the grays as "cancer." As telepathic beings, the grays threaten state and military authority because they dissolve psychic boundaries, just as their physical invasion dissolves physical boundaries. As the novel's central symbol, the dreamcatcher is similarly characterized as a kind of postverbal communication network—while on the one hand it is a literal object, the appropriated Indigenous icon that hangs on the wall in Beaver's hunting cabin, on the other it is the symbol for something that connects minds and events, "some huge pattern, something . . . that binds all the years since [Jonesy, Henry, Pete, and Beaver] first met Duddits Cavell in 1978, something that binds the future as well."[56] In other parts of the novel, King refers to Duddits himself—a man whose Down Syndrome, in combination with his extrasensory perception, positions him as extrahuman—as the dreamcatcher. Duddits is the hub that draws the four friends together, first as teenagers and later as adults, connecting them telepathically and enabling them to "see the line": "He makes them one";[57] together they "catch" (in the sense of spreading or infecting) and enter each other's dreams.

What connects *Dreamcatcher*'s intense focus on embodiment—the permeable and porous body, the body open to invasion and transformation by other agencies—with the novel's organizing metaphor of the dreamcatcher is that both are means of foregrounding the networks and infrastructures that laterally structure urban industrial subjectivity. Like telepathy, water delivery and disposal systems suture bodies to one another, just as visual culture and information technology link minds. And like the "material memoirs" and environmental justice writings that Alaimo examines as examples of trans-corporeality, *Dreamcatcher* makes visible the way human bodies are enmeshed within—and thus accountable to—more-than-human worlds that have their own agency and power to act on the human social world.

Toward an Urban Environmental Gothic

The shifting representation of body and bathroom in these two novels is not unique to King. Rather, it reflects broader shifts across both horror fiction and film toward an urban environmental Gothic that effects what environmental sociologist Elizabeth Shove calls "deroutinization." In *Comfort, Cleanliness, and Convenience: The Social Organization of Normality*, Shove analyzes what she calls "inconspicuous consumption," consumption that takes place as part of the "practices and expectations that constitute the barely detectable gridlines of everyday life." Examples include the water mains and showers that enable habits of daily showering (and a certain standard of cleanliness) and the central heating and air conditioning that regulate indoor climate year-round.[58] In contrast to many environmentalists and policy makers, Shove argues that the majority of environmental devastation results not from conscious, conspicuous acts but from the services and infrastructures taken for granted as part of a standard of living considered inviolable in the urban industrial West—a standard that in the past century has been subject to "distinctive forms of escalation and standardization."[59] As she states, echoing Jonesy in *Dreamcatcher*, "Many environmentally relevant 'choices' do not appear as such. Buried in the realm of . . . practical consciousness, . . . water consumption only penetrates the plane of discursive consciousness when it comes out brown, or in the wrong place, or when the utility bill arrives. . . . Such moments of deroutinization are critical because they enable people to examine and assess their habits from a green perspective."[60]

Similarly, the bathroom horror of the urban environmental Gothic deroutinizes the many infrastructures and networks whose backgrounding keeps us from thinking about what gets flushed, by industries and individuals both, as well as where it ends up and whom it impacts. As Alaimo writes, a risk society means that "true awareness" of how bodies interface with environments "elude[s] most, if not all members."[61] As in the case of toxins disposed of into sewers and waterways and relocated from there back into human and nonhuman bodies, the issue is not so much that powerful interests are able to obscure effects but rather that, by virtue of the logic of flushing, these are impossible for anyone to know. Even as pipes, grids, and networks integrate bodies ever more tightly into the environments that serve as reservoirs and waste sinks, this integration lies beyond social visibility and thus beyond accountability to the requirements of environmental health and the demands of environmental justice.

Refracting the psychoanalysis of bathroom horror through the lens of ecocriticism and environmental sociology complicates the more prevalent view that the body in horror is uncomplicatedly abject and that the bathroom is an inherently uncanny space. Although King himself suggests that the excretory body waiting behind the bathroom door is the "final taboo," the novels and films of the urban environmental Gothic do not simply exploit the taboo status of the body for scares (or pleasure). They also deploy it strategically to point to the ecosocial production of this affect, suggesting in the process that the sewers, drains, toilets, reservoirs, water treatment facilities, and pipes that normalize distance from the body—and invisibilize slow violence in the process—have created an alien and frightening presence out of something at one time intimate, familiar, and ordinary. This is, in fact,

Freud's original concept of the uncanny.[62] In this way, bathroom horror exposes and unsettles ecophobia as much as it reproduces it.

Notes

1. Tony Magistrale, *Abject Terrors: Surveying the Modern and Postmodern Horror Film* (New York: Peter Lang, 2005), 17.

2. This conclusion is based on unpublished research conducted from 2006 to 2010, in which I surveyed bathroom scenes in the top 10 percent of the highest-grossing films each year, starting with *Psycho* in 1960. This resulted in a list of 130 films, which I reviewed to determine how many featured the bathroom as a site for horrific happenings; strikingly, 66 of 130 did.

3. Andrew Tudor, *Monsters and Mad Scientists: A Cultural History of the Horror Movie* (Oxford, UK: Blackwell, 1989).

4. Manuel Aguirre, *The Closed Space: Horror Literature and Western Symbolism* (Manchester, UK: Manchester University Press, 1990).

5. Magistrale, *Abject Terrors*, 73.

6. Ibid.

7. Environmental Protection Agency, "Basic Information About Nonpoint Source (NPS) Pollution," 2018, https://www.epa.gov/nps/basic-information-about-nonpoint-source-nps-pollution.

8. Margaret Morgan, "The Plumbing of Modern Life," *Postcolonial Studies* 5, no. 2 (2002): 171–95.

9. Elizabeth Shove, *Comfort, Cleanliness, and Convenience: The Social Organization of Normality* (New York: Berg, 2003).

10. Simon C. Estok, *The Ecophobia Hypothesis* (New York: Routledge, 2018), 1.

11. Elizabeth Grosz, *Volatile Bodies: Toward a Corporeal Feminism* (Bloomington: Indiana University Press, 1994).

12. George Stade, "The Big Chiller," *The Nation*, February 28, 1987, 262.

13. Stephen King, *It* (New York: Signet Books, 1986), 414.

14. Ulrich Beck, *The Risk Society: Towards a New Modernity*, trans. Mark Ritter (London: Sage, 1992).

15. Joel Tarr, "Water and Wastewater: The Origins of the Piped Society," in *The Composting Toilet System Book: A Practical Guide to Choosing, Planning, and Maintaining Composting Toilet Systems, a Water-Saving, Pollution-Preventive Alternative*, ed. David Del Porto and Carol Steinfeld (Concord, MA: Ecowaters Books, 1999).

16. Manuel Castells, *The Rise of the Network Society*, 2nd ed. (Malden, MA: Wiley Blackwell, 2010).

17. Stephen King, interview, *Dreamcatcher* DVD, 2004, https://www.youtube.com/watch?v=sk6OG1N9bIE.

18. Joel Tarr and Gabriel Dupuy, *Technology and the Rise of the Networked City in Europe and America* (Philadelphia: Temple University Press, 1988).

19. Martin V. Melosi, *The Sanitary City: Urban Infrastructure in America from Colonial Times to the Present* (Baltimore: Johns Hopkins University Press, 2000).

20. Jonas Hallström, "European Water History from a Swedish Viewpoint: Introduction of Modern Water and Sewer Systems in Norrköping and Linköping, 1860–1875," *Vatten* 57, no. 3 (2001): 188.

21. See David Inglis's *A Sociological History of Excretory Experience* (2000) for a full elaboration of this history.

22. Michael Collings, *Scaring Ourselves to Death: The Impact of Stephen King on Popular Culture* (Tuscaloosa, AL: Borgo/Wildside Press, 1997), 24.

23. Rob Nixon, *Slow Violence and the Environmentalism of the Poor* (Cambridge, MA: Harvard University Press, 2011).

24. Tony Magistrale, *Stephen King: The Second Decade* (New York: Twayne, 1992), 110.

25. See Robin Wood's "The American Nightmare" and King's *Danse Macabre* (1981). Both Wood and King agree that horror is centrally about the return of the repressed, although they disagree about the political function of that dynamic. King argues that horror, in its focus on destroying the monster and restoring the status quo, "appeals to the conservative Republican in a three-piece suit who resides within all of us" (39). Wood, however, argues that in fact we identify with the monster and that the horror movie allows us to question the norms that have produced the monster.

26. Nixon, *Slow Violence*, 2.

27. King, *It*, 185.

28. Ibid., 344–45.

29. Ibid., 186.

30. Kevin Anderson, "Marginal Nature: Urban Wastelands and the Geography of Nature" (PhD diss., University of Texas at Austin, 2009), https://repositories.lib.utexas.edu/handle/2152/ETD-UT-2009-12-604.

31. King, *It*, 18.

32. Ibid., 998.

33. Estok, *Ecophobia Hypothesis*, 139.

34. King, *It*, 1051.

35. Estok, *Ecophobia Hypothesis*, 138. For another vision of the ecoliberatory ethics of water in contemporary horror—as post-pastoral and postcolonial rather than urban/Gothic—see Robin L. Murray and Joseph K. Heumann's reading of del Toro's *The Shape of Water* in this collection.

36. King, *It*, 509–10.

37. Ibid., 569.

38. Ibid., 867.

39. Nixon, *Slow Violence*, 15.

40. Ibid., 20.

41. Ibid., 3.

42. Ibid., 15.

43. Ibid., 24.

44. Stacy Alaimo, *Bodily Natures: Science, Environment, and the Material Self* (Bloomington: Indiana University Press, 2010), 2–3.

45. Anthony Giddens, *The Constitution of Society* (Cambridge, UK: Polity, 1984).

46. Alaimo, *Bodily Natures*, 3.

47. Stephen King, *Dreamcatcher* (New York: Scribner, 2001), 137.

48. Ibid., 110.

49. Ibid., 114.

50. Ibid., 160.

51. Ibid., 289.

52. Ibid., 161.

53. Ibid., 563.

54. Ibid., 390.

55. Ibid., 531.

56. Ibid., 272.

57. Ibid., 454.

58. Shove, *Comfort, Cleanliness, and Convenience*, 2.

59. Ibid., 3.

60. Ibid., 7–8.

61. Alaimo, *Bodily Natures*, 19.

62. Sigmund Freud, "The Uncanny," trans. Alix Strachey, *Imago*, Bd. V. (1919), reprinted in *Sammlung*, Fünfte Folge, 1, http://web.mit.edu/allanmc/www/freud1.pdf.

References

Aguirre, Manuel. *The Closed Space: Horror Literature and Western Symbolism*. Manchester, UK: Manchester University Press, 1990.

Alaimo, Stacy. *Bodily Natures: Science, Environment, and the Material Self*. Bloomington: Indiana University Press, 2010.

Anderson, Kevin. "Marginal Nature: Urban Wastelands and the Geography of Nature." PhD diss., University of Texas at Austin, 2009. https://repositories.lib

.utexas.edu/handle/2152/ETD-UT-2009-12-604.
Beck, Ulrich. *The Risk Society: Towards a New Modernity*. Translated by Mark Ritter. London: Sage, 1992.
Castells, Manuel. *The Rise of the Network Society*. 2nd ed. Malden, MA: Wiley Blackwell, 2010.
Collings, Michael. *Scaring Ourselves to Death: The Impact of Stephen King on Popular Culture*. Tuscaloosa, AL: Borgo/Wildside Press, 1997.
Environmental Protection Agency. "Basic Information About Nonpoint Source (NPS) Pollution." 2018. https://www.epa.gov/nps/basic-information-about-nonpoint-source-nps-pollution.
Estok, Simon C. *The Ecophobia Hypothesis*. New York: Routledge, 2018.
Eveleigh, David J. *Bogs, Baths, and Basins: The Story of Domestic Sanitation*. Stroud, UK: Sutton, 2002.
Freud, Sigmund. "The Uncanny." Translated by Alix Strachey. *Imago*, Bd. V. (1919). Reprinted in *Sammlung, Fünfte Folge*, 1–21. http://web.mit.edu/allanmc/www/freud1.pdf.
Giddens, Anthony. *The Constitution of Society*. Cambridge, UK: Polity, 1984.
Grosz, Elizabeth. *Volatile Bodies: Toward a Corporeal Feminism*. Bloomington: Indiana University Press, 1994.
Hallström, Jonas. "European Water History from a Swedish Viewpoint: Introduction of Modern Water and Sewer Systems in Norrköping and Linköping, 1860–1875." *Vatten* 57, no. 3 (2001): 187–93.
Hawkins, Gay. *The Ethics of Waste: How We Relate to Rubbish*. Lanham, MD: Rowman and Littlefield, 2006.
Inglis, David. *A Sociological History of Excretory Experience: Defecatory Manners and Toiletry Technologies*. Lewiston, NY: Edwin Mellen, 2000.
King, Stephen. *Danse Macabre*. New York: Everest House, 1981.
———. *Dreamcatcher*. New York: Scribner, 2001.
———. Interview. *Dreamcatcher* DVD, 2004. https://www.youtube.com/watch?v=sk6OG1N9bIE.
———. *It*. New York: Signet Books, 1986.
Magistrale, Tony. *Abject Terrors: Surveying the Modern and Postmodern Horror Film*. New York: Peter Lang, 2005.
———. *Stephen King: The Second Decade*. New York: Twayne, 1992.
Melosi, Martin V. *The Sanitary City: Urban Infrastructure in America from Colonial Times to the Present*. Baltimore: Johns Hopkins University Press, 2000.
Morgan, Margaret. "The Plumbing of Modern Life." *Postcolonial Studies* 5, no. 2 (2002): 171–95.
Nixon, Rob. *Slow Violence and the Environmentalism of the Poor*. Cambridge, MA: Harvard University Press, 2011.
Shove, Elizabeth. *Comfort, Cleanliness, and Convenience: The Social Organization of Normality*. New York: Berg, 2003.
Stade, George. "The Big Chiller." *The Nation*, February 28, 1987.
Tarr, Joel. "Water and Wastewater: The Origins of the Piped Society." In *The Composting Toilet System Book: A Practical Guide to Choosing, Planning, and Maintaining Composting Toilet Systems, a Water-Saving, Pollution-Preventive Alternative*, edited by David Del Porto and Carol Steinfeld. Concord, MA: Ecowaters Books, 1999.
Tarr, Joel, and Gabriel Dupuy. *Technology and the Rise of the Networked City in Europe and America*. Philadelphia: Temple University Press, 1988.
Tudor, Andrew. *Monsters and Mad Scientists: A Cultural History of the Horror Movie*. Oxford, UK: Blackwell, 1989.
Wood, Robin. "The American Nightmare: Horror in the 70s." In *Horror: The Film Reader*, edited by Mark Jancovich. London: Routledge, 2001.

8.
"This Bird Made an Art of Being Vile"
Ontological Difference and Uncomfortable Intimacies
in Stephen Gregory's *The Cormorant*

Brittany R. Roberts

I found myself fascinated by the cormorant's manners. . . . This bird made an art of being vile. It was somehow endearing, such candour.
—Stephen Gregory, *The Cormorant* (1986)

Stephen Gregory's animal horror novel *The Cormorant* (1986) probes the limits of the intimacies we experience with the animals we "know" best: the companion animals with whom we share our families and homes. Tracing the narrator's increasing fascination with an enigmatic and "haughty"[1] cormorant he receives as an inheritance, Gregory explores the complex relationships that can develop between diversely situated multispecies companions. The cormorant—described as "arrogant,"[2] "rude,"[3] and "vile"[4]—represents something that the family cannot understand but that nonetheless affects them powerfully: an ontological otherness that is both "revolting"[5] and strangely alluring. As the narrator and his toddler, Harry, become increasingly affected by the enigmatic cormorant's "magnetism"[6] and transform into new, more horrifying selves in response to the bird's Otherness, Gregory uses elements of ecohorror to foreground the ontological gulf between the cormorant and its human keepers and the at times unsettling connections that can develop between "owner" and "pet," human and nonhuman. Exploring the importance of ethical responsibility toward animal Otherness and examining the horrific, often violent, outcomes of abandoning such responsibilities, Gregory insinuates that true monstrosity is found not in the strange Others with whom we live but rather in humans who abandon their cross-species kin.

Taking as its central focus the dynamic that informs human-animal relationships, *The Cormorant* represents an entry in the ecohorror subgenre of animal horror, which explores the complex relationships between humans and animals and the philosophical traditions that have established these ontological categories as dualistic opposites.[7] Unlike some forms of ecohorror that deal primarily with harmful relations between humans and the wider ecosystem,[8] animal horror emphasizes interactions between humans and animals and "the relation between 'human' and 'animal' as categories."[9] Invested in the ontological gap between these categories and the Western philosophical heritage that has facilitated their "conceptual separation,"[10] such works highlight the boundary between humans and nonhuman animals, simultaneously subverting and reinscribing this division. As Katarina Gregersdotter, Nicklas Hållén, and Johan Höglund argue, the human/animal binary is dependent both on the ongoing process of differentiating these terms and on their conceptual separation from the larger ecological systems that contain them. Animal horror, for them, reveals the fragility of this philosophical dualism, which "is always on the verge of collapsing, precisely because the differences between human and non-human animals are perhaps not as great as we wish them to be for the sake of our conscience."[11] The subgenre thus prompts us to consider the ambiguous, often unsettling subjectivities of animals and, in turn, our sometimes-violent ecological kinships with them.

It is within this animal horror tradition that *The Cormorant* unfolds. Like its avian horror intertexts "The Birds" (1952) by Daphne du Maurier and that story's 1963 cinematic adaptation by Alfred Hitchcock, Gregory invokes our particular fears of and connections to winged creatures: ancestral memories, for instance, of being "hunted by large birds of prey," which Mary Ellen Bellanca suggests may account for early legends of "mythic monsters with wings, beaks, and claws."[12] Presenting the cormorant as an exaggerated "(monstrous) Other to the Western subject,"[13] a being belonging to that "uncanny . . . species of the frightening that goes back to what was once well known and had long been familiar,"[14] Gregory probes the violent histories and potentialities of human-animal relations while also affirming the ethical obligations that must undergird them. As Gregersdotter, Hållén, and

Höglund insist, animal horror "suggest[s] that if animals exist beyond ethics, this does not change the fact that humans have an ethical responsibility toward animals. Humans' failure to do so often leads to swift punishment."[15] Indeed, within *The Cormorant*, such responsibilities are given a central focus: the failure to uphold one's ethical obligations to the Other will ultimately lead to the novel's horrors.

Animal Subjectivity: The Human and Its Others

Like many works of animal horror, Gregory's novel explores the messy, unpredictable consequences of encounters with animal Otherness. Matthew Calarco, summarizing the opportunities posed by such encounters, writes, "The Other here issues a challenge to my way of life and allows me to recognize that there are Others who are fundamentally different from me and to whom I unthinkingly do violence in my daily life."[16] Here, the recognition of Otherness is viscous: cross-species encounters stick to us, transforming us despite our difference. "Such an experience," Calarco continues, "can sometimes have an uncanny way of sticking with me, getting under my skin, and slowly reworking my subjectivity and existence from within."[17] Because they demand an understanding of the Other as subject, cross-species encounters have the potential to undermine Western philosophies of human exceptionalism that have traditionally positioned only the human as agent, subject, and recipient of ethical address. Due to their intimate relations with humans, companion animals in particular offer a promising point of entry into such ethical considerations: as Erica Fudge argues, forming relationships with nonhuman companions is both a radical post-humanist practice and a subversive act that "can actually undo humanist thought," because "we look at our pets and . . . realize that we do not, cannot, know everything."[18] In *The Cormorant*, Gregory raises such cross-species ethical issues in an unusual manner, creating a richly layered multispecies relationship marked not only by companionship but also—most unsettlingly—by competition, mistrust, and fear. In his animal horror masterpiece, Gregory's enigmatic, ambiguous, and horrific cormorant both probes the limits of such an ethics and affirms its necessity.

Throughout the novel, Gregory's cormorant is emphasized as agent, a being capable of generating effects, and as subject, a fully independent being, thereby highlighting one of Gregory's central concerns: human responsibility toward animal Otherness. As agent, the cormorant—whom the narrator names Archie—represents a shift in traditional narrative roles for animals; as subject, the family's ethical responsibility toward Archie is foregrounded from the outset. Indeed, the cormorant is introduced with certain ethical conditions: it comes to the family as an "inheritance" from Uncle Ian, a surly schoolteacher whom the narrator had seen only at family funerals. Bitter and disillusioned, Uncle Ian leaves the family his cottage in a remote Welsh village and a small sum of money for the couple's son, Harry. The narrator speculates, however, that "something of the mischief of the cormorant had touched [Uncle Ian] as he went through the dreary business of making a will,"[19] for the family is allowed to inhabit the cottage only while they care for the bird, whom Ian had rescued from an oil spill while it was still very young. In their short time together before his death, Ian "had seen that the bird would never learn to support itself": although the cormorant "oozed the stink of fish, the smell of the river" and had developed into "an impressively ugly bird,"[20] it could not be rereleased, for "it had learned to feed from the hand of man."[21] Now dependent on human care for survival, the cormorant and human family must learn to live together despite the family's initial repulsion to the bird.

The cormorant, however, is not the only one changed by the human-animal relationship the novel depicts—the narrator; his wife, Ann; and Harry find themselves similarly transformed by the bird. Through the narrator's daily fishing trips with Archie, his and Ann's bewilderment gives way to a hesitant respect: the cormorant's gluttony and "filthy manners"[22] contrast sharply with the polite English middle-class suburban society from which he and Ann have longed to escape. Drawn by the bird's perceived crudeness and dependent on him for their new rural lifestyle, the narrator, Ann, and Harry must meet the cormorant as full participants in a relationship that is depicted as competitive and precarious and yet necessary to all. If the family wishes to keep their living arrangement, and if the cormorant wishes to survive, they must cultivate an ethics of difference, which demands an awareness of the Other as a fundamentally different being *who yet* demands a response. *The Cormorant*, then, explores foundational questions for animal horror. What kinds of responses can we address to the Other, especially if the Other is occluded? And what are our responsibilities toward the Others with whom we live, particularly when such relationships with Otherness are ambiguous, or even, sometimes, monstrous? Gregory suggests that the potential outcomes of such cross-species relationships may be horrific. Indeed, the cormorant's effects on the subjectivities of the narrator, Ann, and Harry form a central locus of the novel's horrors. As the cormorant lodges itself deeper into their understandings of themselves and into the family's burgeoning cracks, such questions of responsibility and response assume a critical importance.

John Berger's influential essay "Why Look at Animals?" examines an idea central to *The Cormorant*'s depictions of the joys—and horrors—of relationships with companion animals: the animal's ability to awaken something dormant in the human. As Berger notes, "pets" provide their "owners" a private audience before whom the owner can "be to his pet what he is not to anybody or anything else."[23] For Berger, the pet thus "*completes*" the pet owner, "offer[ing] its owner a mirror to a part that is otherwise never reflected."[24] Indeed, as I will explore further, the cormorant exerts a profound influence on the narrator and Harry, who find themselves drawn to the bird's "art of being vile."[25] For them, Archie provides access to another self, awakening something horrific in them that had not been evident before. As Berger cautions, however, such human-pet relationships—though they offer something powerful—can be costly: "Since in this relationship the autonomy of both parties has been lost (the owner has become the-special-man-he-is-only-to-his-pet, and the animal has become dependent on its owner for every physical need), the parallelism of their separate lives has been destroyed."[26] As in the relationship described in Berger's essay, the autonomy of the human family members and young cormorant of Gregory's novel is increasingly lost. With the family's housing secured only by Archie's health and with Archie dependent on the narrator for food, water, and exercise, the lives of all parties are irrevocably entangled and transformed.

The mutual dependence of the family and cormorant and the bird's enigmatic influence raise several questions useful to thinking through horror's place in ecological thought. When we engage in human-pet relationships, who is "keeping" whom? Who do we become when we become-with pets? And with whom, exactly, do we share our families and our homes when we live with other species? Within the context of ecohorror, in which ambiguous, border-crossing relationships among species are of primary concern and in which agency often originates outside the human, such questions are of critical importance. Through its portrayal of the fragile and ever-changing relationship between Archie and his human cohabitants, *The Cormorant* suggests, however, that answers are not so easily forthcoming—the bird's agency, inaccessible subjectivity, and ontological difference contribute to a relationship marked by mistrust and precariousness. The novel's unflinching depictions of the difficulties of navigating cross-species relationships serve as a powerful reminder that many human-pet relationships are characterized more easily by fear than by joy.

Otherness and Malevolence: The Cormorant in Western Thought

Drawing inspiration from the cormorant's long-standing associations in the West with evil and gluttony, Gregory's unusual choice of companion animal contributes to the novel's exploration of the ways in which human-pet relationships can rouse fear. As Richard King notes, the cormorant has long been deployed as a symbol of greed and doom, particularly with regard to shipwrecks.[27] He speculates that "the cormorant as devilish or portentous of some dangerous event likely has its roots in the bird's black plumage, its nearly silent voice, and its snakelike neck. The bird is infamous for the way it stands still . . . while spreading its wings to dry, as if draping a dark Dracula cape."[28] As King implies, the cormorant's black feathers have lent it a sense of otherworldly malice, which Gregory emphasizes throughout the novel: Archie's black feathers, "shot through with green and wet with shit," are prominently featured, even perceived in one pivotal scene as a "weapon."[29] The comparison between the cormorant's black wings and Dracula's cape is also not lost on Gregory, who writes that Archie is "a Heathcliff, a Rasputin, a Dracula" and "a dangerous, black villain of a bird . . . most closely resembling a vampire bat (redolent of fish)."[30] Like crows and ravens, bats have an extensive history in Western iconographies of death, long associated with vampires, creatures of the night, and other undead beings. Gregory draws on the evocative power of these species throughout, referring to Archie as "a sea-crow, *corvus marinus*,"[31] and several times comparing Archie to a bat.[32] These beings, who, as King notes, have similarly "long been associated with death and ill portent, in part because of their color, their mischievous intelligence, and their feeding on carrion—including dead people," lend Archie an air of overdetermined evil that is greater than the sum of his parts.[33]

    The cormorant's status as an evil omen is present throughout the novel, allowing Gregory to conjure an atmosphere of dread that is often, for the human characters, connected with Archie. Indeed, when Uncle Ian dies while at sea with the cormorant, his body is discovered with cheeks "pitted from the blows of the cormorant's beak."[34] The ghastly tale, which unexpectedly places the human in the role of prey, recalls the avian attacks of du Maurier's "The Birds" as well as philosopher Val Plumwood's account of her own near-death experience when she was nearly eaten by a crocodile. As Plumwood powerfully recounts, the experience of being reduced to meat, like any other vulnerable, ecologically embedded being, "threatens the dualistic vision of human mastery of the planet in which we are predators but can never ourselves be prey."[35] Recognizing ourselves as prey, we recognize the inadequacy of Western relations with animals and the environment: such stories remind us not only that we too are edible animals attractive to predators but also that there are Other beings and agencies whom we cannot control.[36]

Gregory's novel similarly overturns traditional human-animal hierarchies in the West, presenting Uncle Ian first as master over Archie and then, finally, as lifeless snack. The image of Ian's bird-pitted cheeks highlights human vulnerability and reinforces the impression of the cormorant as malevolent and gluttonous, a potent portent of doom and a familiar stock character from horror's repertoire: the silent, hulking beast who preys on human flesh. Indeed, as Bellanca muses, "The knowledge that we were preyed upon by birds at one time, possibly for much of that 99 percent of our history before migration out of Africa, casts bird-attack narratives in an interesting new light."[37] In an image that recalls humanity's earliest fears of becoming prey to birds, the narrator reflects on the discovery of Ian's body: "His lips were torn. The tender tissues of his gums were split. One eye remained intact. When they had taken the body away, the bird heaved itself onto the deck of its master's boat. It was seen through the rest of the evening and that warm summer's night, hunched on the top of the cabin. It only blinked and cleaned a few morsels of soft flesh from its beak."[38] The cormorant's portrayal as hunching, lurking, and flesh-eating unsettles traditional Western modes of thinking about pets, not least because of Archie's unconventionality as a pet. Rather than a tame, humanlike companion, Archie is a shadowy form filled with fleshly secrets, a carnivorous "Dracula."[39]

The cormorant's doom-laden portrayal at the novel's outset emphasizes his predatory agency and suggests the existence of a rich, though concealed, inner life, lending Archie an air of what Sigmund Freud, summarizing Friedrich Schelling, diagnosed as the uncanny: that which, like the subjectivity of animals, "was intended to remain secret, hidden away, and has come into the open."⁴⁰ Archie's uncanny subjectivity contrasts sharply with traditional Western views of animals, which have emphasized their soullessness, passivity, and innocence; animals may feel and may think, but they can never be *evil*, can never *scheme*.⁴¹ Gregory's cormorant, however, ruptures this tradition: unlike the innocent, soulless, marginalized animals of Western modernity, who for Berger are placed "in a *receding* past,"⁴² Archie hulks and hunches, lurks and stares. His stubborn fixity places him ever present in the narrator's mind, a threatening presence legally bound to the family. With his menacing appearance and horrifying gaze, Archie is anything but receding and, to the narrator, anything but innocent. Archie's seeming vileness, however, offers an opportunity to consider the animal as subject, restoring to him an inner life that—no matter how maligned—emphasizes his status as subject, as *returner* of the look. Indeed, Gregory writes that "as [Uncle Ian] lay convulsing for just a few seconds, the cormorant sat and watched."⁴³ The novel's use of horror tropes—such as its haunting reminders of Uncle Ian, its dark inheritances, its isolated setting, and its frequent depictions of blood, excrement, and gore—allows Gregory to explore the inverse of Western presumptions about animals: instead of the animal as passive innocent, Gregory delivers the animal as corrupted subject, as dark mirror. The perception of Archie as both subject *and* malevolent being inspires a disturbing sequence of transformations in the human narrator and Harry that serve as a profound and unsettling reminder of the vulnerability of human-animal relationships and of the beings we take into our homes.

The Gaze of the Other

Throughout *The Cormorant*, Gregory carefully traces the family's shifting impressions and understandings of Archie, including their initial expectation of receiving a docile animal akin to the machinelike, innocent beings of eighteenth-century thought. As the narrator recalls, "It was a sure sign of our complacency in receipt of the cormorant that we had opened the white wooden crate in our living-room and expected some kind of plastic, domestic fowl to emerge and be driven quietly out through the back door."⁴⁴ Instead, however, the family receives a fully formed being, replete with inner life. Indeed, Archie's arrival horrifically unsettles the family's "picture of domestic bliss,"[45] introducing an element of unpredictability that defies the narrator's expectations of dominance over the cormorant and reverses traditional ways of thinking about pets as tame and subordinate. Archie literally defiles the human domain of the home, immediately marking the pillows, rugs, and curtains with his excrement and thereby threatening the boundaries between inside and outside, or between what the narrator can and cannot control. As Julia Kristeva theorizes, excrement—like corpses, decay, and disease—poses a threat to human identity from without: it "stand[s] for . . . the ego threatened by the non-ego, society threatened by its outside, life by death."[46] In marking the home with his excrement, Archie violates the boundaries between civilization and wilderness, human and nonhuman; the home—that most sacred of human spaces—is under attack.

Eager to restore peace to his human home and uncertain how best to handle the family's new addition, the narrator studies the cormorant, watching it and "allow[ing] it to watch [him]."[47] Here he acknowledges Archie's subjectivity, thereby departing from traditional Western modes of thinking about animals; his recognition of Archie's subjectivity is, however, tinged by horror. Drawing attention to the cormorant's "enigmatic eye,"[48] Gregory emphasizes the irreducible gap between the cormorant and his human handler, thereby foregrounding Archie's status as both subject and menacing figure of difference. In *The Cormorant*, the animal unexpectedly—and unsettlingly—looks back. In a scene that recalls philosopher Jacques Derrida's account of finding himself the object of his cat's gaze, during which Derrida was struck by the alterity of this being whose existence "refuses to be conceptualized,"[49] Archie's assertion of his own inscrutable gaze stakes his claim to subjectivity while simultaneously marking him as an uncertain, possibly threatening Other. Indeed, for Derrida, the uncomfortable feelings aroused by the cat's return of his gaze reminded him of "a bottomlessness, at the same time innocent and cruel perhaps, perhaps sensitive and impassive, good and bad, uninterpretable, unreadable, undecidable, abyssal and secret."[50] But though Archie's gaze, like that of Derrida's cat, is illegible, it prompts the narrator to recognize Archie's subjectivity with a name. He muses, "I would call the cormorant Archie. It was harsh, like the sound the bird repeatedly croaked. There was something cocky and irreverent about it."[51] Although the narrator does not fully understand—or even like—the cormorant, he recognizes the bird's singular subjectivity, its unique voice.

If Gregory emphasizes Archie's subjectivity, however, he also warns that the subjectivity of pets and other intimate strangers can be unsettling. Ann, for instance, is frightened and "bewildered" by the cormorant, in whom she recognizes a complete being that she cannot "understand."[52] Indeed, she feels called to protect Harry from Archie, turning the boy's eyes away from the bird and, at one point, removing her son from the cottage entirely to break the sway of the bird's "demonic arrogance."[53] The family, then, acknowledges the legitimacy of Archie's inner space, even granting that Archie experiences emotions: the narrator, for instance, ponders the bird's "unpredictable temper"[54] and, later in the text, its "panic of impatience."[55] His assessment of Archie's emotions, however, must be approximated from across the ontological gulf between humans and animals. With the "impressive weapon"[56] of the bird's beak on display throughout, and with any certain access to Archie's inner space denied, Gregory undermines the narrator's assumption of mastery over the cormorant and, by extension, the human assumption of mastery over all animals. Archie's ominous presence suggests enclaves of animality that escape human domination, spaces of thought and subjectivity withdrawn from human access. It is this very unpredictability that, for the narrator, makes Archie a "hazard";[57] his subjectivity is a source of horror.

Archie's status as both intimate housemate and ontological stranger makes his position within the family uncertain throughout the novel, underlining the precariousness of the multispecies relationship the text examines. Is Archie brother, fellow, friend—or foe? As Donna J. Haraway observes, cross-species cohabitation can be an uncomfortable, ambiguous, and intimate process, "involving agencies of many sorts and stories that do not lend themselves . . . to an assured outcome for anybody. Co-habiting does not mean fuzzy and touchy-feely."[58] It is the very uncertainty of this human-animal relationship that leads to the family members' varied reactions: Ann remains largely repelled by Archie, but the narrator and his young son find themselves fascinated, even *called* by him, affirming Archie's status as both subject and agent. In a scene that disturbs both the narrator and Ann, Harry wanders into his parents' room, gazing out the window to where Archie awaits in the yard, "head and beak erect, wings outstretched. Utterly motionless. Utterly black."[59] As the narrator, Ann, and Harry watch Archie, Harry surprises his parents by "suddenly hiss[ing] loudly, forcing the air like steam."[60] Reaching to touch the windowpane beyond which Archie waits,

Harry stands as though summoned by the bird, leaving only once the bird departs and walking between his parents "as though [they] were invisible to him."[61] The child's rapt attention to the bird leaves his parents disconcerted. As the narrator bemoans, "For a few minutes, . . . Archie had been more important to Harry than we were. He had watched and signalled to the cormorant, oblivious to our presence."[62] The bird's mysterious connection with Harry unsettles the narrator and his wife—Archie calls and is heard, but to what end? As Gregory icily insinuates, the relationship forming between bird and human is "multiform, at stake, unfinished, consequential."[63] Here, the bird's agency threatens.

The horror evoked in Ann and, at times, the narrator as they watch Harry's increasingly agitated fascination with Archie recalls Haraway's admonition that relationships between beings are relationships of "significant otherness":[64] they demand not only respect but also the unceasing awareness that one is relating to an essentially unknowable Other with whom one nonetheless shares a profound bond. She writes, "The recognition that one cannot *know* the other or the self, but must ask in respect for all of time who and what are emerging in relationship, is the key."[65] In the case of Archie and the narrator, who and what emerge across this multispecies divide is at times hopeful but more often disturbing—a recognition that cohabitation is, indeed, not always "touchy-feely."[66] As Gregory emphasizes throughout, multispecies companionship is often marked by competition and violence. With the haunting images of Archie's sharp beak and Uncle Ian's broken, pitted face looming large throughout the text, Gregory reminds us that such relationships are not always under human control; one can participate in but not always predict the relationships one forms with Others.

Significant Otherness and Multispecies Companionship

As *The Cormorant* demonstrates, the inability to access the inner lives and ontological spaces of animals does not prevent humans from forming intimate relationships with animals or from attempting to learn to live with them. Indeed, throughout the novel, Archie and the narrator communicate—at times haphazardly—through nonverbal means, gradually allowing a relationship to form that changes both participants. As their relationship demonstrates, influence and agency do not originate solely from the human—animals transmit too. What is less certain, however, is *what* is emerging from the relationship between the narrator and Archie. As their intimacy develops, Gregory portrays the narrator's transformation in response to the cormorant, using the bird's presence to highlight the narrator's increasing selfishness and appetite. With Archie looming larger and larger in the narrator's mind, the text's atmosphere grows more sinister as the narrator becomes increasingly aware of a presence around Archie, the haunting reminder of Uncle Ian, whose foul personality is recalled to the narrator again and again, often accompanied by the "clinging scent of a dead cigar."[67] As the intimacy between Archie and the narrator grows, these recollections of Uncle Ian affect the narrator more and more, first with a sense of bitterness and then, increasingly, of sympathy. Through the ominous presence of the dead, "malicious"[68] Uncle Ian, Gregory suggests that what is emerging from the human-animal relationship the novel examines may, in fact, be something horrific: an intimate but cruel bond.

The relationship between the narrator and Archie begins its most significant development when Ann—frightened by Archie's influence over Harry—decides to leave town with the toddler for a week. During this time, the narrator takes Archie out frequently to exercise in the Menai Straits while he gathers firewood. Archie moves from the back of the narrator's van to the passenger seat, marking the narrator's acknowledgment of Archie as an equal partner. Archie, too, seems to recognize this when he brings the narrator the "gift" of a dying fish. Gregory writes,

> The bird waddled forward and held up its bill to me. I instinctively withdrew my hands. In the half-light, I could not be sure what Archie was carrying, and I would never really trust the hooked beak. Archie craned forward again and put down a fish by my green wellingtons. It was a dab, still alive and convulsing, its gristly body arched with cramp. I bent to pick it up. "Thank you, Archie. Thank you very much."[69]

Noting the cormorant's "determination to offer its prize to me,"[70] the narrator turns Archie's appetite and expertise in fishing to his own, human advantage, keeping the fish Archie catches while allowing Archie to keep any eels. During their fishing trips, the narrator's feelings toward Archie begin to change. He muses, with an unexpected pleasure that emphasizes the cormorant's growing, pernicious impact on him, "I was enjoying the raffish company of the cormorant."[71]

"This Bird Made an Art of Being Vile"

Archie's gift-giving signals a departure from the stereotype of the greedy, gluttonous cormorant that opens the novel while also marking a turning point in the cross-species relationship emerging between bird and human. As Archie becomes more sympathetic to the narrator, the narrator appreciatively notes Archie's curiosity, mischievousness, and apparent generosity. The narrator, too, begins to change, thinking with scorn about the domestic suburban life he has left behind in England and admiring the developments that have taken place in his character since cohabiting with Archie:

> I smiled when I thought how I had changed in the last few months since leaving the Midlands. What would my old headmaster say if I were to meet him, by some absurd coincidence, in the harbour car park in Caernarfon? I was used to wearing a jacket and tie for school; here I was, parking a smelly van on the quayside, stepping out in tattered jeans and wellington boots, . . . in a waterproof spotted with fish scales and containing in one pocket the corpse of a forgotten flatfish; to crown the effect of such scruffy clothing, on opening up the back of the van, a dangerous, black villain of a bird would spring out, a cross between a raven and a pelican but most closely resembling a vampire bat (redolent of fish). And the hunt for food: taking the bird with its leash and collar, filling a bag with fresh fish, while other people stood stupidly in a supermarket queue.[72]

The narrator, indeed, is becoming the man he's always dreamed of being, recalling Berger's assessment that "the pet *completes* [the pet owner], offering responses to aspects of his character which would otherwise remain unconfirmed."[73] The narrator notes that as a child he had dreamed of "possessing a falcon."[74] Now, as an adult, he is "reaping pocketfuls of flatfish from the mudbanks of the Menai Straits, seizing them from the beak of the cormorant, alive with bone and gristle."[75] Even his beard and fingernails have been left to grow wild, as he imagines himself to have become: "Instead of being closely razored under my chin and on my cheeks, I had left [my beard] to crawl over my throat and disappear below my ears. The fingernails, which were once so immaculately filed and cleaned, were now neglected."[76] Gregory suggests, however, that such transformations may be horrific, as the narrator becomes aware of a mysterious spectator watching his expeditions with Archie, a man who greets the narrator's and Archie's successes with "slow, sarcastic applause."[77] The gray figure, obscured from sight but for the butt of his cigar, haunts the narrator, prompting him to consider "what else was included in the inheritance."[78] Made sinister by the dark presence of Uncle Ian, the narrator's transformation and newfound rusticity, Gregory implies, may be part of a darker design.

Gregory further cements these impressions of the narrator's transformation by setting them against a backdrop of interspecies violence. Archie's beak is repeatedly emphasized throughout the novel, underscoring both the fragility of the bird-human relationship and the potential for violence to erupt at any moment. Indeed, this potential is actualized more than once in the novel: Archie kills the family cat, attacks the narrator on several occasions, and, in a particularly gruesome scene, injures a family guest, Mr. Knapp, on Christmas Day. This last occurrence marks a shift in the text, when the tension building between Archie and his human keepers erupts, fully, into violence; it also highlights the narrator's growing admiration of Archie's unpredictable temperament and capacity for bloodshed. Indeed, the narrator almost wills the injury, showing the cormorant to Mr. Knapp out of a perverse desire to impress his neighbor with his conquest of the imposing animal. As Jonathan Burt notes of animals on film, the image of the violent animal carries the capacity to infect humans who perceive it, as Archie's violence does to the narrator. Burt explains, "The violent animal image . . . has a significance that extends beyond simply representing the uncivilized (both in the sense of the 'natural' and the 'barbarous'), and, like a form of propaganda, is assumed to have the power to cause the repetition of such an action."[79] Indeed, when the bird strikes Mr. Knapp, the narrator reacts with silent encouragement: "Something told me that the beak was destined for the finger, just as Archie closed its eyelids and swooned in the luxury of the man's caresses. There was something so inevitable about it at that moment that I had been unable to speak a word of warning. So I simply watched."[80] Viewing the bird as a symbol of his own unsociable impulses, the narrator approves of Archie's violence, thus underscoring the cormorant's sinister impact on the narrator and in turn the uncertain nature of their relationship as a whole. As the narrator becomes increasingly cruel, projecting onto Archie his repressed desires and drawing inspiration from Archie's aggressive behaviors, the violence brewing within their human-animal relationship threatens to emerge in unsettling and unexpected ways.

If trust is established between the narrator and Archie, then, it is a cruel and unpredictable trust that can be severed at any moment, most notably by violence—either Archie's or, increasingly, the narrator's own. The growing violence between them is foreshadowed early in the novel, shortly after Archie kills the family cat. Gregory writes,

> The bird came at me in two leaps, brandishing the heavy beak, punishing the night shadows with the power of its wing beats. There was blood on its bill. . . . I kicked out with my slippered foot and the bird flapped backwards, long enough for me to take up some slack around my wrist and reel it in. . . . Archie resisted, skidded forward on slippery feet. As I fumbled with the latch, the cormorant struck hard at my hand.[81]

As Gregory highlights throughout the stages of the cross-species relationship between Archie and the narrator, these are kin who do not fit together easily and are yet bound to each other—the narrator legally and Archie by force of being raised in captivity. As Haraway warns, making kin—particularly multispecies kin—requires us to consider "to whom one is actually responsible."[82] She asks, "Who lives and who dies, and how, in this kinship rather than that one? What shape is this kinship . . . ? What must be cut and what must be tied if multispecies flourishing on earth . . . [is] to have a chance?"[83] As Gregory examines the pressure points in the multispecies kinship between Archie and his human family, the responsibilities we bear toward others are highlighted again and again. Archie's sinister influence on the narrator and Harry suggests that the cross-species intimacies that cut across our more-than-human world are not always pleasant; as mortal lives of different species intersect, such intimacies often invite unexpected consequences and unwelcome responsibilities.

Responsibilities to the Other

If the narrator and Archie are engaged in a relationship of becoming-with—each becoming more dependent on the other—then Harry and Archie are also becoming-with, albeit in far more ambiguous ways. Throughout the text, Harry becomes animated only in Archie's presence, lapsing into listlessness when parted from the bird. Even more significantly, Harry appears to be *transformed* by the cormorant: he is described as "suffused with the malice of the sea-crow," as "hissing" and "croaking" in the same manner as Archie, and as experiencing a "union"[84] with the bird. Following an incident on Christmas Day in which Harry sneaks into the cormorant's cage to sleep, Ann is too mortified to consider keeping Archie any longer. As she leaves with Harry for the second time, it becomes clear that the novel's tensions have reached a breaking point. The narrator must choose between his son and Archie.

Although the family—especially Ann—project their fears and superstitions onto Archie, detecting in him an almost supernatural malevolence, Gregory emphasizes throughout *The Cormorant* that Archie is merely an ordinary bird, a victim forced into captivity due to an unordinary, unnatural, and ecohorrific oil spill. He is enigmatic and unsettling but demonstrates no supernatural abilities, no capacity for enacting the doom that seems to follow him. Far from the devilish associations that plague the cormorant in the West, Archie demonstrates both trust and respect for the narrator at multiple points, following his human companion without a leash and even, in one touching scene, nuzzling the narrator's hand "as affectionate[ly] as a dog."[85] It is not Archie, then, who falls short of his ethical responsibilities toward his human kin. Rather, it is the narrator, fueled by anger and resentment over the strain in his family, who abandons his ethical responsibilities toward Archie, corrupting the ethical relations between human and bird.

On Christmas night, the narrator, drunk and blaming Archie for Ann and Harry's departure, grabs a hot poker from the fire and beats Archie until the bird's wing is badly broken, revealing the injured bone. Locking Archie outside in his crate for the night, the narrator contemptuously urinates on Archie before passing out, not realizing—or perhaps not caring—that a magnificent blizzard has been gathering on the horizon. Awakening the next morning to an ecohorrific landscape "erased by the deadening blanket of snow,"[86] he discovers that Archie's cage has been snowed under; the cormorant, severely injured and unable to seek shelter, has frozen to death.

Rather than the monstrous being that the human characters have perceived Archie as, the bird, in death, is fragile. In a depiction that elicits disgust for the narrator's actions, Gregory writes, "The neck was folded to enable the cormorant to press its face into its breast feathers, the beak was partly hidden under one wing. Eyes closed. One wing tucked away, the other awry."[87] The novel does not treat Archie's death as a victory, as in more conservative animal horror narratives such as Steven Spielberg's *Jaws* (1975), but instead as a moment of profound loss. Emphasizing Archie's vulnerability, Gregory reverses the script on the monster narrative, generating sympathy for Archie and making clear that the narrator's interspecies abuse is unjustifiable. Indeed, the narrator himself regrets his behavior, "tenderly" holding the cormorant as he tries to "infuse some life through the warmth of [his] hands." Archie, however, remains "stiff beyond the powers of [his] warming."[88] By rendering the murder of the cormorant a tragedy, Gregory reveals the novel's true monster: the human pet owner who violates his bond with his animal companion.[89] The "fragile relic of the cormorant,"[90] thawed and decaying, levels an accusation at all who fail their cross-species kin.

Underscoring the questions of kinship that motivate the novel's horrors, the death of the animal in *The Cormorant*—as in many other animal horror texts—is tied to the death of a human. But unlike in more conservative animal horror texts, in which a vicious predatory animal must be killed in atonement for the human's loss, the loss in *The Cormorant* is more ambiguous: with the cormorant dead, there is no animal to enact the human's death. Instead, it is the violation of the bond between Archie and the narrator that leads, albeit indirectly, to the loss of Harry, reinforcing the ethical judgment the novel performs. If the narrator is able to violate his bond with Archie, Harry cannot; when Ann decides to "clean"[91] the yard so recently occupied by the cormorant through a "cleansing by fire,"[92] the boy, seized by an urge to run into the blaze in which the cormorant's crate is melting, cannot be contained. As Gregory describes, "He dropped to the ground, cat-like among the blaze. With a shout, he sprang forward . . . and immersed himself in the flames of the white wooden crate. Engulfed by the fire, the little figure was tearing and rummaging at the remaining panels of the box."[93] Harry, like Archie, is consumed by fire, his last effort a desperate attempt to retrieve Archie's body from the burning crate until all that remains are the "blistered bones of bird and boy."[94] Harry's horrific death points toward the potentially horrific outcomes of such intimacies: like "all true lovers, of whatever species,"[95] Harry and the cormorant are connected by a bond that does not always have desirable outcomes. In the ecological relations that govern all cross-species encounters, such intimacies can be—and often are—fatal.

Toward an Ethics of Becoming-With

The tragedy of Harry's and Archie's losses demonstrates how deeply we are impacted by the animals with whom we share our lives, suggesting the transformative power of our relationships with the nonhuman beings with whom we are most intimate. On a planet full of such intimate cross-species relationships, the destructive potential of human-animal relationships—especially those that are most intimate—demands attention. As Gregory's ecohorror novel shows, animals can haunt us, reshaping our senses of our selves, our families, and our homes. The frequency with which human and animal lives collide, often in our most intimate spaces, demonstrates the necessity of understanding both the positive and, at times, horrific outcomes of cross-species cohabitation. On the finite spaces of an increasingly small earth, such considerations are not a choice but a responsibility. If we are ecologically bound, Gregory suggests, then so too are we ethically bound. Thus, if there is evil to be found in *The Cormorant*, it lies not in the ontological Others with whom we share our lifeworlds but in the moment in which we break our ethical responsibilities toward Others. In assuming that we can attempt to exercise violent control over animals, in favoring one kinship over another, we violate the bonds between "owners" and "pets," humans and nonhumans.

In a gesture that violently sutures the gap between humans and animals, the novel closes with one final encounter, a mutual acknowledgment of pain that once more bonds man and bird. The narrator stands in the yard, still stunned by the double loss of Archie and his son, "alone in the garden. Until the gulls came."[96] In a passage whose imagery again evokes the avian frenzy of du Maurier's "The Birds," Gregory writes,

> At first a solitary bird came skimming over the plantation and peered down at the garden. Its laughter rang hollow against the hillsides. Until another gull appeared, and another, and the hysterical mirth increased. I stood still, my face upturned. And my sky became a blizzard of whirling white birds. They dived towards me, their throats gulping with the effort of screams. Their wings made the air quiver. A patter of droppings rained on the slated path and settled like tears on my cheeks. I never raised my hands to wipe the tears away: I let them trickle to the corners of my mouth. Then, when the turmoil was too much and in my head there was nothing but the snowstorm of gulls, I could dismiss them. . . . They wept a little and were gone.[97]

The gulls, presented as unholy familiars to Archie throughout the novel, share their "tears" with the narrator, excrement which, significantly, he refuses to wipe away. If Gregory constructs the ontological gulf between human and nonhuman as impenetrable, it is a gulf across which bonds and connections can nonetheless be forged. In the finite space of the planet on which we are all cohabitants, the task, Gregory intimates, is to establish ethical bonds, ones attentive to the dynamics of otherness-in-relation, which are always precarious, always uncertain. As Haraway notes, "We become-with each other or not at all."[98] To this, I add simply that we must become-with ethically—as strangers and, more importantly, as neighbors.

Notes

1. Stephen Gregory, *The Cormorant* (New York: St. Martin's Press, 1986), 25, 67.
2. Ibid., 8, 89, 122.
3. Ibid., 8, 23.
4. Ibid., 15, 123.
5. Ibid., 64.
6. Ibid., 42.
7. See chapter 12 by Carter Soles in this volume for more on the animal horror subgenre and its relationship to ecohorror.
8. Katarina Gregersdotter, Nicklas Hållén, and Johan Höglund, introduction to *Animal Horror Cinema: Genre, History, and Criticism*, ed. Katarina Gregersdotter, Johan Höglund, and Nicklas Hållén (New York: Palgrave Macmillan, 2015), 4; Stephen A. Rust and Carter Soles, "Ecohorror Special Cluster: 'Living in Fear, Living in Dread, Pretty Soon We'll All Be Dead,'" *ISLE: Interdisciplinary Studies in Literature and Environment* 21, no. 3 (Summer 2014): 509–10.
9. Gregersdotter, Hållén, and Höglund, introduction to *Animal Horror Cinema*, 4.
10. Ibid.
11. Ibid., 12.
12. Mary Ellen Bellanca, "The Monstrosity of Predation in Daphne du Maurier's 'The Birds,'" *ISLE: Interdisciplinary Studies in Literature and Environment* 18, no. 1 (Winter 2011): 28.
13. Gregersdotter, Hållén, and Höglund, introduction to *Animal Horror Cinema*, 10.
14. Sigmund Freud, *The Uncanny*, trans. David McLintock (New York: Penguin Books, 2003), 124.
15. Gregersdotter, Hållén, and Höglund, introduction to *Animal Horror Cinema*, 7.
16. Matthew Calarco, *Thinking Through Animals: Identity, Difference, Indistinction* (Stanford, CA: Stanford University Press, 2015), 31.
17. Ibid., 32.
18. Erica Fudge, *Pets* (Stocksfield, UK: Acumen, 2008), 46.
19. Gregory, *Cormorant*, 8.
20. Ibid.
21. Ibid., 9.
22. Ibid., 78.
23. John Berger, *About Looking* (New York: Pantheon Books, 1980), 12–13.
24. Ibid., 12, 13.
25. Gregory, *Cormorant*, 15.
26. Berger, *About Looking*, 13. See chapter 11 by Sharon Sharp in this volume for more on the ethics of human–companion animal relationships.
27. In his study of the cormorant's status in Western thought, King devotes a few paragraphs to *The Cormorant*, writing, "Gregory's novel . . . reinforce[s] that enduring, deep-seated, cultural antipathy toward the cormorant in Britain, Ireland, and North America" (66). I contend, however, that the novel's important exploration of the at times challenging and confusing dynamics of multispecies interaction renders it worth further consideration.
28. Richard J. King, *The Devil's Cormorant: A Natural History* (Lebanon: University of New Hampshire Press, 2013), 54.
29. Gregory, *Cormorant*, 71.

30. Ibid., 16, 54–55.
31. Ibid., 16.
32. Ibid., 8, 13, 54–55, 108, 114.
33. King, *The Devil's Cormorant*, 54. For more on the evocative, ecohorrific image of the seabird, see Keri Stevenson, chapter 4 in this volume.
34. Gregory, *Cormorant*, 11.
35. Val Plumwood, "Being Prey," in *The New Earth Reader: The Best of* Terra Nova, ed. David Rothenberg and Marta Ulvaeus (Cambridge, MA: MIT Press, 1999), 88.
36. Sharon Sharp, in chapter 11 in this volume, also considers the ontological ramifications of becoming prey. In her discussion of the television series *Zoo*, Sharp writes that narratives that feature animal consumption of humans emphasize similarities between humans and animals on the grounds that they are both edible.
37. Bellanca, "Monstrosity of Predation," 37.
38. Gregory, *Cormorant*, 11.
39. Ibid., 16.
40. Freud, *The Uncanny*, 132.
41. As Berger argues, Descartes's pronouncement of animal "soullessness," or lack of inner life, constituted a "decisive theoretical break" in Western thinking about animals, through which "the animal was reduced to the model of a machine" (*About Looking*, 9). Writing a century later, the influential zoologist Georges-Louis Leclerc, Comte de Buffon, built upon Descartes's declaration by articulating a perceived contrast between the soullessness of animals and the spiritual anguish of humans, which for Leclerc imparted to animals an aura of innocence (Berger, *About Looking*, 10). The animal's soullessness and subsequent innocence has formed part of a long tradition of thought toward animals in the Judeo-Christian West.
42. Berger, *About Looking*, 10.
43. Gregory, *Cormorant*, 10.
44. Ibid., 13.
45. Ibid.
46. Julia Kristeva, *Powers of Horror: An Essay on Abjection* (New York: Columbia University Press, 1982), 71.
47. Gregory, *Cormorant*, 16.

48. Ibid., 31.
49. Jacques Derrida, *The Animal That Therefore I Am*, trans. David Wills (New York: Fordham University Press, 2008), 9.
50. Ibid., 12.
51. Gregory, *Cormorant*, 16.
52. Ibid., 112.
53. Ibid., 19.
54. Ibid., 16.
55. Ibid., 46.
56. Ibid., 16.
57. Ibid.
58. Donna J. Haraway, *The Companion Species Manifesto: Dogs, People, and Significant Otherness* (Chicago: Prickly Paradigm, 2003), 30.
59. Gregory, *Cormorant*, 38.
60. Ibid.
61. Ibid.
62. Ibid., 39.
63. Haraway, *Companion Species Manifesto*, 30.
64. Ibid., 16.
65. Ibid., 50.
66. Ibid., 30.
67. Gregory, *Cormorant*, 45.
68. Ibid., 36.
69. Ibid., 48.
70. Ibid., 49.
71. Ibid., 55.
72. Ibid., 54–55.
73. Berger, *About Looking*, 12.
74. Gregory, *Cormorant*, 54.
75. Ibid.
76. Ibid., 55.
77. Ibid., 60.
78. Ibid., 61.
79. Jonathan Burt, *Animals in Film* (London: Reaktion Books, 2002), 140.
80. Gregory, *Cormorant*, 99.
81. Ibid., 34.
82. Donna J. Haraway, *Staying with the Trouble: Making Kin in the Chthulucene* (Durham, NC: Duke University Press, 2016), 2.
83. Ibid.
84. Gregory, *Cormorant*, 19, 38, 86, 110.
85. Ibid., 60.
86. Ibid., 127.
87. Ibid., 133.
88. Ibid.

"This Bird Made an Art of Being Vile"

89. As Kristen Angierski similarly notes in chapter 10 of this volume, "Ecohorror exists in the revelation of horrific truths about human treatment of nonhuman others" (225).
90. Gregory, *Cormorant*, 133.
91. Ibid., 142.
92. Ibid., 143.
93. Ibid., 144.
94. Ibid., 145.
95. Haraway, *Companion Species Manifesto*, 50.
96. Gregory, *Cormorant*, 147.
97. Ibid., 147–48.
98. Haraway, *Staying with the Trouble*, 4.

References

Bellanca, Mary Ellen. "The Monstrosity of Predation in Daphne du Maurier's 'The Birds.'" *ISLE: Interdisciplinary Studies in Literature and Environment* 18, no. 1 (Winter 2011): 26–46.

Berger, John. *About Looking*. New York: Pantheon Books, 1980.

The Birds. Directed by Alfred Hitchcock, performances by Tippi Hedren, Rod Taylor, and Jessica Tandy. Alfred J. Hitchcock Productions, 1963.

Burt, Jonathan. *Animals in Film*. London: Reaktion Books, 2002.

Calarco, Matthew. *Thinking Through Animals: Identity, Difference, Indistinction*. Stanford, CA: Stanford University Press, 2015.

Derrida, Jacques. *The Animal That Therefore I Am*. Translated by David Wills. New York: Fordham University Press, 2008.

du Maurier, Daphne. "The Birds." In *The Birds and Other Stories*, 7–43. New York: Penguin Books, 1968.

Freud, Sigmund. *The Uncanny*. Translated by David McLintock. New York: Penguin Books, 2003.

Fudge, Erica. *Pets*. Stocksfield, UK: Acumen, 2008.

Gregersdotter, Katarina, Nicklas Hållén and Johan Höglund. Introduction to *Animal Horror Cinema: Genre, History, and Criticism*, edited by Katarina Gregersdotter, Johan Höglund, and Nicklas Hållén, 1–18. New York: Palgrave Macmillan, 2015.

Gregory, Stephen. *The Cormorant*. New York: St. Martin's Press, 1986.

Haraway, Donna J. *The Companion Species Manifesto: Dogs, People, and Significant Otherness*. Chicago: Prickly Paradigm, 2003.

———. *Staying with the Trouble: Making Kin in the Chthulucene*. Durham, NC: Duke University Press, 2016.

Jaws. Directed by Steven Spielberg, performances by Richard Dreyfuss, Roy Scheider, and Robert Shaw. Universal Pictures, 1975.

King, Richard J. *The Devil's Cormorant: A Natural History*. Lebanon: University of New Hampshire Press, 2013.

Kristeva, Julia. *Powers of Horror: An Essay on Abjection*. New York: Columbia University Press, 1982.

Plumwood, Val. "Being Prey." In *The New Earth Reader: The Best of Terra Nova*, edited by David Rothenberg and Marta Ulvaeus, 76–91. Cambridge, MA: MIT Press, 1999.

Rust, Stephen A., and Carter Soles. "Ecohorror Special Cluster: 'Living in Fear, Living in Dread, Pretty Soon We'll All Be Dead.'" *ISLE: Interdisciplinary Studies in Literature and Environment* 21, no. 3 (Summer 2014): 509–12.

9.
The Shape of Water and Post-pastoral Ecohorror

Robin L. Murray and
Joseph K. Heumann

When Colonel Richard Strickland (Michael Shannon) of the secret Occam Aerospace Research Center introduces General Hoyt (Nick Searcy) to Guillermo del Toro's latest monster, Amphibian Man, in *The Shape of Water* (2017), he highlights both its monstrous qualities and its connections with environmental issues rooted in post-pastoral concerns. Referring to the creature, Strickland exclaims, "Ain't that something? Ugly as sin. The natives in the Amazon worshipped it.... They were primitives, sir. Tossed offerings into the water—flowers, fruit, crap like that. Tried to stop the oil drill with bows and arrows. That didn't end too well." The throwaway line about oil drilling explicitly demonstrates how the creature's capture is inextricably connected with environmental resource exploitation and the figurative cannibalism of colonial manifest destiny. But it also connects *The Shape of Water* with ecohorror and what anthropologist Jack D. Forbes calls the weitiko/wendigo disease: "the disease of exploitation." As Forbes asserts, "Imperialism and exploitation are forms of cannibalism and, in fact, are precisely those forms of cannibalism which are most diabolical or evil."[1] That is, imperialism and exploitation are symptoms of a wendigo disease linking the horrors of cannibalism with the figurative consumption of the South American frontier.

The film's connections with the colonial spaces of the Amazon complicate its approach to the nature/culture binary, moving traditional pastoral ideals toward the postcolonial, dark, and/or post-pastoral, as when Strickland transforms a pastoral Amazonian paradise into an oil field and an amphibian god into an ugly creature.[2] Whereas most critics see *The Shape of Water* as a fairy tale with traditional pastoral elements rather than as a monster movie, del Toro blurs the boundaries between these genres and thus moves the film toward this "darker" post-pastoral vision that combines the ecology of the pastoral with the horror of exploitation. Terry Gifford suggests that the post-pastoral negotiates a resolution between traditional pastoral and its anti-pastoral opposite. Instead of attacking idealized pastoral visions of nature by invoking contrasting features such as harsh and unattractive realism, the post-pastoral "recognises the dangers of a complacent view of our fragile relationship with nature, seeking to avoid hubris"[3] and the exploitation that traditional pastoral texts celebrate. *The Shape of Water* promotes a similar recognition through a mixed-genre approach that stresses interdependence.

Del Toro illuminates the reasons for this blurring of genres that move the film toward post-pastoral ecohorror when he claims the two genres are "very similar," so much so that "the original *Cinderella* is a horror story, so is *Red Riding Hood* and so forth. I think that horror and the fairy tale walk hand in hand."[4] By drawing on visuals of horror—including low-key lighting and cool colors—and on what del Toro calls the "mechanics" of the fairy tale, *The Shape of Water* defines a post-pastoral ecohorror rooted in colonialism and the wendigo disease. As Rob Nixon asks in *Slow Violence and the Environmentalism of the Poor*, "What happens when memories of colonial space intrude upon pastoralism, disturbing its pretensions to national self-definition and self-containment?"[5] For Nixon, the answer to this query highlights a new kind of pastoralism, the postcolonial pastoral, which "refracts an idealized nature through memories of environmental and cultural degradation in the colonies."[6] *The Shape of Water* seems to agree. Amphibian Man clearly draws on this version of the pastoral, as a victim of resource exploitation by literal and economic colonizers in the Amazon. But the creature also offers a post-pastoral solution based in interspecies love. Terry Gifford asserts that such a view of the post-pastoral "might be able to nudge us into some ways of answering the most crucial question of our time: what is the right relationship by which people and planet can live together?"[7] By combining the monster of the horror genre with the pastoral idealism of the fairy tale, *The Shape of Water* offers a path beyond the disease of exploitation toward interdependence and what del Toro calls love.

Incorporating post-pastoral elements, *The Shape of Water* not only highlights how wendigo-driven violence against the natural world limits the relationship between human and nonhuman but also blurs distinctions between the human and the more-than-human to promote ecological awareness. As del Toro explains, the film provides "an antidote to the skepticism of living"[8] and is also "about beauty and love. . . . The creature is the shape of love, in a way." According to Victoria Nelson's *Gothicka: Vampire Heroes, Human Gods, and the New Supernatural*, del Toro called his connection with creatures outside the human realm "a spiritual reality as strong as when people say, I accept Jesus in my heart. Well, at a certain age, I accepted monsters into my heart."[9] Through such genre-mixing, *The Shape of Water* pulls us toward a post-pastoral vision of nature, asking us to rethink our relationship with the natural world and choose love over exploitation and terror, interdependence over fear.

Most reviewers note del Toro's powerful genre-mixing without connecting it with environmental concerns,[10] but Kenneth Turan of the *Los Angeles Times* elucidates possible ecocritical connections with the film. Turan explores the multiple genres evident in *The Shape of Water*, showcasing how the film draws on the creature feature, spy drama, film noir, and musical. But Turan also highlights ways the film's merging of genres quietly addresses social, cultural, and environmental ills, suggesting that "plot elements involving racial and sexual differences allow *Shape of Water* to deftly work in a subtext about how society treats the other in its midst, whether it be otherworldly or the ordinary folks next door."[11] Turan explores exploitation from racism and ableism to homophobia and classism while also illuminating how inserting the "otherworldly" Amphibian Man in the mix highlights the film's potential environmental message, primarily because this creature so closely parallels that of the *Creature from the Black Lagoon* (1954). *Creature* tells the story of a scientific expedition to the Amazon to investigate the origins of a strange fossil of a hand with webbed fingers. The narrative reaches its climax in the Black Lagoon, when the scientists disrupt a lone fish-man's home and battle one another over both the creature's fate and Lawrence's (Julia Adams) romantic future. But the film leaves unanswered questions about the fish-man, such as an evolutionary missing link, relying on melodrama to justify science's exploitation of the lagoon and its more-than-human inhabitant.

When del Toro viewed the film as a small boy, he had other questions that broach post-pastoral possibilities in *The Shape of Water*: "Why — he wondered even then — did the creature never get the girl? Why, indeed."[12] Doug Jones, who plays Amphibian Man, amplifies Turan's claims. According to Jones, del Toro "fell in love with" Julia Adams and the Gill-man during a scene in which "Julia Adams . . . swims while the Gill-man follows several feet below."[13] *The Shape of Water*'s take on the "monster" offers a genre-blended affirmation of the power of love that's missing from *Creature from the Black Lagoon*. By blending horror, classic "nature attacks" ecohorror, and fairy-tale pastoral, *The Shape of Water* points toward interconnected relationships between human and nonhuman nature that benefit both.

The Shape of Water and/as Horror

The most obvious element of horror in *The Shape of Water* is its monster, the most essential ingredient of the horror genre, according to Noël Carroll's iconic *The Philosophy of Horror: Or, Paradoxes of the Heart*, Jeffrey Jerome Cohen's *Monster Theory*, Maria Beville's *The Unnamable Monster in Literature and Film*, and Robin Wood's "An Introduction to the American Horror Film." Clearly del Toro appreciates monsters, from the Judas Breed of *Mimic* (1997) and the Faun and Pale Man of *Pan's Labyrinth* (2006) to the vampire hunter Blade of *Blade II* (2002), Hellboy and Abe Sapien of *Hellboy I* (2004) and *II* (2008), and the *kaiju* of *Pacific Rim* (2013). But humans also morph into monsters, both figuratively and literally, as we see in the transformations of a loving grandfather into a vampire seeking eternal life in *Cronos* (1993) or of suffering children and women into ghosts seeking revenge in *The Devil's Backbone* (2001) and *Crimson Peak* (2015).

Del Toro's exploration of the monster reaches its apex in *The Shape of Water*, where the monstrous aligns with the gendered, sexualized, and racialized Other and where Strickland's character both counters and parallels Amphibian Man. Set against the backdrop of 1960s Cold War–era America in the hidden, high-security Occam Aerospace Research Center, *The Shape of Water* highlights how Amphibian Man (a secret, classified experiment) changes the lives of both the predator Strickland and those he exploits: mute janitor Elisa (Sally Hawkins); her African American coworker, Zelda (Octavia Spencer); her disgraced gay neighbor, Giles (Richard Jenkins); and scientist and Soviet spy Dr. Robert Hoffstetler (Michael Stuhlbarg). By juxtaposing the character of a traditional creature-feature monster (Amphibian Man) with that of middle-class patriarch Strickland, *Shape of Water* places constructions of the monster at its center, rewriting and expanding them for the film's post-pastoral take on ecohorror.

Characters' reactions to the creature amplify his role as monster in the film. Because Dr. Hoffstetler resembles mad scientists in big bug movies such as *Bug* (1975) and *The Nest* (1988) and in creature features like *Swamp Thing* (1982), his responses to the creature align with theirs. In these earlier films, scientists become enthralled by the creatures they study, ultimately transforming them with tragic consequences. Hoffstetler may have more positive intentions, but he too is awed by Amphibian Man's biology, declaring, "This creature, Sir, I've never seen anything like it. Ever. It can alternate between two entirely separate breathing mechanisms." For Hoffstetler, the creature is a way to gain knowledge, for "long-term survivability in space," as he explains to General Hoyt, and he provides the correct greens for the creature's habitat in Elisa's bathtub after he is freed from his laboratory prison. Zelda also emphasizes the creature as a "thing" and looks shocked when she realizes Elisa sees him as a romantic partner. Even when Zelda warns Elisa that Strickland is coming to her apartment, she tells Elisa she must leave and "take the thing with you" to emphasize its still-monstrous difference.[14] Giles witnesses this monstrous side when the creature grows curious and explores his apartment. After watching part of a *Mr. Ed* episode in which the horse hero volunteers as an astronaut, the creature notices a cat and wants to hunt it. When Giles finds the creature feeding on his pet in the living room, he yells out in anger, frightening the creature, who slashes Giles's arm and runs.

The Shape of Water draws on traditional character and narrative elements from the horror genre, including its critique of Cold War rhetoric and irresponsible science in the hands of the military and its construction of villains as monstrous "things." It also highlights multiple visual motifs of the genre. In the underground realm of the research center, faces are lit from below and the lighting changes from browns and yellows to ghastly blues and greens, exaggerating the whiteness of Strickland's and his assistant Fleming's (David Hewlett) faces. This underworld, with its massive chains and baroque torture chamber vault, recalls Expressionist films such as *Nosferatu* (1922) and *Metropolis* (1927) as well as Hollywood's *Frankenstein* (1931) and *Bride of Frankenstein* (1935).

Somber lighting, flash camera movements promoting shocking introductions to characters, and settings that create a sense of total secrecy and enclosure also heighten the horror of the film. Low-key lighting enhances the murky underground and promotes shadows in Giles's and Elisa's apartments. By nearly concealing the faces of these two characters in scenes that highlight their status as outsiders separated from the norm by their sexuality, social class, or literal or figurative lack of voice, this low-key lighting visually suggests a question that Gifford proposes as a post-pastoral call for environmental activism: "Is the exploitation of our planet aligned with exploitation of human minorities?"[15] Low-key lighting in Hoffstetler's apartment draws on both film noir and horror conventions, emphasizing Soviet intrigue and portending horrific violence. Flash camera movements most obviously elicit the fear associated with horror, as when Elisa first meets Amphibian Man and shows the shock of terror when a webbed hand slaps the glass in its tank. The throwback to traditional Hollywood editing amplifies Elisa's emotional response, with an establishing shot that emphasizes potential terror before a quick shot of the webbed hand hitting the tank. These stylistic conventions complicate the fairy-tale elements in the film's opening and Elisa's role as fairy-tale princess.

Because horror settings tend to be interior, domestic spaces, the camera takes viewers into a variety of "homes" violated by the film's human and nonhuman monsters, expanding on Bernice M. Murphy's view of the cabin as an American replacement for the Gothic haunted castle in horror film and literature.[16] The domestic spaces and relationships of victims take center stage in *The Shape of Water*, emphasizing its adherence to visual motifs of the horror genre. The prisonlike conditions of the monster's large tank filled with murky green swamp water draw on such horror settings and reinforce a corporate office structure that promotes exploitation. In this horrific setting, manual laborers are separated from scientists in their white lab coats, and military/corporate elite in their crisp suits or officers' uniforms contrast with the men and women drably dressed and waiting in long lines to punch the time clock. This factory may be deep underground and full of strange experiments, but the everyday men and women are as drone-like as those in *Metropolis*. The infinite corporate structure that encloses the monster is no more oppressive than are the working conditions of the wage slaves carrying mops and buckets to clean up messes left by the various experiments that we not only see but also know must be happening down the endless corridors. These physical structures reify ideological and economic constraints and amplify the wendigo role that Strickland plays in the film, that of a colonizer willing to confine the creature and exploit humanity and the more-than-human for profit and power, figuratively consuming them to assuage his greedy hunger for a control as unlimited as that of a prison warden.

As in all his creations, del Toro's control over the film's mise-en-scène, color, and cinematic strategies is combined with a carefully constructed soundscape to enhance horror. The eerie rattling of the creature's chain evokes discomfort, promising the shock of grotesque monsters or ghosts, but the sound itself hurts the ears, emulating the pain of captivity. On- and offscreen shrieks from Amphibian Man parallel Strickland's yells of pain when the creature retaliates and amputates his fingers. The film amplifies these sounds of fear and pain by juxtaposing them with scenes of Elisa's lack of voice and Strickland's craving for a silence that moves him to cover his wife's mouth with his bleeding injured hand during their lovemaking. Muffled voices from the movie theater and television emphasize this literal and figurative silencing found throughout the film, as when Giles and an unnamed African American couple are ousted from the Dixie Pie Restaurant and when Zelda struggles to be heard both at work and in her own home. By juxtaposing screams of pain from Strickland and the creature with gestures that silence women, gay men, and African Americans, the soundscape again illuminates the film's integration of post-pastoral ideals that align exploitation of humanity with exploitation of the more-than-human.

Readings of the idea of the monster amplify the post-pastoral elements implicit in horror conventions. By drawing on environmental roots and conflicts between human and nonhuman nature, such views of the monster as those of Paul Wells and Noël Carroll offer a space for the post-pastoral and its emphasis on our complex relationship with the natural world. Wells takes an interdisciplinary approach to horror, asserting that horror film "has interrogated the deep-seated effects of change and responded to the newly determined grand narratives of social, scientific, and philosophical thought."[17] Carroll also highlights the genre's connection with a disrupted natural world when he declares, "In works of horror, the humans regard the monsters they meet as abnormal, as disturbances of the natural order."[18]

These environmentally grounded views of horror are also tied to post-pastoral elements. Wells, especially, offers a definition of horror emphasizing features of the post-pastoral. By combining Karl Marx's critique of classicism and exploitation of the powerless with Darwin's theories of evolution, Wells brings to mind Gifford's suggestions regarding the alliance of human and nonhuman exploitation in post-pastoral approaches, a connection *The Shape of Water* showcases by linking Amphibian Man with Elisa, Giles, and Zelda. But Carroll's focus on monsters as disturbances of the natural order also lines up with post-pastoral concerns, including its focus on how "our inner nature echoes [our] outer nature"[19] and how we might "heal our alienation from our home."[20] In *The Shape of Water*, Strickland's dead fingers—part of his outer nature—are echoed by an inner nature focused on vivisecting a living creature. But Elisa's merger with Amphibian Man brings her home. Aligning these conventions of horror with environmental questions begins to shift *The Shape of Water* toward post-pastoral ecohorror, a shift reinforced by its fairy-tale elements.

Fairy Tales and the Pastoral in *The Shape of Water*

As post-pastoral ecohorror, *The Shape of Water* connects visions of the monster with conventions of classic fairy tales and their complex interrogations of the pastoral and post-pastoral.[21] Connecting horror with the fairy tale moves the film's traditional pastoral elements toward a post-pastoral vision, opening a space for an ecohorror promoting interdependence and what del Toro calls "beauty and love." Del Toro explicitly aligns *The Shape of Water* with the fairy tale, integrating multiple stylistic and narrative elements that complicate traditional pastoral views. Steven Swann Jones lays out four primary narrative elements we see in *The Shape of Water*: fantasy or magic used "to underscore and affirm a moral propriety in the universe,"[22] a heroic quest of sorts, a happy ending, and "a good and deserving, albeit modest and somewhat ordinary, person, who is being unfairly afflicted by a problem."[23] Amphibian Man clearly represents the film's magical quality and moral center. And Elisa, Giles, and Zelda not only represent good and deserving persons but also perform a successful heroic quest when they free the creature from Strickland, his would-be vivisector and, from a post-pastoral perspective, colonizer and figurative wendigo.

The film's happy ending also showcases a story structure found frequently in the fairy tale, one beginning with "once upon a time" and ending with "they lived happily ever after." The film opens and closes with a voice-over narration from Giles that explicitly connects the story's authentic 1960s US civil rights and Cold War themes with the fantastical setting and characters of the fairy tale. Giles's opening voice-over sounds like the "once upon a time" frequently found in fairy tales, even including a fair prince and a faraway fantastic setting. Giles declares, "Would I tell you about the time? It happened a long time ago, in the days of a fair Prince's reign. Or would I tell you about the place? A small city near the coast but far from everything else?" And Giles's narration also establishes Elisa's role as a fairy-tale princess: "Or would I tell you about her? The princess without voice?" The opening ends by introducing the film's fairy-tale themes of love, monsters, and a happily-ever-after ending: "Or perhaps I would just warn you about the truth of these facts and the tale of love and loss and the monster that tried to destroy it all." The film's concluding narration reinforces this fairy-tale structure, with Giles exclaiming, "If I told you about it, what would I say? That they lived happily ever after? I believe they did. That they were in love—that they remained in love? I'm sure that is true." This opening and closing clearly connects with the "Once upon a time" beginning and "They lived happily ever after" ending of most fairy tales. But it also runs parallel with more traditional pastoral ideals that separate nature from the real world in which we live. Elisa transforms into a princess only in the fantastic realm Giles and the creature create, a world outside the exploitative workplace and 1960s milieu.

Other fairy-tale elements more explicitly connect the film with the environmental issues and post-pastoral leanings on display. Ann Gadd explores the use of mirrors in fairy tales "as the gateway between this world and other realms or levels of consciousness," for example, emphasizing their transformation from looking glass to "tool of a seer" in tales like "Snow White and the Seven Dwarfs"[24] or like the reflective waters of the Amazon River from which colonizers extract Strickland's Amphibian Man "asset." The Amazon forest and river also align with Jack Zipes's suggestion that in many fairy tales, "the forests are often enchanted," like the magical "emerald forest of the Amazon where the creature was worshipped by natives as a God" and where "lakes, ponds and seas that are difficult to cross . . . serve as the home for supernatural creatures."[25] In *The Shape of Water*, a mirror also becomes such a gateway when it reflects back Giles's growing hairline after Amphibian Man touches his head. Because Amphibian Man is ripped from his Amazon River home, *The Shape of Water* explicitly integrates these fairy-tale tropes.

Even more powerfully, water is the source of life as we know it. In fact, Amphibian Man's life depends on submersion in water, a point highlighted from the opening submerged underwater shots. According to David Burne, it is the "medium of life" and "at some point, all biogeochemical cycles involve water, because water forms the fluid environment inside all living things [to our knowledge]. But water also moves in a cycle of its own."[26] Water, then, both sustains and is contained by life, and, of course, it contains life forms of its own as an ecosystem—a biogeochemical cycle—in which plant and animal life thrives. We see this biogeochemical cycle disrupted in *The Shape of Water* when Strickland and Hoyt exploit Amphibian Man and the Amazon's resources and the cycle restored when Elisa, Zelda, Giles, and Hoffstetler rescue and release him. As David T. Mitchell and Sharon L. Snyder note, "Water's fluidity takes the shape of its container while also shifting the boundaries of that which attempts to bracket it."[27] And it is water that in the end saves Elisa, in the arms of her subaquatic lover.[28]

These fairy-tale elements promote a more complex post-pastoral vision that encourages interdependent relationships between humans and nonhuman nature and moves beyond initial literary definitions such as those Terry Gifford provides: "The specifically literary tradition, involving a retreat from the city to the countryside . . . , more generally, 'any literature that describes the country with an implicit or explicit contrast to the urban'; and the pejorative sense in which 'pastoral' implies an idealisation of rural life that obscures the realities of labour and hardship."[29] These last two kinds of pastoral might dominate the narrative of *The Shape of Water* if separations between Amphibian Man and humanity were maintained. But their literal and figurative merger moves the film beyond traditional pastoral definitions and toward the post-pastoral. Gifford suggests that a post-pastoral approach might promote environmental awareness and action for readers (and viewers) by emphasizing features such as "humility in the face of the creative-destructive forces of nature,"[30] "accepting our responsibility for our relationship with nature and its dilemmas,"[31] and recognizing "that the exploitation of nature is often accompanied by the exploitation of the less powerful."[32]

The Shape of Water explicitly addresses multiple post-pastoral questions evoked by Gifford's definition, moving readers and viewers from exploitation toward environmental activism. It emphatically answers yes to the question, "Can awe in the face of nature (e.g., Landscapes) lead to humility in our species, reducing our hubris?"[33] Amphibian Man illuminates the possibilities of awe in the face of nature and does lead to humility in humanity, thus reducing our hubris. Clearly Elisa, Zelda, and Giles respond with humble awe when encountering Amphibian Man. But, by the film's climax, even Strickland recognizes the creature's awesomeness, exclaiming, "Fuck, you ARE a god."

Most emphatically, the film addresses the last and perhaps most complex of Gifford's post-pastoral questions: "Is the exploitation of our planet aligned with our exploitation of human minorities?"[34] Amphibian Man and Strickland serve as "monstrous" foils for each other. But after freeing him, Elisa, Zelda, and Giles also connect with the creature and the natural world he represents. Strickland most explicitly exploits Elisa, Zelda, and Amphibian Man, highlighting their alignment not only as their bully of a boss but also as a violent predator who intimidates and threatens to assault Zelda and sexually harasses Elisa, just as he exploits the natural world. As the patriarch of a heterosexual nuclear family, Strickland is also overtly linked with a wider mainstream middle-class white culture, a culture that exploits anyone outside its limited parameters. Strickland's two children even watch an episode of *The Many Loves of Dobie Gillis* (1959–63) focused on Maynard G. Krebs's (Bob Denver) desire to travel to the Amazon jungle in South America, accentuating Strickland's roles as literal and figurative colonizer—literally conquering the Amazon for its oil and nonhuman assets and figuratively subjugating his family and employees. Post-pastoral questions of awe and exploitation merge in the film's last scenes when, in a fit of rage, Strickland kills both Elisa and Amphibian Man in a figurative rape of nature but is awestruck when the creature reawakens,[35] pointing the way toward the ecocritical possibilities of the post-pastoral mode.

The Shape of Water and/as Post-pastoral Ecohorror

By blending classic horror tropes with pastoral elements of the fairy tale, *The Shape of Water* embodies a more complex definition of ecohorror, one suggesting that embracing our interdependent relationships with nonhuman nature may save us all. The work of ecocritics and ecocinema and media scholars underlines this complex view of ecohorror. In their introduction to a special issue of *ISLE* focused on ecohorror literature and media, Stephen A. Rust and Carter Soles argue for "a more expansive definition of ecohorror" that includes "analyses of texts in which humans do horrific things to the natural world."[36] We apply a similar definition through a variety of lenses in *Monstrous Nature*, showcasing the human causes of ecohorror while also emphasizing solutions based in organismic approaches to ecology. Combining horror with post-pastoral elements of the fairy tale promotes the love del Toro believes will heal the wendigo disease by highlighting the multiple ways nature is constructed as monster in *The Shape of Water*, but this combination also demonstrates what connects these seemingly divergent generic approaches: a human cause and a biotic solution. Humanity may contribute to the malevolent elements of nature on the big screen, moving us toward a definition of ecohorror that "is fundamentally predicated upon a relationship between humanity and nature that does not allow for their interconnectedness."[37] And, as Christy Tidwell declares, "human and nonhuman are never truly separate."[38]

Strickland's responses to Amphibian Man illustrate more violent approaches to ecohorror. For example, he views Amphibian Man as a monster despite evidence that illustrates how much they resemble each other, rejecting anthropomorphic relationships based on either violence or compassion. Strickland also highlights the power of human ecology, demonstrating the monstrous metamorphosis that an environment destroyed by war may cause. He sees the creature as an evolutionary aberration and menace and takes a hypermasculine approach to its plight, viciously attacking it with his cattle prod and threatening to vivisect it for the military. For him, water is not a life source but a tool, providing him not only with Amphibian Man's "secrets" but also potentially with a silent sexual partner. In fact, he deliberately spills his water to bring Elisa upstairs to mop it for him. "I bet I could make you squawk a little," he tells her as she cleans. As the film's figurative wendigo, Strickland sees both nature and women's bodies as "landscapes" there for the taking for much of the film, changing his attitude only fleetingly when the creature surprises him with awe.

Elisa, Zelda, Giles, and Hoffstetler, however, demonstrate more positive takes on ecohorror, highlighting how the film's genre-mixing may invite interdependent resolutions. For example, instead of condemning Amphibian Man as an evolutionary aberration, they rescue him, choosing what Joseph Meeker calls a comic evolutionary narrative that recognizes the power of relationships—with one another as well as with the natural world.[39] In a more positive take on anthropomorphic approaches to ecohorror, they also each move beyond seeing Amphibian Man as a horrific monster and highlight to varying degrees how ecohorror might address post-pastoral questions. Hoffstetler represents a more positive vision of science than in most ecohorror stories and wishes to learn from the creature rather than destroying it, as Strickland, Hoyt, and Hoffstetler's Soviet bosses would prefer. He even declares to Hoyt, "You cannot under any circumstance kill this creature!" Zelda participates in the rescue because she supports her friend but also seems to connect his plight to her own, a more positive approach to human ecology and a response to the post-pastoral question "Is the exploitation of our planet aligned with our exploitation of human minorities?"[40] Giles also participates out of loyalty to Elisa, realizing she alone stands by him and accepts his sexuality as a positive contrast to Strickland's hypermasculinity. Yet he also seems to recognize that he is "part of nature's creative-destructive processes,"[41] telling the creature, "Maybe we're both just relics." Elisa fully embraces Amphibian Man as an anthropomorphic partner, teaching him sign language, sharing music, dancing with him, and joining him in an aquatic marriage bed.

Lee Gambin's exploration of *The Creature from the Black Lagoon* as ecohorror most clearly highlights the possibilities of del Toro's genre-mixing. Gambin argues that *Creature* fulfills the requirements of ecohorror, drawing on both evolution and anthropomorphism for its critique of irresponsible science.[42] By suggesting its fish-man may serve as an evolutionary link between nonhuman and human nature, the film also suggests the potential healing power of interdependence, especially as del Toro rewrites its creature through a loving lens. Del Toro takes this "ancestor" ecohorror film and transforms its tropes in *The Shape of Water*, creating an interdependent solution to ecohorror issues by merging classic monster horror features with fairy-tale and post-pastoral elements. The film explicitly connects with *Creature*, nearly looking like an unlikely sequel to its ancestor. Both films highlight webbed hands, but instead of the fossil in *Creature*, *The Shape of Water* first shows us a living hand with webbed fingers slamming on its glass aquatic tank when Elisa places both her hands on its surface. But when Elisa dumps her bucket of water to flush out blood under a piece of machinery, she discovers two of Strickland's fingers, highlighting how hands brutally link him to Amphibian Man. In a parallel scene, the creature takes on a similar predator role when he stalks and slaughters one of Giles's house cats, shocking Giles and racing away with the cat's blood on his hands. The bloody webbed handprint he leaves outside a movie theater reinforces this tie to *The Creature* and to Strickland.[43]

To stress the possibilities of such a biotic community based in interdependence, *The Shape of Water* intertwines elements of the horror genre with those of the post-pastoral. The film opens and closes with underwater scenes that merge the cool color schemes and lighting of horror with the post-pastoral and the human and nonhuman aquatic worlds. During the opening dream sequence, fish and algae accompanied by a musical theme float under a low-key overhead kitchen light, but the camera pans toward an opening door that reveals floating furniture surrounded by fish. While a voice-over introduces Elisa and her role as hero in both fairy tale and horror, Elisa swims through the scene before an alarm clock jolts us from the dream in which she literally joins with nonhuman aquatic nature. The green color scheme of the film enhances the bonds between these worlds and the multiple genres they signify, from the more post-pastoral bright greens of Elisa's and Giles's apartments and the horror-driven darker gray-green of the lab and Hoffstetler's apartment to the comic pastoral yellow-green of Elisa's sweater and multiple slices of key-lime pie and the blue-green teal of Strickland's Cadillac and suburban ranch-house decor. And, of course, Amphibian Man explicitly aligns these green elements with the nonhuman natural world using his own green coloring broken by an erotic sparkle of blue. Stacy Alaimo asserts that this image "suggests coral reef fishes, or more particularly, deep sea creatures that communicate via bioluminescent flashes."[44] As a literal connection between colonized and colonizer, Amphibian Man also embodies the promise of interdependence revealed when ecohorror meets the post-pastoral—a focus on life and love for humanity and the natural world.

The film reinforces this spotlight on life and love born of interdependence, made more possible from a genre-blended perspective, by integrating eggs as symbols of fertility and rebirth in multiple scenes. Scenes with boiled eggs highlight the growing bond between Elisa and Amphibian Man as well as the merging of horror with the post-pastoral. Elisa's first offering of an egg draws on horror imagery. In the lab, Amphibian Man hides underwater when Elisa enters, and a rattling chain serves as the only evidence of his presence. When she offers the first egg, the "creature" even screams, using his own fear of humanity to scare her away and jolt viewers. Ultimately, though, he takes the egg when Elisa remains calm, juxtaposing the initial horror of the scene with post-pastoral questions. As she shares her lunch with a creature who should frighten her, Elisa seems to ask, "What are the implications of recognising that we are part of nature's creative-destructive processes?"[45] The links between horror and the post-pastoral associated with the egg imagery also include Strickland in subsequent scenes. While Strickland calls the creature an affront out of the river muck in South America and merely an asset the military might use against the Russians, Amphibian Man places eggshells beside his pool and purrs. In multiple scenes after this, Elisa and Amphibian Man share eggs to highlight their growing bond, reinforced by the egg's symbolism of nonhuman nature, fertility, and rebirth. Strickland, however, grows more and more like those broken shells, his rotting fingers signifying his own embodiment of a figurative cannibal. As Hoyt declares, he is becoming "lost to civilization . . . unborn, unmade, and undone," a prediction confirmed by Strickland's death at the story's end.[46]

By combining horrific elements with a post-pastoral approach, *The Shape of Water* moves ecohorror toward environmental activism based in organismic approaches to ecology. Ultimately, *The Shape of Water* leaves us with a horrific fairy-tale ending that confirms the power of post-pastoral ecohorror and offers a path toward interdependence. The film provides the opportunity for del Toro's dream crush to come true, since the creature finally gets the girl. Although Elisa's romantic connection with Amphibian Man comes at a monstrous cost, evolutionary changes hurried along by the creature's cuts to her throat scars allow her to breathe in her new underwater home. By tackling both the monster of ecohorror and the difficult questions raised by the post-pastoral, *The Shape of Water* also offers possible solutions to the wendigo disease Strickland and Hoyt represent. The film does not erase humanity or destroy the traditional monster. It instead suggests something new. We can rethink our relationship with the natural world and, as del Toro asserts, choose love.

Notes

1. Jack D. Forbes, *Columbus and Other Cannibals: The Weitiko Disease of Exploitation, Imperialism, and Terrorism* (New York: Seven Stories Press, 1992), xix, 24.

2. According to Kristen Angierski's "Superpig Blues: Agribusiness Ecohorror in Bong Joon-ho's *Okja*," chapter 10 in this volume, "To answer the well-worn critiques of the pastoral mode, Terry Gifford theorizes a 'post-pastoral' that 'bypasses the British critical dead end for pastoral by identifying a version of continuity that is itself aware of the dangers of idealized escapism while seeking some form of accommodation between humans and nature'" (220). As Angierski explains, "Post-pastoral is a self-aware pastoral that imagines transspecies accommodation; it emphasizes interrelationality and knotty entanglements instead of estrangement and fear" (220).

3. Terry Gifford, "Pastoral, Antipastoral and Postpastoral as Reading Strategies," in *Critical Insights: Nature and the Environment*, ed. Scott Slovic (Ipswich, MA: Salem Press, 2012), 56.

4. Guillermo del Toro, "Making Monsters," *PressReader.com*, December 7, 2017,

https://www.pressreader.com/uk/fortean-times/20171207/282166471491749.

5. Rob Nixon, *Slow Violence and the Environmentalism of the Poor* (Cambridge, MA: Harvard University Press, 2011), 245.

6. Ibid.

7. Gifford, "Pastoral," 46.

8. Del Toro, "Making Monsters."

9. Victoria Nelson, *Gothicka: Vampire Heroes, Human Gods, and the New Supernatural* (Cambridge, MA: Harvard University Press, 2012), 220.

10. According to Olly Richards of *Empire*, "At his very best, del Toro's work holds dream, nightmare and realism in perfect balance, pulling you into terrible worlds, holding your hand just tight enough that you feel safe. From those fantasy worlds he looks out at our world, in all its cruelty." Steve Persall of the *Tampa Bay Times* calls *The Shape of Water* "a fairy tale of Eros, horror and whimsy, a creature feature doubling as a swooning romance, its bloodiness pumped straight from the heart of master fantasist Guillermo del Toro."

11. Kenneth Turan, review of *The Shape of Water*, directed by Guillermo del Toro, *Los Angeles Times*, December 8, 2017, http://www.latimes.com/entertainment/movies/la-et-mn-the-shape-of-water-review-20171207-story.html.

12. Ibid.

13. Eric Francisco, "'Shape of Water' versus 'Creature from the Black Lagoon': Why 'The Shape of Water' Oscar Win Is Historically Creepy; How the Release of 'Creature from the Black Lagoon' Connects," *Inverse*.com, March 5, 2018, https://www.inverse.com/article/41900-shape-of-water-oscars-2018-creature-black-lagoon-release-date. As Jones asserts, "It was a beautiful and terrifying scene . . . , and [del Toro] said it was in that moment that he fell in love with both of them. He had a crush on Julia Adams, and he had a crush on the creature." Jones even asserts that del Toro's obsession with this possibility grew "to the point of drawing doodles of Julia Adams and the Gillman holding hands on a beach or riding a bicycle or having a picnic."

14. When Zelda sees Elisa smiling uncharacteristically at work, she exclaims, "Stop looking like that," and asks her a series of questions that amplify her disbelief and alarm: "What happened? Why? How? How? Does he? Have a?" And only after Elisa demonstrates the creature's sexual technique does Zelda accept their spectacular connection, but even then with grudging acceptance. Zelda's offhand remark about the creature's "flat down there" sexual anatomy also highlights his difference from other men.

15. Gifford, "Pastoral," 59.

16. Bernice M. Murphy, *The Rural Gothic in American Popular Culture: Backwoods Horror and Terror in the Wilderness* (London: Palgrave Macmillan, 2013), 15–47.

17. Paul Wells, *The Horror Genre: From Beelzebub to Blair Witch* (London: Wallflower Press, 2000), 1.

18. Noël Carroll, *The Philosophy of Horror: Or, Paradoxes of the Heart* (New York: Routledge, 1990), 16.

19. Gifford, "Pastoral," 57.

20. Ibid., 59.

21. Cristina Bacchilega, *Fairy Tales Transformed? Twenty-First Century Adaptations and the Politics of Wonder* (Detroit: Wayne State University Press, 2013), 120.

22. Steven Swann Jones, *The Fairy Tale: The Magic Mirror of the Imagination* (New York: Routledge, 2002), 13.

23. Ibid., 13–17.

24. Ann Gadd, "Fairytales and Symbols," blog, last modified December 1, 2014, http://www.anngadd.co.za/2014/12/fairytales-symbols/.

25. Jack Zipes, "Introduction: Towards a Definition of the Literary Fairy Tale," in *The Oxford Companion to Fairy Tales*, ed. Jack Zipes (Oxford: Oxford University Press, 2016), http://www.oxfordreference.com/view/10.1093/acref/9780199689828.001.0001/acref-9780199689828-miscMatter-7.

26. David Burne, *Get a Grip on Ecology* (London: Weidenfeld and Nicholson, 1999), 18.

27. David T. Mitchell and Sharon L. Snyder, "Room for (Materiality's) Maneuver:

Reading the Oppositional in Guillermo del Toro's *The Shape of Water*," *JCMS: Journal of Cinema and Media Studies* 58, no. 4 (Summer 2019): 156.

28. In "Hydro-eroticism," Jeremy Chow and Brandi Bushman highlight how the "bonding waters and (re)imagining intimacies" of hydro-eroticism in *The Shape of Water* can deconstruct "concepts of the abject, the inhuman, and the brutally violent that are systematically wielded against queer sexuality to discover and amplify a wet, queer futurity" (111).

29. Greg Garrard, *Ecocriticism* (London: Routledge, 2004), 33.

30. Gifford, "Pastoral," 56.

31. Ibid., 57.

32. Ibid., 59.

33. Ibid., 56.

34. Ibid., 59.

35. In chapter 2 of this volume, "Spiraling Inward and Outward: Junji Ito's *Uzumaki* and the Scope of Ecohorror," Christy Tidwell connects this awe in the face of nature to cosmic horror.

36. Stephen A. Rust and Carter Soles, "Ecohorror Special Cluster: 'Living in Fear, Living in Dread, Pretty Soon We'll All Be Dead,'" *ISLE: Interdisciplinary Studies in Literature and the Environment* 21, no. 3 (Summer 2014): 509.

37. Christy Tidwell, "Monstrous Natures Within: Posthuman and New Materialist Ecohorror in Mira Grant's *Parasite*," *ISLE: Interdisciplinary Studies in Literature and the Environment* 21, no. 3 (Summer 2014): 539.

38. Ibid.

39. Joseph Meeker, *The Comedy of Survival: Literary Ecology and the Play Ethic* (Tucson: University of Arizona Press, 1997).

40. Gifford, "Pastoral," 59.

41. Ibid., 57.

42. Lee Gambin, *Massacred by Mother Nature: Exploring the Natural Horror Film* (Baltimore: Midnight Marquee, 2012).

43. When Elisa sees this print on the Orpheum Theater door, she shows relief rather than fear, illustrating how del Toro's Amphibian Man differs from the Creature. The scene also hints at a possible interspecies relationship that reifies the interdependence stressed in *The Shape of Water*.

44. Stacy Alaimo, "Wanting All the Species to Be: Extinction, Environmental Visions, and Intimate Aesthetics," *Australian Feminist Studies* 34, no. 102 (2019): 407.

45. Gifford, "Pastoral," 57.

46. Strickland's confrontation with the creature parallels Dawn Keetley's vision of tentacular ecohorror found in chapter 1 of this volume. For Keetley, tentacular ecohorror is nonhuman nature that snatches and snares people it meets. In *The Shape of Water*, the creature's hand serves a similar purpose.

References

Alaimo, Stacy. "Wanting All the Species to Be: Extinction, Environmental Visions, and Intimate Aesthetics." *Australian Feminist Studies* 34, no. 102 (2019): 398–412.

Bacchilega, Cristina. *Fairy Tales Transformed? Twenty-First Century Adaptations and the Politics of Wonder*. Detroit: Wayne State University Press, 2013.

Beville, Maria. *The Unnamable Monster in Literature and Film*. New York: Routledge, 2013.

Blade II. Directed by Guillermo del Toro, performances by Wesley Snipes, Kris Kristofferson, and Ron Perlman. New Line Cinema, 2002.

Bride of Frankenstein. Directed by James Whale, performances by Boris Karloff,

Elsa Lanchester, and Colin Clive. Universal Pictures, 1935.

Burne, David. *Get a Grip on Ecology.* London: Weidenfeld and Nicholson, 1999.

Carroll, Noël. *The Philosophy of Horror: Or, Paradoxes of the Heart.* New York: Routledge, 1990.

Chow, Jeremy, and Brandi Bushman. "Hydro-eroticism." *English Language Notes* 57, no. 1 (2019): 96–115.

Cohen, Jeffrey Jerome, ed. *Monster Theory: Reading Culture.* Minneapolis: University of Minnesota Press, 1996.

Crimson Peak. Directed by Guillermo del Toro, performances by Mia Wasikowska, Jessica Chastain, and Tom Hiddleston. Double Dare You Studios, 2015.

Cronos. Directed by Guillermo del Toro, performances by Federico Luppi, Ron Perlman, and Tamara Shanath. CNCAIMC Studios, 1993.

del Toro, Guillermo. "Making Monsters." *PressReader.com*, December 7, 2017. https://www.pressreader.com/uk/fortean-times/20171207/282166471491749.

The Devil's Backbone. Directed by Guillermo del Toro, performances by Marisa Paredes, Eduardo Noriega, and Federico Luppi. El Deseo Studios, 2001.

Forbes, Jack D. *Columbus and Other Cannibals: The Weitiko Disease of Exploitation, Imperialism, and Terrorism.* New York: Seven Stories Press, 1992.

Francisco, Eric. "'Shape of Water' versus 'Creature from the Black Lagoon': Why 'The Shape of Water' Oscar Win Is Historically Creepy; How the Release of 'Creature from the Black Lagoon' Connects." *Inverse.com*, March 5, 2018. https://www.inverse.com/article/41900-shape-of-water-oscars-2018-creature-black-lagoon-release-date.

Frankenstein. Directed by James Whale, performances by Colin Clive, Mae Clarke, and Boris Karloff. Universal Pictures, 1931.

Gadd, Ann. "Fairytales and Symbols." Blog. Last modified December 1, 2014. http://www.anngadd.co.za/2014/12/fairytales-symbols/.

Gambin, Lee. *Massacred by Mother Nature: Exploring the Natural Horror Film.* Baltimore: Midnight Marquee, 2012.

Garrard, Greg. *Ecocriticism.* London: Routledge, 2004.

Gifford, Terry. "Pastoral, Antipastoral and Postpastoral as Reading Strategies." In *Critical Insights: Nature and the Environment*, edited by Scott Slovic, 42–61. Ipswich, MA: Salem Press, 2012.

Hellboy I. Directed by Guillermo del Toro, performances by Ron Perlman, Doug Jones, and Selma Blair. Revolution Studios, 2004.

Hellboy II: The Golden Army. Directed by Guillermo del Toro, performances by Ron Perlman, Doug Jones, and Selma Blair. Universal Pictures, 2008.

Jones, Steven Swann. *The Fairy Tale: The Magic Mirror of the Imagination.* New York: Routledge, 2002.

Meeker, Joseph. *The Comedy of Survival: Literary Ecology and the Play Ethic.* Tucson: University of Arizona Press, 1997.

Metropolis. Directed by Fritz Lang, performances by Brigitte Helm, Alfred Abel, and Gustav Frohlich. Universum Film, 1927.

Mimic. Directed by Guillermo del Toro, performances by Mira Sorvino, Jeremy Northam, and Alexander Goodwin. Dimension Films, 1997.

Mitchell, David T., and Sharon L. Snyder. "Room for (Materiality's) Maneuver: Reading the Oppositional in Guillermo del Toro's *The Shape of Water.*" *JCMS: Journal of Cinema and Media Studies* 58, no. 4 (Summer 2019): 150–56.

Murphy, Bernice M. *The Rural Gothic in American Popular Culture: Backwoods Horror and Terror in the Wilderness.* London: Palgrave Macmillan, 2013.

Murray, Robin L., and Joseph K. Heumann. *Monstrous Nature: Environment and Horror on the Big Screen.* Lincoln: University of Nebraska Press, 2016.

Nelson, Victoria. *Gothicka: Vampire Heroes, Human Gods, and the New Super-*

natural. Cambridge, MA: Harvard University Press, 2012.

Nixon, Rob. *Slow Violence and the Environmentalism of the Poor*. Cambridge, MA: Harvard University Press, 2011.

Nosferatu. Directed by F. W. Murnau, performances by Max Schreck, Alexander Granach, and Gustav von Wangenheim. Jofa-Atelier Berlin-Johannisthal, 1922.

Pacific Rim. Directed by Guillermo del Toro, performances by Idris Elba, Charlie Hunnam, and Rinko Kikuchi. Warner Bros., 2013.

Pan's Labyrinth. Directed by Guillermo del Toro, performances by Ivana Baquero, Ariadna Gil, and Gergi Lopez. Estudios Picasso, 2006.

Persall, Steve. "'Shape of Water' Mixes Horror, Humor, and Romance in a Creature Feature." *Tampa Bay Times*, December 19, 2017. http://www.tampabay.com/features/movies/-Shape-of-Water-mixes-horror-humor-and-romance-in-a-creature-feature_163711678.

Richards, Olly. Review of *The Shape of Water*, directed by Guillermo del Toro. *Empire*, February 12, 2018. https://www.empireonline.com/movies/shape-water/review/.

Rust, Stephen A., and Carter Soles. "Ecohorror Special Cluster: 'Living in Fear, Living in Dread, Pretty Soon We'll All Be Dead.'" *ISLE: Interdisciplinary Studies in Literature and the Environment* 21, no. 3 (Summer 2014): 509–12.

The Shape of Water. Directed by Guillermo del Toro, performances by Sally Hawkins, Octavia Spencer, and Michael Shannon. Bull Productions, 2017.

Tidwell, Christy. "Monstrous Natures Within: Posthuman and New Materialist Ecohorror in Mira Grant's *Parasite*." *ISLE: Interdisciplinary Studies in Literature and the Environment* 21, no. 3 (Summer 2014): 538–49.

Turan, Kenneth. Review of *The Shape of Water*, directed by Guillermo del Toro. *Los Angeles Times*, December 8, 2017. http://www.latimes.com/entertainment/movies/la-et-mn-the-shape-of-water-review-20171207-story.html.

Wells, Paul. *The Horror Genre: From Beelzebub to Blair Witch*. London: Wallflower Press, 2000.

Wood, Robin. "An Introduction to the American Horror Film." In *Robin Wood on the Horror Film: Collected Essays and Reviews*, 73–110. Detroit: Wayne State University Press, 2018.

Zipes, Jack. "Introduction: Towards a Definition of the Literary Fairy Tale." In *The Oxford Companion to Fairy Tales*, edited by Jack Zipes. Oxford: Oxford University Press, 2016. http://www.oxfordreference.com/view/10.1093/acref/9780199689828.001.0001/acref-9780199689828-miscMatter-7.

Part 4
Being Prey, Being Food

10.
Superpig Blues
Agribusiness Ecohorror in Bong Joon-ho's *Okja*

Kristen Angierski

A more expansive definition of ecohorror . . . includes analyses of texts in which humans do horrific things to the natural world.
—Stephen A. Rust and Carter Soles (2014)

Bong Joon-ho's 2017 Netflix film *Okja* opens with the funereal sound of church bells. Abruptly replacing this ominous, somber song is a light acoustic melody one might expect to introduce a romantic comedy rather than a film about factory farming, GMOs, neoliberalism, corporate greed, and the sociopathic streak slithering through capitalism's most hallowed institutions. This opening aural gesture signals *Okja*'s dizzying affective manipulation and its unruly mixing of genres. As one critic puts it, "South Korean *Okja* could be described as an anticorporate animal-rights children's horror comedy."[1] Indeed, this film about a girl and her pig fighting against cruel and corrupt agribusiness keeps viewers unsteady even as it treads the somewhat familiar ground of child and animal kinship narratives.

What differentiates *Okja* from, for example, *Free Willy* (1993) is its centering of a farmed and genetically modified animal in the context of the Anthropocene: the age in which humans have become a geological entity capable of altering planetary forces once thought to be unalterable. *Okja* delivers a particularly biting critique of Concentrated Animal Feeding Operations (CAFOs), also called factory farms, which are one of the leading causes of environmental devastation globally.[2] Critic Mikaella Clements emphasizes the film's ecological focus, arguing that *Okja* "builds traditional movie tropes around a sharp criticism of neoliberalism and the gross environmental impact of capitalism."[3] *Okja* represents the factory farm as the horrific but logical end point of the capitalist values of maximization and infinite growth at the expense of marginalized beings and precarious ecologies. Thus, *Okja* meets at least the semantic requirements of ecohorror by focusing an unflinching spotlight onto the horrific things humans do to the natural world. Including films such as *Okja* under the dark umbrella of ecohorror does more than expand the genre, however. It also prompts a productive reevaluation of the terms on which standard definitions of ecohorror tend to rely—such as *revenge*, *agency*, *resistance*, and even *horror* itself.

First, *Okja* illustrates the necessity of thinking of agricultural antipastoral narratives *as* ecohorror in the Anthropocene. If ecohorror is about the frightening and violent nature of which humanity is part and to which it has "trans-corporeal" connections,[4] then texts examining agribusiness have their place in theorizing the genre. While the film arguably meets the central criterion of traditional ecohorror—it centers nonhuman resistance and revenge—*Okja* troubles the genre as well, urging (re)consideration of which kinds of nonhuman resistance are efficacious and independent enough to be considered manifestations of ecohorror. In the context of the factory farm, an agricultural modality that controls every aspect of farmed animal life, large-scale nonhuman revolution like that in Jeff VanderMeer's *Annihilation* (2014) or M. Night Shyamalan's *The Happening* (2008) seems improbable. Consequently, *Okja* helpfully reorients the generally grand, even cosmic, vision of ecohorror, directing it toward ecorealism and the small, the incremental, and the largely unsuccessful—farmed animals often die—resistance occurring on CAFOs with and without the help of human allies: allies who work to undermine the "us versus them" dichotomy at the heart of much ecohorror.[5]

Second, *Okja* reveals the potentialities and limitations of satirical ecohorror. Rarely considered a funny genre, ecohorror in *Okja* includes the absurd as an avenue to heavy-handed messaging about the grotesque dissonances that pervade contemporary thinking about animals. The film's morbid humor and campy irreverence potentially puts *Okja* in the category of "bad environmentalist" texts, which Nicole Seymour defines as works that eschew typical environmentalist affects (for example, didacticism, guilt, and shame) in favor of queerer ones: "irreverence, ambivalence, camp."[6] Although queerer eco-affects can productively challenge the gloom-and-doom tone of contemporary environmentalism, there is a risk. Here I highlight how blending satire with ecohorror potentially undermines *Okja*'s animal rights messaging but also asks vitally productive questions of largely white and Western vegan studies.

Third, *Okja* suggests another possible signification of the term *ecohorror*: a satirical one parodying the sensationalizing term *ecoterrorist*. That is, the greatest "ecohorror" of all to the film's villains is a group of quick-to-cry young people who care about animals. Again, the film veers between high sincerity and the absurd, a disorienting high-low swing that echoes the strange rhetorics surrounding vegans and animal rights activists: taking them too seriously and, at the same time, not seriously enough.

Implicit in this interwoven series of arguments are questions I only begin to answer: What is the relationship between ecohorror, vegan studies, and critical animal studies? How can the context of the slaughterhouse productively interrogate ecohorror's definition of resistance—of what counts? How do *Okja*'s aesthetic formulas take on the hyperobject[7] that is factory farming, and how does that demand a (re-)evaluation of what ecohorror is, should be, and can be as a genre inescapably tied to environmental ethics in the Anthropocene?

Okja opens in New York City with a perky Lucy Mirando (Tilda Swinton) attempting to rehabilitate the reputation of Mirando, an agribusiness corporation akin to Monsanto. Echoing Monsanto's well-documented rebranding rhetoric, Lucy Mirando insists that the days of ecodevastation are behind them. Mirando's new core values are "environment and life." She goes on to explain, with the eco-buzzwords "Eco-friendly," "Natural," and "Non-GMO" on a screen behind her, that Mirando is taking on the problem of world hunger by studying and mating superpiglets, a species that first mysteriously appeared in remote Chile. Twenty-six of these pigs will be sent to farmers all over the world, and each will raise their pig for ten years with the goal of growing the "Best Superpig."

Fast-forward ten years and into the mountains of South Korea, where young Mija (An Seo Hyun) has enjoyed the decade-long companionship of her superpig, Okja. When the Mirando corporation's goons, most notably the bizarre Dr. Wilcox (Jake Gyllenhaal), show up to take Okja to New York (Mija had no idea her friend was destined for slaughter) as the Best Superpig, Mija rebels. Refusing the golden pig figurine her grandfather gives her to replace Okja, Mija sprints down the mountain into Seoul and, with the help of the Animal Liberation Front (ALF), eventually frees Okja, though the superpig is strategically recaptured after the ALF fits her with cameras meant to capture Mirando's deceptions and animal abuse. Ultimately, the ALF exposes Mirando, and Mija gets her pig back when she purchases her from the slaughterhouse. As they are leaving the slaughterhouse, an imprisoned superpig pushes a superpiglet into Okja's path. Okja hides the piglet in her mouth, and they escape back to South Korea, presumably to live happily ever after. The system is not exploded, but a post-credit scene assures us that the ALF will continue their work.

Okja's critique of factory farming and Monsanto-style corporate capitalism places it firmly in the tradition of the anti-pastoral, a satirical inversion of the pastoral tradition that represents nature as stable, beautiful, and fertile. Ecocritics often question the environmentalist utility of the pastoral form due to its aestheticization of living landscapes.[8] To answer the well-worn critiques of the pastoral mode, Terry Gifford theorizes a "post-pastoral" that "bypasses the British critical dead end for pastoral by identifying a version of continuity that is itself aware of the dangers of idealized escapism while seeking some form of accommodation between humans and nature."[9] Post-pastoral is a self-aware pastoral that imagines transspecies accommodation; it emphasizes interrelationality and knotty entanglements instead of estrangement and fear.

Interestingly, this critical conversation generally neglects the question of farming. When scholars of the pastoral mention agribusiness at all, it is implied that industrialized agriculture does not fit within the post-pastoral's vision of human-animal accommodation.[10] It would seem, then, that an agribusiness version of the pastoral would have to be its opposite and its negation: the anti-pastoral.

The anti-pastoral looks suspiciously on the pastoral's vision of idyllic nature and injects a heavy dose of ecorealism and often satire into representations of nature-human interrelationality. It is not insignificant that a recent volume on the anti-pastoral, *Dark Nature: Anti-Pastoral Essays in American Literature and Culture,* does not emphasize farming, factory or otherwise, though the volume's editor, Richard J. Schneider, does offer "a uniquely dark view of the agriculturalist perspective" through his fascinating close reading of a novel full of miserable farmer families.[11] Nowhere in this collection, however, is the anti-pastoral linked to factory farming, in part because the volume is more interested in stories of nature attacking humans than in a more literal understanding of anti-pastoral not as antifarming but as that which challenges the pastoral trance under which agribusiness strives to put consumers.

The enormous gap between pastoral farming imagery and the reality of the factory farm is at the center of *Okja*. This version of the anti-pastoral is also inevitably ecohorror because it highlights both the violence enacted on sentient beings and the slow violence enacted on the environment:[12] a violence that will come back to haunt us in the form of escalating global climate disruption. As Stephen A. Rust and Carter Soles argue, ecohorror "assumes that environmental disruption is haunting humanity's relationship to the non-human world."[13] Indeed, the ghosts of climate change future haunt *Okja*'s iteration of an ecohorrific anti-pastoral.

I am thus using *anti-pastoral ecohorror* to describe a filmic world that uses sentimentality and satire to critique factory farming as an ethical and environmental horror against which nonhumans and their human allies resist. In what follows, I engage in a close reading of the film's arguably most emotional denunciations of factory farming, but rather than condemning the sentimental or opposing it in favor of a more "mature" post-pastoral[14]—a condemnation that carries with it the gendering of empathetic feeling—I prefer to read these scenes' emotionality as strategic and competent storytelling. The "mating" scene and the slaughterhouse ending "reveal the silences in those too-comfortable visions of pastoral that are manufactured for an urban readership" or, in this case, a majoritarian omnivorous food community fed images of "happy cows."[15]

Okja's anti-pastoral ecohorror not only smartly comments on the gaps between pastoral imagery and the reality of factory-farmed animal lives but also highlights the links between animal cruelty and sexual violence. The "mating" scene illustrates this linkage most clearly. At this point in the film, Okja has been taken from her home and brought to New York City to be presented as the Best Superpig. The ALF has attached a camera to Okja in hopes of catching Mirando's cruelty on film. As Okja enters the dark holding facility, she encounters deformed superpigs in cages. Dr. Wilcox—the "animal lover"—is the first to greet her. Holding a bottle of alcohol, he explains that Okja will be meeting her "boyfriend," Alfonso, another superpig. The term *boyfriend* occludes the reality of Okja's refusal of consent, masking with language the fact that her desire for this other, unknown pig is irrelevant to those mating her. She is pushed forward with electric prods, a common tool of CAFOs that "delivers the same shock as a live electric fence."[16] After being prodded, Okja is mated against her will. This rape scene is shown to viewers piecemeal, in upsetting glimpses, signifying the near unbearableness of its viewing.

This scene draws on decades of ecofeminist theorizing that argues for an intersectional conception of human and nonhuman oppressions. As Carol J. Adams argues in *The Sexual Politics of Meat*, sexual violence against farmed animals and sexual violence against human women are interlinked, tied together by the process of "objectification, fragmentation, and consumption" that "permits an oppressor to view another being as an object" that can be reduced to body parts and consumed.[17] *Okja* makes the connection between masculinity, meat, and sexual violence when Red, the only woman member of the ALF, has the most severe reaction to the footage, digging her nail into the skin of her hand until it draws blood.

After the deeply upsetting assault scene, Okja is subjected to yet another gendered violation when an increasingly drunk Dr. Wilcox complains, "Lucy Mirando says I'm not supposed to harm you in here. Well, at least not visibly. She wants you perfect for her big telecast. But . . . when a woman humiliates a man in front of his own colleagues, a man is inclined to make his own decisions!" Dr. Wilcox's drunken speech connects the reassertion of bruised masculinity and violence against a (female) animal, again imbricating patriarchal logics of dominance with violence against animals and highlighting the transspecies nature of oppression.[18] Dr. Wilcox then uses a meat extractor to get samples of Okja's flesh, saying, "It's used on beef. I mean, live cows." The verbal slippage from food to animal signals the strategic ways in which farmed animals and their bodies are discussed: *meat* instead of *flesh*, *veal* instead of *baby cow*. Karen Davis explains how journalistic discourse tends toward the same euphemistic practice: "Journalists do not always feel obligated to adhere to standards of precise language where farmed animals are concerned."[19] The mating scene paints an ecohorrific portrait of the gendered underpinnings and euphemisms used to mask the violence of animal exploitation.

The slaughterhouse scene is the pinnacle of the film's emotional antipastoralism, and its portrayal of the abattoir suggests that the industrial slaughterhouse is the consummate ecohorror setting: an edifice set at a purposeful remove from the lights of "civilization," the industrial slaughterhouse and its myriad ecological, human, and nonhuman ills represent a flash point of Anthropocene terrors. A distraught Mija enters the farming complex and passes rows of superpigs behind electric fences, imagery evoking a concentration camp. It is nighttime, emphasizing the secrecy of CAFOs and government support of that secrecy in the form of "Ag-Gag" policies that criminalize the exposure of inhumane agricultural practices.[20] After managing to sneak into the highly securitized building, Mija runs past blood-spattered Spanish-speaking workers, a nod to the "young, male, and/or Hispanic" and vulnerable immigrant majority of the slaughterhouse workforce.[21]

Mija is visually accosted with slabs of superpig flesh, a pool of blood, and superpigs strung up by their legs, stunned and slaughtered. She reaches Okja just as the worker presses the stun gun against Okja's forehead. Desperate, Mija shows the worker a picture of herself and of her childhood companion as a superpiglet. Ultimately, Mija trades her golden pig for Okja, buying her, speaking the only language a corporation understands. But of course, the factory farm remains, and all the superpigs Mija searched through to get to her Okja are left behind. Even as she helps one superpiglet escape, the ending does not feel triumphant. (Most people with whom I've viewed the film cry as Mija and Okja leave the industrial farm.) In this scene, then, the film is resolutely anti-pastoral ecohorror, a deeply sentimental portrait of an ongoing violent food system.

Although the assault and slaughterhouse scenes are not about the environment explicitly, they speak to one of the central catalysts of climate disruption: industrial agribusiness. Moreover, the knotty entanglement of factory-farmed animals and the agro-ecologies in which they've been placed makes wrenching them out of the natural world untenable. Stacy Alaimo's influential understanding of an imbricated human and other-than-human existence encourages and even necessitates consideration of the ecological ties that bind farmed animals to the social and economic ecologies in which they are involuntarily situated. "Agricultural anti-pastoral ecohorror" is thus nearly redundant in the agribusiness context.

While I have focused primarily on Okja's victimization here and the horrific realism of her torture, Okja also resists; she screams, she moves away, and she fights the stream of superpigs into the abattoir. Although her ultimate escape is facilitated by humans—and necessarily so given the capitalist paradigm to which nonhumans are entirely subject and in which they have the legal status of property—Okja is still defiant. The unnamed superpig who hands over her calf to Okja and Mija is also resisting, as well as providing a heart-wrenching portrait of nonhuman parental love. *Okja*'s anti-pastoral ecohorror therefore lies not only in its emotional critiques of CAFOs but also in its depiction of the nonhuman resistance that exists both in the world of the film and the world outside of it, nonhuman resistance I identify as ecohorror, though its scale is smaller and its independent success less recognizable than, for example, the violent, beak-poking revenge of Hitchcock's *The Birds* (1963). As Sarat Colling asserts in an article about real farmed animal escapees, "Nonhuman animals, like human resistors, seek liberation from human exploitation, yet their stories often go unheard."[22] *Okja* tells these stories and foregrounds farmed animals' capacity to protest.

The phrase "anti-pastoral ecohorror" thus *assumes* the presence of farmed animal resistance. It *witnesses*. It automatically grants nonhuman attachment to life and aligns with vegan studies' emphasis on farmed animal agency. Anti-pastoral ecohorror in its very terminology centers nonhuman defiance, small and invisible as that defiance may be, and as such can be understood as a vegan genre in the Anthropocene and in the context of sentimental slaughterhouse narratives like *Okja*.

But *Okja* is not a documentary, and it is neither adequate nor accurate to describe the film as straightforward ecohorror. It is also wacky and satirical, using high exaggeration to parody the co-optation of environmentalist language for corporate gain. Whereas thus far I have emphasized sentimental factory-farming realism, here I center the representational exploitation of farmed animals. Corporate-created imagery and narrative collude with consumers' wishful thinking to fuel CAFOs and mask the prerequisite of meat: a living animal.

In *Okja*, the two CEOs of Mirando, both played by Tilda Swinton, embody the ways in which corporations invested in morally questionable operations rebrand to appeal to a public with ethical concerns. It is clear by the film's end that Lucy and Nancy are two sides of the same coin; Lucy's pig-pink outfits and attempts to distance herself from Nancy ("We are very different people. . . . We have very different business ethics") are revealed to be a corporate greenwashing distraction from what is really more of the same. Indeed, Lucy is behind the violent superpig enterprise. She also dresses in a Korean *hanbok* in a condescending and appropriative attempt to relate to Mija at the Superpig Festival. In short, Lucy represents a greenwashed version of her sister. She is embodied corporate camouflage—a mask. Nancy at the very least is an honest representation of Mirando. When Mija asks why they want to kill Okja, she answers, "We can only sell the dead ones."

Okja also satirizes the perverse use of animal imagery in the selling of animal products. The film's persistent use of pig-pink—in Lucy's dress as well as in decorations—underscores how wishful narratives of complicity drive the marketing of animal products. That is, by putting animal faces and bodies onto animal-based products, agribusiness corporations strive to create a pleasant pastoral narrative in which nonhumans are happy to be farmed. (Perhaps the most flagrant real-world example of this is the 2000 California "Happy Cows" campaign, which created the well-known tag line: "Great cheese comes from Happy Cows. Happy Cows come from California."[23])

Okja highlights the strangeness of marketing animals with animals most overtly during the Superpig Festival, an event with a parade and "pink streamers, pink fireworks." The parade includes floats with women sitting on hay bales and wearing costume pig ears and sausage necklaces. They throw sausage samples into the crowd. Furthering the pastoral imagery, the women are pulled by a tractor. Cheerleaders with pink pom-poms precede a giant pig float pulled by men also dressed as pigs and actively consuming the superpig sausage. The irony of consuming a being whom you are dressed as goes unmentioned. The pig-people additionally provide a visual evocation of the empathy gap between humans and nonhuman animals. Unable to imagine themselves in the hooves of the other (even while costumed as that other), they cannot perform the imaginative labor of empathy. Moreover, they embody the horrific and *cannibalistically* self-destructive nature of CAFOs in the Anthropocene. Happily eating themselves to ecological death, the parade participants pull a giant corporate symbol above their heads, being led, if the climate change metaphor holds, to violence against others and the self.

By allowing viewers to witness the moment of consumption—the anticlimactic moment of chewing at the end of the various tortures that make up the process of superpig production—*Okja* makes the existence of factory farming a communal responsibility. The film disperses blame, and it accuses. The ridiculous hyperevil of Nancy and Dr. Wilcox is in the final instance a result of consumer demand for their product. The comic-book villains of Mirando create a false narrative, yes, but the consumers are complicit in wanting to believe it. If ecohorror exists in the revelation of horrific truths about human treatment of nonhuman others, then this moment of satire exponentially multiplies the horror by placing responsibility for Okja's terror and pain in the hands of many, not just those of a malevolent few at the top of the capitalist food chain.

And it goes beyond food. During Okja's initial transport in Korea, a Mirando executive scolds employees trying to get a picture of the Best Superpig: "I don't want to see this on Instagram or Facebook, okay?" But when the transport truck door closes, he himself takes a smiling selfie with Okja, holding up one side of her mouth to make it seem as though she were smiling: another "happy cow." Poked, prodded, and made a symbol and media spectacle without her consent, Okja's traumas subtly comment on the use of nonhumans as self-serving entertainment.[24] It is worth mentioning that Mija serves a similar role at the Superpig Festival. Mirando demands that, in exchange for Okja's life, Mija participate in the corporation's self-serving drama that poses Mirando as the benevolent organizer of Mija and Okja's reunion rather than as the reason for their separation. Embedded in the film's critique of the use of animals in entertainment, then, is a comment on the use of nonwhite, female, and children's bodies in global corporate marketing campaigns, a strategic optic that muddles the realities of exploitation and, in some cases, actual child labor.

In sum, *Okja*'s satire highlights the dissonances in representational patterns involving farmed animals; marketing tools collude with consumer hopes for farmed animals to create a pastoral narrative that conflicts starkly with reality. *Okja*'s anti-pastoral ecohorror is thus heightened through satire rather than minimized. The satire refuses viewers a sigh of relief by shining a bright light on discomfiting questions. For instance, can one be "an animal lover" and eat animals? To call *Okja* a vegan film, however, would be to misread its ethics, which seem more post- than anti-pastoral. That is, the film's advocacy for animals is more nuanced than the strict negative ethics—one shall not eat meat—implicit in the anti-pastoral.

To begin with, Okja does not neatly "stand in" for all farmed animals. She is a visual composite of many animals: a hippo, a dog, a pig, and a cow. Although a more generous reader might interpret her amalgamative being as commentary on the effects of nonhuman exploitation beyond the farmed animal, one could also take a cynical approach. Plotwise, of course, Okja is genetically modified and therefore "unnatural." She seems to have humanlike intelligence, at one point using the logic of physics to save Mija from a fatal fall off a mountain cliff. She is therefore exceptional and profoundly charismatic. A recent study published in *Biological Conservation* by Agathe Colléony and her colleagues found that people's donations to conservation programs were largely determined by animal charisma (often code for humanness but also for beauty, cuteness, and predatory prowess).[25] Ernest Small echoes this conclusion in *Biodiversity*, noting that, "for most species, conservation efforts are being determined by qualities that humans admire or dislike."[26] Whether an animal matters, then, is tied to animal charisma, and Okja has plenty.

Her charisma is further heightened by the protagonist's attachment to her. Mija, the heroine, is the only wholly sympathetic character in this film. Unlike the goons of Mirando and the ALF, Mija is steadfastly sincere and honest. Moreover, most would agree that companion animals should not be killed and used for food, so Okja's domestication is an ethical out that can curb deeper thinking about farmed animal lives.[27]

The protagonist's consumption of meat further emphasizes Okja's exceptional status. The film objects to factory farming and animal mistreatment but not to meat-eating entirely. Chicken and fish are not given moral consideration, but neither are they tortured or even portrayed as farmed animals. Indeed, Mija's grandfather's technique for growing Okja was simple; he just "let her run around." This logic represents the film's moral center: let animals be free, treat them well, and, if one must kill them, do it humanely. This style of animal rights thinking is "welfarist," a term often associated with philosopher Peter Singer, who argues that animals "are not self-aware and do not really care *that* we use them but only about *how* we use them."[28] In the context of welfarism, *Okja* is not morally contradictory but rather departs from an abolitionist vegan approach (associated with Rutgers law professor Gary Francione) that takes issue with any unnecessary killing of nonhumans and deems veganism a moral baseline. That Okja is believed to deserve a full life and not "humane slaughter" signals Okja's distance from other farmed animals.

Okja's welfarist approach confirms its post-, rather than purely anti-, pastoralism by rejecting the supposedly extremist position of vegan animal rights activists who argue that there is no ethical consumption of nonhuman bodies. Gifford writes in *Pastoral* that a "'mature environmental aesthetics' would need to recognise that some literature has gone beyond the closed circuit of pastoral and anti-pastoral to achieve a vision of an integrated natural world that includes the human."[29] In Korea, Mija and her grandfather live a balanced life with their environment, an idyllic pastoral existence that is interrupted only when Mirando comes knocking.

In keeping with the retreat-and-return logics of the pastoral, Mija returns to Korea and resumes her integrated life with Okja, the calf, and her grandfather, signaling a post-pastoral that is "mature": integrated and including death but not cruelty, a sobering acknowledgment of the fact that "we can't live and avoid killing."[30] The problem with this vision of farming from a vegan studies point of view is that it is essentially nonexistent; factory farming is so much the norm that it can reasonably be called farming. Ultimately, the welfarist and post-pastoral ethic and aesthetic of *Okja* combine to provide a moral out for Western omnivores, encouraging the consumption of humanely raised meat rather than an outright rejection of speciesism.

Finally, the film's comparison of the ALF to Mirando challenges a straightforward vegan reading. For example, both Mirando and the ALF are shown to be a little ridiculous. ALF activist Silver tries to avoid all exploitation in his consumption habits and thus lives on the edge of starvation; the ALF make sure their corporate foes buckle their seatbelts before jumping their truck; and they exclaim "This is history!" when following the transport vehicle to the Mirando experimental facility, connoting a self-righteous blend of immaturity and self-importance. The most sinister tie between Mirando's cartoonish villains and the silly animal rights superheroes of the ALF, however, is the transgression of consent. Mirando took Okja from Mija without her consent; Okja was "mated" and abused without her consent; and the ALF returned Okja to Mirando (in order to get footage to "fuck Mirando") without Mija's consent, albeit mostly by accident. A Korean American ALF member, K, purposely mistranslated Mija's words and was thereafter exiled from the group, only to return at the end with a tattoo stating, "Translation is sacred." Clearly, the ALF's harsh punishment of K marks an important difference between the two entities pulling, like a tug-of-war, at Mija and her animal companion. Beating and exiling K, the ALF takes K's transgression seriously, and yet the dichotomous structure of the film's central conflict maintains the equation of the ALF and Mirando. The film's description on Netflix clarifies the us-versus-them binary at its heart: "A gentle giant and the girl who raised her are caught in the crossfire between animal activism, corporate greed and scientific ethics."

Thus, while it is clear that the ALF is not entirely villainous, it is even clearer that Mija is *the* heroine, along with Okja. And Mija is not vegan—we see her enjoying her fish stew with her grandfather on a pastoral mountaintop in Korea. Mikaella Clements contends that in *Okja*, "vegans are hilarious, . . . rolling gleefully around as stereotypes of privileged, slightly soft teenagers easily moved to tears."[31] And yet, she writes, they are also ethically correct, and it is easier to laugh at them than to argue with their moral system. Perhaps, but Mija arguably emerges as the moral paragon of the film; she is never ridiculous. *Okja*'s satirical depiction of ridiculous vegans and a reasonable protagonist omnivore complicates its stance on animal life. It is more welfarist than abolitionist, more post- than anti-pastoral, and as such it moderates the anti-pastoral ecohorror that assumes nonhuman resistance and desire to continue living—fish and chickens too.

"Translation is sacred," however. It is at best problematic and at worst racist to demand that Mija's rural Korean lifeways and epistemology fit perfectly into a Western, largely white vegan paradigm as represented by the largely white ALF. Mija's foodways ultimately do reduce nonhuman pain. If vegans take seriously the challenges that plant studies and Indigenous studies pose to vegan studies and can acknowledge that "there may be no moral *destination*, but rather a moral *direction*" that does not require individualist self-designations such as "vegan" or the problematic rhetoric of rights, then perhaps *Okja* can be understood as a productive challenge to vegan studies rather than as a strictly speciesist film.[32]

It is my claim here that *Okja* posits a "contextual moral veganism" that seeks to reduce nonhuman pain without trampling on world views that would, for example, consider the primary part of vegan diets—plants—another kind of kin.[33] Ultimately, *Okja* is anti–factory farming but pro-interrelationality, and the film shines a satirist's light on the problem of moral inflexibility, particularly when the moral instructors are white American vegan activists. Context matters. As Greta Gaard eloquently explains,

> Ecofeminism's contextual moral veganism offers a useful strategy for making decisions about ethical eating for humans, plants, and animals; its contextual aspect is not a form of moral relativism, nor is it a universal rule. A critical ecofeminism encourages a shift in our thinking and in our being, from a humanist perspective of dominance to an awareness and participation in relations of mutuality and reciprocity that resituate humans in the cycles of planetary life.[34]

This is not to say, of course, that factory farming is fine. It is to say that *Okja*'s apparent moral inconsistency is only such under an unbending vegan paradigm that might expand to include other epistemologies of kinship, relationality, and dependence. Much like Guillermo del Toro's *The Shape of Water*—discussed in chapter 9 of this volume—*Okja* gestures toward interdependence and affirms humanity's place in the creative-destructive processes of nature.[35] *Okja*'s version of this critical ecofeminist approach through Mija implicitly critiques the ALF. But the ALF, while deserving of critique, is not the enemy.

After Okja's initial ALF-assisted escape and return to her corporate captors in Korea, Mirando executives back in New York City sit around a TV, watching news coverage of the escape and visually mirroring the famous photograph of President Barack Obama and staff in the Situation Room hearing news of Osama bin Laden's death on May 1, 2011. The visual equates al-Qaeda and the ALF: one a fundamentalist militant organization and the other a group of five young people (one always on the verge of fainting) who stole a pig. Lucy Mirando refers to the theft as "this terrorism thing." The hyperbole here alludes to the strategically inflated rhetoric of "ecoterrorism," a discourse that has long been directed at environmental and animal rights activists to justify surveillance, intimidation, and long-term imprisonment. The FBI considers groups such as the ALF to be the "number one domestic terror threat," a criminalization of protest that, as Will Potter explains in his 2011 *Green Is the New Red: An Insider's Account of a Social Movement Under Siege*, reveals the collusion between corporate agribusiness and the US government. He describes the gap between ecoterrorism and actual environmental activism as well as the private interests reifying the absurdist rhetoric:

> The animal rights and environmental movements, like every other social movement throughout history, have both legal and illegal elements. . . . *None* of these activists, though, have ever injured a human being. . . . This disproportionate, heavy-handed government crackdown on the animal rights and environmental movements, and the reckless use of the word "terrorism," has had dangerous consequences. . . . The entire animal rights and environmental movements, perhaps more than any other social movements, directly threaten corporate profits.[36]

By referring to activists as terrorists, American surveillance apparatuses can cut legal corners to safeguard the state. Transforming animal rights activists into outlaws equivalent to fundamentalist groups with a verified history of violence keeps agribusiness interests safe.

Rob Nixon's public talk series on "environmental martyrdom" highlights the threat environmentalists pose to corporate interests and the murderous lengths to which governments and corporations will go to protect those interests. In his lecture "Environmental Martyrdom and the Defenders of the Forest," Nixon discusses environmental martyrs of the Global South, including Berta Cáceres, a Honduran activist who was assassinated in 2016 because of her efforts to protect a sacred section of forest from the construction of the Agua Zarca dam. The environmental martyrs in *Okja*—the ALF—represent a more secular sacrifice that is unlikely to gain significant media attention. Although members of the real ALF have gone to prison, the threat of assassination does not seem particularly significant because of the relative inconsequentiality of their activism: taking several chickens from a farm, rescuing puppies from puppy mills, knocking over hunting towers. While these acts surely mean the world to the animals saved, this microactivism does not pose a terroristic level of threat to Big Agriculture. To call these acts *terrorism* is to redefine the word.

In short, *Okja* highlights the absurdity and the strategy of labeling animal activists as terrorists. In so doing, the film suggests another signification of the term *ecohorror*, a parodic one that makes good but serious fun of the hyperbole ("The horror!") placed on the bodies of eco-activists such as Jay, Red, and Silver, who are harmless because they never instigate violence but dangerous because they reveal abuse and violence. They are a horror to corporate interests: public enemy no. 1. *Okja*'s ALF is ridiculous, sentimental, and silly but also terroristic and extremist. (This rhetorical swing echoes the language often directed at vegans, who are described both as serious threats to the state and as dismissible anemic "soyboys" in the American context.)[37] Ultimately, then, *Okja*'s ecohorror is a many-faced monster, revealing serious ecological horrors but also satirizing the hyperbole that leads to the criminalization of animal rights activism.

Agribusiness anti-pastoral *is* ecohorror in the Anthropocene; the genre acknowledges farmed animals' existence within ecologies, considers the grave ecological impacts of factory farming, and recognizes the ever-present resistance enacted by farmed animals, with or without human help and with or without human witnesses. *Okja* helps us to remember the losing battles being fought by nonhumans every day on factory farms, even though law, distance, and myriad other factors prevent us from seeing them. On the front lines of maniacal capitalistic obsessions with productivity and efficiency, the always resistant and resisting farmed animal emerges as a tragic hero, whose story emerges only once the grand, cosmic vision of ecohorror comes back down to earth.

An attenuation of ecohorror's most typical scale and focus might lead to a reconsideration of what counts as human resistance too. The viral popularity of a video of a man saving a tiny bunny from a raging California wildfire suggests that dramatic, life-or-death wild animal rescue pulls on our collective heartstrings. But *Okja* asks us to consider more boring, less dramatic moments of resistance when it is unclear that anyone is being saved at all. Does eating vegetarian or vegan really make a difference? Although infographics abound with statistics favorably comparing the environmental impact of a vegan versus an omnivorous diet, to the vegan herself it can remain frustratingly unclear. She never meets the supposed one animal per day that her diet "saves." In other words, eating like it makes an ecological difference requires an act of vision that is also an act of faith. Ecohorror texts such as *Okja* can have a significant hand in creating the cognitive-affective bridges that might encourage more ethical relations with the nonhuman world, including vegetarian and vegan eating. Even as the film encourages viewers to laugh at the silly personalities and inflexibilities of the ALF vegans, it is much harder to argue with them.

And it is the ALF that gets the last word of the film. Although the group undeniably reflects some of the many problems of animal rights activism and veganism (e.g., whiteness at the center, a white male at the helm, and contextual blindness), it is nonetheless linked to futurity. While Mija, Okja, and the superpiglet are enclosed in a happy ending, the ALF's great work is only beginning—and expanding. The post-credit scene follows Jay, fresh out of jail, as he is welcomed back into the now-more-diverse ALF fold; wasting no time, Jay and the rest don their trademark black ski masks on their way to interrupt a Mirando event. They invite a confused older woman on the bus to join them, which is an invitation to the audience too: come with us; come see. The final gesture is an ALF member, Blonde, pointing to something unseen, allowing viewers to fill in the blanks: "There it is," he says. The gesture of pointing demands that we *look*. Pointing requires, and this is a crucial term both for farmed animal activism and for anti-pastoral ecohorror, *witnessing*: the witnessing not only of horrors but also of the small acts of resistance on behalf of and by farmed animals that will continue, whether we see them, hear them, feel them, and consider them or not: "There it is."

Notes

1. Elena Razlogova, "Cannes 2017: Border Crossings in 'Jupiter's Moon' and 'Okja,'" *Popmatters*, May 20, 2017, www.popmatters.com/cannes-2017-border-crossings-okja-and-jupiters-moon-2495391587.html.

2. Gowri Koneswaran and Danielle Nierenberg, "Global Farm Animal Production and Global Warming: Impacting and Mitigating Climate Change," *Environmental Health Perspectives* 116, no. 5 (2008): 578–82, National Center for Biotechnology Information, https://doi.org/10.1289/ehp.11034.

3. Mikaella Clements, "How Movies 'Okja' and 'Carnage' Laugh at Vegans but Ultimately Prove Them Right," *Highsnobiety*, last modified August 8, 2017, www.highsnobiety.com/2017/08/08/okja-carnage-veganism/.

4. Stacy Alaimo, *Bodily Natures: Science, Environment, and the Material Self* (Bloomington: Indiana University Press, 2010).

5. Christy Tidwell, "Monstrous Natures Within: Posthuman and New Materialist Ecohorror in Mira Grant's *Parasite*," *ISLE: Interdisciplinary Studies in Literature and Environment* 21, no. 3 (Summer 2014): 541.

6. Nicole Seymour, *Bad Environmentalism: Irony and Irreverence in the Ecological Age* (Minneapolis: University of Minnesota Press, 2018), 4.

7. Timothy Morton, *Hyperobjects: Philosophy and Ecology After the End of the World* (Minneapolis: University of Minnesota Press, 2013).

8. Greg Garrard, "Wordsworth and Thoreau: Two Visions of Pastoral," in *Thoreau's Sense of Place: Essays in American Environmental Writing*, ed. Richard J. Schneider (Iowa City: University of Iowa Press, 2000).

9. Terry Gifford, "Pastoral, Anti-Pastoral, and Post-Pastoral," in *The Cambridge Companion to Literature and the Environment*, ed. Louise Westling (Cambridge: Cambridge University Press, 2013), 26.

10. Thomas M. Wilson, "Post-Pastoral in John Fowles's *Daniel Martin*," *Organization and Environment* 18, no. 4 (2005): 487.

11. Richard J. Schneider, "The Dark Side of Two Nature Writing Genres: Nature Noir and *Wisconsin Death Trip*," in *Dark Nature: Anti-Pastoral Essays in American Literature and Culture*, ed. Richard J. Schneider (Lanham, MD: Lexington Books, 2016), 111.

12. Rob Nixon, *Slow Violence and the Environmentalism of the Poor* (Cambridge, MA: Harvard University Press, 2011).

13. Stephen A. Rust and Carter Soles, "Ecohorror Special Cluster: 'Living in Fear, Living in Dread, Pretty Soon We'll All Be Dead,'" *ISLE: Interdisciplinary Studies in Literature and Environment* 21, no. 3 (Summer 2014): 510.

14. Terry Gifford, *Pastoral* (London: Routledge, 1999).

15. Wilson, "Post-Pastoral," 478.

16. Temple Grandin, *Temple Grandin's Guide to Working with Farm Animals* (North Adams, MA: Storey, 2017), 106.

17. Carol J. Adams, *The Sexual Politics of Meat: A Feminist-Vegetarian Critical Theory* (London: Continuum, 1990), 58.

18. Greta Gaard, *Critical Ecofeminism* (Lanham, MD: Lexington Books, 2017).

19. Karen Davis, "The Disengagement of Journalistic Discourse About Nonhuman Animals: An Analysis," in *Critical Animal Studies: Towards Trans-Species Social Justice*, ed. Atsuko Matsuoka and John Sorenson (London: Rowman and Littlefield, 2018), 75.

20. Leighton Akio Woodhouse, "Charged with the Crime of Filming a Slaughterhouse," *The Nation*, July 31, 2018, https://www.thenation.com/article/charged-crime-filming-slaughterhouse/.

21. United States Government Accountability Office (USGAO), "Workplace Safety and Health: Safety in the Meat and Poultry Industry, While Improving, Could Be Further Strengthened," January 2005, www.gao.gov/new.items/d0596.pdf.

22. Sarat Colling, "Animal Agency, Resistance, and Escape," in *Critical Animal Studies: Towards Trans-Species Social Justice*, ed. Atsuko Matsuoka and John Sorenson (London: Rowman and Littlefield, 2018), 22. In chapter 11 of this volume, Sharon Sharp demonstrates how fictional ecomedia also tend to deemphasize the existence of farmed animals, a strategic forgetting.

23. "Happy Cows Campaign," *Blogspot: Marketing Campaign Case Studies*, last updated April 21, 2008, marketing-case-studies.blogspot.com/2008/04/happy-cows-campaign.html.

24. For more on the exploitation and abuse of nonhuman animals for entertainment, see Sharon Sharp's withering critique of the CBS television series *Zoo* in chapter 11 of this volume.

25. Agathe Colléony et al., "Human Preferences for Species Conservation: Animal Charisma Trumps Endangered Status," *Biological Conservation* 206 (February 2017): 263–69, https://doi.org/10.1016/j.biocon.2016.11.035.

26. Ernest Small, "The New Noah's Ark: Beautiful and Useful Species Only; Part 2, The Chosen Species," *Biodiversity* 13, no. 1 (March 2012): 37, https://doi.org/10.1080/14888386.2012.659443.

27. For a darker reading of pet ownership, see Brittany R. Roberts's discussion of Stephen Gregory's *The Cormorant* in chapter 8.

28. Gary L. Francione, "Peter Singer: 'Oh My God, These Vegans...,'" *The Abolitionist Approach*, last updated May 23, 2007, www.abolitionistapproach.com/peter-singer-oh-my-god-these-vegans/.

29. Gifford, *Pastoral*, 148.

30. Lori Gruen, "Facing Death and Practicing Grief," in *Ecofeminism: Feminist Intersections with Other Animals and the Earth*, ed. Lori Gruen and Carol J. Adams (New York: Bloomsbury, 2014), 132.

31. Clements, "How Movies."

32. Deane Curtin, quoted in Gaard, *Critical Ecofeminism*, 38.

33. Gaard, *Critical Ecofeminism*, 38.

34. Ibid., 43.

35. See Robin L. Murray and Joseph K. Heumann, chapter 9 in this volume.

36. "Green Is the New Red," accessed July 1, 2018, http://www.greenisthenewred.com/blog/about/.

37. Laura Wright, *The Vegan Studies Project: Food, Animals, and Gender in the Age of Terror* (Athens: University of Georgia Press, 2015).

References

Adams, Carol J. *The Sexual Politics of Meat: A Feminist-Vegetarian Critical Theory*. London: Continuum, 1990.

Alaimo, Stacy. *Bodily Natures: Science, Environment, and the Material Self*. Bloomington: Indiana University Press, 2010.

Clements, Mikaella. "How Movies 'Okja' and 'Carnage' Laugh at Vegans but Ultimately Prove Them Right." *Highsnobiety*. Last modified August 8, 2017. www.highsnobiety.com/2017/08/08/okja-carnage-veganism/.

Colléony, Agathe, Susan Clayton, Denis Couvet, Michel Saint Jalme, and Anne-Caroline Prévot. "Human Preferences for Species Conservation: Animal Charisma Trumps Endangered Status." *Biological Conservation* 206 (February 2017): 263–69. https://doi.org/10.1016/j.biocon.2016.11.035.

Colling, Sarat. "Animal Agency, Resistance, and Escape." In *Critical Animal Studies: Towards Trans-Species Social Justice*, edited by Atsuko Matsuoka and

John Sorenson, 21–44. London: Rowman and Littlefield, 2018.

Davis, Karen. "The Disengagement of Journalistic Discourse About Nonhuman Animals: An Analysis." In *Critical Animal Studies: Towards Trans-Species Social Justice*, edited by Atsuko Matsuoka and John Sorenson, 73–93. London: Rowman and Littlefield, 2018.

Francione, Gary L. "Peter Singer: 'Oh My God, These Vegans. . . .'" *The Abolitionist Approach*. Last updated May 23, 2007. www.abolitionistapproach.com/peter-singer-oh-my-god-these-vegans/.

Gaard, Greta. *Critical Ecofeminism*. Lanham, MD: Lexington Books, 2017.

Garrard, Greg. "Wordsworth and Thoreau: Two Visions of Pastoral." In *Thoreau's Sense of Place: Essays in American Environmental Writing*, edited by Richard J. Schneider, 194–206. Iowa City: University of Iowa Press, 2000.

Gifford, Terry. *Pastoral*. London: Routledge, 1999.

———. "Pastoral, Anti-Pastoral, and Post-Pastoral." In *The Cambridge Companion to Literature and the Environment*, edited by Louise Westling, 17–30. Cambridge: Cambridge University Press, 2013.

Grandin, Temple. *Temple Grandin's Guide to Working with Farm Animals*. North Adams, MA: Storey, 2017.

"Green Is the New Red." Accessed July 1, 2018. http://www.greenisthenewred.com/blog/about/.

Gruen, Lori. "Facing Death and Practicing Grief." In *Ecofeminism: Feminist Intersections with Other Animals and the Earth*, edited by Lori Gruen and Carol J. Adams, 127–41. New York: Bloomsbury, 2014.

"Happy Cows Campaign." *Blogspot: Marketing Campaign Case Studies*. Last updated April 21, 2008. marketing-case-studies.blogspot.com/2008/04/happy-cows-campaign.html.

Koneswaran, Gowri, and Danielle Nierenberg. "Global Farm Animal Production and Global Warming: Impacting and Mitigating Climate Change." *Environmental Health Perspectives* 116, no. 5 (2008): 578–82. National Center for Biotechnology Information, https://doi.org/10.1289/ehp.11034.

Morton, Timothy. *Hyperobjects: Philosophy and Ecology After the End of the World*. Minneapolis: University of Minnesota Press, 2013.

Nixon, Rob. "Environmental Martyrdom and Defenders of the Forest." Lecture given at the 2017–18 Environmental Humanities Lecture Series, Cornell University, Ithaca, NY, May 1, 2018.

———. *Slow Violence and the Environmentalism of the Poor*. Cambridge, MA: Harvard University Press, 2011.

Okja. Directed by Bong Joon-ho, performances by An Seo Hyun, Jake Gyllenhaal, Paul Dano, and Tilda Swinton. Plan B Entertainment, 2017.

Potter, Will. *Green Is the New Red: An Insider's Account of a Social Movement Under Siege*. San Francisco: City Lights Books, 2011.

Razlogova, Elena. "Cannes 2017: Border Crossings in 'Jupiter's Moon' and 'Okja.'" *Popmatters*, May 20, 2017. www.popmatters.com/cannes-2017-border-crossings-okja-and-jupiters-moon-2495391587.html.

Rust, Stephen A., and Carter Soles. "Ecohorror Special Cluster: 'Living in Fear, Living in Dread, Pretty Soon We'll All Be Dead.'" *ISLE: Interdisciplinary Studies in Literature and Environment* 21, no. 3 (Summer 2014): 509–12.

Schneider, Richard J. "The Dark Side of Two Nature Writing Genres: Nature Noir and *Wisconsin Death Trip*." In *Dark Nature: Anti-Pastoral Essays in American Literature and Culture*, edited by Richard J. Schneider, 107–18. Lanham, MD: Lexington Books, 2016.

Seymour, Nicole. *Bad Environmentalism: Irony and Irreverence in the Ecological Age*. Minneapolis: University of Minnesota Press, 2018.

Small, Ernest. "The New Noah's Ark: Beautiful and Useful Species Only; Part 2, The Chosen Species." *Biodiversity* 13, no. 1 (March 2012): 37–53. https://doi.org/10.1080/14888386.2012.659443.

Tidwell, Christy. "Monstrous Natures Within: Posthuman and New Materialist Ecohorror in Mira Grant's *Parasite*." *ISLE: Interdisciplinary Studies in Literature and Environment* 21, no. 3 (Summer 2014): 538–49.

United States Government Accountability Office (USGAO). "Workplace Safety and Health: Safety in the Meat and Poultry Industry, While Improving, Could Be Further Strengthened." January 2005. www.gao.gov/new.items/d0596.pdf.

Wilson, Thomas M. "Post-Pastoral in John Fowles's *Daniel Martin*." *Organization and Environment* 18, no. 4 (2005): 477–88.

Woodhouse, Leighton Akio. "Charged with the Crime of Filming a Slaughterhouse." *The Nation*, July 31, 2018. https://www.thenation.com/article/charged-crime-filming-slaughterhouse/.

Wright, Laura. *The Vegan Studies Project: Food, Animals, and Gender in the Age of Terror*. Athens: University of Georgia Press, 2015.

11.
Zoo
Television Ecohorror On and Off the Screen

Sharon Sharp

In the summer of 2015, viewers of the television event series *Zoo* (CBS 2015–17) were confronted with scenes of human-animal relationships usually invisible on television. In the title sequence, images of pig carcasses in a slaughterhouse, distressed exotic animals in cages, hunters holding dead animals, and animal experimentation labs were accompanied by a voice-over querying human exploitation of other animals. "For centuries," the narrator intoned, "mankind has been the dominant species. We've domesticated animals, locked them up, killed them for sport. But what if, all across the globe, the animals decided, no more? What if they finally decided to fight back? To bite back?" Days before the debut of *Zoo*'s second season the following year, a full-page PETA ad that ran in the *New York Times*, the *Los Angeles Times*, and the *Wall Street Journal* made another troubling aspect of human-animal relationships visible. Featuring a digital chimpanzee handcuffed with strips of celluloid film gazing at the reader, the full-page ad protested the use of live animals in the series' production, declaring, "Some shows hold more than an audience captive. CBS: Use CGI to free all animals from 'Zoo.'"[1]

The "question of the animal," to use Cary Wolfe's phrase, posed by *Zoo* through the generic imagery of horror is a timely one.[2] Television and scholarly literature regularly supply evidence of the breakdown of once secure distinctions between humans and other animals. Yet even as we witness in nonhuman animals behaviors and capabilities often thought to be exclusively human, human relationships with other animals in contemporary times have, as Jacques Derrida notes, resulted in "unprecedented proportions" of the "subjection of the animal."[3] *Zoo*'s representation of animal rebellion draws on the ecohorror genre, which Stephen A. Rust and Carter Soles broadly define as including texts "in which humans do horrific things to the natural world" or that "promote ecological awareness, represent ecological crises, or blur human/non-human distinctions more broadly."[4] Although ecohorror has not been a prolific genre on television, what ecohorror shows there have been have since the 1960s critiqued human-animal relationships. For instance, several of *The Twilight Zone*'s (CBS 1959–64) horror episodes critique human mistreatment of other animals with estrangement techniques in which humans become food or zoo specimens. The *X-Files* (Fox 1993–2002, 2016, 2018) blurred human and nonhuman boundaries in a number of episodes. The SyFy channel's popular cycle of animal horror films that began in the 2000s regularly parodies human-animal relationships and environmental issues. Most recently, the zombie apocalypse series *The Walking Dead* (AMC 2010–present) and *Fear the Walking Dead* (AMC 2015–present) explore human/nonhuman boundaries and human vulnerability on a dystopian, ruined earth. Yet human-animal relationships in ecohorror television have often been overlooked in scholarship on horror television, which tends to focus on other issues, as well as in ecocritical analyses, which mainly concentrate on cinema rather than television. Moreover, while ecocritical scholarship explores the environmental impacts of the exploitation of natural and human resources in media production and consumption, it often ignores the exploitation of nonhuman animal labor in fictional media. But to more fully understand television ecohorror, human-animal relationships both onscreen and off must be considered.

Zoo makes a productive case study for such an analysis, as it has participated in popular debates about human-animal relationships in both its narrative and its production practices. The series, based on the bestselling novel by James Patterson and Michael Ledwidge and produced by CBS Television Studios as direct-to-series summer programming for CBS, is "about a wave of violent animal attacks against humans sweeping the planet."[5] In publicity for the series, executive producer Jeff Pinkner explained, "The premise is basically Alfred Hitchcock's *The Birds* but writ across the whole animal spectrum."[6] As Pinkner's comments make clear, the series draws on the nature-run-amok subset of the ecohorror genre, identified by Lee Gambin, which Rust and Soles summarize as texts in which humans are attacked by animals and plants "that have been altered or angered by humans in some way."[7] *Zoo* is also a televisual variant of animal horror cinema, a horror subgenre that Katarina Gregersdotter, Nicklas Hållén, and Johan Höglund define as films "where the animal seeks to challenge the predominance of the human through physical, sometimes consumptive, violence. In this way, it is the dangerous and transgressive animal that elicits suspense and fear in animal horror cinema."[8] Referencing animal and ecohorror, CBS promoted *Zoo* as a popular ecocritical text and a television event, a summer blockbuster for the small screen "with a wider message" about human-caused environmental change.[9] James Patterson, who served as a producer on the series, suggested that "the notion is, we're next for extinction and maybe we deserve it. The animals are the heroes here, and they're mad for the right reasons."[10] The series was the most watched CBS summer series in its first season and the second-most watched in its second season, but it was canceled after its third season, which had low ratings.[11] *Zoo* also gained notoriety when it became a sustained site of protest by animal advocacy groups for its use of live animals in production.

In this chapter, I examine the representation and labor of animals in the *Zoo* series and its paratexts. I argue that *Zoo* plays on ecohorror's blurring of the distinction between humans and other animals to critique human exploitation of other animals and the anthropogenic causes of environmental destruction. Although *Zoo* calls attention to these issues and suggests continuities between humans and other animals, the representation and labor of animals in the series reaffirm human sovereignty over the more-than-human world, which limits the ecocritical potential of the series.

Animal Rebellion from Novel to Screen

The television adaptation shares its basic premise and focus on human-animal relationships with the novel on which it was based, but the book's explicit critique of human culpability in environmental destruction is diminished in the television adaptation, which expands the human characters and focus across its three seasons. In the novel, which an *Entertainment Weekly* review describes as a "glibly written page-turner that mixes speculative science, current events, and environmental concern," the invasion narrative focuses on narrators Jackson Oz, a zoologist investigating a global animal uprising, and his chimpanzee Attila, who participates in the rebellion.[12] The novel focuses on the environmental destruction unwittingly caused by scientific developments as it proposes that "the recent buildup of hydrocarbon-rich petroleum products, coupled with radiation from cellular phones, has caused changes in the environment."[13] The hydrocarbons "have morphed into a substance that many animals' sensory faculties interpret as a pheromone, altering these animals' behaviors."[14] The new pheromone acts like an airborne pollutant that causes "animals to swarm together and attack human beings."[15] Anthropogenic causes of environmental destruction are directly linked to the animal rebellion, since in order to stop the global pandemic, humanity must completely stop polluting the planet and refrain from using modern technologies. The novel concludes on a grim note, with the narrator Oz indicting humanity for an environmental apocalypse, as humans, unwilling to stop using polluting technologies for more than a few days, face a likely extinction, leaving the earth to a nonhuman animal population.

In order to meet the demands of series television and to stretch the story out across multiple seasons, the television series adds additional protagonists to the invasion plot and departs significantly from the novel's representation of the animal rebellion. Rather than narrating the story through both nonhuman and human subjectivities as the novel does, the television adaptation is focused on a human team of experts investigating the animal uprising. The team consists of Chloe Tousignant (Nora Arnezeder), a French intelligence operative and team leader; Jamie Campbell (Kristen Connolly), a reporter following the animal rebellion story; Mitch Morgan (Billy Burke), a veterinary pathologist; Abraham Kennyata (Nonso Anozie), a safari guide; and Jackson Oz (James Wolk), an animal behavior expert. The novel's premise of a globally spreading animal pandemic was adapted into narratively complex television, which, as Jason Mittell notes, "redefines episodic forms under the influence of serial narration—not necessarily a complete merger of episodic and serial forms but a shifting balance. Rejecting the need for plot closure within every episode that typifies conventional episodic form, narrative complexity foregrounds ongoing stories across a range of genres."[16] The *Zoo* series' complex narrative, described by executive producer Josh Appelbaum as "genuine human emotion plus batshit crazy," combines the novel's overarching animal pandemic story arc with monstrous animal invasions in each episode.[17] After the first season, the series departed from the novel. As the series progressed over the next two seasons, its narrative complexity spun an unwieldy story line about animal invasion that undermined the critique of human-animal relationships presented in the novel and the series' first season. Further, although the novel's focus on anthropogenic climate change is not a radical critique of the larger power dynamics of human-animal relationships within the Anthropocene, the television adaptation was careful to represent human-animal relationships in ways that were even less likely to potentially alienate CBS's audiences and advertisers, which resulted in a contradictory and convoluted narrative.

When Animals Bite Back: Human-Animal Distinctions and Inversions

To some degree, *Zoo* plays on the divisions separating humans from other animals by interrogating and defamiliarizing the power dynamics of human consumption of animals. The premise of the series is structured around the question central to the animal horror genre: what if humans became prey or meat? In *Zoo*, humans are no longer at the top of the food chain, no longer apex predators. Instead their position has been usurped by other animals whose aberrant mutations have enabled them to work together to better prey on humans. As animal horror, *Zoo* foregrounds the genre's reliance on the fear "of being eaten by the animal, of being consumed—the fear of finding ourselves in a position where our position as apex predator is challenged; that we as a species are no longer the consumer but the consumed."[18] By depicting humans as prey, the series challenges the concept of human identity that, as Val Plumwood explains, "positions humans outside and above the food chain, not as part of the feast in a chain of reciprocity but as external manipulators and masters of it: Animals can be our food, but we can never be their food."[19] In the representation of humans becoming prey or meat, the series reminds viewers that humans are like animals and animals are like humans because they share a coexistence as edible beings.

Zoo's depiction of humans as meat aligns with human-animal studies scholars who question what Melanie Joy and others have identified as the rationalization and naturalization involved in carnism. Meat-eating is estranged through the human fear of being consumed, which is seen throughout the series, most explicitly in the episode "This Is What It Sounds Like" (CBS 8/4/15). In the episode, a middle-aged white woman is terrorized by a brown bear that has inexplicably invaded her upscale Parisian kitchen. The frightened woman is explicitly equated with food as she is shown hiding in the pantry while the bear prowls around the kitchen. Her equivalence with animals as prey and as potential meat asks the viewer to consider the terrifying experiences of other animals when they become meat, a process that is invisible to consumers, since animals arrive in the domestic space of the kitchen already dead and packaged as meat. The frightened woman as potential meat makes visible what Carol J. Adams identifies as the absent referent in meat: animals are made absent as animals in order for meat to exist when they become transformed into food after being killed and butchered.[20] The episode implies that animals, like the woman, are sentient beings, and it makes visible a portion of the animal experience involved in the horrific process of becoming meat.[21]

But the series limits its critique of food consumption to an individualized model of predation and leaves the industrial production of meat and large-scale animal suffering unquestioned as it focuses on predatory megafauna and ignores the ten billion domesticated animals farmed for meat, such as cows, pigs, and chickens. This is a significant blind spot in a series promoted for its wider environmental message given that agribusiness practices are the "leading cause of every significant form of environmental damage: air and water pollution, biodiversity loss, erosion, deforestation, greenhouse gas emissions, and depletion of fresh water."[22] In ignoring farmed animals, *Zoo* replicates the ways in which the production of meat is made invisible in the United States at factory farms and animal-processing plants in liminal spaces made further inaccessible by ag-gag laws that suppress whistleblowers from revealing the cruelty of factory farms to the public.

In addition to the limited questioning of food-based consumption through the representation of humans as meat or prey, *Zoo* also critiques the subjection of other animals for human consumption in entertainment practices, highlighting the confinement of animals and the controlling anthropocentric gaze that disempowers animals. In "Fight or Flight" (CBS 7/7/15), the human domination involved in the entertaining experiences of the circus is underscored as a couple and their young son watch and applaud the spectacle of tigers in a circus's big cage being coerced into performing for them by a trainer who whips them into submission. The episode calls out the human domination involved in animal performance when the mother exclaims that it is "unnatural—forcing a creature to do something that doesn't come instinctively." Later in the episode, the gaze of the human spectator and its power dynamic is destabilized by the predatory gaze of the caged tigers who menace (but do not attack) the couple's son as he wanders alone around the circus fairgrounds.

Similarly, the series critiques the zoo's institutional practices of animal captivity for human entertainment by focusing on cages and the power dynamics of the human gaze. In the inaugural episode, "First Blood" (CBS 6/30/15), a pair of lions escape from captivity at the Los Angeles Zoo by attacking their trainer and then later prey on two drunk men urinating in a dark alleyway. The episode directly links the violence inflicted on the humans to the violence experienced by the lions, as the veterinary pathologist Morgan explains that the lions, Nick and Eddie, were siblings captured in the Serengeti at eight months old and were the real victims because they were raised in cages. By reversing the category of victim from human to lion, the episode makes visible the violence involved in the imprisonment of non-human animals in zoos for human entertainment. As Randy Malamud has asserted, "The zoo experience is voyeuristic, imperialistic, inauthentic and steeped in the ethos of consumer culture, which is antithetical to nature and ecology, and hence dangerous to animals."[23] In addition, as John Berger has argued, the structures of looking involved in the human spectator's gaze at caged animals in the zoo disempowers and marginalizes them.[24] The objectification of animals as zoo specimens is critiqued in the depiction of the lions preying on their human victims. The lions are framed above the two men in a dark alley as they stalk them from higher ground for food and amusement, which reverses the gaze and the hierarchy between humans and other animals. The scene pokes fun at human interest in watching animals engaging in entertaining natural behaviors at zoos while disempowering humans by making them not just the object of the animals' controlling gaze but, eventually, their prey.

Zoo also explores another human-animal relationship forged by human dominance and consumption—the companion animal (or pet, as companion animals are referred to in *Zoo*)—in frightening ways that estrange this common relationship.[25] As Yi-Fu Tuan has noted, the domestication of animals into pets involves domination.[26] Although relationships with companion animals are often viewed as positive experiences for humans and other animals, Brett Mills reminds us that "pets are equally at the mercy of human whims and priorities" and that they "might represent the logical conclusion of human dominance over animals, especially as it is a form of dominance which humans manage to convince themselves is for the animals' own good."[27] In addition, the 6.5 million unwanted companion animals that enter animal shelters and the 1.5 million that are euthanized each year in the United States illustrate the overconsumption of companion animals as well as ways animals are subject to human priorities.

Throughout the first season, the series exploits for horror the boundary-crossing nature of the companion animal that is at once alien and familiar in ways that question human dominance within this relationship. Companion animals are most often represented as rebelling against human dominance in the series, from an homage to *The Birds* in which a clowder of cats once considered members of the family uncannily assemble in a tree for attack to dogs that kill and eat their owners. In "Fight or Flight," for example, the family's pet dog escapes, leads the father to his death by mauling by a pack of feral dogs, and then returns home to snuggle with the mother and son. The dog's transformation from a beloved pet into a duplicitous predator defies the human terms of the pet relationship in which companion animals live according to human priorities.

That said, just as the series issues only a limited challenge to human consumption of animals as food, *Zoo* draws the line at individual acts of consumption in terms of the human domination of animals involved in the circus, the zoo, and pet keeping. The series largely ignores the pet, fur, and illegal wildlife trades as well as agriculture, biomedical research, and human overpopulation that contribute to species extinction. The series does not directly critique the larger systemic anthropological machine, a "series of institutions and apparatuses that capture and reproduce but also constrain and kill animal life," which could potentially turn off broadcast viewers and advertisers.[28] Instead, *Zoo* focuses on easy targets that do not stray too far from mainstream public sentiments about human-animal relationships that can be televisually exploited for horror.

In addition to destabilizing select consumption-based human-animal power relationships, *Zoo* challenges human exceptionalism by representing animals in the first season as "subjects with complex and substantial subjectivity" or as having "agency," a quality often thought to be exclusively human.[29] Although animal minds remain off-limits to viewers, unlike in the novel, which was partly narrated by a chimpanzee character, the show figures animals both as members of cooperative interspecies communities and as individuals, with implied agency as they threaten humans. Throughout the first season, animals of diverse species are represented as possessing intelligence that enables them to coordinate attacks on humans based on their understanding of humanity. In the second episode, for instance, Jackson Oz's mother, medical doctor Elizabeth Oz (Bess Armstrong), discovers that African lions adapted their killing behavior to induce maximum pain and suffering in two dozen safari victims by severing their femoral arteries rather than killing them more efficiently by tearing at their throats ("Fight or Flight"). Similarly, bats swarm solar panels at a research station in Antarctica (causing the human inhabitants to freeze to death), crash a plane in Japan, and chew through power lines to disable humans in Brazil. The bat behavior is explained by veterinary pathologist Morgan as a development of hyperintelligence that enables them to understand the key to humanity's status as apex predators: reason and technology ("Blame It on Leo" [CBS, 7/28/2015]). Animals are also represented as emotional beings, like humans, and are shown to harbor anger against humans and demonstrate empathy for animals of other species. In one scene, camels, a baby warthog, and a serval—natural enemies in the wild—band together to threaten the team of experts. Their behavior is explained—again by Morgan—as emotional contagion, the phenomenon in which human emotional states spread from one person to another ("Emotional Contagion" [CBS, 9/1/15]). The ability of animals of various species to share this human emotional capability enables them to cooperate in order to eliminate the human species. Whereas these violent incidents are grounded in speculative fiction in the series, the referencing of animal intelligence and emotions is in tune with the insights of contemporary ethology, which understands animals as "capable of tasks as complex as tool making and tool use, category formation, spatial memory, deceptive behavior, social sophistication, cognitive adaptability, symbolism, the communication of abstract feelings, and 'if-then' or 'purposive' thinking and behavior."[30]

After the first season, however, animal agency is constrained by a plot twist: the animal mutation has been engineered by a mad scientist, Dr. Robert Oz (Ken Olin), the leader of a group of rogue scientists, the Shepherds, who want to return the earth to nonhuman animals and protect the earth from environmental degradation caused by humans. The agency enabled by accelerated evolution does not come from the process of natural selection but by artificial human manipulation of nonhuman animal genetics, which contradicts the first season's representation of animal agency. From the second season onward, animals are represented as extensions of human agency, because they instinctively act only in response to accelerated evolutionary mutations caused by human genetic engineering and return to their normal behaviors once cured. Although the evolutionary nature of animal agency presented by the series implies that a humanlike agency may be inevitable and develop over time, in focusing on the mad scientist plot twist, the series shifts to ideas of biological determinism, which reduces behaviors and actions to genes. In this sense, *Zoo* retreats to a reductionist understanding of animal behavior as determined solely by biology, removing the possibility of animals acting as authors of their own lives in meaningful ways. Any notion of intentionality initially evoked by the series is recuperated as animals are "endumbed," a term Mills coined to describe the way in which television "renders animals voiceless by insisting they have nothing to say, and no ability to say anything; and it renders them as stupid precisely because they are depicted as lacking that ability."[31] Rendering animals as dumb, without agency, over the course of the second and third seasons ultimately reifies human exceptionalism and justifies human dominance of the nonhuman world, because in the series' later seasons only humans are shown to possess the ability to act with agency in the world.

Zoo's turn toward mad science becomes more troubling as the series turns away from saving the animals to saving humanity. In the third season, the show's take on blurred human-animal distinctions becomes hyperbolically reactionary, as Jackson Oz discovers he has a sister, Abigail Westbrook (Athena Karkanis), a human-animal hybrid created by their mad scientist father, Robert Oz. As the final season's villain, Westbrook, the new leader of the Shepherds, plans to unleash hybrid animals that carry a virus able to infect the recently cured animals and turn them into hybrids to rid the planet of humanity. In Westbrook, we see human-animal hybridity represented as monstrous because it is not fully human and is tied to a radical misanthropic ecoterrorism that prioritizes the nonhuman over the human. In its race toward absurdity, *Zoo*'s final episode ends with hordes of Westbrook's hybrid beasts breaking through a barrier to wipe out humanity as the team tries to save the last human infant on earth. Since *Zoo* was canceled after its third season aired, its complex narrative about human-animal relationships never definitively concluded. The series' examination of the horrors of animal exploitation and human-caused environmental destruction has some ecocritical import, but *Zoo* falls short in its anthropocentric focus. In the context of the current human-caused climate crisis and the looming mass extinction of many of the species featured in *Zoo*, the narrative turn to saving humanity from the monstrous more-than-human world derails the series' ecocritical potential.

From Animal to Digital Rendering: *Zoo*, Animal Labor, and Offscreen Horror

Zoo's ideological inconsistencies regarding animal exploitation and environmental damage were underscored when its on-screen representations of ecohorror collided with its offscreen publicity and production practices that involved the horrifying realities of working with real animals. According to the *Los Angeles Times*, *Zoo*'s animal representations for the first season were produced by using "nearly 2,000 live animals" as well as computer-generated effects.[32] Publicity for the series premiere played up human fears of animal alterity in discussing the practice of using real animals—a practice no longer dominant in media production, given the increasing reliance on computer-generated imagery, but still not uncommon—to amplify the terrifying nature of human-animal confrontations on-screen. *Zoo* producers and cast members also discussed the use of animals in the series' production to bolster the realistic depiction of the on-screen animal horror. As executive producer Michael Katleman told a *Times-Picayune* reporter visiting the New Orleans set during filming of the first season, "Our approach is always, 'Can we do it real?'"[33] According to Katleman, in order to produce a more believable effect, *Zoo* producers chose whenever possible to work with real animals that can be trained instead of using CGI effects that can "look off."[34] *Zoo* producers emphasized the use of live exotic animals such as lions and bears over CGI options to highlight the dangerous conditions of working with predators and to reference the series' animal rebellion story line. In an interview with *TV Guide*, executive producer Jeff Pinkner claimed he was able to achieve better performances from the human cast because "when there are real animals on the set, all the actors just behave differently. [The animals are] scary, and they're unpredictable."[35] In another interview, he elaborated: "There's just a level of respect and a level of fear in the eyes when you are acting with an 800-pound bear. Even though it's perfectly safe and controlled, you'll never get the same level of acting if it's, 'Pretend that there's a bear over there and we'll put it in later.'"[36] In a press junket before the premiere of the first season, Pinkner said of the exotic animals used on set, "One of the fun things is they're actors, but they're animals. And so . . . they can be trained, but when the moment happens, they don't necessarily behave the way you're expecting."[37] Such comments were echoed by cast members who repeatedly discussed their fear while working with predators. As star James Wolk told reporters, he didn't need to fake fear when facing a pack of lions: "It's exciting from an actor's standpoint too. Your palms start to sweat, your heart starts to beat and you can't help that when you're around a lion."[38] The comments of the producers and cast are part of a familiar industry publicity strategy in which promotional articles discuss the human-animal encounters as dangerous—risky to human actors in particular—to play up the realism of the productions and to generate viewer interest. The publicity's emphasis on human fear, however, elides the distress animals might experience from the potentially horrific conditions involved in the production of the series.

The industry practice of "doing it real" reveals the paradox of creating narratives about human-animal relationships in ecohorror by using animals: *Zoo*'s use of real animals to critique human exploitation of them engages in the practice of exploitation. CBS and the producers of *Zoo* as well as others who use live animals in horror productions are deeply invested in "animal capital," Nicole Shukin's term describing how animal labor has been rendered to create both material wealth and cultural meanings.[39] Without question, the political economy of animal capital in contemporary media industries has material consequences for animal life. Even in the best circumstances, the agency of animals in media production is heavily circumscribed: just as the fictional animals in *Zoo* ultimately do not make the decision to bite back, the animals captured on-screen did not make the decision to participate in the production of *Zoo*. Rather, an animal's performance in *Zoo* or in any media production is crafted by the human-animal relationships involved in captivity and training practices. Such practices can have adverse effects on animals, particularly exotic animals and other noncompanion species. For instance, industry practices necessitate the removal of animals from natural habitats through captive breeding or the illegal animal trade.[40] In addition, natural animal behaviors are constrained by captivity itself and by training practices. Some trainers use humane training practices, but frequent reports of animal mistreatment and death related to the use of live animals reveal the real-life horror some animals experience in media productions and illustrate the problems inherent in animal captivity and training.[41]

The ecological damage and everyday horrors animals experienced in the production of this ecohorror series were exposed when the animal advocacy organizations PETA and Born Free USA called out *Zoo* for its use of exotic-animal labor. According to the two organizations, CBS met with them to discuss the use of real animals in the production and made promises to use CGI and other alternatives whenever possible.[42] But after the show's publicity and CBS debut called attention to its production practices, PETA and Born Free USA took issue with *Zoo*'s use of real lions through extensive publicity campaigns across social and legacy media outlets. In a statement, PETA argued, "Lions belong in the wild, not confined to tiny cages and forced to perform tricks, often under the threat of beatings. CBS should employ only humane and versatile computer-generated imagery, as so many other productions have done." PETA cited the films *Noah* and *The Jungle Book* and the television series *The Walking Dead* as examples of productions that used accessible digital technology to create convincingly realistic animals.[43] PETA enlisted celebrity animal activist Bob Barker, who wrote a letter to CBS urging them to "adopt a network-wide policy banning the use of wild animals in future CBS programming."[44] Similarly, a Born Free USA press release chided the network for using live animals as "props" when "technological innovations can so easily be substituted" and cited the physical suffering animals endure in captivity.[45] By questioning the industry logic of "doing it real," the protest campaign drew attention to the frightening realities of the animal lives involved in the production of ecohorror in *Zoo*.

The television industry's response to the protest highlights how the industry rationalizes the use of real animals in ecohorror productions while downplaying the environmental impacts of their production practices. CBS and the series' producers reframed the issue from one of ethics to one of animal welfare by emphasizing the safety of animals on set. In a CBS statement made on behalf of *Zoo*, producers noted that "the care, safety and overall well-being of any animal on our set is a top priority of the production."[46] In order to deflect criticism of the use of real animals in producing ecohorror, assurances were made that a representative of the Film and Television Unit of the American Humane Association (the organization funded by SAG-AFTRA and the Alliance of Motion Picture and Television Producers responsible for monitoring animals in media productions) was on set. Trainers and animal suppliers who provided animals for the production were called on to reassure viewers that the animal training and supplier industry is heavily regulated and had given up the inhumane animal training practices cited by PETA. Animal trainer Steve Martin, whose company

Working Wildlife supplied exotic animals for the show, assured viewers that his company uses only positive reinforcement: "Can you imagine beating a 1,000-pound bear or a 500-pound lion and take [sic] him on a set where 200 people are standing around with lights and cameras and have [sic] this animal be cooperative and want to do the job? I don't think so."[47] In addition to marshaling statements about animal welfare, the producers also emphasized technical mastery over animals and how the use of special effects such as split-screen photography protected both human and nonhuman actors on set. But *Zoo* producer Pinkner's comments at a Comic-Con panel organized to promote the first season of the series might have revealed the producers' actual attitude: he made light of animal advocacy groups' concerns by affirming that animal actors were safer than human actors, saying, "PETA has been concerned about the treatment of animals; we're more concerned about the treatment of [*Zoo* star] Billy [Burke]."[48] As Mills has observed, "ameliorative statements" by animal suppliers and regulators in the media industries "function primarily to reduce concern among human cultures. The notion of concern that motivates such communication is anthropocentric, responding to humans' worries about the treatment received by animals they see on-screen."[49] Such assurances by the *Zoo* producers attempted to deflect questions about the ethics and environmental impacts of using animal labor in the production of ecohorror in order to assuage any human concerns that could interfere with the profitability of the series.

Zoo's turn in the third season toward the exclusive use of computer-generated animals for the production of ecohorror appears to have been an attempt to deal with these knotty issues surrounding animal labor. While the producers did not specify that their shift in production practices was a response to the protests, they discussed their use of computer-generated imagery in producing ecohorror in similar anthropocentric terms, highlighting how the technology enabled human mastery over animals both practically and narratively. Computer-generated imagery was presented as a solution to the challenges of working with real animals, who might not understand or want to participate in human production practices. As executive producer Josh Appelbaum explained before the premiere of the third season, "Working with live animals, as great as they could be, you can't get a performance out of them. . . . And now I think you'll see we've been able to really direct performances with the CG creatures. . . . If we want them to . . . give a menacing glare, we can get all these great things that we were never able to do when it was a real bear on set or a dog or whatever."[50] Further, in their rationalization for using computer-generated imagery, the Zoo producers justified symbolic violence toward animal life because it is produced digitally and can enhance the production of ecohorror while minimizing human discomfort with violence toward real animals. Appelbaum noted that it was "tricky" to see humans firing at actual animals but that using computer-generated hybrid animals put the show in a "*Jurassic World* territory where these guys are villains and they're trying to kill us and tear us to shreds, so we can engage with them more in combat, so to speak, and not feel like, 'Oh, no, you're shooting Bambi.'"[51] Thus, computer-generated imagery was promoted by the Zoo producers as solving the problem of animal agency in the production of ecohorror for humans as well as providing a distancing effect that ameliorated human uneasiness with killing animals.

The symbolic violence toward computer-generated hybrid beasts represented as monsters, as completely nonhuman and unlike the other animals, signals the reactionary politics of *Zoo*'s ecohorror, which has implications for animals offscreen. As Robin Wood observes in his discussion of the political categorization of horror films as progressive or reactionary, the progressiveness of horror "depends partly on the monster's capacity to arouse sympathy." And "the presentation of the monster as totally nonhuman," for which "one can feel little," tends to reinforce rather than question dominant ideologies.[52] In this way, *Zoo*'s reactionary computer-generated images, as distancing as they might be, are not without consequences for real animals. If television is one of the primary ways humans interact with other animals, then if animals are represented as dangerous beasts that want to "kill us" and "tear us to shreds" we might be less likely to want to protect them and their habitats. *Zoo*'s portrayal of animals as dangerous predators bent on destroying humans may have an effect similar to that of *Jaws*' representation of "great white sharks as vengeful predators that could remember specific human beings and go after them to settle a grudge." After that film was released, public perceptions of great white sharks changed, which led to decimation of the worldwide shark population.[53] The replacement of real animals with computer-generated ones may reduce the real-life horror of animal labor in the production of ecohorror, but the material consequences of on-screen violence directed toward animals remain an alarming reality for animals offscreen.

Conclusion

In the end, *Zoo*'s narrative and production practices demonstrate Hal Herzog's assertion that it is "hard to think straight about animals."[54] *Zoo* recapitulates our contradictory relationship with other animals and eviscerates its own environmental themes. The series' complex and paradoxical narrative critiques human domination of other animals in limited ways by inverting and estranging consumption practices and granting animals agency, but it ultimately reinforces human exceptionalism and naturalizes human exploitation of the nonhuman world. *Zoo*'s attempts to raise questions about human-animal relationships within the ecohorror genre are undermined further by the real-life horrors of animal labor on which *Zoo* depended. Even as the production shifted to computer-generated imagery, the producers demonstrated that they were more concerned with mastery over animal representations to tell human horror stories than with the material realities of animal lives or of environmental destruction. Although *Zoo* is unable to think beyond the human, its shift from animal to digital rendering demonstrates how the television industry is in the process of rethinking its production practices that involve animal labor. Perhaps this moment of technological change and divestment from animal labor will pave the way for ecohorror television to imagine answers to the question of the animal from perspectives of the more-than-human world.

Notes

1. PETA, "Ad Blitz Targets CBS' *Zoo* for Live Animal Exploitation," June 21, 2016, https://www.peta.org/media/news-releases/ad-blitz-targets-cbs-series-zoo-live-animal-exploitation/.

2. Cary Wolfe, *Animal Rites: American Culture, the Discourse of Species, and Posthumanist Theory* (Chicago: University of Chicago Press, 2003), 8.

3. Jacques Derrida, *The Animal That I Therefore Am* (New York: Fordham University Press, 2002), 25.

4. Stephen A. Rust and Carter Soles, "Ecohorror Special Cluster: 'Living in Fear, Living in Dread, Pretty Soon We'll All Be Dead,'" *ISLE: Interdisciplinary Studies in Literature and Environment* 21, no. 3 (Summer 2014): 509–10.

5. CBS, "About *Zoo*," accessed February 1, 2017, www.cbs.com/shows/zoo/.

6. Bill Keveney, "Primal Fears Are Realized in CBS' 'Zoo,'" *USA Today*, June 30, 2015, Proquest.

7. Rust and Soles, "Ecohorror Special Cluster," 510.

8. Katarina Gregersdotter, Nicklas Hållén, and Johan Höglund, introduction to *Animal Horror Cinema: Genre, History and Criticism*, ed. Katarina Gregersdotter, Johan Höglund, and Nicklas Hållén (New York: Palgrave Macmillan, 2015), 5.

9. Keveney, "Primal Fears."

10. T. L. Stanley, "How James Patterson's *Zoo* Became a Series for CBS," *Los Angeles Times*, May 5, 2015, www.latimes.com/entertainment/tv/la-ca-st-tvpreview-zoo-20150531-story.html.

11. Lesley Goldberg, "*Zoo* Cancelled at CBS After Three Seasons," *Hollywood Reporter*, October 23, 2017, https://www.hollywoodreporter.com/live-feed/zoo-canceled-at-cbs-3-seasons-1051252.

12. Jeff Jensen, review of "*Zoo*," *Entertainment Weekly*, July 3, 2015, 50.

13. James Patterson and Michael Ledwidge, *Zoo* (New York: Little, Brown, 2014), 432.

14. Ibid.

15. Ibid.

16. Jason Mittell, *Complex TV: The Poetics of Contemporary Television Storytelling* (New York: New York University Press, 2015), 18.

17. Kathie Huddleston, "EP Promises Tonight's SC Premiere Will Be 'A Crazy New Chapter in the Saga of *Zoo*,'" *SYFY Wire*, June 29, 2017, http://www.syfy.com/syfywire/ep-promises-tonights-s3-premiere-will-be-a-crazy-new-chapter-in-the-saga-of-zoo.

18. Gregersdotter, Hållén, and Höglund, introduction, 9.

19. Val Plumwood, "Surviving a Crocodile Attack," *Utne Reader*, July–August 2000, www.utne.com/arts/being-prey?pageid=8#PageContent8.

20. Carol J. Adams, *The Sexual Politics of Meat: A Feminist-Vegetarian Critical Theory* (London: Continuum, 1990), 40.

21. See chapter 2, by Christy Tidwell, and chapter 10, by Kristen Angierski, in this volume for more on the horror of eating nonhuman animals.

22. Melanie Joy, *Why We Love Dogs, Eat Pigs and Wear Cows: An Introduction to Carnism* (San Francisco: Conari, 2010), 85.

23. Randy Malamud, *An Introduction to Animals and Visual Culture* (New York: Palgrave Macmillan, 2012), 115.

24. John Berger, *About Looking* (New York: Pantheon Books, 1980), 24.

25. See Brittany R. Roberts, chapter 8 in this volume, for an extended analysis of the ethical considerations involved in pet relationships.

26. Yi-Fu Tuan, *Dominance and Affection: The Making of Pets* (New Haven, CT: Yale University Press, 1984), 2.

27. Brett Mills, *Animals on Television: The Cultural Making of the Non-Human* (London: Palgrave Macmillan, 2017), 149.

28. Matthew Calarco, *Thinking Through Animals: Identity, Difference, Indistinction* (Stanford, CA: Stanford University Press, 2015), 64.

29. Sarah McFarland and Ryan Hediger, "Approaching the Agency of Other Animals: An Introduction," in *Animals and Agency: An Interdisciplinary Exploration*, ed. Sarah McFarland and Ryan Hediger (Leiden, NL: Brill, 2009), 16.

30. Margo DeMello, *Animals and Society: An Introduction to Human-Animal Studies* (New York: Columbia University Press, 2012), 359–60.

31. Mills, *Animals on Television*, 20.

32. Stanley, "How James Patterson's *Zoo*."

33. Dave Walker, "On the New Orleans Set of *Zoo*, the Gorillas Gone Wild Summertime Series Coming to CBS in June," *Times-Picayune*, April 9, 2015, www.nola.com/tv/index.ssf/2015/04/zoo_james_patterson_cbs_james.html.

34. Dave Walker, "In CBS' '*Zoo*' the Attacking Animals Are More Real Than You Would Expect," *Times-Picayune*, June 26, 2015, www.nola.com/tv/index.ssf/2015/06/cbs_zoo_real_animals.html.

35. Liz Raftery, "*Zoo*: What's It Like to Run a Show Where the Extras Are Animals?," *TV Guide.com*, June 29, 2015, www.tvguide.com/news/zoo-cbs-animals-james-wolk/.

36. Bryan Cairns, "'*Zoo*s' Jeff Pinkner Envisions Rampaging Animals, Global Panic in New CBS Series," *CBR.com*, June 30, 2015, www.cbr.com/zoos-jeff-pinkner-envisions-rampaging-animals-global-panic-in-new-cbs-series/.

37. Lisa de Moraes, "PETA Targets CBS over Botched Assurances on '*Zoo*,'" *Deadline Hollywood*, June 29, 2015, deadline.com/2015/06/peta-zoo-tv-series-controversy-lions-cbs-ames-patterson-1201461430/.

38. Maane Khatchatourian, "Peta Protesting Use of Real Animals in CBS' 'Zoo,'" *Variety*, June 29, 2015, https://variety.com/2015/tv/news/peta-protesting-zoo-cbs-1201530440/.

39. Nicole Shukin, *Animal Capital: Rendering Life in Biopolitical Times* (Minneapolis: University of Minnesota Press, 2009), 6–7.

40. Alan Green, *Animal Underworld: Inside America's Black Market for Rare and Exotic Species* (New York: Public Affairs, 1999); Jason Hribal, *Fear of the Animal Planet: The Hidden History of Animal Resistance* (Petrolia, CA: CounterPunch, 2010).

41. According to PETA, one report involved an animal supplier to the *Zoo* series. CBS dropped their plan to use lions, tigers, leopards, and baboons from Canada's Bowmanville Zoo as well as the services of the zoo's owner Michael Hackenberger after PETA circulated a video of Hackenberger whipping a tiger (Fricker). For more on recent reports of animal abuse in film and television, see the exposé "Animals Were Harmed: Hollywood's Nightmare of Death, Injury and Secrecy Exposed," in *The Hollywood Reporter*, December 6, 2013.

42. Khatchatourian, "Peta Protesting"; Born Free USA, "Born Free USA Condemns CBS Television for Continuing to Use Live Animals in *Zoo*: Network Puts Animals, the Show's Cast, and the Crew at Risk; Ignores Requests to Consider Humane Alternatives," last updated June 29, 2016, https://www.bornfreeusa.org/2016/06/29/born-free-usa-condemns-cbs/.

43. Khatchatourian, "Peta Protesting."

44. James Hibberd, "Bob Barker Urges CBS to Make 'Zoo' Changes," *Entertainment Weekly*, June 23, 2016, http://ew.com/article/2016/06/23/bob-barker-cbs-zoo/.

45. Born Free USA, "Born Free USA Condemns."

46. Dave Walker, "Animal Trainer for CBS 'Zoo' Responds to PETA's Charges of Abuse, Exploitation," *Times-Picayune*, July 7, 2015, www.nola.com/tv/index.ssf/2015/07/cbs_zoo_peta_charges.html.

47. Ibid.

48. Marisa Roffman, "Comic Con: 'Zoo' Co-creator Jokes About PETA Uproar," *Hollywood Reporter*, July 9, 2015, www.hollywoodreporter.com/live-feed/comic-con-2015-zoo-peta-807516.

49. Mills, *Animals on Television*, 158.

50. Huddleston, "EP Promises."

51. Ibid.

52. Robin Wood, "An Introduction to the American Horror Film," in *Robin Wood on the Horror Film: Collected Essays and Reviews*, ed. Barry Keith Grant (Detroit: Wayne State University Press, 2018), 103.

53. Charles Choi, "How *Jaws* Forever Changed Our View of Great White Sharks," *Live Science*, June 10, 2010, https://www.livescience.com/8309-jaws-changed-view-great-white-sharks.html.

54. Hal Herzog, *Some We Love, Some We Hate, Some We Eat: Why It's So Hard to Think Straight About Animals* (New York: Harper Perennial, 2011), 1.

References

Adams, Carol J. *The Sexual Politics of Meat: A Feminist-Vegetarian Critical Theory.* London: Continuum, 1990.

Adelson, Steven A., dir. *Zoo*. Season 1, episode 5, "Blame It on Leo." Written by Jay Faerber. Aired July 28, 2015, on CBS.

Anderson, Brad, dir. *Zoo*. Season 1, episode 1, "First Blood." Written by Josh Applebaum, André Nemec, Jeff Pinkner, and Scott Rosenberg. Aired June 30, 2015, on CBS.

Berger, John. *About Looking.* New York: Pantheon Books, 1980.

Born Free USA. "Born Free USA Condemns CBS Television for Continuing to Use Live Animals in *Zoo*. Network

Puts Animals, the Show's Cast, and the Crew at Risk; Ignores Requests to Consider Humane Alternatives." Last updated June 29, 2016. https://www.bornfreeusa.org/2016/06/29/born-free-usa-condemns-cbs/.

Cairns, Bryan. "'Zoo's' Jeff Pinkner Envisions Rampaging Animals, Global Panic in New CBS Series." *CBR.com*, June 30, 2015. www.cbr.com/zoos-jeff-pinkner-envisions-rampaging-animals-global-panic-in-new-cbs-series/.

Calarco, Matthew. *Thinking Through Animals: Identity, Difference, Indistinction*. Stanford, CA: Stanford University Press, 2015.

CBS. "About Zoo." Accessed February 1, 2017. www.cbs.com/shows/zoo/.

Choi, Charles. "How *Jaws* Forever Changed Our View of Great White Sharks." *Live Science*, June 10, 2010. https://www.livescience.com/8309-jaws-changed-view-great-white-sharks.html.

DeMello, Margo. *Animals and Society: An Introduction to Human-Animal Studies*. New York: Columbia University Press, 2012.

de Moraes, Lisa. "PETA Targets CBS over Botched Assurances on 'Zoo.'" *Deadline Hollywood*, June 29, 2015. deadline.com/2015/06/peta-zoo-tv-series-controversy-lions-cbs-ames-patterson-1201461430/.

Derrida, Jacques. *The Animal That I Therefore Am*. New York: Fordham University Press. 2002.

Fricker, Peter. "Animals in Film, TV Productions Need Protection." *The Province*, January 27, 2017. https://theprovince.com/opinion/opinion-animals-used-in-tv-and-film-production-need-protection.

Gambin, Lee. *Massacred by Mother Nature: Exploring the Natural Horror Film*. Baltimore: Midnight Marquee, 2012.

Goldberg, Lesley. "*Zoo* Cancelled at CBS After Three Seasons." *Hollywood Reporter*, October 23, 2017. https://www.hollywoodreporter.com/live-feed/zoo-canceled-at-cbs-3-seasons-1051252.

Green, Alan. *Animal Underworld: Inside America's Black Market for Rare and Exotic Species*. New York: Public Affairs, 1999.

Gregersdotter, Katarina, Nicklas Hållén, and Johan Höglund. Introduction to *Animal Horror Cinema: Genre, History and* Criticism, edited by Katarina Gregersdotter, Johan Höglund, and Nicklas Hållén, 1–18. New York: Palgrave Macmillan, 2015.

Herzog, Hal. *Some We Love, Some We Hate, Some We Eat: Why It's So Hard to Think Straight About Animals*. New York: Harper Perennial, 2011.

Hibberd, James. "Bob Barker Urges CBS to Make 'Zoo' Changes." *Entertainment Weekly*, June 23, 2016. http://ew.com/article/2016/06/23/bob-barker-cbs-zoo/.

Hribal, Jason. *Fear of the Animal Planet: The Hidden History of Animal Resistance*. Petrolia, CA: CounterPunch, 2010.

Huddleston, Kathie. "EP Promises Tonight's SC Premiere Will Be 'A Crazy New Chapter in the Saga of Zoo.'" *SYFY Wire*, June 29, 2017. http://www.syfy.com/syfywire/ep-promises-tonights-s3-premiere-will-be-a-crazy-new-chapter-in-the-saga-of-zoo.

Jensen, Jeff. Review of *Zoo*. *Entertainment Weekly*, July 3, 2015.

Joy, Melanie. *Why We Love Dogs, Eat Pigs and Wear Cows: An Introduction to Carnism*. San Francisco: Conari, 2010.

Katleman, Michael, dir. *Zoo*. Season 1, episode 2, "Fight or Flight." Written by Jeff Pinkner and Scott Rosenberg. Aired July 7, 2015, on CBS.

Keveney, Bill. "Primal Fears Are Realized in CBS' 'Zoo.'" *USA Today*, June 30, 2015. Proquest.

Khatchatourian, Maane. "Peta Protesting Use of Real Animals in CBS' 'Zoo.'" *Variety*, June 29, 2015. https://variety.com/2015/tv/news/peta-protesting-zoo-cbs-1201530440/.

Malamud, Randy. *An Introduction to Animals and Visual Culture*. New York: Palgrave Macmillan, 2012.

McFarland, Sarah, and Ryan Hediger. "Approaching the Agency of Other Animals: An Introduction." In *Animals and Agency: An Interdisciplinary Exploration*, edited by Sarah McFarland and Ryan Hediger, 1–20. Leiden, NL: Brill 2009.

Mills, Brett. *Animals on Television: The Cultural Making of the Non-Human*. London: Palgrave Macmillan, 2017.

Mittell, Jason. *Complex TV: The Poetics of Contemporary Television Storytelling*. New York: New York University Press, 2015.

Moore, Christine, dir. *Zoo*. Season 1, episode 10, "Emotional Contagion." Written by Jeff Faerber. Aired September 1, 2015, on CBS.

Patterson, James, and Michael Ledwidge. *Zoo*. New York: Little, Brown, 2014.

PETA. "Ad Blitz Targets CBS' *Zoo* for Live Animal Exploitation." June 21, 2016. https://www.peta.org/media/news-releases/ad-blitz-targets-cbs-series-zoo-live-animal-exploitation/.

Plumwood, Val. "Surviving a Crocodile Attack." *Utne Reader*, July–August 2000. www.utne.com/arts/being-prey?pageid=8#PageContent8.

Raftery, Liz. "*Zoo*: What's It Like to Run a Show Where the Extras Are Animals?" *TV Guide.com*, June 29, 2015. www.tvguide.com/news/zoo-cbs-animals-james-wolk/.

Roffman, Marisa. "Comic Con: 'Zoo' Co-creator Jokes About PETA Uproar." *Hollywood Reporter*, July 9, 2015. www.hollywoodreporter.com/live-feed/comic-con-2015-zoo-peta-807516.

Rust, Stephen A., and Carter Soles. "Ecohorror Special Cluster: 'Living in Fear, Living in Dread, Pretty Soon We'll All Be Dead.'" *ISLE: Interdisciplinary Studies in Literature and Environment* 21, no. 3 (Summer 2014): 513–25.

Shukin, Nicole. *Animal Capital: Rendering Life in Biopolitical Times*. Minneapolis: University of Minnesota Press, 2009.

Solomon, David, dir. *Zoo*. Season 1, episode 6, "This Is What It Sounds Like." Written by Carla Kettner. Aired August 4, 2015, on CBS.

Stanley, T. L. "How James Patterson's *Zoo* Became a Series for CBS." *Los Angeles Times*, May 5, 2015. www.latimes.com/entertainment/tv/la-ca-st-tvpreview-zoo-20150531-story.html.

Tuan, Yi-Fu. *Dominance and Affection: The Making of Pets*. New Haven, CT: Yale University Press, 1984.

Walker, Dave. "Animal Trainer for CBS 'Zoo' Responds to PETA's Charges of Abuse, Exploitation." *Times-Picayune*, July 7, 2015. www.nola.com/tv/index.ssf/2015/07/cbs_zoo_peta_charges.html.

———. "In CBS' 'Zoo' the Attacking Animals Are More Real than You Would Expect." *Times-Picayune*, June 26, 2015. www.nola.com/tv/index.ssf/2015/06/cbs_zoo_real_animals.html.

———. "On the New Orleans Set of *Zoo*, the Gorillas Gone Wild Summertime Series Coming to CBS in June." *Times-Picayune*, April 9, 2015. www.nola.com/tv/index.ssf/2015/04/zoo_james_patterson_cbs_james.html.

Wolfe, Cary. *Animal Rites: American Culture, the Discourse of Species, and Posthumanist Theory*. Chicago: University of Chicago Press, 2003.

Wood, Robin. "An Introduction to the American Horror Film." In *Robin Wood on the Horror Film: Collected Essays and Reviews*, edited by Barry Keith Grant, 73–110. Detroit: Wayne State University Press, 2018.

12.
Naturalizing White Supremacy in *The Shallows*

Carter Soles

This elusive quality it is, which causes the thought of whiteness, when divorced from more kindly associations, and coupled with any object terrible in itself, to heighten that terror to the furthest bounds. Witness the white bear of the poles, and the white shark of the tropics; what but their smooth, flaky whiteness makes them the transcendent horrors they are? That ghastly whiteness it is which imparts such an abhorrent mildness, even more loathsome than terrific, to the dumb gloating of their aspect. So that not the fierce-fanged tiger in his heraldic coat can so stagger courage as the white-shrouded bear or shark.
—Herman Melville, *Moby-Dick* (1851)

The Shallows (2016) is a low-budget ($17 million) shark attack thriller whose surfer protagonist Nancy (Blake Lively) drops out of medical school to visit a remote, unnamed Mexican surfing beach important to her surfer mother, who recently died from cancer. After hitching a ride there with local resident Carlos (Óscar Jaenada) and surfing the waves with two male Mexican surfers (Angelo Josue Lozano Corzo and Jose Manuel Trujillo Salas), Nancy takes one last run alone and is attacked by a great white shark. Trapped on a rock two hundred yards from shore, Nancy sutures her leg wound and spends a harrowing night exposed on the rock, stalked by the shark. That same night a fat, drunk Mexican on the beach (Diego Espejel) steals her possessions and is subsequently killed by the shark. The next morning, after the two surfers return and are also violently killed, Nancy devises a scheme to defeat the shark by using the navigational buoy in the bay to her advantage. She swims to the buoy, kills the shark, and then returns home to Galveston, Texas, to complete medical school and make amends with her estranged father (Brett Cullen).[1]

White sharks such as the one in *The Shallows* are frightening to us because they function in our monstrous representations of them as an "embodiment of broken boundaries—that is, sharks embody the uncanny."[2] Herman Melville and others make clear that the white shark's uncanniness is to some extent attributable to its whiteness, both physical and figurative: "There yet lurks an elusive something in the innermost idea of this hue, which strikes more of panic to the soul than that redness which affrights in blood."[3] Indeed, in the paradigmatic *Jaws* (1975), sharks are characterized by shark hunter Quint (Robert Shaw) as essentially undead beings with "lifeless eyes, black eyes, like a doll's eyes." Quint's (and the film's) view of the white shark is as "an uncanny, vampiric creature, ambiguously positioned between living organism and machine, life and death"—a creature to be feared, conquered, and killed.[4] Even Hooper (Richard Dreyfuss), who claims to love sharks, calls the great white "a perfect engine—an eating machine," reducing a complex animal to purely mechanistic functions, an "evil and mindless killing machine devoid of any complexity."[5] This places *Jaws* and its successors in opposition to concerns about animal welfare.[6]

The Shallows echoes *Jaws* in its unforgiving attitude toward white sharks. Both films stage a battle with a monstrously exaggerated shark and spare no time for animal rights sentiments: "The struggle to kill the beast forges ahead, deaf to . . . environmental discourses that advocate granting fellow predators space rather than obliterating them."[7] *The Shallows* renders its great white shark scary by making it huge and showing it engaging in only two behaviors: hunting and feeding. The very first image we see of the shark, as Carlos's son watches GoPro helmet-cam footage taken by one of its victims, is its open mouth full of sharp teeth. Such limited representations of sharks "risk reducing all sharks to 'Shark' and then subsequently to fin and jaws. . . . The fin, bite, and death become the dominant sign of their character."[8] *The Shallows* follows this pattern, showing little empathy for the shark.

Yet *The Shallows* reveals an even greater fear of and lack of empathy for the subaltern Mexicans, who barely feature in this scenario except as vaguely sketched stereotypes. The white shark is a fellow apex predator, a formidable adversary worthy of the mixture of fear and admiration humans reserve for sharks,[9] whereas the Mexicans are portrayed as stereotypical foreign menials (Carlos and his son) and/or menaces (the thieving, fat drunk and the ambiguously depicted surfers). In this way, the film promotes US imperialism founded on white supremacy.

By deploying a killer shark in a wilderness locale, *The Shallows* evokes ecohorror, a mode depicting conflict between the human and nonhuman to generate fear.[10] Ecohorror functions as both a genre and a mode, taking many forms across genres and media; it has identifiable characteristics of its own but also appears in other genres. Ecohorror is a rich and capacious category in part because horror writ large is predominantly a rural- or wilderness-centered genre. Monsters usually dwell in or come from the wilderness. They terrorize privileged city dwellers who deserve their fate, since "the city approaches the country guilty," as a "metaphoric rapist" of the country and its resources.[11] Thus, the country-city divide sets up horror's ubiquitous revenge theme, often along class-based lines. Similarly, a common variant of ecohorror or "natural horror" centers on the "revenge of nature" plot, which most commonly features a large predatory animal or great horde or swarm of creatures that kills and terrorizes "harmful, abusive, ignorant, and self-involved human beings" who are made to "pay at the hands of Mother Nature."[12] Despite our pleasure in seeing self-involved humans get their comeuppance, though, ecohorror narratives of this type ultimately align our sympathies and point of view with these same (almost always white) humans. As Maja Milatovic describes this phenomenon in Australian animal horror films, "Mobile, travelling and individuated whiteness camping in remote beaches" or other wilderness locales "is positioned in direct contrast to homogenous, fixed and static portrayals of 'Otherness,' enforced through the imperialist concept of 'wilderness.'"[13] This chapter fleshes out this imperialist concept of wilderness as it relates to ecohorror in *The Shallows*, exposing how the nonhuman of *The Shallows* isn't really the shark—the animal nonhuman—but a more conceptual nonhuman that includes the abject Mexicans. This conceptual boundary between white humanity and all other living beings arises from a white Euro-American culture that views itself as superior to other cultures and species.

Animal horror films such as *The Shallows* dramatize in particularly dynamic and violent terms the interspecies conflicts arising from white humanity's presumed superiority. Animal horror is an enormously influential and popular ecohorror subgenre that usually begins by showing how humans, knowingly or otherwise, travel unprepared into areas or habitats they shouldn't, such as the ocean in shark attack movies. The typical animal horror film then "tells the story of how a particular animal or an animal species commits a transgression against humanity and then recounts the punishment the animal must suffer as a consequence."[14] In *The Shallows*, the action begins when a great white shark attacks Nancy for entering its feeding ground, stranding her on a rock in the middle of the bay. The rest of the film consists of Nancy's attempts to fight back against the shark and escape. The film's most terrifying moments are the shark's attacks, exemplifying that "the horror that most animal horror cinema depicts turns on an attack on human beings by an animal": in this case, a very ferocious and determined white shark.[15]

Few animals have been as enduringly sensational in animal horror as white sharks. As Matthew Lerberg writes, "The collision of fear and admiration places sharks in a paradoxical position where they remain one of the most maligned, yet captivating, animals in art and film."[16] The white shark functions symbolically as a projection of human fear of "loathsome" extreme whiteness, but metonymically it is a great white shark, and its depiction in popular shark attack movies such as *The Shallows* has real material consequences for its well-being as a species.

Although little is known about white shark biology and feeding behaviors, the species' cultural image problem makes the public unsympathetic to them, impeding real-life shark conservation efforts. Writing about shark populations in general, Lindsay French notes that "about 100 million sharks and rays are killed each year by fisheries," concluding that "the somber truth is that the world's shark populations are actually in decline, or exist at greatly reduced levels, as a result of over-fishing and habitat loss.... There is a pressing need to conserve these animals and their associated habitats to ensure their sustainability in the long term."[17] Melville's text and films like *The Shallows* convert white sharks' natural, biological whiteness into cultural whiteness, anthropomorphizing and abstracting the real shark out of existence. The shark becomes a vilified monster, a frightening boundary between human and nonhuman, its terror-enhancing whiteness understood only in anthropocentric, Euro-American cultural terms. By portraying sharks as embodiments of white horror, films like *The Shallows* sustain the white shark's popular image as a ferocious monster, thus enabling shark-killing practices to continue unchecked and making it difficult for shark conservation advocates to achieve their aims.

Animal horror films like *The Shallows* ignore white sharks' real-life vulnerabilities, instead framing the fish as deadly foes threatening their human interlocutors, unwittingly pushing those humans toward personal catharsis. Indeed, *The Shallows*' human protagonist Nancy is an updated version of the lone wilderness hero, traditionally male, who uses wilderness adventures to "recover an essential, authentic masculinity" and reassert the hegemony of the white masculine subject "not only over non-human nature, but also over his ethnic, racial, and gender subordinates."[18] Privileged white men and women go into nature to test or purify themselves: "Nature has again become a scene in which traditional ideals of American manhood are tested and reaffirmed, and the natural world brings out in the [masculine subject] a primitive, regenerative violence."[19]

Yet routinely in horror movies, white women are tougher and more likely to survive than men are, especially men of color. This is a common horror trope, inherited from the Gothic and seen most consistently in modern times as Carol J. Clover's ambiguously gendered Final Girl of the slasher genre, a type that exists outside slasher films, for example in *Alien*'s Ripley.[20] Just as Ripley outlives everyone else aboard the space vessel *Nostromo*, the last survivors in the shark attack films *Open Water* (2003), *The Reef* (2010), *47 Meters Down* (2017), and *The Shallows* are white women. *The Shallows* substitutes a white female heroine for the traditional male hero yet maintains the Eurocentric pecking order, asserting the white woman's superiority over her nonwhite "subordinates."[21] Animal horror, in the form of a huge, aggressive great white shark, is fused with the horror of extreme, deathly whiteness, while Nancy's normal whiteness is validated via her resistance to the shark. Her ability to vanquish the shark using the presumptively positive qualities of her whiteness sets her apart from the extreme-white shark on the one hand and the abject Mexicans on the other.

Nancy is a cinematic descendant of Chrissie Watkins (Susan Backlinie), the blonde woman swimmer who dies horribly in the opening scene of *Jaws* (1975). In that sequence, Chrissie is visually fetishized with underwater shots from below, simulating the great white shark's point of view, and then brutally killed in a sequence Antonia Quirke calls a "screen rape": "As the shark moves in on Chrissie it's almost as though he's stepping in, knowing she's been let down by a lover," that is, the drunk teenaged boy Chrissie leaves passed out on the beach.[22] Near the end of this violent scene, Chrissie tries in vain to cling to a buoy and scream for help, but the passed-out boy doesn't hear, and the shark pulls Chrissie under for the final time. The shark's symbolic rape and real murder take Chrissie out of the action (except as autopsied remains) five minutes into *Jaws*. A lap dissolve from the stretch of ocean where she dies (next to the ominously clanging buoy) to the view from Chief Martin Brody's window indicates Chrissie's story has been handed over to Brody (Roy Scheider). He will avenge her.

In *The Shallows*, no Brody figure vanquishes the shark. Instead, Nancy becomes Clover's Final Girl, seizing phallic power and fighting back against the monster stalking her. Nancy is proactive and exerts agency in ways denied to Chrissie, most significantly by using the intertextually significant buoy as a base from which to antagonize the shark with a flare gun. *The Shallows* reworks *Jaws*' opening sequence, exploring what it would be like if *Jaws*' Chrissie had been allowed to fight the shark herself. Nancy not only survives but outright destroys the shark, tricking it into mortally impaling itself on some sharp, protruding metal fragments at the bay bottom.[23] After remorselessly killing the shark, Nancy floats to shore and has an out-of-body experience that includes a benedictory vision of her dead mother. By the film's "One Year Later" denouement, she has returned to being a doctor in Houston in good favor with her paternalistic father.

Although Nancy is ultimately (in terms of narrative position) a gendered-masculine patriarchal agent, she shows a maternal side as well, in line with Stacy Alaimo's claims about women in ecohorror films: "Women, it seems, must serve as the border zone between nature and culture, keeping nature safely at bay in order that men can be fully human."[24] Nancy acts as a protective mother figure, defending her American family (and Carlos's Mexican one) against the monstrous, extreme-white killer shark that inhabits the bay. In so doing she demonstrates not only her white superiority but her fitness to replace her deceased mother as the protector of her younger sister Chloe (Sedona Legge), with whom she surfs in the film's Texas-set denouement.[25] Like Shirley Temple in *Wee Willie Winkie* (1937), Nancy is a young, flexible mediating figure who helps bring US imperialism, represented by her hidebound, conservative father who wants her to return to medical school, to the film's Mexican milieu.[26] When explaining her interest in the secret bay to Carlos, Nancy tells him that it was where her mother came when she found out she was pregnant with her: "I've never been, but it's kind of our beach," she tells him. It is as though she lays claim to the place on the basis of maternally transmitted right. Upon arriving at the beach, she sees an offshore landmass that looks to her like a supine pregnant woman and names it "The Island of the Pregnant Woman." When Carlos pushes back against her pronouncement, saying he doesn't see what she sees, Nancy insists that even if that isn't the land feature's actual name, "it is to me." Nancy's claiming of the beach as "our beach" and cavalier naming of the landmass over local resident Carlos's protests draw together two themes: maternal femininity and colonialist expansion of territory. The scene fuses Nancy's maternal tendencies with her imperialist ones, indicating that Nancy's whiteness and place in the Euro-American imperial hierarchy complicates her status as a Final Girl and woman hero.[27]

Furthermore, viewers are implicated in the film's entwining of woman-centeredness and imperialism via our connection to Nancy. The film's story is told almost exclusively from Nancy's point of view, and via a diegetic video chat and subsequent confessional video recording the film charges her relationships with her sister and father with tears and emotional weight.[28] This emphasis on heightened emotions within the family sphere denotes melodrama, a pathos-driven mode "focused on victim-heroes and the recognition of their virtue."[29] Most important in melodrama is "the feeling of righteousness, achieved through the sufferings of the innocent."[30] In Linda Williams's terms, Nancy is the melodramatic victim-hero whose suffering at the whims of the monstrous shark ennobles her. By surviving and fighting back, Nancy displays "a goodness that is inextricably linked to suffering," thereby symbolically restoring her purity and innocence in the film's melodramatic scheme.[31] Conversely, the shark is given no emotional sympathy or regard, and, apart from a few lurking, underwater camera shots early on, we never share its point of view.

Melodrama is a traditionally feminine mode with ties to the soap opera and the woman's film. Yet, while Nancy's gender matters, progressing from eroticized feminine object (Laura Mulvey) to melodramatized victim-hero (Williams) to masculinized "hero" (Clover), the film more strongly emphasizes Nancy's national and racial identity: she is a white American—a Texan no less. Texas is a former Confederate state and an iconic conservative American stronghold, the adopted home of the Bushes (originally from New England). Texas is also the setting for countless Westerns, and white Texans are often framed as being anti-Mexican due to the state's proximity to the border and the legacy of the US defeat at the Alamo. Furthermore, the state is known as a pro-gun haven whose unofficial motto (seen on ubiquitous bumper stickers) is "Don't mess with Texas!"[32]

In addition to her character's status as a Texan, Blake Lively's real-life history of racial insensitivity contributes to the film's portrayal of Nancy as a vaguely conservative, casually racist all-American woman. In 2012, Lively married her husband Ryan Reynolds at Boone Hall, a real-life plantation in South Carolina, complete with nine original slave cabins known as "Slave Street." Then, in 2014, she posted a spread called "The Allure of Antebellum" to her lifestyle website *Preserve*, in which she celebrates the fashion choices of Civil War–era Southern belles.[33] Lively's presumably unconscious public racism—which despite some criticism has not impeded her film career—supports the interpretation of *The Shallows* as a pro-white-American narrative sustaining the imperialist concept of wilderness founded on the unifying master idea of whiteness. Indeed, as Richard Dyer writes, the most important vehicle for the exercise and display of white dynamism—white enterprise—is imperialism.[34] Lively's extrafilmic business and lifestyle pursuits show her to be enterprising and racially insensitive—a true imperialist and marketplace feminist.[35] *Bitch Magazine* cofounder Andi Zeisler defines marketplace feminism as a commodified form of feminism that emphasizes superficial lifestyle choices over activism, centered on finding and sustaining heterosexual relationships, marriage, and economic success that don't challenge existing capitalist structures.[36] Nancy's (and the film's) marketplace feminism, expressed in her commitment to surfing, a sport which requires expensive equipment and often necessitates travel, functions as a smokescreen for the film's anti-shark and anti-Mexican fearmongering in the service of US imperialism.

Nancy's blonde hair, white skin, Texas roots, and "bossy" attitude (as noted by Carlos) establish her as a near-ideal American subject—only her femininity obstructs her rise to the top of the imperial hierarchy. Yet her status as a surfer codes her as masculine and white.[37] As Krista Comer writes, women who surf are "about ocean-going physical power and the serious mental game it [takes] to sustain that."[38] That "serious mental game," which Nancy clearly possesses, keeping calm and maintaining her mental focus throughout her shark attack ordeal, aligns with two of Dyer's key traits of whiteness: willpower and mind over matter. The coded-white character traits of "energy, enterprise, discipline and spiritual elevation, and even the white body, its hardness and tautness," are also surfer-girl traits Nancy possesses.[39]

The Shallows first establishes Nancy's athleticism and toughness via early surfing sequences similar to those seen in the women's surfing documentary *Blue Crush* (1998).[40] The scene where Nancy paddles out, which is set to inspirational instrumental music, and the first surfing sequence could be mistaken for sequences from that documentary, except that the surfing itself in *Blue Crush* is much more impressive and sustained. Eschewing the documentary's long takes of surfing prowess, *The Shallows* favors rapid montage, an abstract approach suggesting surfing. Furthermore, use of a low-angled underwater camera to show the surfers passing by overhead, which echoes shots in the *Jaws 2* waterskiing and parasailing sequences, suggests the point of view of the shark, the lurking predatory monster of horror. Yet these shots simultaneously evoke the underwater footage of surfers (without the implied presence of monsters) in *Blue Crush*. Thus, despite its nods to impending horror, *The Shallows* here foregrounds the excitement of surfing in an exotic locale, bonding the viewer to Nancy via shared participation in this exhilarating action spectacle.

Beyond establishing Nancy's surfer bona fides, *The Shallows'* early sequences also highlight the beauty and appeal of the natural surroundings of the bay, located in real life on Lord Howe Island, an ecotourism resort located off the east coast of Australia. As Nancy diegetically engages in surfer tourism, the film's viewer engages in optical tourism of the kind documented by Ella Shohat and Robert Stam: "The camera [penetrates] a foreign and familiar zone like a predator, seizing its 'loot' of images as raw material to be reworked in the 'motherland' and sold to sensation-hungry spectators and consumers."[41] The film's producers seem to share this same touristic glee. In *Finding the Perfect Beach: Lord Howe Island*, a behind-the-scenes documentary on *The Shallows* DVD, one of the film's producers, Lynn Harris, discusses the need to discover in Australia "a beach that looked Mexican or Latin American or Costa Rican—an isolated, tropical, magical place." Or as locations manager Duncan Jones puts it, fetishizing the locale in colonialist terms, Lord Howe's "water was uniquely tropical" and the locale "really untouched." The production team's language in describing Lord Howe Island evokes a pastoral fantasy of pristine, Edenic wilderness. In *The Shallows*, the cinematography encourages this same interpretation, portraying

Nancy's Mexican beach as an isolated paradise, featuring several overhead panoramic shots of the entire bay that mimic scenic travel photography, specifically publicity photos and tourism videos on Lord Howe Island's official website. David Ingram notes that Hollywood films tend to follow such aesthetics of pristine wilderness cinematography, omitting from natural landscape images "all signs of human intervention in nature."[42] Until the shark shows up, *The Shallows* adheres to this dominant Hollywood visual trend, in which "nature tends to be shown at its pristine best, a tourist gaze from which what is undesirable or ugly is omitted."[43]

In line with the surfing sequence's visual commodification of surfing and the tropical surroundings, Nancy's white, female body is also placed on erotic display. The montage where she first prepares her surfboard on the beach features close-ups of her bare stomach and bikini-clad breasts, an especially gratuitous shot of her zipping her wetsuit top over her cleavage, and a provocative long shot from behind of her dropping her jean shorts to reveal her bikini bottoms, thus coding her body for "strong visual and erotic impact."[44] But Nancy's sexuality is complicated by her whiteness. White women inhabit the paradoxical position of being seen as both sexual and sexually pure: their sexuality, coded as "dark," functions as "a disturbance of their racial purity."[45] In their role as sexual beings they act as vessels for reproduction, thus guaranteeing the continuance of the so-called white race, but to retain their white purity they must remain "unsullied by the dark drives that reproduction entails."[46] In line with these contradictory cultural mandates, Nancy is portrayed as sexy but not sexual—she possesses "to-be-looked-at-ness" without possessing sexual relationships, interest, agency, or desire.[47] To further reinforce this, Nancy's body is fetishized as she paddles out on her surfboard, with more shots from behind displaying her buttocks, interspersed with lurking underwater point-of-view shots, waterline shots, and sinister music. These underwater shots in particular generate ecohorror, in this case fear of the nonhuman, via terror of the water and what lives in it, providing a specific context for what threatens Nancy's exposed body. This sequence sets up Nancy as a potential victim of a (sexual) predator waiting just below the waterline.

Nancy paddles out and meets the two male Mexican surfers, whose nonwhiteness provides a visual contrast to Nancy's blonde hair and white skin. Being a (white) woman in the company of two (Mexican) men, Nancy treats them warily as they chat about where she's from and the quality of the waves.

Having been unable to pry the beach's name out of Carlos, she again tries to learn the place's local name, asking the darker-skinned surfer. He refuses, building on Carlos's two similar refusals during the car-ride sequence to again highlight the invasive nature of Nancy's request. Furthermore, the surfer's response of "If I tell you, I would have to kill you" makes him seem possibly menacing: even as a joke this could come true, given the conventions of the horror/thriller genre. This discussion with the surfers is the last time Nancy is called out for her privileged American attitude, though. Until the shark appears, Nancy acts like a presumptuous tourist, and the film pokes fun at her imperialistic behaviors via Carlos's and the surfers' comments. But once the shark attacks her, providing her personal melodrama with its true villain, she is ennobled. Through its extreme, bestial whiteness, the shark draws out her noble, sympathetic white qualities.

Tourists and Vagabonds

Unlike *Jaws*, in which the shark comes to the US Atlantic Coast to terrorize fictional Amity Island, *The Shallows* takes place in an exoticized, unnamed bay in rural Mexico to which Nancy journeys alone. Nancy's status as a medical student and aspiring doctor is a plot convenience (allowing her to know how to stitch herself up), but it also affirms her high socioeconomic status: she is from the American upper middle class, a tourist—both literally, as a white tourist in Mexico, and figuratively, in Zygmunt Bauman's sense of being an upwardly mobile global "tourist" who travels to fulfill her consumerist desire as a sensation gatherer.[48] For Bauman, *mobility* is a key measure of one's status under global capitalism: "one difference between those 'high up' and those 'low down' is that the first may leave the second behind—but not vice versa."[49] Privileged, sensation-gathering tourists like Nancy "are satisfied that they travel through life at their heart's desire and pick and choose their destinations according to the joys they offer," while impoverished vagabonds like *The Shallows*' Mexicans "are the waste of the world which has dedicated itself to tourist services."[50] Such disenfranchised vagabonds remain stuck in place until "pushed from behind" by the forces of global capitalism, at which time they are "thrown out from the site they would rather stay in."[51] This is why Carlos and the two surfers are guarded about telling Nancy the beach's name—if word gets out, more privileged tourists will be attracted to the area and the locals will be conscripted into wage slavery and/or pushed out altogether.

By presenting its protagonist and principal antagonist as two white anomalies in an otherwise exotically coded environment, *The Shallows* calls attention to whiteness as a privileged cultural category. Dyer argues that "the category of whiteness is unclear and unstable, yet this has proved its strength. Because whiteness carries such rewards and privileges, the sense of a border that might be crossed and a hierarchy that might be climbed has produced a dynamic that has enthralled people who have had any chance of participating in it."[52] Whiteness is internally hierarchical, with normal, "non-extreme, unspectacular, plain whiteness" at the top and less desirable extreme whiteness fearfully resisted and denied by presumptively normal whites.[53] Thus, ordinary and extreme whiteness are mutually constitutive, each containing certain elements of its counterpart. For example, both forms are enterprising, but extreme whiteness is seen to take that tendency too far, to a psychotic, monstrous, and/or obsessive point (e.g., murderous tendencies and world domination), whereas normal whiteness is seen to be ambitious in just the right amount. In *The Shallows*, ordinary whiteness, represented by the good-hearted, strong-willed Texas surfer girl, defeats and destroys the monstrously extreme great white shark. The shark's monstrosity is in part a projection of ordinary whiteness's terror of its counterpart. That the target of this projection is a wild animal facilitates this anthropocentric devaluation, since nonhuman animals are already thought of as "dumb" and "gloating," in Melville's words; their whiteness merely amplifies their horrifying animal otherness. *Jaws*, the "paradigmatic shark film,"[54] poses the same dichotomy, pitting the all-white residents of the "archetypal American coastal town" of Amity against the monstrously devouring shark from "the uncontrollable, formless wilderness" of the sea beyond the shoreline.[55]

The film speaks not only of ordinary whiteness and of extreme whiteness but also of a third kind of whiteness seen in the nonwhite Mexicans who serve as *The Shallows*' supporting characters. Dyer argues that liminally white ethnic groups sometimes contingently included in whiteness and at other times excluded—"a category of maybe, sometime whites"—create a buffer between the purely white and the emphatically nonwhite, that is, the Black, the Indigenous, and the savage.[56] In *The Shallows*, the Mexican locals occupy the ambiguous space between Nancy's civilized, proper human whiteness and the shark's savage, Indigenous otherness. For while the shark is a white shark, its nonhuman animality—its exaggerated, monstrous shark-ness—allows it to be dismissed and destroyed as a savage force. The film's Mexicans help demonstrate this, for although they turn out mostly to be just minor threats to Nancy, all of them except Carlos and his son get brutally killed by the monstrous white shark.

The most developed of the Mexican characters, Carlos, is a benign magical minority character whose sole purpose in *The Shallows* is to selflessly help Nancy achieve her goals. He exists outside of any community of his own and is not recognized in any significant way by the white community to which the protagonist belongs.[57] Carlos gives Nancy a free ride to the bay on a rough dirt track through dense tropical foliage and then rescues her once his son finds her GoPro recording asking for help. We know nothing about him except that he lives nearby and is named Carlos. That said, Carlos fleetingly offers some moments of resistance when he is pleasantly cagey about refusing to reveal the beach's real name and takes advantage of Nancy's lack of facility with Spanish to call her "bossy" without her knowing it. He also refuses to let her pay him for the ride, which could be seen as an assertion of his economic autonomy. Yet in absolute terms, her monetary offer, compounded with her ability to reach this remote corner of Mexico in the first place, makes clear that she is of a higher class status than Carlos. Using Bauman's terms for globalized consumers, Nancy is an economically and geographically mobile "tourist" able to capitalize on global flows (of money and travel), while Carlos is a lower-class "vagabond" confined to the local region.[58] Carlos's initial cleverness pokes fun at Nancy's economic privilege and cultural insensitivity, yet the film undermines his critique, emphasizing Carlos's provincialism by joking that he is unaware of Uber. "How you getting out from here?" he asks Nancy. "Uber," she replies. "Who is Uber?" he asks. Beyond Carlos, the other Mexican characters in *The Shallows* are depicted only as drunks, thieves, and potential sexual predators whose ultimate function is to play victim to the killer shark.

White Death

Once the two surfers leave the beach and Nancy is left alone, she sees and paddles out to a floating whale carcass. The whale carcass is a nice touch on three levels. First, it is ecohorrific in its own right, showing off the ecohorror of death and decay.[59] Second, it helps explain the shark's presence in the bay at this time. White sharks scavenge on whale carcasses, a well-documented phenomenon[60] seen, for example, in the white shark documentary *Blue Water White Death* (1971) and in an appearance by the white known as Deep Blue off Hawaii in mid-January 2019. Third, along with the underwater point-of-view shots and the Mexican surfer's "I'd have to kill you" joke, the carcass is another harbinger of the lurking shark, indicating its feeding ground.

But the presence of a seaborne whale carcass, which may drift for several weeks while exuding "a continuous slick of blood and oil that can attract sharks from long distances,"[61] throws into question why the shark spends so much time hunting Nancy when there is an abundant, preferred food source available. It's not that some sharks might not prefer the taste of some humans, but the shark that circles Nancy's rock all night and ultimately attacks a buoy to get at her is shark-as-monster, not shark-as-shark.

When the shark attacks, it comes in with a wave, knocking Nancy off her board as she is surfing. The shark works together with the wave, implicating the wave and the water in this ecohorrific strike—as Keri Stevenson argues in chapter 4 of this collection, the sea is often deployed as a monster in ecohorror, "swallowing up the world with a radical ability to conquer time and space, feeding on the earth with no satiation of its appetite possible."[62] Antonia Quirke similarly argues that shark attack films are among several subgenres that inflect "the whole of a landscape with fear,"[63] and surely a core part of the human fear of white sharks is that encounters with them by definition take place in their element, the water.[64] Furthermore, the shark's attack is sudden and violent and takes place near shore at the water's surface in daylight, as do most documented real-life white shark attacks on humans.[65] That is, the shark attacking Nancy in this way is both cinematically spectacular—inside the wave, we see the shark's dark profile cruise up behind Nancy—and essentially believable.

Indeed, *The Shallows* takes some pains to couch its monstrous, horror-movie white shark in terms that make its behavior at least somewhat credible. It is a superficial realism placed in the service of "melodramatic passion and action,"[66] but it does align with certain known traits and behaviors of white sharks. For example, Nancy's status as a surfer contributes to this sense of the shark's verisimilitude. Although the exact reasons for this remain opaque, white sharks most frequently attack humans who participate in board sports and who are isolated from other groups of humans.[67] Thus, as a lone surfer, Nancy makes a relatively probable target for a white shark attack.

As the film unfolds, however, the shark is increasingly portrayed as a hostile, monstrous force, attacking relentlessly, killing three locals, stalking Nancy overnight, and ultimately attacking a buoy to get at her. It is a psychotic killer shark, a fantastical, ecohorrific movie creation. Simply by being itself (if that can be said of a computer-generated shark in a Hollywood movie), it is, in Dyer's words, too excessively white: mechanistic, deadly, relentless—Hooper's "perfect eating machine." The white shark is *too* good at what it does, *too* effective an apex predator, so humans fear it and want to destroy it because we anthropomorphically project our own hated, extreme-white qualities onto it.

As if to amplify the anthropomorphized extremity of its whiteness, the shark reserves special rancor for its Mexican victims. *The Shallows* depicts the deaths of at least two of the shark's nonwhite victims in especially terrifying and gruesome terms, therefore reifying the film's American imperialist racial hierarchy. The darker skinned of the two surfers, who speaks less English and needs his lighter-skinned buddy to translate, suffers the longest on-screen death. His drawn-out death scene—he is initially attacked and then dragged through the water only to be fatally pulled under right in front of Nancy—is the most reminiscent of Chrissie's in *Jaws*. Nancy watches in horror as the surfer is killed, and thus his death is used to generate more pathos for her. On day one, he is threatening due to his lack of facility with English and his dark brown skin; on day two, he is a feminized, hapless target for the killer shark, weaker and less savvy than Nancy, whose whiteness and narrative position render her superior to him.

Nancy's mildly xenophobic attitude, though misapplied to the surfers, is well founded when it comes to the other Mexican character in the film—the fat, drunk ne'er-do-well sleeping on the beach. That night Nancy sees him lying next to an empty tequila bottle, and she screams to get his attention. He awakens, rummages through her backpack, and steals her cell phone and cash. He then wades into the water to steal Nancy's surfboard. Even though he just robbed her, she nobly tries to warn him out of the water, but he is too stupid to heed her warnings. The shark gets him, and he suffers the goriest on-screen death of any character. He is severed in half at the waist, and we see his detached top half crawling up the beach in three-quarter profile shot. He is in abject pain and groans horribly throughout. While the viewer takes pleasure in the grotesque death of this unsympathetic, stereotypical character, Nancy shows her ordinary, decent, human whiteness by being horrified and saddened at the shark's ruthless deeds.

Nancy's perseverance in battling the white shark and trying to help its Mexican victims is framed as a normal, sympathetic, culturally valorized quality of whiteness infused with enterprising "white spirit."[68] Furthermore, it is a whiteness strongly associated with masculinity. Nancy's morally purifying white toughness and willpower is most memorably displayed in the scene in which she sutures her own leg wound. A tough survivor, she sews herself up with an earring chain sans anesthesia, evincing her whiteness by exerting determination, coldness of will, and mind over matter. This is grotesque, gory, and horrific, showing graphically the damage done by the shark attack. It also echoes self-repair scenes in hard-bodied action films such as *First Blood* (1982) and *The Terminator* (1984). Like John Rambo in *First Blood*, Nancy may unconsciously wish to die—she takes risks due to an unconscious desire to obliterate herself, a punishment for not being able to save her mother. But once the shark attacks her, she is galvanized into action, resisting her dark desire for self-destruction and using her medical training to stitch her own wounds and save herself. In later scenes, Nancy remains calm and cool under pressure, using her watch timer to calculate time and distances dispassionately when plotting against the shark and clinically reporting her injuries on the video recording she makes for her family. These scenes masculinize Nancy, and as she becomes more coded-masculine she rises up in the imperial hierarchy. That is, as the Final Girl of the horror genre she moves progressively into a structurally masculine role as "hero,"[69] and this, coupled with her whiteness, makes her an ideal imperial subject.

The shark tries to consume Nancy—that is, it tries to do to her what she does to the beach, the landscape, and its denizens. In this, *The Shallows* follows a traditional revenge-of-nature/animal horror pattern. Yet in its singular focus and ferocity, and in the particularly gruesome deaths it inflicts upon the film's Mexicans, *The Shallows*' white shark embodies a projection of the "dark side" of whiteness, those death-inflicting qualities intrinsically possessed yet abhorred and denied by ordinary whites. By reducing the shark to a horrific, sensationalized, anthropomorphized projection of extreme whiteness, the film represses the "real" shark, reducing it to an empty signifier that is really a reflection of human faults such as "rapaciousness, greed, and voraciousness" that are cleanly divorced along species lines from the film's noble, white, human protagonist.[70]

Conclusion

In the chapter's opening epigraph from *Moby Dick*, Melville describes an elusive, ambiguous quality that "causes the thought of whiteness, when divorced from more kindly associations, and coupled with any object terrible in itself, to heighten that terror to the furthest bounds."[71] This suggests that humans find sharks inherently "terrible" but that our terror of white sharks is heightened by their whiteness—a whiteness they share with white people. The great white shark represents the appalling mildness of extreme (human) whiteness, too perfect, too cold, too lethal—a reflection of (human) white "deathliness."[72] This deathly, abhorrent whiteness we share with other creatures such as the shark points to Stacy Alaimo's idea that horror makes us at least temporarily, in the messy middles of horror movies, "entertain the fear that humans are part of the nature they destroy" and thus confront the permeability of the boundary between human and nonhuman.[73] Indeed, in analyzing the similarities between *Jaws* and subsequent slasher movies such as *Halloween* (1978), Dawn Keetley contends that both films

> disclose the terrifying confrontation with the nonhuman (the inexplicable, irrational, and implacable) at the heart of horror. That the Great White becomes Michael Myers, moreover, suggests that there is no firm line between that nonhuman force and the human. The nonhuman that stalks the horror film, that the horror film is so devoted to exploring, is (also) in the human. *Jaws* made it clear, before the slasher sub-genre really got going, that what was at the heart of the slasher was this nonhuman force—and sometimes it looked human.[74]

That nonhuman force, at least in the examples Keetley raises, is whiteness. Does not Michael Myers's bleached-white mask have the same mildly abhorrent effect that Melville describes in the white shark?[75] Dyer writes that when it comes to whiteness, "horror films have their cake and eat it: they give us the horror of whiteness while at the same time ascribing it to those who are liminally white. The terror of whiteness, of being without life, of causing death, is both vividly conveyed and disowned."[76] Human slasher killers stripped of their humanity and nonhuman animals such as sharks make ideal targets for this act of white disavowal.

In the end, despite its revision of Chrissie's narrative from *Jaws* and some market-feminist gestures, *The Shallows* reinforces "a diehard, historically dominant culture's determination to keep living in denial, to sustain an unsustainable condition of contorted innocence."[77] It's an innocence bought with nonwhite lives and with the lives of killed and bycaught sharks. Nancy is ultimately willing to murder a member of a threatened species in order to survive. She never even considers a live-and-let-live attitude toward the shark that stalks her, despite her momentary sympathy for the shark when she sees it has a hook in its mouth: "They got you," she muses, then enacts her plan to reach the buoy and kill the shark. Val Plumwood's well-known essay "Being Prey" offers a contrast to Nancy's approach, suggesting that humans should learn to see themselves as part of the food chain rather than outside or above it. Noting that encounters with large predator species present "an important test" for us, Plumwood writes that when they are allowed to live freely, "these creatures indicate our preparedness to coexist with the otherness of the earth, and to recognize ourselves in mutual, ecological terms, as part of the food chain, eaten as well as eater."[78]

Conversely, in *The Shallows*, Nancy's survival is bought with the shark's life and with the lives (and GoPro camera) of the Mexicans. All our sympathies go to Nancy, our white, Texan, surfer-girl protagonist, a melodramatic avatar of contemporary whiteness and an embodiment of "American culture's (often hypocritical) notion of itself as the locus of innocence and virtue."[79] *The Shallows* thus maintains the Eurocentric pecking order, ultimately endorsing Nancy's anthropocentric, capitalistic view of the bay as a commodified tourist destination that serves only as a backdrop to her test of wills and survival. As a work of marketplace feminism, *The Shallows* makes its heroine appealing, capable, and cool, but it portrays her as neither an intentional feminist nor an environmental activist. All her enterprise and willpower goes toward destroying the shark and reconciling with her patriarchal family unit. *The Shallows* updates the wilderness-survival-film/animal-horror-film formula by featuring a victorious female heroine, yet its ecohorrific, Othering depiction of the natural world and its nonhuman animals follows a playbook familiar to viewers of *Jaws* (1975), *The Birds* (1963), and the nuclear-tinged creature features of the 1950s.

Notes

1. I thank several colleagues whose comments made this chapter better: Kom Kunyosying, Sara L. Crosby, Bridgitte Barclay, Isaac Rooks, and Christy Tidwell.
2. Nichole Neff, "The Belly of the Beast: The Uncanny Shark," *Gothic Studies* 18, no. 2 (November 2016): 53.
3. Herman Melville, *Moby-Dick* (New York: Harper and Brothers, 1851; New York: Penguin Classics, 1992), 205. Citations refer to the Penguin Classics edition.
4. David Ingram, *Green Screen: Environmentalism and Hollywood Cinema* (Exeter, UK: University of Exeter Press, 2000), 89.
5. Matthew Lerberg, "Jabbering *Jaws*: Reimagining Representations of Sharks Post-*Jaws*," in *Screening the Nonhuman: Representations of Animal Others in the Media*, ed. Amber E. George and J. L. Schatz (Lanham, MD: Lexington Books, 2016), 36.
6. Ingram, *Green Screen*, 88.
7. Stacy Alaimo, "Discomforting Creatures: Monstrous Natures in Recent Films," in *Beyond Nature Writing: Expanding the Boundaries of Ecocriticism*, ed. Karla Armbruster and Kathleen R. Wallace (Charlottesville: University Press of Virginia, 2001), 281.
8. Lerberg, "Jabbering *Jaws*," 35.
9. Ibid.
10. Stephen A. Rust and Carter Soles, "Ecohorror Special Cluster: 'Living in Fear, Living in Dread, Pretty Soon We'll All Be Dead,'" *ISLE: Interdisciplinary Studies in Literature and Environment* 21, no. 3 (Summer 2014): 510.
11. Carol J. Clover, *Men, Women, and Chain Saws: Gender in the Modern Horror Film* (Princeton, NJ: Princeton University Press, 1992), 128–29.
12. Lee Gambin, *Massacred by Mother Nature: Exploring the Natural Horror Film* (Baltimore: Midnight Marquee, 2012), 24.
13. Maja Milatovic, "Consuming Wildlife: Representations of Tourism and Retribution in Australian Animal Horror," in *Animal Horror Cinema: Genre, History and Criticism*, ed. Katarina Gregersdotter, Johan Höglund, and Nicklas Hållén (New York: Palgrave Macmillan, 2015), 84.
14. Katarina Gregersdotter, Nicklas Hållén, and Johan Höglund, introduction to *Animal Horror Cinema: Genre, History and Criticism*, ed. Katarina Gregersdotter, Johan Höglund, and Nicklas Hållén (New York: Palgrave Macmillan, 2015), 3.
15. Ibid. While often referred to in popular parlance as the "great white shark," the most common name used by marine biologists and other scientists for members of the species *carcharodon carcharias* is simply white shark—I default to this usage throughout.
16. Lerberg, "Jabbering *Jaws*," 35.
17. Lindsay A. French, "Yearly Worldwide Shark Attack Summary 2017," *International Shark Attack File* (ISAF), last modified February 6, 2018, www.floridamuseum.ufl.edu/shark-attacks/yearly-worldwide-summary/.
18. Ingram, *Green Screen*, 36.
19. Ibid., 37.
20. Clover, *Men, Women, and Chain Saws*, 39–40, 63.
21. Ingram, *Green Screen*, 36; Ella Shohat and Robert Stam, *Unthinking Eurocentrism: Multiculturalism and the Media*, 2nd ed. (New York: Routledge, 2014), 113.
22. Antonia Quirke, *Jaws* (London: BFI, 2002), 11.
23. This outcome, modeled upon the exploding shark at the end of *Jaws*, is more common in bigger-budget, action-oriented, male-centered shark films like *Deep Blue Sea* (1999) and *The Meg* (2018) but seen less often in the films *The Shallows* more closely resembles, lower-budget shark thrillers in which usually female protagonists barely escape with their lives (*The Reef*, *47 Meters Down*) or don't survive at all (*Open Water*).
24. Alaimo, "Discomforting Creatures," 283.
25. In a private correspondence, ecocritic Sara L. Crosby has provocatively suggested that the shark may represent Nancy's dead mother's ghost come to haunt her in animal form.

26. Shohat and Stam, *Unthinking Eurocentrism*, 113.

27. Nancy's status as a woman who mediates between wild nature and civilization is reinforced by her maternal relation to Steven Seagull, a wild bird with an injured wing she nurses back to health while stranded on the rock. The seagull is framed as a quasi-domestic, pet-like wild animal and enjoys more sympathetic screen time than the shark or any of its Mexican victims.

28. *The Shallows* is somewhat unique among shark attack films for its single-protagonist focus. Most shark attack movies feature small groups of human victims (*Jaws*, *Deep Blue Sea*, *The Reef*) or at least couples (*Open Water*, *47 Meters Down*).

29. Linda Williams, "Melodrama Revised," in *Refiguring American Film Genres*, ed. Nick Browne (Berkeley: University of California Press, 1998), 66.

30. Ibid., 62.

31. Ibid., 54.

32. Texas also has a history of prominent women leaders, mostly liberal—for example, former Governor Ann Richards and former State Senator Wendy Davis. While Nancy clearly does not reflect the politics of such figures—her in-film characterization (xenophobic toward Mexicans, ultimately a dutiful daddy's girl) plus Lively's star text code her as centrist-leaning conservative—the tradition of politically powerful women in Texas could resonate in Nancy's depiction, at least superficially, making her seem more feminist and/or progressive than she actually is. While the phrase "Don't Mess with Texas" originated as a slogan for a statewide anti-littering campaign launched in 1986 and retains its associations to that campaign, it has also entered general parlance as an expression of Texan defiance and/or pride.

33. Allie Jones, "Blake Lively's Fall Fashion Inspiration Is Slaveowners," *Gawker .com*, October 13, 2014, https://gawker.com /blake-livelys-fall-fashion-inspiration-is -slaveowners-1645661587.

34. Richard Dyer, *White* (New York: Routledge, 1997), 31.

35. Andi Zeisler, *We Were Feminists Once: From Riot Grrrl to CoverGirl, the Buying and Selling of a Political Movement* (New York: PublicAffairs, 2016), xiii.

36. Ibid., xv.

37. See also Hilary Radner's *The New Woman's Film* and Virginia Luzon-Aguado's "The Wild Bunch" for more on women-centered survival narratives.

38. Krista Comer, *Surfer Girls in the New World Order* (Durham, NC: Duke University Press, 2010), 66.

39. Dyer, *White*, 21.

40. Not to be confused with the 2002 fiction film of the same name.

41. Shohat and Stam, *Unthinking Eurocentrism*, 107.

42. Ingram, *Green Screen*, 26.

43. Ibid.

44. Laura Mulvey, "Visual Pleasure and Narrative Cinema," *Screen* 16, no. 3 (Autumn 1975): 11.

45. Dyer, *White*, 29.

46. Ibid.

47. Mulvey, "Visual Pleasure," 11.

48. Zygmunt Bauman, *Globalization: The Human Consequences* (New York: Columbia University Press, 1998), 83, 92.

49. Ibid., 86.

50. Ibid., 86, 92.

51. Ibid., 92.

52. Dyer, *White*, 19–20.

53. Ibid., 222.

54. Graham Benton, "Shark Films: Cinematic Realism and the Production of Terror," in *This Watery World: Humans and the Sea*, ed. Vartan P. Messier and Nandita Batra (Newcastle upon Tyne, UK: Cambridge Scholars, 2008), 123.

55. Jonathan Lemkin, "Archetypal Landscapes and *Jaws*," in *Planks of Reason: Essays on the Horror Film*, ed. Barry Keith Grant and Christopher Sharrett, rev. ed. (Lanham, MD: Scarecrow Press, 2004), 322, 323. Unlike *Jaws* and *The Shallows*, which conflate (eco)horror with extreme whiteness, some horror/thrillers like *Surviving the Game* (1994) and *Get Out* (2017)—both by Black directors—have tried to point out the monstrosity inherent to relatively "ordinary" whiteness, via the militant racism of the

white hunters in the first film and the paternalistic faux-liberalism of the rich bidders in the second.

56. Dyer, *White*, 19.
57. Audrey Colombe, "White Hollywood's New Black Boogeyman," *Jump Cut* 45 (Fall 2002), www.ejumpcut.org/archive/jc45.2002/colombe/index.html.
58. Bauman, *Globalization*, 85–86.
59. See Chelsea Davis, chapter 5, and Ashley Kniss, chapter 3, in this volume for more extensive analyses of the repulsion and attraction of rot, decay, and corpses in ecohorror.
60. Douglas J. Long and Robert E. Jones, "White Shark Predation and Scavenging on Cetaceans in the Eastern North Pacific Ocean," in *Great White Sharks: The Biology of Carcharodon Carcharias*, ed. A. Peter Klimley and David G. Ainley (San Diego: Academic Press, 1996), 296, 306.
61. Ibid.
62. Keri Stevenson, "The Death of Birdsong, the Birdsong of Death" (chapter 4 of this volume), 91.
63. Quirke, *Jaws*, 44.
64. Many shark attack film titles, such as *Open Water*, *Deep Blue Sea*, *The Shallows*, and *47 Meters Down* suggest that watery locales are intrinsically ecohorrific. Ecohorror movie sharks are part of this terrifying environment, framed as elemental forces of (monstrous) nature.
65. George H. Burgess and Matthew Callahan, "Worldwide Patterns of White Shark Attacks on Humans," in *Great White Sharks: The Biology of Carcharodon carcharias*, ed. A. Peter Klimley and David G. Ainley (San Diego: Academic Press, 1996), 459, 460.
66. Williams, "Melodrama Revised," 67.
67. Burgess and Callahan, "Worldwide Patterns," 461, 466.
68. Dyer, *White*, 15.
69. Clover, *Men, Women, and Chain Saws*, 60–61.
70. Neff, "Belly of the Beast," 52, 59.
71. Melville, *Moby-Dick*, 205.
72. Dyer, *White*, 208.
73. Alaimo, "Discomforting Creatures," 280.
74. Dawn Keetley, "Jaws, the Slasher, and the Encounter at the Heart of Horror," *Horror Homeroom.com*, July 5, 2015, http://www.horrorhomeroom.com/jaws-the-slasher-and-the-encounter-at-the-heart-of-horror/.
75. In this connection it is noteworthy that the original Michael Myers mask used on *Halloween*'s set in 1978 was a modified Captain Kirk mask. As the white captain of the *Enterprise*, both Kirk's characterization and the ship name designate him as the ideal embodiment of masculine, imperialistic, spirited whiteness, at the top of a rigidly hierarchical, multiethnic crew. Only slight alteration converted his iconic visage into an emblem of white death and horror.
76. Dyer, *White*, 210.
77. Rob Nixon, *Slow Violence and the Environmentalism of the Poor* (Cambridge, MA: Harvard University Press, 2011), 187.
78. Val Plumwood, "Being Prey," *Utne Reader*, July–August 2000, https://www.utne.com/arts/being-prey.
79. Williams, "Melodrama Revised," 50.

References

Alaimo, Stacy. "Discomforting Creatures: Monstrous Natures in Recent Films." In *Beyond Nature Writing: Expanding the Boundaries of Ecocriticism*, edited by Karla Armbruster and Kathleen R. Wallace, 279–96. Charlottesville: University Press of Virginia, 2001.

Bauman, Zygmunt. *Globalization: The Human Consequences*. New York: Columbia University Press, 1998.

Benton, Graham. "Shark Films: Cinematic Realism and the Production of Terror." In *This Watery World: Humans and the Sea*, edited by Vartan P. Messier and Nandita Batra, 123–32. Newcastle upon Tyne, UK: Cambridge Scholars, 2008.

Burgess, George H., and Matthew Callahan. "Worldwide Patterns of White Shark Attacks on Humans." In *Great White Sharks: The Biology of Carcharodon carcharias*, edited by A. Peter Klimley and David G. Ainley, 457–69. San Diego: Academic, 1996.

Clover, Carol J. *Men, Women, and Chain Saws: Gender in the Modern Horror Film*. Princeton, NJ: Princeton University Press, 1992.

Colombe, Audrey. "White Hollywood's New Black Boogeyman." *Jump Cut* 45 (Fall 2002). www.ejumpcut.org/archive/jc45.2002/colombe/index.html.

Comer, Krista. *Surfer Girls in the New World Order*. Durham, NC: Duke University Press, 2010.

Dyer, Richard. *White*. New York: Routledge, 1997.

French, Lindsay A. "Yearly Worldwide Shark Attack Summary 2017." *International Shark Attack File* (ISAF). Last modified February 6, 2018. www.floridamuseum.ufl.edu/shark-attacks/yearly-worldwide-summary/.

Gambin, Lee. *Massacred by Mother Nature: Exploring the Natural Horror Film*. Baltimore: Midnight Marquee, 2012.

Gregersdotter, Katarina, Nicklas Hållén, and Johan Höglund. Introduction to *Animal Horror Cinema: Genre, History and Criticism*, edited by Katarina Gregersdotter, Johan Höglund, and Nicklas Hållén, 1–18. New York: Palgrave Macmillan, 2015.

Ingram, David. *Green Screen: Environmentalism and Hollywood Cinema*. Exeter, UK: University of Exeter Press, 2000.

Jones, Allie. "Blake Lively's Fall Fashion Inspiration Is Slaveowners." *Gawker.com*, October 13, 2014. https://gawker.com/blake-livelys-fall-fashion-inspiration-is-slaveowners-1645661587.

Keetley, Dawn. "Jaws, the Slasher, and the Encounter at the Heart of Horror." *Horror Homeroom.com*, July 5, 2015.

http://www.horrorhomeroom.com/jaws-the-slasher-and-the-encounter-at-the-heart-of-horror/.

Lemkin, Jonathan. "Archetypal Landscapes and *Jaws*." In *Planks of Reason: Essays on the Horror Film*, edited by Barry Keith Grant and Christopher Sharrett, 321–32. Rev. ed. Lanham, MD: Scarecrow, 2004.

Lerberg, Matthew. "Jabbering *Jaws*: Reimagining Representations of Sharks Post-*Jaws*." In *Screening the Nonhuman: Representations of Animal Others in the Media*, edited by Amber E. George and J. L. Schatz, 33–46. Lanham, MD: Lexington Books, 2016.

Long, Douglas J., and Robert E. Jones. "White Shark Predation and Scavenging on Cetaceans in the Eastern North Pacific Ocean." In *Great White Sharks: The Biology of Carcharodon carcharias*, edited by A. Peter Klimley and David G. Ainley, 293–307. San Diego: Academic, 1996.

Luzon-Aguado, Virginia. "The Wild Bunch: Women's Survival Narratives." Presentation at A Clockwork Green: Ecomedia in the Anthropocene: An ASLE-Sponsored, Nearly Carbon-Neutral Symposium, June 2018. http://ehc.english.ucsb.edu/?page_id=17731.

Melville, Herman. *Moby-Dick*. New York: Harper and Brothers, 1851. Reprint, New York: Penguin Classics, 1992.

Milatovic, Maja. "Consuming Wildlife: Representations of Tourism and Retribution in Australian Animal Horror." In *Animal Horror Cinema: Genre, History and Criticism*, edited by Katarina Gregersdotter, Johan Höglund, and Nicklas Hållén, 76–93. New York: Palgrave MacMillan, 2015.

Mulvey, Laura. "Visual Pleasure and Narrative Cinema." *Screen* 16, no. 3 (Autumn 1975): 6–18.

Neff, Nichole. "The Belly of the Beast: The Uncanny Shark." *Gothic Studies* 18, no. 2 (November 2016): 52–61.

Nixon, Rob. *Slow Violence and the Environmentalism of the Poor*. Cambridge, MA: Harvard University Press, 2011.

Plumwood, Val. "Being Prey." *Utne Reader*, July–August 2000. https://www.utne.com/arts/being-prey.

Quirke, Antonia. *Jaws*. London: BFI, 2002.

Radner, Hilary. *The New Woman's Film: Femme-Centric Movies for Smart Chicks*. New York: Routledge, 2017.

Rust, Stephen A., and Carter Soles. "Ecohorror Special Cluster: 'Living in Fear, Living in Dread, Pretty Soon We'll All Be Dead.'" *ISLE: Interdisciplinary Studies in Literature and Environment* 21, no. 3 (Summer 2014): 509–12.

Shohat, Ella, and Robert Stam. *Unthinking Eurocentrism: Multiculturalism and the Media*. 2nd ed. New York: Routledge, 2014.

Williams, Linda. "Melodrama Revised." In *Refiguring American Film Genres*, edited by Nick Browne, 42–88. Berkeley: University of California Press, 1998.

Zeisler, Andi. *We Were Feminists Once: From Riot Grrrl to CoverGirl, the Buying and Selling of a Political Movement*. New York: PublicAffairs, 2016.

Contributors

Kristen Angierski holds a PhD from Cornell University, where she studied and taught environmental literature, eco-horror, ecofeminism, and occult environmentalism. Her work has also appeared in *Gothic Nature* and *ISLE: Interdisciplinary Studies in Literature and Environment*. In the fall of 2020, she began a new career as a high-school English teacher. She lives with her two familiars—her cats—in South Carolina.

Bridgitte Barclay is associate professor and English department chair at Aurora University. She also serves on the Executive Council of the Association for the Study of Literature and Environment (ASLE) and as coleader of their Ecomedia Special Interest Group. Bridgitte writes and teaches about intersections of gender, science fiction, and the environment in the English, environmental studies, and gender studies departments. She recently coedited *Gender and Environment in Science Fiction* with Christy Tidwell, and her other recent work is on museum habitat dioramas as ecomedia, extinction narratives in contemporary women's science fiction, and midcentury women making popular science ecomedia.

Marisol Cortez, PhD, a community scholar and creative writer, occupies the space between academic, activist, and artistic worlds. She has been involved in environmental justice movements for twenty years, which informed her doctoral research at UC Davis. After an ACLS New Faculty Fellowship at the University of Kansas, she returned home to San Antonio to write and research in service of movements to protect *la madre tierra* and create alternatives to parasitic forms of urban "development." With environmental journalist Greg Harman, she coedits *Deceleration,* an online journal of degrowth thought and praxis. For more information on publications and projects, visit mcortez.net.

Chelsea Davis holds a PhD in English from Stanford University, where her research focused on narrative representations of violence—from horror film to war fiction to apocalyptic writings to the literary Gothic. Her dissertation developed a theory of anti-genre by illuminating the surprising absences, parodies, and repudiations of Gothic tropes in early fiction about the American Revolutionary and Civil Wars. As an independent scholar, she has published on film adaptations of Henry James, social class in horror, and island Gothic narratives. She is currently at work on a series of essays about the intersections of horror and comedy.

Joseph K. Heumann is professor emeritus of communication studies at Eastern Illinois University, where he continues to teach various film courses. He has coauthored six books exploring ecocinema with Robin L. Murray: *Ecology and Popular Film: Cinema on the Edge* (SUNY Press, 2009); *That's All Folks? Ecocritical Readings of American Animated Features* (University of Nebraska Press, 2011); *Gunfight at the Eco-Corral: Western Cinema and the Environment* (University of Oklahoma Press, 2012); *Film and Everyday Ecodisasters* (University of Nebraska Press, 2014); *Monstrous Nature: Environment and Horror on the Big Screen* (University of Nebraska Press, 2016); and *Ecocinema and the City* (Routledge, 2018).

Dawn Keetley is professor of English, teaching horror/Gothic literature, film, and television at Lehigh University. She is the author of *Making a Monster: Jesse Pomeroy, the Boy Murderer of 1870s Boston* (University of Massachusetts Press, 2017); editor of *Jordan Peele's "Get Out": Political Horror* (Ohio State University Press, 2020); and coeditor (with Angela Tenga) of *Plant Horror: Approaches to the Monstrous Vegetal in Fiction and Film* (Palgrave, 2016) and (with Matthew Wynn Sivils) of *The Ecogothic in Nineteenth-Century American Literature* (Routledge, 2017). Keetley writes regularly for a horror website she co-created, www.HorrorHomeroom.com.

Ashley Kniss is a senior lecturer in the English department at Stevenson University. Her current research and writing explores human foodiness, the corpse as evidence of trans-corporeality, human decomposition, green burial, waste, materiality, and human reactions of disgust toward the more-than-human.

Robin L. Murray is professor of English at Eastern Illinois University, where she teaches film and literature courses and coordinates the film studies minor. She has coauthored six books exploring ecocinema with Joseph K. Heumann: *Ecology and Popular Film: Cinema on the Edge* (SUNY Press, 2009); *That's All Folks? Ecocritical Readings of American Animated Features* (University of Nebraska Press, 2011); *Gunfight at the Eco-Corral: Western Cinema and the Environment* (University of Oklahoma Press, 2012); *Film and Everyday Ecodisasters* (University of Nebraska Press, 2014); *Monstrous Nature: Environment and Horror on the Big Screen* (University of Nebraska Press, 2016); and *Ecocinema and the City* (Routledge, 2018).

Brittany R. Roberts is an instructor in the Department of English at Southeastern Louisiana University. She researches Russian and Anglophone literature, cinema, and culture, particularly speculative fiction and the environmental humanities. She is currently working on her first book project, which conducts a comparative analysis of Russian and American horror literature and cinema focusing on depictions of humans, animals, the environment, and the metaphysical dynamics that link them. Her work has appeared in *The Irish Journal of Gothic and Horror Studies*, *The Spaces and Places of Horror*, *Plants in Science Fiction: Speculative Vegetation* , and the forthcoming *The New Routledge Companion to Science Fiction*.

Sharon Sharp is an associate professor of film, television, and media at California State University, Dominguez Hills. She has published on television, genre, and gender and is currently working on a project on nonhuman animals and media.

Carter Soles is associate professor of film studies in the English department at SUNY Brockport. His research interests include ecomedia studies, identity studies, and film genre studies. He has written on the cannibalistic hillbilly in 1970s slasher films for *Ecocinema: Theory and Practice* (Routledge, 2012), on environmental apocalyptic themes in 1960s horror for *ISLE*, and on petroculture, gender, and genre in the Mad Max franchise for *Gender and Environment in Science Fiction* (Lexington Books, 2019). He is currently writing a book on ecohorror cinema.

Keri Stevenson is an assistant professor of English at the University of New Mexico–Gallup. She has published peer-reviewed articles and given conference presentations on birds in literature and humanity's place among other species in an evolutionary context, and she has taught courses in composition, British Victorian and Romantic literature, and folk and fairy tales. Her dissertation analyzed the use of nineteenth-century evolutionary theory by Victorian atheist and agnostic authors, including Algernon Charles Swinburne, to discuss kinship between humans and animals.

Christy Tidwell, associate professor of English and humanities at the South Dakota School of Mines & Technology, writes about speculative fiction, environmental studies, and gender studies. She is the Digital Strategies Coordinator for ASLE (the Association for the Study of Literature and Environment) and was coorganizer of A Clockwork Green: Ecomedia in the Anthropocene (a nearly carbon-neutral virtual conference). She also coedited *Gender and Environment in Science Fiction* (Lexington Books, 2019) with Bridgitte Barclay and has published on ecohorror in *ISLE*, *Posthuman Glossary* (ed. Rosi Braidotti and Maria Hlavajova), and *Gothic Nature*.

Index

abjection, 87n10, 154–55, 158, 165–66, 170, 182, 259, 261
absent referent, 242
Adams, Carol J., 222, 242
afterlife, 72, 74, 75, 77–82, 84–85, 102, 110, 123
Alaimo, Stacy, 6, 10, 31–32, 54, 62, 86n4, 138, 141, 165, 169–70, 208, 223, 262, 273
Alder, Emily, 15
Alex, Rayson K., 5
American Civil War, 11, 111–12, 114–15, 117, 120, 123–24, 126
Anderson, Kevin, 162
animal
 agency, 176–79, 180–81, 183–85, 218, 223–24, 244–46, 248, 251–52
 behavior, 187, 237, 240, 243, 245–46, 248, 258, 260, 270–71
 capital, 248
 captivity, 13, 46, 188–89, 237, 242–43, 248–49
 charisma, 226–27
 emotions, 183, 193n41, 245
 ethics, 174–77, 190–93
 exploitation, 13, 222, 224–25, 226, 228, 237–39, 246–48, 252, 254n41
 horror. *See* horror: animal
 imagery, 225–26, 239, 247
 kinship narratives, 174–75, 188, 190–92, 217, 230
 labor, 237, 239, 247–52
 rights, 13, 217–19, 226–32, 248–49, 258
animal attacks, 2–3, 8, 133–34, 139, 180, 187, 198, 220, 238, 240, 243–45, 257, 260–61, 264, 267, 270–72, 276n28, 277n63
animality, 45–46, 183, 269
Animal Liberation Front (ALF), 13, 219–20, 221, 222, 227, 228–31, 232–33
animation, 49, 63n8

Anthropocene, 1–4, 6, 14, 15n7, 59, 143, 146, 217–18, 223–25, 231, 241
anthropocentrism, 15n7, 24, 73, 82, 96, 100, 114, 117, 119–20, 122–25, 136, 245–46, 250, 259–60
anthropomorphism, 49, 93, 110–11, 114–15, 117, 119, 121–22, 124–25, 127n5, 206–7, 260, 271–72
anti-Gothic, 11, 111–12, 117, 124, 127n8
anti-pastoral, 13, 196, 218, 220–24, 226–29, 231–32
apocalypse, 50, 58–59, 64n67, 69, 82, 86n6, 96, 133, 143, 145–46, 147n13, 240
assemblage, 34, 64n40
atomic fears, 4, 6, 9, 36n1, 133–34, 136–38, 147n4
Attebery, Brian, 59
awe, 81, 199, 204–6

Baier, Annette, 145–46
Balsamo, Anne, 142
Banks, Peter B., 142
bathroom, 12
 as Gothic, 154, 156, 158
 as setting, 153–54, 156, 160, 166–67, 171n2
 as taboo, 156, 170
 and toilets, 154, 158, 159, 162, 167, 170
 See also horror: bathroom
Bauman, Zygmunt, 267, 269
Beast from 20,000 Fathoms, The, 9, 17n41, 147n4
Bellanca, Ellen, 175, 180
Bennett, Andrew, 121
Bennett, Jane, 34
Bercovitch, Sacvan, 72–73
Berger, John, 178, 181, 186, 243
Berlatsky, Noah, 63n18
Berta, Péter, 110

Beville, Maria, 26, 29, 198
Bierce, Ambrose
  other fiction, 117, 127n8, 128n30
  "Tough Tussle, A," 11, 111–12, 118–26
  views on war, 116–17, 125–26, 129n53
birds, 11–12, 36n4, 99, 116, 144
  cormorant, 174–92, 192n27
  point of view of, 101
  sea-birds, 92, 94, 96–97, 100, 102, 104–6, 179, 276n27
  voices of, 92, 94, 96–97, 100–102, 104–5, 182
Birds, The, 36n4, 175, 180, 191, 224, 238, 244, 274
Blackwood, Algernon, 10, 25–36, 37n18, 64n79
Blair Witch Project, The, 25, 36n7, 62n6
Blue Crush (1998 documentary), 265
body horror. *See* horror: body
Bradford, William, 72
Brady, Lisa, 115
Brinkman, Paul D., 135
Brown, Charles Brockden, 114
Bruni, John, 135
Buell, Lawrence, 124
Burne, David, 203
Burt, Jonathan, 187
Bushman, Brandi, 211n28

Calarco, Matthew, 176
camp, 16n18, 218
Campanella, Thomas J., 113
cannibalism, 46–48, 195, 209, 225
  See also meat: eating
Carroll, Noël, 4, 26–27, 29, 45, 198, 201
Carson, Rachel, 86n6, 148n46
cemetery. *See* graveyard
Chasing Ice, 3
children, 137–39, 158–61, 163–64, 184, 217, 226
Chow, Jeremy, 211n28
circus, 242–43
Civil War. *See* American Civil War
Clasen, Mathias, 24
Clean Water Act, 158
Clements, Mikaella, 217–18, 229
climate change, 2, 4, 6, 14, 59–61, 91, 104, 221, 225, 240–41
Clover, Carol J., 259, 261–63
Clute, John, 1
Cohen, Jeffrey Jerome, 35–36, 61, 198
Colavito, Jason, 2, 43, 136, 140–41
Colléony, Agate, 227

Colling, Sarat, 224
colonialism, 38n32, 114, 195–96, 200, 202, 205–6, 208, 243, 258–59, 262–63, 265–66, 269, 274
Comer, Krista, 264
companion animals, 174, 176, 178, 227, 243–44
computer-generated imagery, 237, 247, 250–52, 271
consolation verse, 73, 77, 99
Cormorant, The, 12, 174–92
corpse, 11, 46, 68–70, 72, 74, 76–78, 81, 83–85, 86n4, 87n10, 99, 103, 111, 118–25, 182
Corstorphine, Kevin, 10
cosmic horror. *See* horror: cosmic
Crawl, 2
creature features, 8, 46, 133–34, 139–42, 145–46, 147n4, 198–99, 274
Creature from the Black Lagoon, 197–98, 207
Cronon, William, 138
Crosby, Sara L., 71–72, 275n25

darkness, 28–29, 77–78, 118, 122
Day of the Animals, 23
death, 11, 69, 76, 79–85, 91, 95–97, 101–2, 104, 115, 190, 271–73
  beliefs about, 72–73, 120, 179
  fear of, 7, 59, 270
Deborah, S. Susan, 5
decay, 68–70, 72, 73, 76, 80–81, 84–86, 103–4, 123, 125–26, 145, 182, 270
decomposition, 68–69, 72, 79, 82, 85, 118, 123, 126
de-extinction, 17n41, 133–34, 136, 139, 142–43, 148n35
dehumanization, 30, 46–48, 63n30
del Toro, Guillermo, 12, 195–98, 201–2, 206–7, 209, 230
denial, 6, 61, 164, 274
deroutinization, 169–70
Derrida, Jacques, 182, 237
Dillon, Sarah, 1–2
disanthropocentrism, 61
disanthropy, 11, 37n22, 92–94, 96–98, 101, 106
disaster, 91, 98, 134, 137, 139, 143, 164
disaster film, 9
dread, 26–27, 30, 77, 116, 179
Dreamcatcher. *See* King, Stephen: *Dreamcatcher*

Dumas, Raechel, 55, 58
du Maurier, Daphne, 175, 180, 191
Duncan, Russell, 117
Dupuy, Gabriel, 156
Dwight, Theodore, 113
Dyer, Richard, 264–65, 268, 271–73

eco-fear, 5
ecofeminism, 222, 229–30
ecogothic, 4, 5, 7, 16n22, 111–12, 117–19, 127n5
   See also urban environmental gothic
ecohorror
   agribusiness and, 13, 222–23, 225–26, 231
   as mode, 3, 10, 259
   definition of, 3, 5–6, 7–8, 14, 25–26, 36n1, 42–43, 45, 60, 68, 110, 146, 205–7, 217–19, 231, 238, 259
   fear of the nonhuman, 110, 266
   landscape as horrific, 143–46, 270
   nature-strikes-back, 3, 23, 42, 68, 198
   revenge-of-nature, 8, 23–24, 36n1, 36n6, 92, 127n5, 218, 224, 237, 238–39, 259, 272
   tentacular, 10–11, 24–36, 59, 211n46
ecophilia, 70–72
ecophobia, 4–6, 12, 14, 16n22, 16n26, 36n2, 70–72, 155–56, 159, 161–62, 164, 171
ecoterrorism, 219, 230–31, 246
Elbert, Monika, 127n5
Eliot, T. S., 94, 96
embalming, 69, 83
embodiment, 32, 75, 156–57, 165, 169, 209, 258, 260
entanglement, 10, 31–36, 59, 135, 138, 178, 181, 220, 223
environmental health, 53–54, 137–39, 144–45, 170
environmental justice, 52–54, 161, 164, 170
Eron, Sarah, 93–94, 96
erosion, 91, 92, 94, 98, 102–4, 106
Estok, Simon C., 4–5, 16n22, 16n26, 36n2, 70, 86n10, 155, 162
estrangement, 3, 13–14, 70, 75, 220, 238, 241, 243, 252
Eveleigh, David, 156–57
event-based horror. *See* horror: event-based
Evernden, Neil, 68
evil, 26–27, 36n1, 38n33, 74, 114, 160, 179–81, 191, 195, 225
evolution, 58, 135, 142, 197, 201, 206–7, 209, 245–46

extinction, 1, 2, 12, 93–94, 96, 106, 134–37, 141, 143, 145–46, 147n13, 239–40, 244, 246
extreme weather, 1, 2, 6, 44, 45

factory farming, 13, 217–21, 223–24, 227–31, 242
fairy tale, 117, 120, 195–96, 200–205, 208–9
fear, 4–6, 54, 62, 70–71, 81, 87n10, 110, 112, 143, 179, 189, 197, 199–201, 239, 247–48, 259–60
Fielder, Pat, 133
film noir, 200
Final Girl, 261–63, 272
Finnegan, Lorcan, 10, 25–32, 34–36, 38n33
Fletcher, Pauline, 95
flowers, 95–96, 98
Fly, The, 42, 52
Forbes, Jack D., 195
forest
   agency of the, 25, 27–28, 31, 116, 119, 124
   enchanted, 203
   fear of the, 10, 24, 26–27, 33, 38n34, 73, 115
   haunted, 110–11, 114, 117–18, 122–23
   Irish, 37n31
Foy, Joseph, 36n1
Francione, Gary, 227
Frankenstein, 2, 136, 143, 199
Freitag, Gina, 10
Friday the 13th, 24, 37n7
frontier, 134–35, 195
Fudge, Erica, 176
fungi, 32, 34, 166
future, 3, 14, 93–98, 126, 139, 145–46, 153, 221, 232

Gaard, Greta, 229
Gambin, Lee, 8, 36n1, 207, 238
Garrard, Greg, 11, 37n22, 92–93
genetic engineering, 217, 226, 245–46
genre, 16n18, 43, 92, 99, 113, 117–18, 125, 141, 153, 196–201, 206–8, 217–18, 224, 238–39, 259
Geostorm, 3
ghosts, 54, 97, 110, 112, 120, 123, 125, 127n3, 145, 160, 164, 186–87, 275n25
Giddens, Anthony, 165
Gifford, Terry, 196, 200–201, 204–5, 209n2, 220, 227–28
Gilman, Charlotte Perkins, 112, 122
Godzilla, 2, 6, 134, 137, 147n4

Index

gothic, 4, 7, 16n22, 69–71, 77–78, 80, 82–83, 85, 111–14, 117–18, 122, 125, 153, 200, 261
    See also anti-Gothic
graveyard, 99, 101–5, 124
green burial, 11, 70, 76, 83–86
greenwashing, 224–25
Gregersdotter, Katarina, 9, 175–76, 239, 260
Gregory, Daryl, 60
Gregory, Stephen, 12, 174–92
Grosz, Elizabeth, 155
guilt, 6, 23–24, 259

Hackett, Jon, 10
Hållén, Nicklas, 9, 175–76, 239, 260
Hallow, The, 38n34
Hallström, Jonas, 157
Happening, The, 15n15, 36n4, 61, 218
Haraway, Donna J., 14, 32, 142, 183–84, 188, 192
Harrington, Seán, 10
haunting, 11–12, 28, 96, 110–12, 114, 118, 122, 127n5, 134–35, 143, 145–46, 148n45, 191, 221, 275n25
Hawkins, Gay, 158
Hawthorne, Nathaniel, 83, 118–19
Hayden, Tyler, 143
Hediger, Ryan, 14
Heise, Ursula K., 3, 134, 146
Hellraiser, 62n3
Herzog, Hal, 252
Heumann, Joseph K., 8, 36n1
Hillard, Tom J., 86n10, 111, 114, 127n5
Hills, Matt, 2–3, 15n15
Hochuli, Dieter F., 142
Höglund, Johan, 9, 175–76, 239, 260
hope, 5, 14, 98, 103, 112
Hornaday, William, 135
horror
    animal, 8–9, 10, 24, 174–77, 189–90, 238–39, 241, 247, 259–61, 272
    atomic, 136, 140
    bathroom, 153–55, 165, 170–71
    body, 11, 42–43, 45, 50–54, 60, 62, 63n40, 153
    Canadian, 10
    of continuation, 97, 98, 101–2, 106, 116
    cosmic, 2, 11, 42–43, 45, 54–62
    definition of, 2, 4, 26, 29, 32–33, 199–200
    event-based, 2, 15n15
    history of, 1, 7
    natural, 8–9, 36n1, 42, 259

oceanic, 10
paranoid, 58, 153–54
planetary, 1–2, 60
plant, 9, 15n15, 36n6, 58–60, 111
postmodern, 64n67, 139
secure, 58
setting of, 7, 118, 133–34, 143, 146, 148n45, 153, 222
supernatural, 31, 112–13, 117, 119–22, 124–25, 128n30, 158
techno-horror, 153
human/nonhuman
    blurred boundaries, 3, 26, 37n15, 42, 47, 49, 52, 68–69, 71, 79–81, 83, 124, 178, 182, 196–97, 206, 246, 273
    communication, 100, 124, 182, 184–85, 189, 208
    difference, 74, 120, 135, 175–77, 184, 192
    equality, 100–101, 180
    hybrid, 45, 47–49, 246
    relationships, 6–7, 12, 13, 34, 119, 146, 175, 177, 181–92, 196–98, 200, 204, 225–26, 232, 237–46, 252
    transformation, 45–49, 52, 71–72, 80, 83, 85–86, 103, 178, 181
    See also interspecies relationships; multispecies: relationships
hymns, 75, 77, 82, 99

impersonal life, 28–30, 34
impurity, 4, 45–46, 102–3, 157
Indigenous peoples, 5, 127n13, 168–69, 195, 229
infrastructure, 155, 158, 159, 162, 166–70
Ingram, David, 261, 266
interdependence, 13, 178, 196–97, 202, 204–9, 211n43, 230
interspecies relationships, 12, 187, 196, 207, 209, 211n43
    See also human/nonhuman: relationships; multispecies: relationships
intimacy, 174, 185, 188, 190
Ireton, Sean, 103
Irving, Washington, 113
It. See King, Stephen: *It*
Ito, Junji, 11, 37n17, 43–62, 63n40

Jancovich, Mark, 140
Japan
    culture of, 48, 50
    environmental history of, 53

science fiction of, 55, 58
See also Minamata disease
Jaws, 7, 61, 64n40, 189, 251, 258, 261–62, 267, 271, 273–74, 275n23, 276n28
Jaws: The Revenge, 23
Jones, Doug, 197, 210n13
Jones, Steven Swann, 202
Joon-ho, Bong, 13
Joy, Melanie, 241
Jurassic World, 10, 251

Keetley, Dawn, 4, 6, 9, 15n15, 59, 120, 273
Kelly, Suzanne, 76–77, 83–86
King, Richard, 179, 192n27
King, Stephen, 12, 164
  biography of, 165
  Danse Macabre, 172n25
  Dreamcatcher, 12, 155, 158, 165–70
  interviews, 156
  It, 12, 155–56, 158–65, 167, 168
Klein, Naomi, 61
Klooster, David J., 117
krakens, 31, 133, 137–39, 146
Kremmel, Laura R., 10
Kristeva, Julia, 69, 87n10, 182

Laist, Randy, 37n17
LaMarre, Thomas, 49–50, 58
landscape, 11–12, 24, 92, 94, 96–98, 104, 106, 111–12, 114, 122–23, 125, 143–45, 189, 206, 220, 266, 270
Lawrence, D. H., 98
Lennard, Dominic, 8–9
Lerberg, Matthew, 260
Levin, Yisrael, 105–6
Levinas, Emmanuel, 28–29, 38n45
live burial, 69–70, 77–80
Loiselle, André, 10
Long Weekend, 23
love, 94–95, 196–98, 202–5, 208–9, 224
Lovecraft, H. P., 31, 43, 54–55, 58, 59–60, 61, 64n65

mad scientist, 2, 136, 140, 199, 245–46
  See also science: mad
Magistrale, Tony, 153–54, 160
Malamud, Randy, 243
manga, 43, 49, 50
Manning, Paul, 110–11
"Man Whom the Trees Loved, The," 10, 25–36

Marder, Michael, 28
marketplace feminism, 264, 274
Marran, Christine, 49–50
Marshall, Jon R., 144
Martinelli, Lucia, 142
McRoy, Jay, 50
McSweeney, Kerry, 98, 102, 103–4
meat
  eating, 13, 46–48, 53, 224–29, 241
  euphemisms for, 222
  and gender, 222, 241–42
  humans as, 47–48, 69, 78, 82, 84, 99, 104, 123, 180, 241–43, 274
Meeker, Joseph, 206
Meier, Kathryn S., 114
melodrama, 4, 197, 263, 270
Melosi, Martin, 157
memory, 111, 113, 116, 126, 134, 159–60, 164–65
Merchant, Brian, 36n1
Merola, Nicola M., 3
Milatovic, Maja, 259
Miller, T. S., 36n6
Mills, Brett, 243–44, 246, 250
Minamata disease, 53, 138–39
Mitchell, David T., 204
Moby-Dick, 257, 260, 268, 273
mollusks, 12, 45–47, 63n18, 133–34, 137, 146n1
monsters, 35–36, 91, 146, 163–64, 174–75, 189–90, 201, 206, 209
  de-extinct, 134, 136–37
  in film, 2, 140, 159, 198–99
  See also nature: monstrous; sharks: as monsters
Monster That Challenged the World, The, 6, 12, 133–43, 145–46
monstrous nature. *See* nature, monstrous
monuments, 92, 113, 127n13, 168
more-than-human, 6, 31, 45, 54–55, 70–71, 85, 163, 165, 169, 188, 197, 200–201, 204
Morgan, Margaret, 154–56, 162
Morris, Roy, Jr., 117
multispecies
  companionship, 174, 184
  relationships, 12, 176, 178, 183–84, 186, 188, 192n27
  stories, 14
  See also human/nonhuman: relationships; interspecies relationships
Mulvey, Laura, 263, 266
Murphy, Bernice M., 10, 23, 36n1, 73, 200
Murphy, Brian, 140–41

289

Index

Murray, Robin L., 8, 36n1
mutation, 37n12, 42, 52, 63n40, 138–39, 241, 245–46

natural attack films, 9, 36n4
nature
  agency of, 23, 25, 30, 31, 119, 122, 127n5, 140, 161–63, 169, 178–79, 180, 184, 218, 224
  as alien, 27, 29, 31–32, 34, 36, 59, 68–69, 73, 86
  control of, 4, 7, 24, 61, 72, 86, 101, 123, 134–38, 140–41, 145, 157, 161–63, 180, 182–83, 191, 218, 239, 242–44, 252
  dirty, 10
  exploitation of, 195–97, 201, 205
  indifferent, 92, 111, 115–16, 120, 124–26
  malevolent, 72, 80, 86, 180–81, 189, 206
  monstrous, 6, 7, 8, 32, 36n1, 46, 71, 73, 240, 247, 277n63
  without humans, 92, 93, 97–98, 105, 115–16, 145, 266
Neale, Steve, 141
Nelson, Victoria, 197
Nickel, Philip J., 145
Night of the Lepus, 2, 46
Nixon, Rob, 144, 159, 161, 164, 196, 231, 274
nonhuman, 5, 47, 121, 195, 258, 259, 268–69, 273
  resistance, 218, 221, 223–24, 229, 231–33, 237, 239, 244
nostalgia, 6, 116, 135
nuclear fears. *See* atomic fears

oceans. *See* sea
O'Connor, M. R., 142
Okja, 13, 217–33
Oksanen, Markku, 142
Oppermann, Serpil, 141
organismic approaches to ecology, 205, 209

Pandey, Rajyashree, 48, 50
paranoid horror. *See* horror: paranoid
parasites, 17n33, 166
Parker, Elizabeth, 10, 36n6
pastoral, 97, 98, 103, 195–96, 202–4, 220–21, 225–28
PETA (People for the Ethical Treatment of Animals), 237, 249–50, 254n41
pet keeping, 174, 178, 180–82, 186, 190–91, 243–44

pets. *See* companion animals
Pilcher, Helen, 148n35
Pinedo, Isabel Cristina, 64n67
Pitetti, Connor, 145
planetary fear. *See* horror: planetary
plant horror. *See* horror: plant
plants, 24, 27, 33, 59–60, 115, 120, 122, 126, 127n5
Plumwood, Val, 47–48, 69, 74, 76, 124, 180, 241, 274
Poe, Edgar Allan, 11, 69–86
  "Colloquy of Monos and Una, The," 11, 69–72, 75, 77–86
  and detective fiction, 71
  and live burial, 77–78, 80
  and religion, 77–78, 80, 82, 85
Poland, Michelle, 39n72
pollution, 2, 4, 6, 36n1, 53–54, 92, 138, 144, 148n46, 158, 161–62, 240, 242
postmodern horror. *See* horror: postmodern
postpastoral, 12, 172n35, 195–205, 207–9, 220–21, 226, 227–29
Potter, Will, 230
prehistoric creatures, 12, 133–37, 145, 197, 207
prey, 180, 241–42, 266, 274
Prince, Stephen, 37n15
Psycho, 153–54, 156, 171n2
psychoanalysis, 154, 160, 170
Punter, David, 39n72
Puritans, 72–73, 80, 86, 114

queer ecologies, 63n18, 218
Quirke, Antonia, 261, 270

racism
  against immigrant workers, 223
  against Mexicans, 13, 258–59, 261, 263–64, 266–67, 269, 271–72
rehorroring, 134, 140, 143, 145–46
resurrection, 70, 74, 75, 77–78, 82, 84, 86, 122, 125, 142–43, 148n35
revenge-of-nature. *See* ecohorror: revenge-of-nature
Richardson, Judith, 112, 123
Riggs, Ransom, 145
Roebeling, P. C., 91
Roosevelt, Theodore, 135
Rosenberg, John D., 92
rot, 11, 68, 85–86, 126, 128n25
Royle, Nicholas, 121
Ruskin, John, 113

Rust, Stephen A., 3, 7, 37n12, 42–43, 45, 47, 139, 146, 205, 217, 221, 238
Ryden, Wendy, 127n5

Sahagun, Louis, 144
Salton Sea, 12, 133–34, 140, 143–46, 148n44
Santilli, Paul, 26–27, 29
satire, 13, 218–21, 224–26, 229
scale, 58–60, 232
   geological, 93, 164, 217
   shifting, 3, 11, 45, 46, 59
   time, 45, 55, 59–60, 69, 81, 83, 85–86, 93, 95, 98, 126, 134, 161, 164
Schell, Jennifer, 5–6, 16n22
Scherer, Agnes, 38n59
Schneider, Richard J., 220
Schoell, William, 8
science, 2, 7, 34, 59–60, 141, 157, 197, 206, 239
   critique of, 134, 137, 139, 141–42, 199, 207
   experimentation in, 2, 12, 78, 133–34, 200
   fear of, 141, 143
   hubris in, 134, 137, 140, 145
   institutionalized, 135–43, 148n46
   mad, 2, 140, 246
   militarized, 136, 140–42, 198–99, 209
sea, 11, 91, 92, 95–99, 102–6, 208, 270
   See also Salton Sea
sewer history, 156–58, 161
Seymour, Nicole, 62n8, 218
Shallows, The, 13, 38n32, 257–74
Shanley, Garrett, 25
Shape of Water, The, 12, 195–209, 230
sharks, 13, 38n32, 63n40
   behavior of, 270–71
   conservation of, 260
   as monsters, 251, 258, 261, 270–71
Sheldon, Rebekah, 139
Shohat, Ella, 265
Shove, Elizabeth, 155, 169–70
Shukin, Nicole, 248
Sigourney, Lydia Huntley, 74
Siipi, Helena, 142
Silent Spring, 3
Silva, Rodolfo, 91
sin, 72, 74, 75, 99–100, 160
Singer, Peter, 227
Sivils, Matthew Wynn, 4, 6, 111, 123, 127n5
slow violence, 144, 146, 148n46, 159, 161–62, 164, 170, 221–22, 231, 243, 270
Small, Ernest, 227

Snyder, Sharon L., 204
Soles, Carter, 3, 7, 36n4, 37n12, 42–43, 45, 47, 62n6, 146, 205, 217, 221, 238
somatophobia, 155, 161
speciesism, 5, 228–29
Spofford, Harriet Elizabeth Prescot, 119
Stam, Robert, 265
sublime, 92, 145
supernatural horror. *See* horror: supernatural
Swinburne, Algernon Charles, 11, 91–106
   "By the North Sea," 92, 94, 98–106
   "Forsaken Garden, A," 92, 94–98, 102
sympathy
   for the monster, 48, 147n30, 172n25, 251, 274
   for the nonhuman, 6, 48–49, 63n26, 189–90, 258

Tarr, Joel, 156, 167
Taylor, Matthew, 70–71, 81
technology, 62n3, 142, 153, 157–58, 161, 245, 249–50, 252
television, 13, 237, 239, 240–41, 246, 249
Tenga, Angela, 9
tentacular ecohorror. *See* ecohorror: tentacular
terraforming, 3, 146
Texas Chain Saw Massacre, 24–25, 62n6
Tezuka, Osamu, 58
Thacker, Eugene, 31, 38n51
Thing, The, 37n15, 38n59, 42
Thunberg, Greta, 5
Tidwell, Christy, 14, 17n33, 23, 54, 110, 206
tourism, 265–69
transcendence, 6, 99
trans-corporeality, 6, 10, 31–32, 54, 86n4, 136, 138–39, 144, 148n46, 165, 167–69, 218
trees, 25–27, 29–30, 35, 38n45, 110, 113, 116
   See also forest
Trowbridge, J. T., 115
Tuan, Yi-Fu, 243
Tudor, Andrew, 58, 153
Turner, Frederick Jackson, 134

uncanny, 31, 36, 59, 87n10, 124, 158, 170–71, 175–76, 180–81, 258
unhaunted, 11, 111–12
urban environmental gothic, 12, 154–56, 164, 169–70
Useless Sea, The, 143–44

Index

Uzumaki, 11, 37n17, 43–44
   as body horror, 50–54, 60
   as cosmic horror, 54–60
   as ecohorror, 45–50, 52–54, 60–62
   as plant horror, 58–60
   publication history of, 43

vegans, 13, 224, 226–30, 232
vegan studies, 219, 228–29
vegetal life, 9, 11, 28, 32, 35, 111–12, 126
   See also horror: plant
vegetation. *See* plants
Vetter, Jeremy, 135
Victorian poetry, 11, 91–106
Videodrome, 62n3
violence, 23–24, 125–26, 140, 153, 159–60, 164, 184, 187–89, 196, 206, 221, 239, 251

Walker, Brett L., 53–54, 138
war, 111–12, 113, 115–16, 123, 125, 138, 142
Washington, W. D. H., 140–41
waste, 83, 103, 144, 154, 156, 158, 160, 163
water, 159–61, 167–68, 170, 203–4, 211n28, 277n63
Watts, Isaac, 75–76
Weisman, Alan, 92–93, 97

Wells, Paul, 201
wendigo, 195–96, 200, 202, 206, 209
whiteness, 13, 232, 258, 264–65, 268, 269, 271–73, 276n55, 277n74
   and female sexuality, 266
white supremacy, 13, 259, 261, 262–63, 268–69, 271–72
wilderness, 72–73, 79–81, 111, 113–15, 119, 124, 126, 128n25, 182, 259, 261, 264–66, 268, 274
   grave as, 73, 79–80
Williams, Evan Calder, 24
Williams, Linda, 4, 263, 270
Without Name, 25–32, 34–36
Wohlleben, Peter, 34
Wolfe, Cary, 237
Wood, Robin, 36n1, 48, 147n30, 172n25, 198, 251
Woodruff, Stuart C., 125
woods. *See* forest

Yacowar, Maurice, 9

Zipes, Jack, 203
Zoo, 13, 234n24, 237–52
zoos, 243, 254n41

Milton Keynes UK
Ingram Content Group UK Ltd.
UKHW010324210224
438187UK00006B/563